The Art of Exploration

Levison Wood is an award-winning author, explorer and photographer, whose books and documentaries have won critical acclaim around the world. Levison is the author of 10 books to date, including *Walking the Nile* and *Walking the Americas*, which were both *Sunday Times* bestsellers, and *Walking the Himalayas*, which was voted Adventure Travel Book of the Year at the Edward Stanford Travel Writing Awards. His book *Arabia* was also chosen by Hudson Books as one of their Top Ten Non-Fiction Titles of 2019 in the USA.

Levison's passion for adventure and discovering more about indigenous ways of life has taken him to over 100 countries. He served for several years as an Officer in the British Parachute Regiment, including an operational deployment to Afghanistan, where he fought Taliban insurgents in Helmand. He is an elected Fellow of the Royal Geographical Society, the Explorers Club and Visiting Fellow at Cass Business School.

He has presented several documentaries, which have aired around the world, including 'Arabia with Levison Wood', which was shortlisted for Best Documentary Series at the Broadcast Awards 2020 and 'Walking with Elephants', which recounts a trek across Botswana following a herd of elephants to the Okavango Delta. Levison is a passionate conservationist and an ambassador for the charity The Tusk Trust.

The Art of Exploration

*Lessons in Curiosity, Leadership
and Getting Things Done*

LEVISON WOOD

Illustrations by the author

HODDER

First published in Great Britain in 2021 by Hodder & Stoughton
An Hachette UK company

This paperback edition published in 2022

1

A CIP catalogue record for this title is available from the British Library

Paperback ISBN 9781529343069
eBook ISBN 9781529343045

Typeset in Bembo by Hewer Text UK Ltd, Edinburgh
Printed and bound in Great Britain by Clays Ltd, Elcograf S.p.A.

Hodder & Stoughton policy is to use papers that are natural, renewable
and recyclable products and made from wood grown in sustainable
forests. The logging and manufacturing processes are expected to
conform to the environmental regulations of the country of origin.

Hodder & Stoughton Ltd
Carmelite House
50 Victoria Embankment
London EC4Y 0DZ

www.hodder.co.uk

All that is gold does not glitter,
Not all those who wander are lost
– J.R.R. Tolkien

For my brother, Peter

Contents

Introduction

Why am I telling you all these examples of exploration and adventure? Because we are all explorers in life, whichever path we follow – Nansen, *Spirit of Adventure*, 1926

I had never been more scared in my life.

'Jump! Just jump!'

I was a child. A terrified seven-year-old child. Since my earliest thoughts I had dreamed of adventure, but now that I looked down at the swirling waters beneath a sheer cliff face, I was beginning to realise that I was not the explorer I had imagined myself to be.

'Jump!'

Right there, in that moment of childhood, I had reached a fork in life's road. I could never have known it then, but to step back from the cliff's edge would have sent me on a very different journey to the life that I live today. If I had backed away from that cliff, I might never have gone on to jump out of planes with the Parachute Regiment or walk through war zones with nothing but my camera. I may not have experienced the differences between the sodden heat of the jungle and the baking sun of the desert; breathed in the smells of Himalayan meadows, or felt the ground move as a herd of elephants passed by.

Would I have ever shared smiles and conversations on the world's frontlines, or in remote villages forgotten by time? I don't believe I would have done.

There is a whole world for us to explore, but it will always be out of reach until we take the first step.

Until we jump.

Fortunately for me, I had my father with me on that cliff top, if you can even call it that. It seemed miles high at the time, and there was no way that I could have mustered the courage to jump into the cold waters below unless my dad had asked, 'Do you trust me?'

I did, and even though I thought we were probably jumping to our deaths, I followed him over the edge, and to adventure. From that point on in my life, I could not be held back. Now, in this book, I want to do for you what my father did for me.

I want to support, guide and encourage you to think like an explorer.

By virtue of the fact you have picked up this book, you have shown that you are a curious individual, and curiosity is what drives exploration. It is the essence of humanity. Our ability to ask questions, to learn and to share that knowledge is what has made our species the most successful on the planet. Exploration is hardwired into our DNA, so if you feel like you are sometimes consumed by an urge to discover new things, to travel or to explore, then you are not alone.

Because it is who we are.

Too often we can feel like passengers in our own lives. This is because we have surrendered our curiosity to other people. We let them make our decisions, and tell us what shape our lives will take. We let fear and mistrust guide us; we become scared of change. We allow ourselves to fall into a rut – our comfort zones – and fail to appreciate new things. We forget that when you retrieve your own curiosity, you can begin to take back control of your life and start sitting in the driving seat .

I can tell you from experience that being a passenger in a car that is out of control is not a good place to be. I was very lucky to survive when the taxi I was travelling in fell hundreds of feet from a Himalayan mountain road. I had no right to survive that accident, and yet here I am. I have been very lucky in many ways in life. I survived the war in Afghanistan too, and some close calls with crocodiles and elephants in Africa. Somehow, I narrowly missed stepping on several bombs in Iraq and Syria. For that, I am very grateful.

I was fortunate to grow up in a stable democracy and I couldn't have asked to be born to better parents, who believed in the value of education and gave me the gift of curiosity. But even with the privilege of a very happy childhood, I had no idea that my dreams of exploring the world would ever become true. We were not wealthy, and I assumed that the only people who could have those kinds of adventures were the very rich. I never imagined that it would be possible to make my living by following my dreams of travel.

Some people are born with the travel bug, others are later bitten by it, but the need to visit far-flung places is not a criteria for reading this book. It is about the importance of allowing yourself to be curious, and to become a student of life.

I'm not trying to convince you to become a professional, full-time explorer, and that's not because I don't want the competition! Part of the explorer's mindset is to be realistic, and even though what appear at first to be obstacles can often provide the answer, there are certain things in our life that restrict our ability to do as we like. If your dreams are to explore full-time, then you already have the explorer's mindset, and I hope you will find in these pages the tools to refine those raw ideas into an art form.

For everyone else, no matter your age or profession, I believe wholeheartedly that these lessons from my travels can help you to fulfill your potential for living a happy life, regardless of your circumstances.

You might feel that you keep getting knocked by the world and the people in it, and you need help to get back on your feet. Or you may be winning at life and constantly looking for ways to sharpen your mental blade. Whatever position you're in, you can always do better. We can always learn. We can always improve. If you have waited sixty years to explore, but start today, that is not failure. The start point will be different for everyone, but the destination will be the same – a happier, more fulfilled life.

I have always tried to learn from my own mistakes and from those of others. I have also learned from the successes of strangers, taking inspiration from people who have done things that I want to do, applying those lessons to create the life of my choice. Life is all about making choices. Being human is all about making choices; but we can only make those choices when we recognise first that we have them by taking ownership of our lives and taking the relevant action. There is much in the world beyond our control, but that it is no reason to surrender the huge amount of power that we *do* have over our own lives.

Affirmative action is a term we used in the military to describe a situation when you need to do *something*, even if you don't know what, in order to progress and avoid getting stuck in a negative pattern. Moving forward breeds success, and the more considered action we take, the more successful we will be in any line of work.

This book sets out to arrange the ways that I have learned to act and think. They are the guiding principles that have given me the best opportunities in my vocation, which is so intertwined with my life that it is impossible to separate the two; nor would I want to, because I love what I do, and I do it because I can't imagine doing anything else. It is my purpose. I used to shy away from the term 'explorer', as it felt a bit old-fashioned and fusty, belonging to an era when men wore pith helmets and shot tigers. Now exploration takes on a new meaning and is far more inclusive. It is about documenting a moment in time, not for the sake of posterity, but for the here and now, so that we can all share in the dissemination of learning, improvement and collective knowledge.

A hundred and fifty years ago, vast swathes of the world remained unexplored. There were countless opportunities to undertake pioneering expeditions. Many rivers had yet to be navigated, almost no great mountains had been summited and the poles were thought to be an impossible dream. Today, you can simply look at your phone and scroll on Google Maps to see any point on our planet. There is no need to worry what will happen when you get there, either – Trip Advisor will fill in all the details. Almost no 'firsts' remain to be conquered. Instead, would-be explorers have taken to adapting the well-trodden paths with new speed records, unassisted or oxygen-free climbs, and eco-friendly adventures. Good for them, I say!

There remain plenty of reasons to travel, beyond verifying what the digital guidebooks say, and finding a new variation on an old route is a worthy undertaking in itself. It is better than not travelling at all, that's for sure. But fear not, there is still one unexplored journey to be had for each and every one of us, and that is in the quest for self-discovery – to live a meaningful life. This kind of exploration traverses more than the physical realm, but the treasures are perhaps even more rewarding.

There are risks, of course, and no GPS can tell you how to live a good life. Therein lies the challenge. In this modern age of chaotic technological advancement, even Google cannot find out who you truly are, and the signposts are perhaps more obscured than ever. That is why it is vitally important to forge your own path and plot a course towards a life of your own making. This is what I have always tried to do and I hope this book will help you to do the same.

To that end, I have included lessons from some of the great explorers and figures in history, but also anecdotes from my own life – from childhood adventures and student wanderings to military scrapes and my encounters as a professional explorer. As you will see, I have never had all of the answers, but fortunately there have been people around me who helped out along the way, and now I want to pass their wisdom onto you. I have been fortunate to travel to more than a hundred countries, and wherever I have gone I have tried to be curious and learn lessons from the people around me. In that sense, exploration never ceases.

I have set out these eleven lessons from the road not as a comprehensive rule book, nor as an autobiographical summary of my own adventures, but simply as a way of showing how the art of exploration can benefit anyone.

This is a book for students, entrepreneurs, career-changers, armchair wanderers and veteran travellers alike. It is about curiosity – and that belongs to us all. It is part philosophy and part smart-thinking, with a smattering of guidance.

Life is a complicated matter and we all have our own path to follow and mission to achieve. For some people, winning comes easy. For others it may take a lifetime. But what is for sure is that we can all be explorers in our own right if only we adopt the right thought process. So forget routine; now is the time to embrace the unknown, step out of your comfort zone and open the gateway to the Art of Exploration.

All you have to do is jump.

Levison Wood
London, January 2021

Sir Richard Burton

I

Know Yourself

Knowing yourself is the beginning of all wisdom – Aristotle

Exploration starts at home

I have a rather unusual name, and a rather unusual career. That often leads people to assume that I grew up somewhere far away and exotic, and that my parents brought me up amongst the local wildlife on some far-flung frontier. They're often disappointed when they hear the truth of where I was born and raised.

Stoke.

Nothing much exciting happened in Stoke in the early 1980s. The coalmines and factories were all but closed, and there was widespread unemployment. People's ambitions were mostly limited to a ten-mile radius and a sense of the foreign was encountered only when the first curry houses started to open. Families were tight and the idea of going off on an adventure was complete anathema.

Not that I'm complaining. Despite having a typical and very average upbringing, Stoke-on-Trent was very good to me. My childhood memories are a bundled collection of passing images: my little brother in a pram being pushed by my Auntie Josie outside my grandparents' house; walking up a cobbled side street in Hanley city centre going shopping with my mum, and standing in a red soldier's uniform in the school play. They are all visions of home; a happy childhood in a safe place, far from exotic, a mundane vision of suburbia.

That said, there are a few moments I do recall that set me upon a path of discovery when I grew up; the first of which came when I was about six years old. It was morning assembly at my primary school, all the pupils sitting cross-legged in the hall, eagerly awaiting

Mr Adams to address us. 'Mr A' as he liked to be known, was our favourite teacher. Kind and funny, he was the only male teacher at the primary school, memorable for being tall and hairy. He let us play and never shouted; he didn't need to, we all did as we were told.

Anyway, we sat in silence, and I remember sitting in the second row to the front at the far left, looking towards the line of chairs where the other teachers, Mrs Rogers and Mrs Watts, were sitting. Mr Adams stood up.

It was story time.

Sometimes we were read a few pages from Enid Blyton's *The Famous Five*. Other times it was a biblical proverb regaling the adventures of some long-lost saint. But this morning Mr Adams had a treat for us. It was a real-life adventure – something that had happened to him personally. When Mr Adams was eight, he had sneaked out of his house with two friends, and walked across the fields in search of an elusive newt pond. Armed only with some jam jars and a net, the boys went off on a voyage of discovery for this mysterious Shangri-La of Stoke-on-Trent.

These were local fields, which I'd heard of myself. He travelled far, crossing over the brook, and climbing over a fence and through a small forest, until it was very late in the afternoon and he realised that he was lost. His friends ran away, abandoning Paul (as he was known to them). As the sun set, Paul followed a hedgerow towards a hill in the distance. At the top he looked out over the forest to the fields beyond, where he thought he could make out the familiar sight of a nearby town.

Looking down, he saw a path between the trees, but that led to a cliff, and beneath it was a gorge through which ran the railway track. He knew it was dangerous to go anywhere near the train tracks, and there were signs everywhere with a skull and crossbones – but he had no choice. He climbed down the little cliff, sending soil and rocks crumbling down the sandstone divide, until he found himself standing, alone, on the gravel embankment. Looking left then right, he stood there for five, maybe ten minutes, fearful that a train might come and crush him at any moment.

Eventually, he made the mad dash, hopping over the metal girders and the wooden beams until he was safe on the far side. From there, he was able to climb up the other bank and follow a path that led him to safety; through the woods, across the fields and towards the town, where he was able to walk home.

I'm sure there must have been some lofty moral to the story. All the other stories, proverbs and biblical extracts we'd been read had a moralistic tone, and this one would have been no different, even if it was real life. However, at the time, this little tale of misadventure left a lasting impression on me. I don't know why I remember it so well, because it wasn't particularly memorable or adventurous, especially when compared to the stories of my own dad or grandad, who had served in the war. But it was probably the first one I'd heard where the protagonist was not an immediate family member, and he got away with doing something naughty.

Either way, the memory stuck. I thought how wonderful it was to be a grown-up boy of eight, who could go off on an adventure and get lost, and be able to climb down cliffs and run over train tracks. It sounded like the height of exploration. I also remember how disappointed I was. I was already six, and I hadn't done anything so extreme or dangerous yet. I felt as if I had wasted my life so far, and promised myself that as soon as I was old enough, I would go off on a perilous adventure. I wanted to be just like him and have my own stories to tell.

But Mr Adams' story was only an idea. We all have those – dreams where we act out the life that we want, rather than accept the one that we lead – and the truth is that I did not run away from home on my own newt-seeking adventure, or risk life and limb to climb down cliffs and cross train tracks at the next opportunity, much to my parents' relief.

Perhaps my dad did recognise something in me, though. A chafing desire to be outside and explore the big wide world. Either way, a few months after I heard Mr Adams' story, my dad took me canoeing and camping for the first time.

It was the height of summer and we paddled down an ancient gorge; suddenly I felt as if I was exploring the world myself, and not hearing about it second-hand through other people's stories. I loved the feeling of floating down the fast-flowing river, my dad telling me to hold on tight – there was a sensation of danger, and it was thrilling.

After some time, we came to a pebble beach under the shade of a tree. My dad pulled us up onto the bank. 'Come on, son, it's time,' he said purposefully.

Time for what? I thought, as we got out of the canoe, but I didn't ask. I could feel we were on the edge of something important, and I didn't want to ruin it with questions.

'Follow me,' he said, and leaving the paddles behind, we scrambled along the water's edge, and up a rough track that ran parallel to the river. My dad helped me up the rocky outcrops, until we were standing on top of a cliff that seemed to tower over the whirling rapids below. I assumed that he'd brought me up here so that I could admire the view.

I was wrong.

'Jump,' he said, still holding my hand.

Jump? It seemed unfathomably high and I could barely bring myself to peer over the edge. Instead I looked at him and started to cry. There was no way I was going over that cliff. I wanted adventure, but it seemed obvious that to jump down there was to die.

'Son,' my dad said, with a patient stare, 'do you trust me?'

I was silent. I had a fear of heights and I didn't much like water, either. The combination terrified me. I could hear the water crashing below. In my mind, it was a mile to the bottom; in reality, it was probably only a few metres.

'Would I ever hurt you?' my dad asked benevolently.

Ashamed of my cowardice, I looked at my feet. 'No . . .'

'We'll jump together,' he said. 'Okay?'

So the decision was made for me. We'd die together, but better death than the shame of letting my father down.

I closed my eyes and hoped that my feet would grow roots into the stone. They did not, and my knees trembled as my dad slowly pulled us towards the edge.

'Jump!'

I held my breath and clenched my hand in his, as we stepped forwards and into the abyss.

The fall seemed to go on forever. My eyes remained closed as I held my breath, waiting for the impact. Everything was silent as I plunged down through the air, my fingers suddenly slipping free, and I could no longer feel the safety of my father's hands.

Whoosh . . . I hit the cold waters and felt my head sucked under the eddy. I wanted to let out a cry of shock as I opened my eyes and saw nothing but white foam whirling all around. I had no concept of up or down. I might have been pulled a mile downstream for all I knew, but I kept holding my breath, hoping for the best. Suddenly, I felt someone grab me from behind and pull me up. I turned around and let out a sigh of relief when I felt my dad close by. He lifted me clean out of the water and had a big smile on his face.

I wanted to cry again, but I didn't – I was safe! The overwhelming sensation changed instantly from terror to relief, which morphed into a visceral bodily pleasure. I found myself inexplicably happy, beaming with confidence and joy. I had done something I never thought I could do, and to top it off, my dad was proud of me!

What did I do next? I swam back across the river, of course, climbed to the top off the cliff and jumped off again, this time on my own, and without a moment's hesitation.

I had conquered my fear, and felt invincible.

The motto of my old high school is *Know Yourself*.

Painsley was a Roman Catholic comprehensive school which drew in a wide range of children from across the surrounding towns and villages due to its good reputation for the sciences, and a stern disciplinarian staff. Mr Tunney, the headmaster, would explain to all the new pupils the importance of knowing yourself.

'Knowing yourself is the beginning of all wisdom,' the head would say, quoting Aristotle, and we would stare back blankly. Everybody knows themselves already, surely? Why would we need to be reminded of that?

Perhaps the school motto was not intended for the children we were then, but for the adults we would grow up to be. It was a reminder that knowing oneself is the key to both success and happiness. Being self-aware means marrying your outward behaviour and actions with your internal ideals and values. Astute self-awareness is a good predictor of success in life; it gives people a clear idea of the opportunities that will suit them and those that won't.

Above all, this ability to see yourself as being separate from your environment can bring you happiness and contentment. As the Chinese philosopher Lao Tzu put it, 'Knowing others is intelligence; knowing yourself is true wisdom.'

Samsara

If I asked you to think of an explorer, His Holiness the Dalai Lama might not be the first person who came to mind, but he is a man who trekked over the Himalayas on foot, travelling at night and in disguise to escape persecution in his homeland. What's more, he has since travelled the world spreading the message of peace, reconciliation and compassion, whilst maintaining his very humble origins. He is a man of boundless energy, infectious enthusiasm and a childlike curiosity – all characteristics of a great explorer.

I was fortunate to meet and speak with the man himself, when I visited India and listened to one of his sermons on the subject of 'Samsara', a central tenet of Tibetan Buddhism. Samsara is a Sanskrit word that translates as 'wandering', but in this context it can also mean rebirth, and life after death – reincarnation. Its essence is a cyclic and circuitous change known in Buddhism as the karmic cycle. It is best understood as 'a cycle of aimless drifting, wandering and mundane existence'. The whole point of our spiritual quest, according to the Dalai Lama, is to be liberated from Samsara, through enlightenment. This can only be achieved through self-awareness, understanding and self-mastery.

For Buddhists, and many others who follow the ancient Eastern philosophies, the meaning of life is simple: to achieve a state of mind that is free from desire, temptation and greed, and to walk a middle path of balance and moderation.

Very few people achieve it, but with dedication and hard work, we are all capable of it. For me, the Art of Exploration is about discovering the world with purpose and intent, and an aspiration of betterment. The starting point for our liberation from aimless wandering is self-knowledge.

The importance of self-awareness

The year 2020 will be remembered as the Great Pause. As the world went into lockdown, billions of people were quarantined in their own homes for weeks and months on end due to the Coronavirus Pandemic. For thousands across the globe it was a time of tragedy, losing loved ones to this terrible disease. For many millions more it was financially ruinous, as jobs and businesses went under and the economy plummeted.

Of course, it affected many people in different ways, but despite its awful impact and terrible consequences, if we were to fathom some positives to come out of the whole mess, it would be fair to say that it brought many communities together, unified in purpose and a desire to help one another get through it. Perhaps even more importantly, it forced a great number of us to take stock and reflect on our lives in a way that we never have before. It certainly did for me.

It is quite remarkable what a few weeks of solitary confinement can do for you. Shakespeare wrote *King Lear* while quarantining from the plague and the playhouses were closed, and the famous seventeenth-century diarist Samuel Pepys documented the impact of the rampant 1665 bubonic plague in London:

> But, Lord! how sad a sight it is to see the streets empty of people, and very few upon the 'Change. Jealous of every door that one sees shut up, lest it should be the plague; and about us two shops in three, if not more, generally shut up.

Seclusion has also afforded a great many writers over the centuries the chance to come up with their finest masterpieces. Dante wrote *The Divine Comedy* whilst in exile, and Cervantes came up with *Don Quixote* whilst behind bars. Dostoyevsky too was inspired to write two of his finest works after spending months in jail, and let's not forget Nelson Mandela, and a whole host of other political leaders. It seems that having one's liberty removed temporarily, if looked at with a positive mindset, can enable you to focus on things that really matter; and that begins with self-reflection and an understanding of oneself.

I am certain that, in time, we will look back at 2020 as being a year of catalytic change in many ways – politically, economically, and socially. We have lived through historic times, and I believe that much of the change to come will be driven by people who have used the time wisely, thinking about what they can do to improve themselves. There are the obvious things that many of us aspire to, such as reading books, getting fit, learning an instrument or a new language, or perhaps taking up a new hobby, whether that's origami or baking. But as well as the 'easy wins', I'm also referring to deep, fundamental changes in how we go about our daily lives, committing ourselves to a new regime of betterment in how we treat ourselves and others – and all this begins with understanding.

I've heard more than one person say that – if not for the losses that so many people have suffered – they were almost glad the pandemic happened, because it gave them the first chance of a break in their lives for decades. If it takes a coronavirus to give you the time to do what you want in life, then that would suggest a strong case for examining how you live; and you can only do that if you are self-aware. We can make big changes at any point in our lives, but we often get distracted because of work, relationships and other external factors, and it is easy to ignore what is happening deep inside of us. As well as taking care of our physical health, we need to carve out time to work on our self-awareness.

There are few times in our lives when we are forced to be still and make peace with our decisions, because we have no choice but to do otherwise. For me as an explorer and professional traveller, the year 2020 was the first time in over a decade that I'd spent more than a couple of months in one place, so it was certainly a big change from the norm.

At first I remember feeling trapped and a bit claustrophobic, stuck in London when all I wanted was to enjoy the freedom of the road. All my trips got cancelled and, like many freelancers, I lost an entire year's worth of wages. It was made harder by the fact that I ended up breaking an ankle, which forced me to stay put, even if there was a temptation at times to escape. It would have been simple to just sit in front of the TV and do nothing, but, instead of moping, I decided to try and use the time wisely and write down some of the lessons I have learned from travel, and in doing so reflect on what I could do better.

It reminded me of the last time I was forced to stay still and take stock in the summer of 2015. It was under slightly different circumstances, but with a rather similar outcome. I remember the date well – it was 19 August. I was on an expedition in the Himalayas, when the taxi I was travelling in took a tumble off the edge of a cliff in the dead of night, and I was plunged into a jungle ravine. Somehow I survived and escaped that time with only a broken arm and a few smashed ribs, but I ended up having to halt the journey for fifty days while I recovered from the accident. I'm sure a close brush with death is enough to give anyone pause for thought, and it forced me to re-evaluate things and ask myself a few questions about my own life, who I was, and where I was going.

Quite often we can get on a path to reach a 'destination', but neglect to re-evaluate the next stage once we get there: we simply keep going in the same direction without thinking. This can happen in business, relationships or in any part of our life. How often do you sit back and think – *really think* – about whether or not the path you are on is the right one? Maybe it was the right choice for you a few years ago, but life changes us, and what works for the person you were *then*, may not be right for the person you are *now*.

Wilful ignorance

Like many young men, I spent much of my teenage years unsure of who I was and where I would fit into the world. I did have a strong idea of what I wasn't about – I disliked routine and knew that a 9–5 office job was never going to satisfy me – but I found it hard to identify something positive that I could sink my teeth into. Back then, I thought that only the really wealthy could live the kind of life that I wanted.

I was fiercely independent, but I was also driven intensely by social approval in ways that I wasn't even aware. In fact, I think a lot of what I thought of as my 'independence' at the time was driven by a need for other people to see me that way. In my desire to be seen as making my own choices, I was making those choices because I was worried what people would think of me!

I was also hugely competitive. I couldn't bear the thought of other people seeing things in the world that I wouldn't see, having experiences that I wouldn't have or being able to do certain things better than me. I wanted to experience *everything*, all at once, and I was consumed by a constant fear of missing out. In my early years, it was fear that drove me. I was scared of being denied experiences, and ironically this led to an almost self-fulfilling prophecy as you cannot be truly grateful and appreciate the experiences that you *do have*, if your mind is whirling at 1000 miles an hour, trying to push you on to the next one. I have definitely been guilty of tick-in-the-box tourism.

As a young man, I started to drift. There are a number of structures that you can pin your efforts to at that age – sports teams, academic exams, and the like – which give you a sense of progress and purpose. But as time goes by, these gradually fall away, like scaffolding coming down to reveal a half-completed building. By my early twenties, I was starting to realise that I'd been going through life accumulating achievements and experiences, clocking up new pins on my mental map of the world in all the countries I'd visited, without ever really asking myself what was the underlying purpose of all this exploring. It took me a long time to figure that out.

Having an explorer's mindset is not about visiting new or challenging places for the sake of visiting them. You have to ask yourself not only where or what you want to explore, but *why*. If you are facing challenges in your life, a bit of travel might seem like one way of getting a sense of perspective on these (more on this later), but it might not, because *you* are *you*, no matter which continent you stand in. Either way, what's important is not where you go or what you do, but the mindset that you travel with. It's important to want to learn about the world around you, but the answers will never fit into place until you understand the person asking the questions.

The First Adventure

Homer's Ancient Greek epic poem, the Odyssey, is perhaps the earliest travel story in Western literature. It tells the adventures of Odysseus, the king of a small Greek island called Ithaca. Odysseus leaves his wife, Penelope, and their baby son at home and sets sail to fight in the

Trojan war. The war drags on for a decade, but that isn't the end of his travels. In his mission to get home, the fraught king encounters all sorts of obstacles. The journey is filled with fantastic tales of passionate affairs, a trip to the underworld and encounters with horrific monsters and demons.

Odysseus is the hero of the story, but he is deeply flawed, and brings a lot of the tale's misfortune upon himself. His hubris after successfully tricking the Cyclops leads to him being cursed by the sea-god Poseidon, and he must wander the Mediterranean for ten years before he can return home to his family. His lack of self-awareness sets him at odds with his own compatriots – the Ithacans. Odysseus is warned not to eat the sun god Helios's sacred cows, but his men ignore this and are shipwrecked as a result, with all but Odysseus dying. Then, when he returns to Ithaca, the man who was presumed dead murders his wife's suitors in a cruel rampage, torturing some, and sparing none. Odysseus is blamed for the deaths of two generations of Ithacans – all because of his egotistical blunderings, and a lack of self-awareness.

This story is foundational to how we imagine adventure, at least in the West. It has underpinned our collective imagination for nearly three thousand years, and the word 'odyssey' – derived from Odysseus – has become synonymous with long journeys. The Ancient Greeks, along with Aristotle, were the first Westerners to explore ideas of self-knowledge in a meaningful way. This is reflected in literature from the period, and is the foundation of what we now call 'philosophy'.

Discover your inner explorer

When we start to ask questions of ourselves, inevitably we get drawn towards the notion of 'purpose'. Why am I here? Where am I going in life? What do I want to achieve? It is important to ask these questions, because without them we drift aimlessly. We might have a good idea of what we need to do to keep going from one day to the next, but without being able to tie this into some higher overarching goal or set of ambitions, we quickly become disillusioned.

We don't all want the same things, and we (quite rightly) have our own personal interpretations of success. That makes it even more difficult when it comes to trying to distil lessons from other people's lives. No one should presume to tell anyone else what they should be striving for, because that is a very personal matter, but for me the successful explorer's mindset begins with a general principle, summarised aptly by Ernest Hemmingway: 'There is nothing noble in being superior to your fellow man; true nobility is being superior to your former self.'

I echo Hemingway's words. I truly believe that success is simply doing better than you were before; we all have a duty to understand ourselves better, and to strive constantly to improve ourselves, because life is about learning lessons. Classical philosophers from Aristotle to the Buddha and Lao Tzu have identified knowing ourselves as the starting point for a meaningful existence, but what does self-knowledge mean? What does it take to know oneself?

To understand our goals, we need to understand our flaws; to understand our flaws, we need to understand ourselves. Our histories (ancestral and personal), our identity, our upbringing, our desires and our values. To begin the journey of self-improvement, we must understand and grapple with the various factors, mistakes, hopes, dreams, strengths and weaknesses that define us as individuals.

This can be very uncomfortable and difficult work, but if we are truly to embrace the mindset of an explorer – someone who can think for themselves, be free of judgement, and aspire to humility and gratitude – then we need to accept that there is something we *can* do to help ourselves.

First, however, we need to understand a little bit more about our own drivers and motivations. As T.S. Eliot famously wrote: 'We shall not cease from exploration / And the end of all our exploring / Will be to arrive where we started / And know the place for the first time.'

It is impossible for us to know our limits and the extent of our powers without testing ourselves, pushing a bit further than we thought possible and delving a little deeper into the unknown, and we don't know who we will be when we return after our own personal odyssey.

Knowing yourself is important no matter who you are, and what you do. Navigating through life has always been difficult, but now we are under constant bombardment from our screens and phones telling us who we should be, and what we should think. We work long hours and are often tired, so it can be very tempting to accept one of these 'one size fits all' personalities that social media tries to hand us.

The problem is that, as humans, there is no one size fits all. We are all unique, and we need to make time and space to ask ourselves the question: what is truly meaningful to us? Without knowing the answer to this question, we cannot be effective, caring, understanding, calm or purposeful in what we do. In the hustle and bustle of modern-day living, we can get swept up in routine, work and family, without spending time to consider who we want to be and where we really want to go.

To live a fulfilled, exciting and happy life, I believe we have to create our own philosophy, whether conscious of it or not.

Sir Richard Burton

One of my personal role models and childhood heroes is the Victorian explorer Sir Richard Burton. Long before I was old enough to be let loose on my own, I read all about his adventures in faraway lands, using my imagination to fulfil my lust for adventure. He was a man of many talents, earning his keep as a soldier, diplomat, spy, translator and author. Far from ordinary, Burton was a troublemaker in his youth, known for clouting a teacher over the head with his violin. He was thrown out of Oxford University for violating dozens of rules (including keeping a pet bear), and left in an enormous huff, flattening the college flower beds on his way out with his horse and carriage.

As he grew up, Burton learned how to behave, but retained a rebellious streak. He hated what he called the 'slavery of civilisation' and rejoiced in shocking polite society. A young vicar once asked if it was true that he had killed a man in the Arabian desert. 'Sir,' Burton replied coolly, 'I'm proud to say that I have committed every sin in the Decalogue.'

But Burton was not merely a hot-headed rogue. He had a sharp intellect and a healthy approach to improving himself; possessing the ability to work hard at subjects that interested him, or that he felt served him. He was a polyglot, with a mastery of multiple European and Asian languages, as well as multiple dialects of Arabic.

Free-spirited by nature, he would remain outspoken throughout his life and his adventures included a contested and controversial journey to search for the source of the Nile. His weather-worn complexion, dark eyes and language skills made him a perfect spy for the East India Company, but perhaps the greatest example of his guile and guts came when he smuggled himself across the deserts of Arabia and into Mecca, which was and is completely forbidden to non-Muslims. Not one to do things by halves, Burton had completed his disguise by getting circumcised.

The explorer once wrote, 'Of the gladdest moments in human life, methinks is the departure upon a distant journey to unknown lands,' to which I can certainly relate. There is no better feeling than the immense anticipation that comes with embarking on a trip of any kind. Burton found life in the desert and in the wilderness – and the risks of getting caught – utterly exhilarating. The idea of this endless inquisitiveness, and of being a brave and fearless risk taker, is what appealed to me as a boy. Burton was forever seeking out new experiences and continually defied expectation. I admire that he accepted his exploratory instincts and embraced his own insatiable curiosity.

In this respect, he is the quintessential Victorian explorer, determined to make his name in the annals of history, and this is often the focus when it comes to Burton. Beneath all of this, though, there is something far more nuanced and that is his enlightened attitude to self-awareness. It is summed up well in the quote, 'Do what thy manhood bids thee do, from none but self expect applause.' It is important to understand that when he wrote this, the word manhood meant 'the condition of being human'.

Burton made great pains and efforts to improve his understanding of the self. He was convinced that the best measure of our success was against ourselves, and that the noblest claim was to adhere to one's own moral compass. He believed that without this understanding, you were no better off than a slave.

Finding your quest

I believe that it was Burton's capacity for introspection and reflection that set him apart from so many others, and that this trait is something worth emulating. Giving ongoing attention to one's internal state and one's inner life is what will make that life rewarding. When it comes to travelling, are we doing it to help answer questions about the world and our place in it? Or, without that introspection, are our travels nothing but vanity – a slide show to let everyone know how adventurous and fortunate we are?

There's a great meme of a couple lounging on a beach with cocktails in hand, and palm trees in the background. The caption reads: 'Oh no, we're still us!' It's meant to be a caution for travellers who think that the simple act of moving from place to place is the remedy for everything.

If your problems exist inside your head and heart, then they will be with you whether you're in the Taj Mahal or a Tesco carpark. You can't outrun thoughts and feelings, but travel can help you process and place them, so long as you approach it with the purpose of self-discovery. Only with an open mind can we learn more about our inner purpose – what we want, what we think and what kind of world we want to leave behind us.

Of course, people travel for all sorts of reasons. The truth is that very few will go to booking.com and put 'somewhere I can find myself and the meaning of life' into the search box. Self-discovery is often a by-product of another venture, at least at first. That is why having an open mind is so important. So long as we put ourselves in positions to learn, and don't fight the revelations when they come, we will grow by osmosis. If you travel to discover new culture, who you are as a person will change. If you travel to learn a language, that ability to connect more deeply to a whole new population will also change you. If you travel for physical adventure, that challenge will change you, too.

There is no right or wrong about the reasons for travel. Even if the sole aim of one's journey is to relax, then that too is sufficient, so long as it gives time for thoughtfulness. Rushing around from sight to sight, ticking off temples and flitting from Instagrammable beach to five-star resort may boost your ego, but ultimately it does little more than send you home more exhausted than before you left. Living this way is seeking other people's approval, not your own.

Honestly, I can only imagine how much more shallow my early travel experiences would have been if social media was around when I was a younger man. Yet I think a spell of tick-in-the-box tourism is natural for most of us. If you grow up in a consumer society, then it is silly to think that the mentality of 'gotta have it all' would not stretch to travel. The key is to recognise when that is happening, because it's a behaviour that you can relapse into at any time.

Did you book a trip to impress someone? Are you spending more time looking at your phone than the sights you came to see? Does your enjoyment of the trip diminish because not enough people comment and like your social media posts about it? We can all slip into these negative loops at any time, unless we are self-aware enough to know that they *will* happen. Don't feel bad when they do. Give yourself a little pat on the back for noticing, and refocus on what is really important; even if you did book a trip for the wrong reasons, that doesn't mean you can't use it as a chance for personal growth while you're there!

You would not be the first person who travels to try and escape their problems. Travel provides a method of escape from the mundane, normal and tragic. Going on a journey has long been seen as the surest way of getting over a broken heart, and everyone knows a good love story that involves the protagonist fleeing his or her breakdown and going off to a faraway land.

Travel is escapism in its rawest form. It is a way of getting away from life's distractions, which in itself can be both good and bad. They say that running away from your problems solves nothing, and whilst this is true, I don't think there's anything wrong with taking a break from your problems, so long as you understand that they will still be there when you get back. When I broke my arm, I knew that at some point I would have a lot of hard work to do in physio, but was I jumping out of bed to do press-ups on day one? Absolutely not! It is okay to rest broken bones, broken hearts and battered minds, so long as we use that rest to prepare ourselves for the hard work that lies ahead.

Sometimes you need to take yourself out of the equation for a while in order to gather your thoughts, gain a new perspective and look at the problem from an alternative angle. You never know, you might have that lightbulb moment that inspires you to make the necessary changes. You might find a random stranger to share your problems with on a train, and they suggest some useful advice; or you might need to go somewhere with a different culture, which offers up a novel outlook. Even if you don't, a change of scenery and a long walk will at least give you the time and space to process what you have left behind. Sometimes you simply need to go away in order to return.

Travel has gifted me endless experiences; it has given me shocks, surprises and tragedies. I have witnessed suffering beyond comprehension, seen poverty beyond words and uncovered awful abuse. I live in a very safe and comfortable corner of the world, and I could stay here and avoid all of the terrible things I have seen, and yet I still travel for the sake of it, and I seek out the hardest places in the world. It has enabled me to formulate my own viewpoints based on real-life experiences, and not merely theories or speculation. When you travel, you realise that all those experiences, both good and bad, teach you a lesson.

Gustav Flaubert once observed, 'Travel makes one modest.' But I think it does so much more. It makes you tolerant, humble and very grateful, too. It makes you recognise that there are many ways of living your life, and no such thing as black and white. By going away on journeys, whether they be short trips or long expeditions, I have learnt to let go of prejudices and accept things the way they are. Away from the constraints of my own society, I have found a contentment like no other, and a reality more authentic than anything I could conceive within the boundaries of those set by myself in an ordinary world.

The more you learn of others, the more you will know yourself.

The stakes are high

While travel gives us an obvious and clearly delineated time to think, it is not enough to adopt this mindset only when travelling. It is a way of thinking and a process that can and should serve us in all areas of our lives. Self-reflection is a must for being honest with oneself, and truly understanding one's own needs and desires.

As humans, our vision of our inner world does not come as naturally to us as our ability to perceive the outside world. If you can learn to understand your inner workings as well as the outer, then you will be emotionally intelligent, have better social skills and be much more motivated. As with anything, some people are born with greater skill at this than others, and one's upbringing also makes a difference, but no matter where you start, everyone has the capacity for self-awareness; like the strength of your muscles, it is something that can be improved upon with practice.

Our self-appraisal mechanism is like a feedback loop: if you welcome information on how you are perceived by others, that is how you will develop. If there is a gulf between your understanding of yourself, your performance and the character you outwardly present, and what others see and know to be true, you will not go as far in life. All of this takes a huge amount of humility and you must have a willingness to put yourself out there, if change is even remotely going to be possible.

Whether consciously or not, I have always enjoyed setting goals for improving myself, but it can be hard and very exposing to put yourself out there and ask for feedback. Alas, it is only by seeking this 'criticism' that you will get to know yourself in the first place, and then have the capacity to grow.

Anyone can do this – it is all about making time for it. Go and write a really honest list of things that you know about yourself. You might have heard of a SWOT analysis. Write down your own Strengths: personal and circumstantial, everything you're good at, as well as your assets. Then list your Weaknesses, and be ruthless here. O stands for Opportunities: what can you see around you that will help you to improve – whether that's a new job, a financial investment, the offer to travel or simply an introduction to a new person. Then finish up with Threats: what is in the way between you and success? Who is the competition for that job you want? Will someone else beat you in the race?

All these things you probably know already, deep down, but sometimes it is important to take the time to reflect on your own situation, where you've come from, and where you're heading. The truth is that if you don't adopt this way of thinking, then you are directly placing yourself as an obstacle between the life you currently have, and the one that you wish you were living. In other words . . .

Know yourself.

That means being truly honest in what we are, and what we want, because without that knowledge we can never know where we want to go next in life. The voyage of self-discovery is often uncomfortable – sometimes downright painful – but what's the alternative? Living a life where you constantly feel lost, and dissatisfied? Personally, I would rather take the path to knowing myself, no matter how painful, because I know what lies at the end of it is a life well lived, and my potential fulfilled. Curiosity, as we'll discover next, is key to exploration.

Remember that to be an explorer means asking questions – of the world, of other people, and most importantly – of yourself.

George Mallory on Everest

2

Be Curious

The difference between an ordinary life and an extraordinary one is only a matter of perspective – Beau Taplin

Escaping the ordinary

Growing up, I was blessed – or cursed – with an insatiable curiosity. I remember reading *Moby Dick* for the first time as a child, Herman Melville's words echoing through my soul: 'As for me, I am tormented with an everlasting itch for things remote. I love to sail forbidden seas, and land on barbarous coasts.'

I had never sailed a forbidden sea, and I don't remember seeing anything particularly more barbarous when we left Stoke for trips to the seaside, but I understood Melville's words as well as I knew my own name. I believed then – and I believe now – that there was something in my soul that demanded I explore.

And I mean, *demand*. There was no subtle hint about it. My head was filled with a raging storm of questions. I couldn't switch it off, and I knew that the only cure was to find answers. I *had* to explore.

Of course, I am far from unique in this respect. Think about the explorers of old.

When George Mallory was asked by a journalist from New York why he wanted to climb Mount Everest in 1924, the hardy mountaineer responded with perhaps the three most famous words in the history of exploration: 'Because it's there.'

Travellers and adventurers of all eras have constantly wondered what is over the next horizon. There seems to be an innate desire in some people to know and learn more, and an aversion to routine and stability. I knew at an early age that I was not cut out for a mundane office job and I wanted to experience something that would provide me with adventure. I always liked surprises.

I also hated the saying 'curiosity kills the cat'. It feels like society is sometimes trying to drum our natural instinct out of us – to make us accept the box that we are born into. If every human had listened to that advice, then there would be no books, no music, no art. I wouldn't have friends all over the world. We wouldn't have medicine. Complacency is what kills the cat – particularly one born with a desire to explore – or as the novelist Paolo Coelho rather astutely put it: 'If you think adventure is dangerous, try routine; it is lethal.'

Danger is not what we should be worried about. It is living a life full of regrets that ought to be a bigger concern. I have thought long and hard about my own reasons for wanting to travel so much. On top of being somewhat in awe of Mr Adam's youthful adventures, I believe a deeper inspiration came from my childhood holidays with my mum and dad.

I was lucky to have parents who were both school teachers. They had long summer holidays and so we were able to travel for at least a couple of weeks twice a year. Because they were teachers, they didn't have a great deal of money, so the holidays usually involved long motorway journeys to places like Scotland, Wales or Cornwall, often with grandparents and extended family in tow – all destined to fill up a caravan, or a great big tent on a muddy campsite. Of course, as a child they were great adventures, which began the moment my mother started packing the suitcases. I knew, even as a toddler, that as soon as we set off, we were into the realms of otherness – an alien world filled with ice creams, audiobooks and service stations.

The anticipation was almost overwhelming. There would be treats and sandcastles and salty water. Coming from the Midlands, seeing the sea was a rare adventure, and it was always exciting to wrestle with my little brother Peter in the back seat of the car for the title of who saw the sea first.

Nothing, though, could beat the thrill of jumping out of the car at our destination, sucking up the fresh coastal breeze, and exploring this new and foreign land. Even at home, my parents fully encouraged me to discover what lay beyond the hedgerows and our garden. They let me build a den in the field and sometimes, if it was warm enough, Peter and I would camp in the garden, imagining we were the very first settlers in this strange environment.

Every time we left the confines of Stoke-on-Trent on a family trip, it felt as if the universe had expanded. A desire to see the rest of the world was cemented in my mind forever. Travel, even as a child, made my little heart sing and kept me wanting more. Those formative holidays, wandering in the Highlands, catching crabs off piers and scrambling around Welsh castles, established a vision of reality beyond my normal comprehension. It was an ethereal existence verging on fantasy, where anything was possible. It didn't so much matter where I went, *as long as I went*, and I immersed myself in the simple experience of being in a new environment away from the routine of home.

Explorers of the South Seas

Thor Heyerdahl was a visionary explorer and anthropologist, who wanted to try and prove that Polynesians originally came from South America and that there was an ancient sea route between that continent and the South Pacific Islands. In 1947, the famous Kon-Tiki expedition was launched. Heyerdahl built a raft made only of materials that would have been available to pre-Columbian society and set sail from the coast of Peru on an epic journey of 5,000 miles across the Pacific Ocean.

Subsequent DNA analysis of the people that inhabit Polynesia has since discredited the Norwegian explorer's hypothesis, and yet his own expedition was a success – proving that with a bit of luck and a steadfast determination, the voyage was indeed possible. What's more, it has been shown that the seafaring people of the South Pacific, whilst perhaps not originating from South America, did in fact travel extraordinary distances on rudimentary rafts. There were no compasses, maps or sextants; they navigated with only the movements and rhythm of the seas and the constellations of the stars.

The Polynesians somehow managed to sail thousands of miles across open water, from the famous Easter Islands to Tahiti, Hawaii and New Zealand, which begs the question: why? As populations on the islands grew, there was a need to search for other islands to inhabit, but the scope of the task was incredible. The islands they colonised seem so tiny when contrasted with the vastness of the ocean that surrounds them, and yet these innate explorers were determined to find out what lay beyond the limited, safe lands that they knew.

The feat of discovering islands in such an expanse of water is nothing short of miraculous, but it was made possible by the insatiable curiosity of those who were willing to set off into the cruel seas against all the odds. Those men and women were rewarded for their inquisitiveness with new lands, rich in resources and devoid of competition, in which to house and feed their families. It is an accomplishment that should leave us all in awe and wondering about our own limits.

Adventure in the genes

Mr Adams used to tell us that only boring people get bored. As a child, I took that as license to let my imagination run free. I was never bored, either in my own company or other people's. I think those early holidays with the family made me aware that there was a whole world waiting to be explored. I knew I wasn't cut out for routine, and travel soon became my passion.

I am far from alone in feeling that way. Travel seems to be a basic human desire, part of our psychological, if not genetic makeup. I get a visceral thrill being somewhere new. For many of us, even the mere anticipation of travel is enough to excite and fill us with a sense of joy, but it begs the question: why are there more than 500,000 people in the air at any one time? Why do we humans, in ever increasing numbers, decide to pack ourselves into flying cylinders and translocate to the other side of the planet simply to take a break?

The vast majority of those half a million flying humans are travelling because they want to, no matter how annoying the airport, or sitting in the middle seat – the excitement and thrill of getting to explore a new place is so addictive. Even as a young man, I wanted to understand where my obsession with movement, newness and adventure came from. What gave me such itchy feet? Why did I appear to have such a deep-rooted and inescapable wanderlust?

The answer may be partly genetic. Studies have shown that a particular allele of the DRD4 gene (which controls our sensitivity to dopamine, effectively the hormone from which we get our kicks), known to geneticists as DRD4 (7R+), is associated with risk-taking behaviours. This allele – dubbed the 'wanderlust gene' – appears to be more prevalent in nomadic communities, who need a drive to explore in order to keep moving and finding new pastures, and less prevalent in settled, sedentary peoples. Globally, around 20 per cent of people carry this allele, so if you feel you are a natural explorer, you might well be a carrier.

That said, the other 80 per cent of us have a drive to explore as well, and the explorer's mindset is relevant to everyone. Regardless of whether it is genetic or not, the desire in many people to explore the world is very real. It is not only me that has a seemingly insatiable need to explore. It is deeply rooted in the human psyche. Ever since early man left Africa, humans have continued to move all around the planet. Cynics might say that they were simply looking for new food and resources, but when there were only a few hundred thousand humans on the planet, there wasn't anywhere near the amount of competition for hunting grounds and grazing that there has been in more recent millennia.

No, there must have been something else that induced these prehistoric explorers to leave the relative safety of their forests and caves to set off into unknown lands and face untold dangers. No doubt the search for food was a factor, as early human populations were at least partially nomadic and their prey came and went with the seasons, but why would a community leave the comfort of the African savannah with its plentiful game and endless opportunities for foraging, to go and seek out the deserts of Arabia, or indeed the harsh, cold wastes of northern Europe and Siberia – let alone brave the perilous sea crossings on bamboo rafts to settle on remote islands in the south Pacific?

One must assume that it was the same motivation that drove generations of successive explorers, conquerors and travellers to venture forth continually in the spirit of exploration to inhabit almost every corner of the earth, from the frozen wastelands of the Arctic to the seemingly impenetrable jungles of South America.

Let's say that there is a wanderlust gene, or at least a basic human need to travel. What could possibly be the benefit to those of us living in the modern world, with all its technological comforts? We live in an age of Google Earth, where the planet reveals its secrets at the spin of a digital globe. We live in the age of TV and online streaming, where we can watch icebergs and steamy rainforests from the luxury of our sofa, so why would anyone bother actually going to such irksome environments themselves?

Why, in England – a country that has long forgotten nomadism – is there still a population of travellers who choose to move from place to place in the same way their ancestors did for hundreds of years? I suppose it might be the same reason that in North Africa and across the Middle East there still exist Bedouin nomads who refuse to settle in one place, in favour of a lifestyle of discomfort and hardship and continual momentum. When there are plenty of occupations that offer financial reward, stability and plenty of other benefits, why do some people choose to become itinerant circus entertainers, roving war photographers or busking yoga instructors? Out of curiosity, that's what.

I could read a thousand studies, or interview a hundred scientists, but the truth of the matter is this: I *feel* I have to explore, and therefore I must. I know myself, and therefore I can match my external action with my internal feelings and thoughts. I *have* to be curious, and explore, because it is who I am.

Sound familiar?

A bit of distance

Solvitur ambulando – 'Everything is solved by walking' – is a phrase first attributed to the ancients, who used to say that all temporal and spiritual conundrums could be figured out by taking a long walk. It was an idea that has been passed down through the ages – from the early Christian pilgrims to modern philosophers and travellers. It is the theory that removing yourself from a problem for a while will give you the headspace required to work things out.

When I was a soldier, one of the key skills we were taught for command was how to detach ourselves from what was happening around us; with all the bangs and the shouting, it was easy to get sucked into what was right in front of you. Through being put into challenging situations, we developed the skill to take a mental step back from the chaos and the noise in order to see the bigger picture, and work out a plan to overcome the situation in front of us.

Travel can be the 'step back' that gives us that detachment. When a problem seems to be 'in our face', it can be difficult to think of any solution to it other than fight or flight. By contrast, when we escape from the place where we spend most of our time, our mind is suddenly made aware of all the errant ideas we had suppressed. We start thinking about obscure possibilities that never would have occurred to us if we had stayed back home. Furthermore, this more relaxed sort of cognition comes with practical advantages, especially when trying to solve complex tasks.

Take the 'Duncker problem', a cognitive test published in 1945, when people are given a cardboard box containing a book of matches, a few drawing pins and a wax candle. They are told to figure out how to attach the candle to a piece of cork board on a wall, so that it can burn properly and no wax drips on to the floor. Nearly 90 per cent of people pursue the same two strategies, even though neither strategy can succeed. They try to pin the candle directly to the board, but this causes the candle wax to shatter; or they try to melt the candle with the matches so that it sticks to the board, but the wax doesn't hold and the candle falls to the floor.

At this point most people surrender, assuming that the puzzle is impossible and the experiment a waste of time. Only a slim minority come up with the solution, attaching the candle to the cardboard box with wax and then pinning the cardboard box to the corkboard. Unless people have an insight about the box – that it can do more than hold drawing pins – they will waste candle after candle. They'll repeat their failures while waiting for a breakthrough. This is known as the bias of 'functional fixedness', since we are typically terrible at coming up with new functions for old things. That is why we are so surprised when we see an everyday object used in a way for which it wasn't designed.

Researchers reported that those who had lived abroad were 20 per cent more likely to solve this problem than those who had never lived outside their country of birth. Why? The experience of another culture endows us with a valuable open-mindedness, making it easier to realise that a single thing can have multiple meanings. Consider the act of leaving food on the plate: in China this is often seen as a compliment, a signal that the host has provided enough to eat. But in America the same act is a subtle insult, an indication that the food wasn't good enough to finish.

In another study, an American psychologist found that people were much better at solving a series of insight puzzles when told that they came all the way from California and not from down the hall in Indiana. The subjects considered a far wider range of alternatives, which made them more likely to solve the challenging brain-teasers. There is something intellectually liberating about distance. In reality, most of our problems are local – people in Indiana are worried about Indiana, not China or California.

This leaves two options: find a clever way to trick ourselves into believing that our nearby dilemma is actually distant, or else go somewhere far away and then rethink our troubles when we get back home. Given the limits of self-deception – we can't even tickle ourselves properly – travel seems like the more practical possibility.

These cultural contrasts mean that open-minded travellers are receptive to ambiguity, more willing to accept that there are different (and equally valid) ways of interpreting the world. This in turn enables them to expand the circumference of their cognitive inputs, as they refuse to settle for their first answers and initial guesses. Of course, this mental flexibility doesn't come from mere distance; increased creativity appears to be a side-effect of difference – we need to change cultures to experience the perplexing assortment of human traditions.

The same details that make foreign travel so confusing – Do I tip the taxi driver? Where is this bus taking me? – turn out to have a lasting impact, making us more imaginative because we're less blinkered. We are reminded of all that we don't know, which is a lot; we are astounded by the constant stream of surprises. Even in this globalised age, slouching toward homogeneity, we can still marvel at all the earthly things that aren't included in the guidebooks and that certainly don't exist back home.

Consider too the impact that distance has on our emotions. How do you feel when you watch a movie on a flight or in the cinema, free from the subconscious restraints and pressures of your home? Why do so many people find love on one-week getaways, when they tell themselves that they can never find it at home? Distance can free us from the self-imposed cages that we have built at home through our routines, the norms of our society and the expectation and opinions of others.

Don't ask, don't discover

Albert Einstein once said: 'I have no special talents. I am only passionately curious.'

We are curious animals, and we forget this simple fact at our peril; it's the key to self-knowledge. We are far more predisposed to ask questions about the world around us than we are to question ourselves, so if we don't do the former, what hope do we have of doing the latter? Exploring gives us the opportunity both to see ourselves through a different lens – comparing our own upbringing to that of someone with a very different lot in life – and to learn things about ourselves by facing challenges we would otherwise not encounter.

This could be anything from climbing a mountain to using a hole-in-the-floor toilet – the important thing is that it is new, and outside of our comfort zone, because no matter how big or small the experience may seem, it contributes to our personal growth. Simply realising that there is no right way or wrong way to live is in itself hugely powerful. Without that knowledge, we succumb to tunnel vision and group think, which shrink our horizons dramatically.

Social/cultural anthropologists, who study different human cultures, have a phrase for this kind of perspective: 'cultural reflexivity'. It describes the ability to recognise that the way we perceive the world is only one of an infinite number of world-views, and that, for example, Western materialism doesn't seem any more strange to a Tibetan monk than a belief in reincarnation might to a Wall Street banker; but it *is* just as strange. By experiencing other ways of viewing the world, we can understand that our own world-view (and its associated stresses and challenges) is in many senses arbitrary.

Without reflexivity, all we can really do when we visit another place or culture is to compare that way of life with our own. This is flawed, because each way of life is unique and rests on its own particular values and life prospects, and we lose any chance we had of learning something from other people. Rather than compare, we need to learn to place ourselves fully in someone else's shoes when we travel. We do this by asking questions before we make any assumptions, and therefore we open ourselves up to infinite veins of wisdom and allow ourselves to tap into new perspectives. How many of our problems could be solved by finding a new way to look at them?

It is not enough simply to get on a plane or visit some unexplored part of the world: if we want to experience the creative benefits of travel and exploration, then we have to rethink its *raison d'être*. Most people escape to Paris *not* to think too hard about anything much; but rather than gorge on that buttery croissant, consider a thought for the person who baked it, and how they might view the world differently to a person from across the channel. As a Brit, we can find the idea of shorter French working hours 'frustrating and lazy', but place yourself in their shoes. What do those extra hours away from work bring? More time with the family, or time to read – the ability to separate work from life?

There is a reason behind everything, and to imagine that we know it without asking questions is foolhardy at best, and jingoistic at worst. Put aside ego – both personal and national – and ask *why*. Then ask again, because the first answer is rarely the correct one.

The truth is that – as nice as it is – you don't need to go to Paris or Peru to do this kind of exploration of the mind and our assumptions. There are many ways we can expand our horizons without needing to leave our home town, or even our home. It could be as simple as trying new cuisines; perhaps visiting community centres, or places of worship that you don't normally associate with, and asking the people there about their beliefs and cultures; or reading books based on the beliefs of other cultures (even other religion's holy texts, if done respectfully) and ethnographies.

Even watching a classic Bollywood film – given how different the traditions of filmmaking are in India from the West – can have a transporting effect, and provide distance from your immediate life. Something as mundane as changing your route into work occasionally will show you people and parts of your town you've not seen before. Be honest with yourself – how well do you *actually* know your town, or your neighbours? For that matter, how well do you know your family, or have you fixed assumptions based on their role in your life?

The larger lesson here is that our thoughts are shackled by the familiar. The brain is a neural tangle of near-infinite possibility, which means that it spends a lot of time and energy choosing what *not* to notice. As a result, creativity is traded away for efficiency; we think in literal prose, not symbolist poetry. A bit of 'distance' (geographical or mental), however, helps loosen the chains of cognition, making it easier to see something new in the old, and the mundane is grasped from a slightly more abstract perspective.

David Livingstone

On the outside wall of the Royal Geographical Society in London is a statue of perhaps the most iconic of all British explorers. His name inspired one of the most famous lines in the annals of Victorian exploration, uttered by another great adventurer, Henry Morten Stanley, who was sent out to find the lost hero: 'Dr Livingstone, I presume?'

Dr David Livingstone was of humble Scottish origins, growing up in Blantyre in a workers' cotton mill to impoverished parents. Against all the odds, he worked hard to become educated and became a medical missionary. He was a man of great conviction and determination to improve not only himself, but all those around him. As a missionary, he was sent to Africa and was a vociferous campaigner against the slave trade. Unlike many explorers of his age, he showed a desire to understand the people he met there, rather than simply convert or exploit them. He learned the local languages and immersed himself in African culture and customs, all the while never losing his zest to explore this uncharted land.

He undertook a number of great expeditions, travelling along the Zambezi river into Central Africa, further than any white man at the time. He also went in search of the source of the Nile and in doing so mapped out much of the Great Lakes region of Tanzania, adding a wealth of new information to the geographical understanding of the time.

That said, he never succeeded in many of his tasks. The source of the Nile remained elusive and his missionary efforts were ultimately futile. But despite the fact that his achievements were far less glorious or impressive than many of his contemporaries, it is his name that stands out, thanks in my view to his endless curiosity about the world. He followed his heart to the extreme and regardless of the outcome, he did what he felt was right.

He was a stern believer in personal change and choice, and always encouraged others to choose the right path, never forcing anyone to his own ideas. Unlike some later Victorian explorers who believed in racial superiority, Livingstone called that attitude 'the most pitiable puerility' and was a staunch believer in equality and human potential. He was a patient, kind and intellectually curious explorer, who embodied the virtues to which most can only aspire.

Seeing things in a new light

When we travel, there is usually a goal behind it, even if it is only to rest and do nothing. However, we often find something that we had no idea we were looking for. This makes sense when we view travel as a learning opportunity, dictated by our circumstances back home. We might be stressed, so go away looking for peace and quiet; we might be interested in history, so go somewhere in search of ancient monuments and landmarks.

It is important to have a goal like this in mind – after all, it is part of being curious and the point of travel in the first place – but on top of these goals, we need to be ready for experiences that we were not expecting. This is how travel and exploration can be truly transformative; they introduce our minds to things and events that previously they couldn't even contemplate.

I've always loved elephants. Ever since I was a kid I wanted to see them in the wild. I was inspired by David Attenborough's documentaries and loved the fact that, against all odds, these enormous gentle giants still roamed across the wilds of Africa. I wanted to see them with my own eyes, So when I was eighteen, I set off on a very clichéd backpacking trip around the world. It was 2001 and going off on a gap year had suddenly become all the rage. I had never travelled on my own before, and it was terrifying.

First stop was South Africa. I got a flight to Cape Town and took a bus along the coast via Durban all the way to the Kruger National Park. I was very much out of my comfort zone, but I put on a brave face, pretending to know what I was doing. At first, I kept myself to myself. There were lots of backpackers in their mid-twenties and I felt like a child, tagging along on a grown-ups' holiday. Then I realised that everyone else was as nervous as I was.

I experimented by talking to strangers and forcing myself to interact. I learned card games and listened to stories and observed how other people acted. I slowly grew in confidence and began to hitchhike as a way of meeting random people. In doing so, I was invited into strangers' homes and shown incredible hospitality and kindness. It established a firm belief in human nature, which I have taken with me ever since.

I found that by putting myself in new situations I would be afforded new opportunities, and that was how I came to be invited on a free safari, where I got to see elephants in the wild. But for me, the biggest reward wasn't seeing the elephants, although they were awe inspiring; it was understanding more about other people, learning new ways of doing things, and discovering more about myself and my own potential.

In hindsight, it was a pretty simple and self-obvious truth that I would learn more about the world in general, and myself in particular, from meeting strangers along the way than I would from seeing a bunch of elephants, but I had to take the trip to grasp that. In itself, that's a great example of how blinkered our brains can become if left to the same old, familiar routines. We forget that we share our planet with seven billion other people, and their lives are so hugely different from our own that each of them has something new and intriguing they can teach us. The trick to netting as much of this collective wisdom as possible is exploring at home and abroad with an open, inquisitive mindset.

Sir David Attenborough

David Attenborough was born in Isleworth in May 1926, and grew up in Leicestershire. From an early age he had a voracious appetite to learn about the world around him, and was fascinated by nature, wildlife and fossils.

Attenborough's curiosity led him to the field of nature filmmaking, beginning with the three-part series The Pattern of Animals in 1953. At time of writing, almost seventy years later, he has yet to hang up his camera, nor has his curiosity been dulled. In 1957, Attenborough founded the BBC's Travel and Exploration Unit, from which he commissioned a huge range of programmes that he could share with his fellow man.

Through the course of his career, Attenborough essentially created the genre of the nature documentary as we know it, and he has become virtually synonymous with this type of programme. He has also become known as a champion of environmental causes and is an ardent campaigner. But Attenborough's curiosity and interests stretch far wider than the field of nature and conservation; during his time as a controller of the newly created BBC Two during the 1960s, he committed to broadening the range of content beyond that shown by traditional broadcasters, commissioning programmes as diverse as Match of the Day and Monty Python's Flying Circus.

Sir David Attenborough has been given more honorary degrees by British universities than any other individual. He also has an extensive list of titles, having been made CBE in 1974, knighted in 1985 and made a Fellow of the Society of Antiquaries in 2007. In a dazzling career that is testament to the rewards of curiosity, perhaps one child-hood incident stands out above the rest: as an eleven-year-old, the young David responded to a request from University College, Leicester, for newts for the zoology department, which he offered to sell to them for three pence each. His source of the newts, unbeknownst to the university, was a pond five metres away from the faculty. A bit of curiosity about the world around you pays dividends!

Look beyond the horizon

It is amazing what bits of information we hear in our childhood, but don't fully come to appreciate until we're older. My grandmother used to say that a change is as good as a rest, which was hard to understand as a child. Now, I couldn't agree with her more.

I've already mentioned a few of the reasons that we explore. The truth, of course, is that there are as many reasons to travel as there are people on the planet, and on top of that you can layer the overlapping circumstances that arise as we do our best to navigate our lives. And yet, I believe there are 'themes', if you will, that must unite us in our exploration, not least of which is the desire for a sense of freedom and liberty, unique to the process of leaving behind one's norm and setting off to somewhere different.

Exploring new horizons is a mindset, as is applying curiosity to all that you do. It's about pushing your personal boundaries and taking the time to see and do new things, wherever in the world you may be. My own childhood emotions of excitement, adventure, a sense of freedom and joy are what still compel me to travel, as I'm sure is the case for many people who pack a bag, or simply walk out of their back door and into their home town that still holds surprises.

There is a sensation that comes with the unfamiliarity of places. A visceral feeling as the senses are crammed with new smells and flavours. You don't just see a place when you travel – you smell it, you touch it and feel it. The hot sand beneath your toes or the wet jungle air in your lungs. Travel is immersive. We go to these places expecting that they exist for our admiration, but quite often it is we who are consumed by the experience. The mosquito that drinks our blood. The villager who makes a sale and sits with the grin of a man who has charged you four times his normal price.

We are not set aside from each new place that we visit. We are a part of it, and we will remain so even after we leave. Our interactions will be remembered by the people who call it home. They were introduced to the new as much as you were.

I love the human connection when I travel. I also like surprises, and the feeling of anonymity of being in a different country. It makes me feel invisible and free. I especially like those sensations when I'm alone. Usually the first thing I do when I get to a new city is go out and walk, with no particular destination in mind; I will happily get lost. I walk the streets without a map and the simple process of walking aimlessly gives me time to reflect, check in and get to know myself once more.

I go to far-flung places to do this, because I grew up travelling the world; I have set my boundaries quite far to start with, so to push them I need to go a long way away. If most of your life has been spent in one country, even one town, then good news: you've got less far to go, at far less cost and effort, to stretch your own boundaries and gain a sense of the unfamiliar. Take it one step at a time, and see where it takes you.

And while not everyone can or wants to 'travel', anyone and everyone can 'explore'. In his book *A Journey Around My Room*, Xavier de Maistre describes the experience of 'travelling' to his sofa and seeing it with fresh eyes, studying it deeply and celebrating the sensation of exploration and discovery without needing to leave his own house.

The same benefits that a traveller gains from exploring the world around them – perspective, novelty, challenge – can be gained simply by adopting a curious, exploratory attitude towards the familiar, everyday things around us. With the explorer's mindset, we can see ourselves through someone else's eyes, and come to know our own limits and aspirations better as a result. In 2020, with prolonged lockdowns, how many people have fully come to know their home for the first time, and the neighborhood that surrounds it? We don't have to wait for a pandemic to make us curious about the place we call our own.

Curiosity opens new opportunities and perspectives to us. A curious mind is the most powerful thing that you own. It broadens our horizons and enables us to reassess our lives in a new light, providing distance from our problems. But more than that, it sets us on a journey towards unlocking our fear of the unknown. Overcoming our fear, in all contexts, is the subject of the next chapter.

Amelia Earhart

3

Do What Scares You

*The cave you fear to enter holds the treasure
you seek* – Joseph Campbell

Take the leap

One hot morning in 2001, I set off from my hostel in Northern
Queensland in search of an elusive waterfall. It has grown in popularity in recent years, but back then it was barely on any maps, and
only the local people knew the way. The waterfall had attained
almost mythical status among young backpackers, because it involved
several hours hiking to get there, and there were no organised treks.
I'd never seen any pictures, but the two or three people I'd met who
had made the journey had described it as one of the most beautiful
they'd ever encountered – consider me sold!

I packed a small backpack including drinking water, sunscreen, a
few snacks, an old film camera and a compass that I always carried.
The hostel owner had given me directions on how to get there
through the forest, but no one else seemed interested in going, so I
set off alone.

At least that was the plan.

I had barely started walking down the road that led into the forest
when I noticed a little dog following on behind. I stopped to pat it
and saw that it was a beautiful grey Staffordshire Bull Terrier and –
being from Staffordshire myself – I took it as a good omen. I tried to
shoo him away, because I didn't want the poor thing to get lost, but
as I carried on walking down the path, the Staffie seemed determined to follow me.

The forest was hot, and seemingly deserted except for myself and
my new companion. I could hear the ocean on the other side of the

trees, but no other people. Then, as the path petered out into nothing, I realised that I was lost. I decided that the best route would be to walk towards the sea and follow the beach north. After hacking my way through the bush, I reached the deserted shoreline, where palm trees cast a short shadow over the brilliant white sands. It was a scene of such beauty that I could hardly believe it existed; the kind of place reserved for postcards and computer screensavers.

Spewing out of the jungle to my left was the estuary of a small river. It seemed to cut a swathe through the sand like a green snake, before pouring into the shimmering ocean. The estuary was perhaps six metres wide, too wide to jump across, and there was no way to tell how deep the water was, or what lurked within – this was Australia, after all.

I stared at the water for a while, but my intense concentration did not conjure up a bridge. So I thought about looking to see if it got any more narrow inland, but that was a no go as I knew that to cut through the thick forest would be virtually impossible.

It was then that I was delivered a sign.

A rusty sign, mind you. It had been hammered into the sand. The sea salt had faded the yellow paint, but its message was clear to see – there was a black drawing of a crocodile. It looked almost comedic, with a curly tail, the kind you see in children's books, not at all menacing. And yet I knew there was nothing laughable about the situation. I'd heard all about the infamous saltwater crocodiles and their fearsome reputation. Some were so massive, they would eat sharks that dared to swim up into the river mouth. What was I going to do?

As I stood on the hot sand, a few stories floated up to me from my past. I remembered the story that Mr Adams had told us at primary school. I couldn't recall the moral of it, but by taking a risk he had found his way to the other side of the railway tracks and made it home. And then I remembered the cliff, my dad and how he'd given me the confidence to jump off it alone.

I looked at my watch. Forty-five minutes had passed while I'd been daydreaming in indecision. The dog was getting impatient now, looking at me as if I were a coward. I decided that there was a simple way to commit myself to action, and threw my rucksack across to the other side of the waters.

Shit, I thought to myself, *there's no going back now*. The Staffie knew that. Wagging his tail, he jumped straight into the river, swam to the other side and gave his coat a shake all over my bag.

Shit.

I walked back a few yards, determined to run up and jump, so that I would spend the least amount of time possible in the water. I came forward, but then stopped at the water's edge: I was scared. I didn't want to die, and particularly not in the jaws of a prehistoric monster. No one would even find my body, only my bag on the sand and a stoic Staffie, who would probably not make the greatest witness at my inquest.

I took a deep breath, and made myself think about the odds. There are a lot of crocs in Australia, and a lot of people, but only a few get eaten a year. The odds were on my side, right? I took a few steps backwards then ran, and launched myself into the air, bracing myself for the hungry jaws that awaited me . . .

But there was only a splash, and a thrashing young man, and then I was out on the other side – and alive. I felt exhilarated and foolish all at once, and then I realised that I'd have to do it all again on my way back. Oh well, I'd cross that bridge – or lack of it – when the time came.

I kept walking up the beach with my companion, and after another hour we reached the waterfall. It was every bit as beautiful and unspoilt as it had been described to me, and the fear I had felt in getting there was washed away.

DISCLAIMER: Now I'm not advocating recklessness here, and I'm sure that there are plenty of parents who will be tutting with desperation at the thought of their gap-year, adventuring offspring taking silly, unnecessary risks because I told them to hop over croc-odile-infested waters.

But . . .

Some measured risk is a crucial part of our development as we grow up. It is something to be sought out, rather than avoided.

Mawe Manhood

There are many different manhood rituals around the world, but one of the toughest and most painful has to be performed by the Mawe. The tribe live as hunter gatherers deep in the Amazonian jungle of Brazil.

It is an unforgiving environment, and they believe that for the younger boys to become men, they must prove that they can endure the most painful experience there is: the sting of the Paraponera clavata, also known as the bullet ant.

It may not surprise you to hear that the bullet ant takes its name from the fact that its sting produces a feeling like being shot. The sting is 4 out of 4 on the Schmidt pain index, with only the bite of a tarantula hawk wasp given the same score in the insect world. It is said to be excruciating and wildly painful, with waves of burning pain lasting up to twenty-four hours. After covering them with a natural sedative, the Mawe weave hundreds of these ants into a pair of gloves made from leaves and vines. Naturally, the ants' stingers are left to face inwards in these mittens of misery.

For the manhood ritual the young boys must place their hands into the ant glove for five minutes, receiving hundreds of stings. Through the process the boys experience muscle paralysis, disorientation, violent shaking and even hallucinations. But once it's over, it's over, right?

Actually, no. To be accepted as men, the boys must perform the ritual up to twenty times, which may take place over months, or years. Once the men have faced the most excruciating pain the jungle has to offer, they have faced their fears and are able to hunt courageously in the rainforest as a man.

Embrace risk

I am not one for putting my hands into gloves of bullet ants, but a big part of my own mindset *is* about allowing curiosity to get the better of fear. There are amazing things, places and people around us in the world, but so often a nagging fear of doing what others find odd, of social rejection, or maybe even financial ruin and physical danger, prevents us from discovering something new. Through practice and confidence, we can all get a grip on our fears and approach the unknown with curiosity and interest.

Believe it or not, I have an innate fear of heights. I'm terrified of flying, in fact, even though I know rationally that it's safe. Because of this, over the years I've forced myself to face that fear. I joined the Parachute Regiment, I've climbed mountains, and I've tried to learn paragliding. I'm still scared of heights, but each time I push myself, I become a little less so. Explorers are sometimes described by journalists as fearless, but it's not true. I think we misappropriate the word, because really those who don't fear are probably either mentally deficient or psychologically maladapted. In fact, there is evidence to suggest that psychopaths have a reduced startle response and that their fear receptors are dulled.

Fear has been given a bad rep. It isn't something to be avoided; rather, it is our life's mission. It's our duty to overcome our fears, whatever they may be. I believe that failure to do so is an abject failure in life itself. With that being the case, what do we have to lose?

Contrary to what we might read in the news, we live in some of the safest times in all of human history. People live longer, we have amazing technology and medicine, and fewer people die from illness and war than ever before. And yet we seem to worry more, and be scared of everything.

I try to remind myself every day that the world is not as dangerous as the media plays it up to be. The threat and fear that is transmitted to our screens twenty-four hours a day is not a fair representation of the seven billion people living in amazing places across the planet. I've found even in the most war-torn countries that fighting and danger exists for only a small amount of people, for a fraction of time. Equally in the most hostile places, you're likely to find the most incredible hospitality. It is up to us to accept our own powers and make up our own minds, and not leave it to someone else.

Fear is a natural human instinct that has evolved as a tool for survival. The fight or flight mechanism in our brains that has been a part of our reptilian core for millions of years still dictates how we deal with stressful and potentially dangerous situations. No matter how clever we think we are, we're still evolved apes, and fear is an essential part of our psychological makeup.

Fear is contagious. This is how terrorism works. It kills very few, but terrifies billions, forcing nations to spend their security budget on preventing panic. Fear can collect and pool in an area, becoming part of the collective consciousness, as it has recently in Paris and

London. This is not just in our minds – there is evidence suggesting that humans emit alarm pheromones when under stress, which send out olfactory signals that can be detected by other humans.

Greed may be the root of all evil, but I believe that fear lies at the root of all greed. One of the seven deadly sins, it is by definition insatiable, making it all the more lethal. Greed amounts to taking more than your fair share, or grasping and clinging onto something that you are scared of losing or not having enough of. Quite frankly, as evolved apes, we cannot always resist these animalistic urges, which explains why most of us have been greedy at some point in our lives. Taking more than one's portion is the subconscious ape telling us that we need to have this or that to survive: more food, more sex, more money, more power. We are basically scared of not having enough – so we take more than we need. We become desirous, and lack control over ourselves.

Having evolved from animals that would be only sporadically successful in bringing down prey, dogs have an instinct to keep eating until their bellies are completely full. In an age where human owners provide all their food for them, domestic dogs are unable to suppress this instinct – meaning that if their owners succumb to the puppy-dog eyes and overfeed them, they can easily become overweight out of a primal fear that their next meal may be some way off.

Thanks to similar instincts, humans often overeat, and also over-indulge in lots of other areas. Our mind loses itself and acts irrationally, defending its actions and saying things such as: 'I need to have that sportscar to feel fulfilled'; 'I need to invade that country to feel safe'; 'I need to kill that person before he kills me'; 'I need to eat that animal, otherwise I won't have enough protein.' Greed is the manifestation of the ego, which is fuelled by fear. In some ways, fear is a manifestation of our greed for safety, which we often think we need more than is good for us.

Greed is the concept of doing more harm than good, or taking more than you give. From an ecological perspective, this couldn't be clearer to me – our greed looks set to be our downfall. It is an exaggeration of fear: the belief, subconsciously or not, that if you don't accumulate, you will not survive. We have become obsessed with material things and with convenience, but it is melting our glaciers and destroying our planet. It is something I have seen first-hand, out in the Himalayas and the Amazon for example, and it's something in which we are all complicit. I don't know what the answers are, but I've become conscious of this greed in my adult life – just because you can do something, doesn't mean that you should.

When we act selfishly or greedily, we make decisions that in the long run are bad for ourselves and bad for society. I'm a firm believer that deep down we all know what is right or wrong, and what we want, but we get a bit lost on our journey to find it. Everyone makes mistakes, and everyone has the opportunity to learn from them. The problem is that when we let our ego control our emotions, we end up holding grudges, fighting with our friends, starting wars or destroying the planet.

Alexandra David-Néel

Alexandra David-Néel lived the life that many explorers dream of. She was an independent, highly intelligent and seemingly fearless woman, who defied all expectations of her time.

Born in 1868 to Belgian-French parents, she ran away from home aged fifteen to learn Buddhism and the ancient arts of the East. An accomplished linguist, she first had to study English so that she could read the translated texts in the British Museum. Determined not to settle for a normal life, she lived with her lover out of wedlock and announced that children would not suit her wandering lifestyle.

In 1924, disguised as a poor pilgrim, she managed to sneak into the forbidden City of Lhasa in Tibet, which was then out of bounds to foreigners on pain of death. She ended up spending two months inside the holy city, where she studied philosophy and became a master Buddhist herself.

Over the course of her life she wrote thirty books about her adventures, as well as academic tomes on history and religion. She travelled her entire life, speaking a dozen languages fluently. At the age of sixty-nine, she travelled through China, where she witnessed the brutal Sino-Japanese war and saw first-hand the horrors it entailed. Her curiosity, though, was never sated, and she was a brave advocate of seeing the world with one's own eyes, rather than simply being a passenger in life.

She once said, 'Who knows the flower best? The one who reads about it in a book or the one who finds it wild on the mountainside?'

Have the courage to live the life of your own making.

Dare to fail

I was only eighteen when I was in Australia, leaping into rivers, and it will come as no surprise to you that teenagers are more likely to take risks than adults or younger children. A teen brain is still undergoing maturation, which makes a lot of us more likely to seek new and novel experiences. The brain has a bias at this age, weighing positive experiences more heavily and negative ones less so. My adult self might have acted differently with the crocodile conundrum.

Effectively, as a teenager you are more accepting of a consequence that is as yet unknown to you. When you capture this mindset and tap into it, you can further broaden your horizons in adulthood. Things are rarely as dangerous as they seem at first glance, and risk is often rewarded. We can always make excuses about why we didn't want to do something, but with that attitude, what would we ever get done, or explore? We would simply stay put in our safe little bubbles, never growing. What a waste.

There is no reward without risk, and certain considered risks ought to be embraced in order to reap rewards. This is all part of being an explorer.

Fortune favours the brave.

Yes, the risk can be scary – it can be downright *terrifying* – but you have to get used to this uncertainty if you are ever to change, innovate or grow. When you take a risk, your brain has an increase of dopamine, and if you learn something new as a result, the neurons form stronger connections. Boldness pays dividends. By taking chances, one can achieve things that other people can't, because they didn't have the bravery to do whatever was required.

On the Victoria Embankment of the River Thames in London, outside the Ministry of Defence, there is a stone plinth topped with a bronze statue of a fearsome-looking beast called a 'Chinthe'.

Resembling a lion, but with the features of a dragon and a dog, this mythical beast is usually found as a stone effigy guarding Burmese temples and pagodas. But during the Second World War it became the symbol of British and Indian Army Special Forces units, who saw action against the Japanese in the jungles of Myanmar.

Nicknamed the 'Chindits' and led by a maverick brigadier called Orde Wingate, these guerilla fighters specialised in attacking the enemy deep behind the front lines. Wingate, a rebel by nature, was very much a budding adventurer himself. As a young officer, he once took six-months' leave to cycle across Europe and Africa to reach his new posting in the Sudan, where he established himself as an expert in desert warfare. He mounted numerous successful operations to capture slave traders and ivory poachers, and in his spare time surveyed North African archeological ruins and published his work at the Royal Geographical Society.

It was the knowledge gained during these early expeditions, and his innate curiosity and ability to overcome fear, that gave him the confidence to become an effective Special Forces commander in Myanmar. The Chindits operations took inspiration from those early forays in Africa and included long marches through extremely difficult terrain, blowing up enemy lines of communication, expedition-style surveying and using guerilla tactics to fight larger forces.

Wingate and his band of irregular fighters were famed across East Asia and feared by the Japanese invaders. It was precisely because they took lots of risk (which was often criticised by other military units) that they had such an effect in undermining the enemy morale and boosting their own forces' efforts.

On the statue in London is written the motto of the Chindits, adopted from the words of Admiral Horatio Nelson: 'The Boldest Methods are the Safest.'

By encouraging risks, we also have a duty to accept mistakes. We must foster an environment where they are not simply tolerated, but encouraged. I like to call this way of thinking 'fail fast, fail early'. This means creating fertile ground for experimentation; we owe it to ourselves to try things out and accept that they might go wrong. There is no time like the present to have a go and get the learning out of the way.

So many people shy away from this foggy arena of mistakes and failure, but only by pushing past your boundaries and limitations can you ever increase them. You are unlikely to achieve greatness if you're safely at home with the doors closed, doing the same thing every day. Routine and regularity are the enemy of pushing boundaries and taking risks. But those who *do* go there – into the arena of risk – can exploit the valuable lessons that come with learning from their mistakes.

Take a look around you in your own life, and at the world at large. I bet that the people or organisations who have grown the most in a short space of time took risks, and those that have stagnated did not. Now, of these, who talks about their stumbles as well as their successful leaps? I believe that organisations and individuals can be divided into two categories: those who conceal their errors and those who confront them.

The aviation industry is a leader in this arena of learning from mistakes. It learns from and interrogates errors, rather than being threatened by them. They install small, robust black boxes in all passenger planes, which record huge amounts of data about the flight and are designed to withstand crashes. Famously, they are rescued from the rubble if an aeroplane has an accident, but they are also used more regularly than this – for instance, if there has been a near miss between two planes, or one has come close to running out of fuel while in a holding pattern, the aviation companies will examine the information. The recorded log, both from the point of view of machinery and people, gets analysed in depth.

The industry has developed a culture of making improvements and reforms, ironing out weaknesses in the system rather than blaming individuals for errors. In aviation, mistakes and accidents are not concealed, but are seen as valuable learning opportunities – crucial in a sector where mistakes come at the cost of human life.

If we fear failure, or allow our fear to stop us taking risks, we cut ourselves off from every chance we have of learning and growing. Organisations and entire industries that are ruled by a fear of failure will stagnate and, ultimately, die out. Leaders who do not create and foster environments in which experimentation is encouraged, where failure is viewed as a learning opportunity, will sacrifice the innovative capacity of their teams and be overtaken by their competitors. Individuals who let fear govern their actions and avoid risky activities over time will not only fail to push their own boundaries, but shrink in on themselves, as the risk-taking, experimental instincts of youth disappear, in favour of the safe predictability of the familiar.

Amelia Earhart

Like many explorers, aviator Amelia Earhart clearly had the desire to win a place in the annals of history. She also had an extremely healthy appetite for risk. As a child, she fashioned a makeshift roller coaster out of crates in her garden, hungry for thrills even at a young age. She loved going to stunt flying exhibitions, watching the hair-raising loop the loops with delight. During one such event, a pilot saw her watching the show and intending to give her a bit of a fright, he dived his aircraft down towards her, swerving only at the last moment, but brave young Amelia sat tight. She said later that she believed the little airplane had said something to her as it whizzed by, enticing her into a life of aeronautical adventure.

In her early twenties, she finally went up in a plane herself. She reflected that she knew immediately – a few hundred feet off the ground – that she had to learn to fly herself. Amelia did not observe conventional limits, which is all the more remarkable given that she was born in Kansas, USA, before the turn of the last century. A time when a great number of limits were a feature of a woman's life.

Flying had not even been around for twenty years, but that did not deter Earhart, who dropped out of nursing school and tracked down one of the best aviators of the time. Neta Snook was the first woman to have a flying school and she agreed to teach Amelia – for a fee, of course, and after a lot of begging. The airfield was a fair distance from Earhart's home, a long bus ride followed by a six-kilometre walk, but she stuck to her training and it paid off; after only two years, she became the sixteenth woman in the US to be issued with a pilot's license. Earhart worked multiple jobs to support her dream – as a lorry driver, a photographer and a stenographer – saving every cent she could spare. After six months she was able to afford a biplane of her own.

From then on, Amelia Earhart began setting world records, and soon became a celebrity. By 1932 she became the first woman – and the second person – ever to fly across the Atlantic. It was a dangerous and testing flight that included an emergency landing. A few years later, Earhart set her sights on the ultimate goal; she wanted to become the first woman to circumnavigate the globe by aircraft.

It was an enormous risk with a huge amount of unknowns: she would be vulnerable to icy conditions, heavy winds or technical problems with the plane. She would need to fly 47,000 kilometres around the equator, which could take weeks, but Earhart was well aware of the hazards. Accompanied by her navigator, she took off from Miami in 1937, and made good headway on the first legs of her journey. A month later, Amelia Earhart had made it to Papua New Guinea, where she took off for the next section of the journey – aiming for Howland Island in the Pacific.

But the formidable explorer never made it. A few distress signals were detected, but the plane and Amelia were never seen or heard of again. In a testament to her popularity, the President of the USA, Franklin D. Roosevelt, sent out a search party. It went on for two years until the teams were forced to give up, and she was declared lost at sea.

Though it is not known what happened to her in the end, Amelia was a trailblazer who has left a legacy of pushing the boundaries and being bold. I read her inspiring tales as a young lad and I have tried to adopt her attitude towards taking risks. Amelia herself said, 'Flying may not be all plain sailing, but the fun of it is worth the price.' She saw risk as something that was an important and necessary part of life, and something that would reap an immense reward – the freedom and euphoria of flying your own aircraft.

As she put it: 'Decide whether or not the goal is worth the risks involved. If it is, stop worrying.'

Keep pushing boundaries

In 2004, at the age of twenty-two, I hitchhiked along the ancient silk road from Europe to India. It was one of the most terrifying and yet exhilarating times of my life. I was fresh out of university and full of the zest for life. Unfortunately, my bank account wasn't full of anything at all. In fact I was attempting to travel for almost five months on just £500, which as you can imagine was stretching things a bit thin.

I decided that I had no choice but to believe in the inherent goodness of people. I was travelling overland all the way from England to the Himalayas and had already crossed Europe, Russia, the Caucasus, Turkey and Iran. By the time I reached the Afghan city of Herat I was out of cash, and had no hope of more till I reached Kabul. I hitched rides in beat-up minibuses and sometimes walked, and one day I reached the small town of Chaghcharan, deep in the central mountains of Ghor province. I knew nobody there, and there were no hotels.

Eventually I met a young man whose family turned out to be opium smugglers. He invited me to stay in his house until I could get another onward ride over the mountains to the capital. I explained that I had no money, but Usman, my new host, explained that in Afghanistan the code of hospitality was clear: if you come upon a stranger in need, then you are bound by duty and religion to assist them. In Afghanistan, the usual Islamic practice of hospitality to guests is taken to an even greater level, where guests should be protected at all costs, even against your own neighbours.

I ended up staying at their home for a couple of nights, sitting on top of Usman's roof, looking out across to the snow-capped Hindu Kush mountains beyond. I was glad that I'd taken the risk to make it to Afghanistan, which was catching its breath after the toppling of the Taliban, and I was glad that I had put enough store in human nature, and someone else's culture, to enable me to have these experiences.

There was a blip in my faith, though. I must admit that when I was about to leave, young Usman asked me for some payment. I'd already explained that I had no money, but he really wanted a gift. I had nothing with me except the bare essentials, but I felt so bad that I had nothing to give that I ended up parting with my sleeping bag.

He seemed happy with that, but then the fear crept over me . . . what if I found myself stranded in the mountains? I might have just signed my own death warrant.

I told myself that I had barely used it since leaving Europe, and tried to put the image of freezing to death from my mind. I reminded myself that the sleeping bag was merely my comfort blanket, both physically and metaphorically. It represented fear and a guard against the unknown. But now, without anything to protect me against the elements, I was entirely at the mercy of the kindness of strangers. I had no option but to go out there and put my faith in other people. If I didn't, I would die of exposure, because now there was no plan B.

It turns out I needn't have worried. From that point on, I was taken in wherever I went and didn't need to sleep out at all until I reached the safety of India. I let go of my comfort blanket, cast my fear aside, and good things happened in return.

The Vine of the Soul

The Quechua people of Peru and dozens of other indigenous Amazonian tribes have a ceremony unlike any other.

Ayahuasca, or yagé, as it's also known, is a hallucinogenic tea made from a mix of vine, leaves and roots found only in certain parts of the Amazon rainforest. Nobody knows how the first indigenous people came across this strange potion, but it's believed to have been in use as a traditional plant medicine for thousands of years.

Shamans, or medicine men, prepare the brew by chanting poetry and singing icaras, or chants, while blowing sage smoke over the mixture in a highly formalised and ceremonial way before the tea is administered.

While the medicine has gained popularity in recent years amongst curious Westerners, who travel far and wide to partake in the ceremony, it has traditionally been reserved as a means to help people suffering from undiagnosed mental health issues. It is reputed to be extremely beneficial for those struggling with depression, anxiety and PTSD, with no known side effects.

I spoke to a Colombian shaman, who explained to me that the medicine is useful for many physical ailments too, but only if the recipient is open-minded and willing to accept responsibility for their own problems.

It sounded strange to me – how can you accept that an illness is your own fault? It goes against everything that Western medicine states. Despite the cultures being extremely geographically distant, the Shaman's outlook on karma struck me as similar to the Buddhist way of thinking; he told me that at the root of all of life's problems was fear.

Ayahuasca works best when we overcome our fears. The medicine is ingested to the accompaniment of music, singing and chanting, sending the person into a psychedelic trance. What happens next is hard to explain, even after witnessing it first-hand. The individuals first seemed to writhe around, groaning before vomiting in the noisiest way possible. Some participants cried and screamed as if they were possessed by demons. Then, hours later, as the music became more upbeat, the crying stopped and everyone began to smile, sitting or lying still with their eyes closed. Some even stood up to dance and looked like they had found the most awesome rapture.

When I spoke to them afterwards, everyone explained that they felt like they had been on a journey to the depths of hell, having confronted their deepest fears and traumas head on. They continued to explain that through the medicine they had been cleansed of their worries and felt as if they had been reborn.

Whatever this might sound like to the Western mind, it was certainly real to those who took part. This tribal ceremony was centred around overcoming fear and facing whatever demons are hidden within. Only then can the weight of worry be lifted, and true peace found.

Heading off into the darkest Amazon to find inner peace through an hallucinogenic brew might not be everybody's cup of tea, so to speak, but it's true that only by confronting your fears can you grow and develop your true potential, in any walk of life.

Don't believe the hype

There is a big difference between real risk and perceived risk. Familiarity is a big part of how we perceive the two. If you've been doing the same kind of thing for years, you are bound to take on a new, similar risk with more gusto. Playing rugby can be dangerous, but if you started in childhood, you are conditioned to the game by the time you reach adulthood. Banging into each other at full speed would seem much more of a risk if you first started playing in your thirties, but if you're used to risking your body, then going from rugby to parachuting doesn't seem like much of a leap. In my own life, jumping off the 'cliff' as a child was scary, and so was jumping out of planes as an adult, but I was able to do it because I had increased my exposure to risk incrementally throughout my life.

There are people who think it is perfectly reasonable to avoid risk in any sense, but doing so will stunt your personal growth and likely lead to a pretty boring and uninspiring life. Risk is crucial for our development and is how we gain novel experiences and learn.

When I go travelling, I face a constant battle with other people in trying to convince them that where I am going is safe. My career as a writer and photographer has taken me across the globe to all sorts of conflict zones, war-torn regions and places that are in the news for all the wrong reasons. I often find myself in disputes with lawyers, health and safety consultants and other litigious types, who are wary of accepting the 'risk' of sending me off to somewhere like Afghanistan, Iraq or Syria.

I understand that they are just doing their job, but what they often fail to consider is that because a country is perceived as a war zone, it doesn't automatically mean that I will get shot. Conflict is usually localised – the whole of Iraq isn't at war, all at the same time. There are parts of Afghanistan that are perfectly safe for travellers to visit. The Wakhan corridor, a narrow valley in the far north-east of the country, is ethnically very different to the rest of Afghanistan. There are no Taliban there, it's been free from any fighting, and no visitor has ever been harmed in that area during the War on Terror.

I learned that, even as a soldier on 'the frontline', you spend far more time drinking tea and chatting with your friends than you do exchanging bullets with the enemy. Worry is often futile; the chances of something happening to you are really low. There's a clichéd statistic, but I think it is one worth remembering: you are far more likely to die by being trampled by a cow in a field than you are to be killed by a terrorist. You're also more likely to be injured by a toilet than struck by lightning, and you're more likely to be struck by lightning than attacked by a shark. You have higher odds of being born with eleven fingers or toes than all of the above.

The truth, as I've found out at my own expense, is that you are far more likely to be involved in a car accident while travelling than you are of being mugged, shot at or beaten up.

The media loves bad news. Moreover, the average Western person reading a newspaper doesn't care that much about how happy people are in Nigeria, or about the vibrant hipster scene in Damascus, or how literate the women are in Northern Pakistan, or the progressive nature of Iranian culture.

Don't believe everything you're told. Take the risk and see things for yourself. We must fight our stereotypes and approach ideas with an open mind, and we can only do that by embracing a certain level of risk. When we do so, we expand our field of vision and therefore our own limits – by risking more, we can fear less. I was lucky that I could go out and experience the world in order to formulate my own ideas. My conclusion is that most people are generally pretty good; even in the most 'unlikely' places, I have often found an almost overwhelming level of hospitality.

By closing your mind, you are assuming that you already have all the answers to life, which is rather arrogant when you think about it. Having an open mind doesn't mean that you don't hold any convictions, but that you are willing to be challenged on what you think is the truth, and to change your mind accordingly, as you are exposed to new places, new people and new ways of thinking. It is accepting that the process of learning, which you so embraced as a child, doesn't stop until the day that you die. Without the risk of being wrong, you will never be able to learn, and get closer to being 'right.'

All that said, risk-taking does not have to be an extreme sport; you needn't gamble all your cash on the Grand National or jump out of a plane (although I'd recommend the latter). Instead, we can get better at taking risks by making 'mistakes' less of a taboo. We should embrace risk while being prepared for mistakes, rejection or 'failure' – and I use quotation marks because is it even failure unless you give up?

We can build incremental steps in our lives to hone our capacity for risk-taking, such as visiting some place new, or switching up your regular routine – even striking up a conversation with a stranger if you are naturally shy or introverted. It may sound mundane, but these experiences will build up a tolerance and those new neuron connections will start to form. This is the explorer's mindset. We seldom explore our home cities in the way that we might when we are travelling. If you have a small choice that you need to make, try making a snap decision; leave it to the toss of a coin if you have to.

Seek things out that are *just* beyond your reach, in the foggy arena of risk-taking. Little by little you will acquaint yourself with life outside of your comfort zone. If you don't put yourself out there, vulnerable to the risk of failure, then there is no chance of progress.

Fear is a primal biological reaction. This means it is very powerful, but also that it isn't always suited to our modern lives. Like food, we tend to crave more safety than we actually need, but if we can learn to overcome our fears, we can continue to open up to the world; embracing and learning more for all of our lives. By taking risks, we learn that the world isn't as scary a place as we thought it was.

Do not underestimate the power of this realisation, as this positivity has an infectious, snowballing effect – the less we fear, the more positive we become; the more positive we become, the less we fear. And, as we're about to see in the next chapter, a positive outlook can change not only our own lives, but the world.

Annie Londonderry

4

Back Yourself With a Smile

It pays to be a winner – British Army unofficial slogan

Opportunity knocks

My grandfather served in the British Army. So did my father. After spending a few years wandering and backpacking, and loathing the prospect of a 9–5 job, I decided to follow in their footsteps. Both of them had served in the infantry – the footsloggers who carry the fight to the enemy – and it felt only natural that I would keep this family tradition going.

I passed the army's commissioning board, which meant that I could join as an officer, and command men; something I found both exciting and daunting. A young officer's training takes place at the Royal Military Academy Sandhurst and when I arrived there, aged twenty-three, I still wasn't sure where I wanted to end up. After visiting as many units as they want, to see where they might fit in, officer cadets can select two regiments to have interviews with in their final term.

It is a difficult task, as each regiment has a different role. The Cavalry might not charge about on horses anymore, but they do drive around in massive battle tanks; the Royal Military Police do everything from locking up naughty soldiers to providing special armed guards for the royal family. If you become an officer in the Logistics Corps, you could find yourself in charge of feeding front-line troops, or working out how many blankets are required in a far-off barracks.

Before going to Sandhurst, I went on a few visits to the Staffordshire Regiment, my local infantry unit, and when I was at the academy I was also interested in the Intelligence Corps. It was a very tough decision, which would impact the course of my entire life, and it weighed on me heavily during my time there. Sandhurst was hard work, and the late nights ironing my uniforms, the parades and long academic essays were only part of it. There was a lot of running, marching and being shouted at, along with field exercises, rifle ranges and blowing things up; as well as learning the more subtle arts of officership – fancy dinners, the intricacies of letter writing and knowing the Debrett's guide to etiquette inside out. It was an interesting and varied education.

I also took up boxing. Everyone had to be part of a sports club at Sandhurst, and given I wasn't into rugby or rowing, boxing seemed like a decent choice. Initially I hated the 4.30 a.m. starts, but as the fitness started to impact on me and I felt myself improving, I came to relish the early-morning alarm calls. Plus, there was the added carrot of the annual 'fight night', in which the most dedicated, committed boxers were chosen to fight, watched by the whole academy, as well as a string of generals, politicians and VIP guests.

I was incredibly proud to be chosen as one of those fighters, and on 9 November 2005, I stood in a ring surrounded by over a thousand people, face to face with Officer Cadet Mortimer. I won the fight by knocking my opponent to the ground, but I'm not retelling this story to discuss the win – I had a huge respect for my opponent, and the opportunity that came next arose simply from having stood in the arena.

After the fight, all of the boxers were invited to the Sergeants' Mess (a club of sorts, where many of our training instructors lived). This was a huge honour, because this particular mess was usually out of bounds, and the sergeants themselves were only seen in their context as authoritarian figures, all muscle, tattoos and shaved heads. The fact that we privileged few were allowed into their private domain was viewed with absolute envy by the other cadets.

The sergeants crowded round the fighters and congratulated us all on our performance, victors and defeated alike. As I finished my second pint of beer, I found another one thrust into my hand. Looking up I saw that it was Captain Truett, the Sandhurst representative of the Parachute Regiment.

'Congratulations, Wood. Which regiment are you joining?' he said sternly.

I hesitated momentarily before replying, 'I'm not sure, sir, I was looking at the Staffords, or the Int Corps.'

'Sod that,' he said. 'You should join the Paras.'

My look of surprise must have been quite apparent. The Paras were the most fearsome soldiers in the British Army. *I'm not good enough to get into the Paras*, I thought. You needed to be a muscle-bound machine to get in, surely? It wasn't even on my radar.

'Sit down,' the captain barked. I sat on one of the little stools by the bar, beer still in hand. 'The first two rounds of interviews have already been done,' he told me. 'We had over a hundred applicants and now we're down to twenty. I don't do this very often, and I won't ask you twice, but do you want an interview?'

I sobered up pretty quickly. My entire future rested in the balance and all sorts of thoughts crossed my mind: what about the Staffords, they seemed a nice enough bunch – and the Intelligence Corps, they did some interesting spy-related work? It could be a good start to my career, and would allow me to travel too. When it came to the Paras, there were a lot of unknowns. As a regiment, they are shrouded in mystery and are considered to be one of the country's – if not the world's – most elite military units. I didn't know what to expect and I didn't think I was capable of joining their ranks. The temptation was to play it safe and stick with a more achievable goal. I knew what I was getting with the Staffords.

If I agreed to an interview with the Paras, I would automatically have to turn down one of the other options, since you can only interview with two regiments, and the Paras had the toughest selection of all, just peaking the Intelligence Corps. If I turned down the Staffords and failed the board for the others, I ran the risk of not getting any of my choices – I could end up being a blanket stacker in the Logistics Corps for the rest of my career.

The captain was staring at me.

'I'd like to interview, sir,' I told him, expecting that it would take place in the coming weeks.

Nope. Captain Truett launched into a formal interview right there at the bar, grilling me about my own motivations, experiences, education and skills. After fifteen minutes he stood up, shook my hand and told me to report to his office at 6 a.m. the next morning. And that's what I did, hangover and all. I was fast-tracked into the final eight, and then at the last interview – with a panel headed by some of the most senior figures in the British Army – I was offered a place in the Parachute Regiment.

That's how I got into the Paras. It would probably have been easier to get into the Staffords, or even the Intelligence Corps, but looking back, I'm glad that I let optimism overcome my doubts about joining one of the most elite units in the world. A unique club, which opened more doors than I could have ever imagined.

Ed Stafford Walking the Amazon

Inspiration can come in many forms, and many of my own examples have been explorers from long bygone eras, but when I was in the process of leaving the army, one man's journey in particular stood out as a feat of endurance unlike anything I had heard about in the modern age.

Ed Stafford, like myself, had left the British Army as a captain some years earlier. He spent time working as a security consultant in Afghanistan and the Middle East before embarking on a walking journey that was to set the bar very high indeed. In April 2008, he set off from the southern coast of Peru with the intention of travelling the entire length of the Amazon River on foot. It was an expedition that had never been completed before. Despite his companion leaving after only a few weeks, Ed carried on, often alone, sometimes with local guides, along the course of the mighty river.

His journey was fraught with challenges; he pushed himself to the limits of human endurance, dealt with endless bureaucracy, battled deadly wildlife, narco-traffickers and the ever-present thugs working for illegal logging and mining companies. The walk took a mind-boggling 860 days (two years and four months) due to the difficult terrain.

In his book, Ed describes the emotional turmoil he went through during that period, leaving behind everything to commit to finishing a challenge he had set himself. But, and this is something I can empathise with, he was never in any doubt that he would complete it. He gave himself no option for failure, no plan B, and no safety blanket. Sometimes, only by throwing all of your eggs in one basket and risking everything, can you achieve the seemingly impossible.

Positivity breeds success

A positive mental attitude has an enormous impact on your life. Optimism will allow your mind to soar, making you open to more and more positive ideas and opportunities. It will free your mind into an ascending spiral of positive emotions, which will give you new approaches to the world and new ways of thinking. This is a huge part of being an explorer: on an expedition you need people who are constantly looking for opportunity, seeing things through a positive lens and focusing on the best. That is not to say that you don't have a sensible and healthy understanding of the negative things that might befall an adventure, but it's about hoping for the best in *spite* of that knowledge.

If you can couple optimism with enthusiasm – bringing joy, energy or genuine interest to what you do – you will go far. My thoughts resonate with those of Roald Dahl, who said:

> I began to realise how important it was to be an enthusiast in life . . . If you are interested in something, no matter what it is, go at it at full speed ahead. Embrace it with both arms, hug it, love it and above all become passionate about it. Lukewarm is no good. Hot is no good either. White hot and passionate is the only thing to be.

Enthusiasm will make people listen to you; it is contagious and energising. If you're a leader with enthusiasm, you are more likely to be followed without question, and people will call you a visionary. Enthusiasm keeps you focused and delivers results. Certainly, in my experience as a traveller, you'll have a lot more fun if you stay positive, instead of whingeing and whining about every little issue; if you see the funny side of life, you'll soon realise things aren't so bad. At the very least, *smile* – some research shows that you can even smile yourself into a better mood.

Optimism is undeniably good for our mental health, making us more resilient. This gives us the ability to cope with change or a crisis and get ourselves back to a pre-crisis state more quickly. In fact, having a positive attitude in challenging circumstances is shown to make you recover more quickly from adversity. Resilient people will translate negative feelings into positive ones, and are better at regulating their emotions. They tend to view difficult challenges as a chance for growth, rather than a threat to their wellbeing.

Studies are showing that optimism may even be good for your health. Heart transplant patients who are optimistic about surgery are making better recoveries, and optimism has been linked to a reduced risk of dying from cancer. Another recent study looked at the expectations of students about their course – how well they expected to do in exams and how optimistic they were feeling about it. It measured cell-mediated immunity, the number of immune cells that flow to an area in response to an invasion by a virus or bacteria. It found that as the participants got more optimistic, they would have a larger immune response, but when they were more pessimistic about their prospects, their immune response was slower and more delayed.

The study did not look at general outlook on life; in other words, it was not about a student's general mindset and approach, but about their specific attitude towards their course. What this means is that by being optimistic about your success in an important part of your life, you may create higher immunity against infection. It is also a crucial factor when it comes to negative health behaviours, which are things like smoking – optimists are less likely to engage in them, and more likely to be successful when they choose to quit.

Winston Churchill once said: 'Success is going from failure to failure without losing your enthusiasm.' I believe that positivity is key to success in whatever situation you find yourself. If you stay positive, then half the battle is already won.

Enthusiasm, optimism and confidence all go hand in hand to make tough circumstances bearable and give the best chance of a good outcome. Psychologists spend their whole careers looking at this, delving into how optimism increases quality of life, and perhaps more importantly, how anyone can learn to improve it for themselves. Clinical studies show that optimists are healthier, happier and more successful in life than pessimists, and this is put down to three main differences in their outlook on the world.

The first is that optimists do not personalise negative events; they view them as external, brought about by circumstances or other people. Effectively, optimists will ascribe a negative situation to causes outside of themselves, meaning that failure or struggle is not their own fault. A pessimist, on the other hand, will see their struggles and setbacks as a reflection of something that they have done themselves, or because of something internal to them. What this means is that optimists tend to be more confident, believing what they do is *in spite* of what happens around them, rather than because of it.

This confidence breeds confidence. Whether you are a soldier, a teacher, a chef or an explorer, your confidence in what you do will be picked up by the people around you. How would you feel if you went to see a doctor and they said, 'I'm not really sure what I'm doing, but I suppose I'll give it a bash.' Contrast that with, 'Don't worry, I've done this thousands of times. You're in safe hands.'

Another main difference between the optimist's and pessimist's outlook on the world is described as the pervasiveness of the situation. For a pessimist, a bad situation applies universally to all parts of life; failing in one thing will be framed as failure in life as a whole. An optimist will see this as one specific failure, and though they may feel that they are incapacitated in one area, they will have the ability to compartmentalise this. Optimists also benefit from the fact that they let positive experiences have a knock-on effect of positivity across all parts of their life, and not only that specific area.

For instance, an optimist who completed a 10K run may think to themselves, *I completed a physical challenge that I set for myself, so I know that I can succeed in that business I want to launch*.

The pessimist mindset might think, *I completed a 10K run, sure, but what's that got to do with starting a business? I'll never be able to do it*.

The third and final difference in outlook is the most crucial, and pertains to the question of permanence. If an optimist is facing a challenge, they will see this negative event as something temporary, telling themselves, *This too shall pass*. On the other hand, if you look at things through a pessimistic lens, you are assigning yourself to an immutable outcome on something that not even time can change. If things are final or viewed as a foregone conclusion, why would you bother making an effort to overcome them?

Nobunaga

There was once a powerful Japanese warrior called Oda Nobunaga who, because of his leadership prowess and great ability to motivate those around him, became known to history as the Great Unifier. There is one particular story about Nobunaga when the warlord was at the head of his army and, faced with an overwhelmingly superior enemy force, he knew he needed some divine intervention to muster his men to fight.

On the eve of battle, he visited an ancient Shinto shrine, where he prayed out loud for victory. After he finished, he went to his captains and told them that the spirit world had informed him that he should toss a coin. If it landed on heads, his army would be victorious, and if it was tails, then they should face defeat: 'Destiny holds us in its hands.'

Nobunaga prayed again in front of his troops before flipping the coin high into the air as everyone waited with bated breath. The coin landed on heads to a deep sigh of relief, and the army, emboldened by the backing of the gods, went forward and crushed the enemy. 'No one can change the hand of destiny,' remarked Nobunaga's assistant sagely, after the battle was over.

'Indeed not,' said the leader, handing him the coin that had been tossed. It was a double-headed forgery.

Never despair

Pessimism leads us into a trap where we think that everything is hopeless, and we stop looking for ways that we can influence situations positively. I have travelled to plenty of places where showing a bit of zeal and having a sense of humour has relieved me of some fairly sticky situations. I once had to go for lunch and drink moonshine with Guatemalan gangsters, in order to prove I wasn't an American spy. While in places like Afghanistan, you will often be served goat's brains and eyeballs as a delicacy by the local chief, the real test is to see if you're made of tough enough stuff and are polite enough to deserve hospitality.

One dangerous test took place the first time that I visited South Sudan, in the spring of 2011. It was a turbulent time, shortly before the country got its independence from the Arab North, and tensions were mounting as nobody knew what would happen. I had been invited on an expedition by my friend Chris Mahoney, an American who was part of the East Africa expat community. He'd been told that the UN high commissioner for South Sudan was recruiting a team of explorers to join him, and a famous water guide called Pete Meredith, to raft down the River Nile from the Ugandan border at Nimule, all the way to Juba. It was supposed to be the start of a blossoming tourism trade for this new nation.

The Sudanese civil war had raged through the 1970s and 1980s and the whole area was filled with lethal landmines and unexploded ordnance. What's more, the tribes were fighting each other again – the Dinka and the Nuer had been skirmishing over cattle and land, and the police had been up to their usual tricks of pillaging passing traders.

Despite that, I wasn't too worried, as we had a good team. There was the head of the UN mission, David Gressly, plus a bunch of other ex-pat misfits, including a a helicopter pilot, a barman, a doctor and a lion tracker.

I had some nerves, of course – crocodiles, hippos and irritable tribesmen awaited. But the only reason I'd been invited on the trip was because I was 'The Paratrooper' and with that comes a great reputation, and responsibility; so I got stuck in, helping fix up the rafts, reassuring the less experienced members of the team that things were going to be OK, and making sure that everyone's kit was strapped down properly.

For a few days we made good progress towards Juba, South Sudan's main town and soon-to-be capital city. Then, ten miles south of the outskirts of the ramshackle town, as we were relaxing and looking forward to reaching our destination and a cold beer, we were met with a nasty surprise.

There was a commotion on the river bank to our left and I could hear shouts from the bushes. I looked to the west and noticed half a dozen semi-naked tribesmen shouting and waving angrily. One was clasping a large spear that glinted in the sunlight. The men began to run along the river bank trying to catch up with us, and I couldn't help noticing that many of them were armed with AK-47 machine guns. It was clear they wanted us to stop, but even if we had wanted to, there was no chance – the current was too strong.

Crack! It sounded as if someone had taken an enormous whip and slapped it across the river.

'Shit, they're shooting at us!' shouted David.

'Paddle harder!' replied Pete.

The men on the bank fired another shot in our direction. It went over our heads, but just when I thought we were getting out of range, more tribesmen appeared, and they were directly ahead of us. There were dozens of them now – on both banks, too. Then a dugout canoe appeared from behind an island, and on second glance I made out another – not one, but two canoes, filled with angry gunmen. They were paddling hard, chasing us downstream.

'Stop paddling,' said Pete, calmly now. 'If we try to escape they will kill us. Stay composed, they're going to get us.'

Pete let go of his oar and let it drag in the river, raising his hands. We all did the same. The men in the canoes were still shouting and aiming their rifles directly at us. Eventually they caught up with us and took hold of our dinghy ropes.

As we sat there in sheer terror, now captives to these unknown assailants, we waited to see what would happen as we got dragged to the west bank.

'Get out!' one of the men screamed, with an anger that I hadn't seen before, his scarred face dripping with sweat.

We all did as we were told, clambering out of the raft with our hands still above our heads. The gunman shoved us one by one against the river bank and made us kneel down. Were they going to beat us or torture us? All sorts of horrors ran through my mind – maybe they would even execute us. This was a place where human life was cheap, and the population deeply traumatised after decades of war.

'You are mercenaries!' screamed our captor, as we were surrounded by more and more of the men. 'You are here to invade our country!'

David tried to explain that we were simply on an expedition. He protested that we were not mercenaries, that we had permission from the president himself, and that all our paperwork was in order (which it was).

The man was having none of it. 'I am the chief of police here!' he yelled. 'I am the boss here, so shut up.'

He didn't look like the chief of police, that's for sure, but who were we to argue?

'If I want to kill you all, then I will.'

What do you say to that? Nothing, is my advice. We stayed quiet. I'd been taught about how to act in this sort of situation whilst in the army, during our lessons in the art of survival and extraction from hostage situations. You are more likely to be killed if you agitate your captor, so it's important to remain calm and in no way attempt to fight or be aggressive – especially if he is being irrational and waving a loaded gun in your face.

You are also far more likely to be killed when your attacker is able to dehumanise you mentally, so it is important to try to be collected and measured, which is sometimes hard when you have a gun trained on the back of your head. To keep calm in a crisis, you have to slow down and think things through. It can seem counterintuitive but giving your next decision as much time as possible can make all the difference. Collect as much information as you can, be observant: look around and assess the situation.

In order to keep us safe, I knew that I had to remain optimistic. Focus on one small positive thing, instead of letting your mind wander into the endless possibilities of negative outcomes. If I had been standing there panicking and wondering 'what if', things might have ended very differently.

I looked over at David. He was very calm, but I could tell he was trying to do something covertly. I looked down at his hand and I saw he was grasping something. It was a satellite phone. Of course! He had somehow managed to get it out of his bag when we'd first got into trouble, but he needed to make a call, or at least alert his team we were in trouble. I had to buy him time and somehow distract the gunmen. Luckily I had just the trick – something I'd learnt on my travels.

Always carry a packet of cigarettes, even if you don't smoke. I looked at the nearest policeman, and made a gesture of smoking. He looked around to make sure the chief wasn't looking, and nodded. I took out the packet, handed him one, and took one myself. As I suspected, the chief stormed over, but before he could say anything, I held the pack open towards him and with as much confidence as I could muster, I forced a big smile, looking him hard in the eyes.

He lowered his gaze. Suddenly, I was human again. He snatched the cigarettes and took my lighter, but I kept my smile big and I could tell that he was warming to it, no matter how reluctantly.

Sometimes it is the little things that can break down barriers, and perhaps even save your life. While everyone was grinning and smoking, David managed to send out an SOS signal, and half an hour later a UN helicopter arrived filled with soldiers. We were rescued, and even allowed to carry on in our boats down river towards Juba. I wouldn't go so far as to say I made new friends, but everyone walked away unharmed, and I put that down to staying positive.

If we had all started pleading for our lives – or worse, decided that death was imminent, and so rushed our attackers – then the situation could have resulted in a bloodbath. By holding fast to the idea that an opportunity would present itself, but also that these people were not evil and intent on killing us, we came away with nothing more than some shaken nerves, and a story.

Touching the Void

In 1985, Joe Simpson and Simon Yates became the first mountaineers to climb successfully the summit of Peru's Siula Grande via the indomitable west face, but on their descent, disaster struck.

Simpson slipped and fell down an ice cliff, badly breaking his right leg. The men were already behind schedule, and had little fuel to melt snow, nor did they have any snow around them that they could drink. The pair were surrounded by ice, and Yates would have to lower Simpson down the rest of the mountain. Not only that, but they would have to do it in total darkness, and with a storm raging around them so loudly that the men couldn't even hear each other.

It is no surprise that things got worse from there, and Yates accidentally lowered Simpson off the edge of a cliff. Simpson tried to climb back up, but due to severe frostbite, he couldn't tie the required Prusik knot properly, and dropped one of the cords he needed to ascend. He was suspended over a sheer drop with one leg broken, with no way of communicating with his partner, and certainly no way of reaching him.

Above him, the weight of Simpson was beginning to pull Yates from his belay seat. Yates knew that he would plummet to his death if he didn't take action. Wracked with guilt, knowing that he was sending his friend to his death, Yates cut the cord.

Simpson fell away, but against all odds he survived the landing, and found himself deep inside a crevasse. He was suffering badly from frostbite and his broken leg, but he was alive, and would not give in to despair. He found a route through the crevasse and onto the glacier, and from there – over the course of three days, and with barely any water or food – Simpson hopped and crawled his way across the eight kilometres to base camp. He reached it exhausted and delirious, only hours before Yates was about to depart.

The survival instinct in humans is very strong, but even so, it still beggars belief that Simpson didn't succumb to despair. From the moment he broke his leg onwards, he knew his chances of survival were next to zero, yet somehow he persevered, remaining optimistic in the face of unthinkable odds. Here we see the power of the human mind at work. Aiming for a goal with composed execution can overcome even the greatest odds.

Probability thinking vs possibility thinking

If Joe Simpson had been a 'probability thinker', he might have given up and died on the mountain. Only a focus on what's possible can pull you through an experience like that.

I find myself encountering these kinds of mindsets a lot when planning expeditions. In 2016, I started planning for a circumnavigation of the Arabian Peninsula, through thirteen Middle Eastern countries. Some of these nations have notoriously tight borders, and many others were warzones. Before we could begin to think about the probability or possibility of potential danger on the ground, we had to persuade each of these countries not only to let us in, but to grant us visas and permission to film. Many times I was told that it was unlikely we could get the requisite visas, or sufficient access to some of the countries that we wanted to include, but the members of my team and I preferred to believe it was still very much in the realm of the possible – and it was.

By engaging in 'possibility thinking', we open our perspective to entertain new ideas that were previously beyond our expectation or knowledge. In this case, the new, improved and adjusted world-view meant that I got to see the 'ground truth' in the Middle East with my own eyes, transforming my perception of the region beyond comprehension.

Now I'm not saying that one of these approaches is right, and the other is wrong – as we know from assessing risk, you need to be thinking about the probability of an incident – but I find that probability vs possibility thinking is a useful framework through which to view people's mindsets.

Of course, one person can engage in both possibility thinking *and* probability thinking, making this more of a behaviour style than a personality type. In fact, I'd say that in order to be successful, it's crucial to employ both approaches, or at least to try and hold both in mind. Once you've done your blue-sky thinking, and picturing what you would like to achieve if there were no limits, you have to return to some rational probability thinking, in order to strategise or – as is so often the case for me – plan the actual expedition.

In my experience, most people have a natural predisposition to one or the other way of thinking. It is crucial to understand this when it comes to functioning as a group, and knowing the styles you have in your team.

When I tell people about my expeditions, I can divide them into two camps based on their responses. Firstly, there are those who see them as hare-brained schemes that are bound to fail, or at least be filled with multiple challenges, which will be difficult if not impossible to overcome. They weigh up everything that could possibly go wrong, and run an analysis on whether the expedition vision is remotely probable or likely. These people are probability thinkers; they look at what *may* be. This approach of taking a reality check is logical and sensible, but because the laws of probability tell us that events and outcomes follow a cause-and-effect linearity, these people tend to be more likely to sit back and wait for an outcome.

The downfall of this way of thinking is that our ego makes us capable of doing an analysis based only on what we have done, seen or experienced in the past. Maybe the probability thinker I'm chatting to has heard only stories of drastic failed adventures, or crocodiles ripping explorers apart. It is a rear-view perspective that is based on what was possible or happened then, rather than what is possible or could happen now, or in the future.

That latter way of thinking is the realm where possibility thinkers live. For these folks, anything is possible; they look at what *can* be. Possibility thinkers are enthused by hope and have faith that things are doable. When I tell these people about an upcoming expedition, they see the boundless options and ways to enhance it; perhaps this location would be a great addition, perhaps this route might make it easier. Thinking big, bold and ambitious visions can cause our ego to panic, nervous that we are straying out of reality and into fictions that are impossible to achieve, but possibility allows you to see the opportunities and growth instead.

There is no right and wrong here. Rather, whether you are planning an expedition, or your own life, I would advise seeking out people with each mindset. The truth, as with so much in life, often lies between the two extremes.

Annie Londonderry

Possibility thinking and positive spirit lived in many explorers of days gone by, but perhaps none more so in my eyes than explorer Annie Londonderry, who was famous for being the first woman to cycle the globe. Born Annie Kopchovsky in Latvia in 1870, her parents emigrated to the United States when she was just a girl, and by her early twenties Annie was settled in Boston with a family of her own.

Annie's call to adventure came in 1894. A man had recently cycled around the world, and two gentlemen bet each other $10,000 that a woman could not do the same. It's not clear how Annie came to be the one who took up the challenge, but she did — even though she'd never ridden a bike before! The conditions of the challenge were that she must *start the journey with no money, and that she must finish it in under fifteen months.*

Annie assembled five hundred or so people to see her off and used this as a publicity opportunity. As well as fundraising for the whole trip on her own, the savvy young woman had arranged for sponsorship from a water company called Londonderry Lithia. They would pay her to put an advertising plaque for their brand on her bicycle, as well as change her surname to Londonderry. Annie got a representative of the company to hand over the $100 in front of the crowds, and this gained her a lot of applause and attention.

In France, Annie's bike was promptly confiscated by customs and the French press wrote insulting stories about her unladylike clothing. Undeterred, Annie continued on and made it to Egypt, Jerusalem, the port of Aden in Yemen, then across to Colombo, Singapore, Hong Kong, Korea, Russia and Japan before taking a boat back to America. Annie collected signatures from the American ambassador in each country, and made it back to America fourteen days under the allotted time. Apparently, she never got on a bicycle ever again!

Annie Londonderry was not without controversy, though. She certainly knew how to bend the rules, hopping on the odd train or ferry and taking her bike with her, on the basis that the rules stipulated she travel 'with' her bicycle. As well as this liberal approach to transport, it turned out that the wager was entirely fictitious – there were no two gentlemen betters. While there are some slightly questionable elements to the trip, there is no doubt that Annie worked hard and took things into her own hands, creating her own luck.

She was the ultimate hustler, putting her bike out to tender for advertising space in return for cash to keep herself going as she rode through towns. At one stage even her clothing was covered top to toe in adverts, a mobile billboard. She developed her own line of merchandise, selling autographs and photos of herself, as well as giving cycling demos.

Annie was a phenomenal saleswoman and a captivating storyteller: she knew exactly which juicy and gory details of her adventures to share with her growing audience.

She was astute and talented at making the most of the media and a master of public relations. On the second half of her journey, she earned extra pocket money by delivering lectures about her adventures. Resourceful and enterprising, her enthusiasm and possibility thinking made her arguably the world's first international cycling star.

Discovering optimism

Optimism and pessimism, like fear and the fight-or-flight reflex, operate on subconscious levels, but we can use our conscious minds to rewire these reflexes. For example, we can visualise the best possible versions of ourselves, and describe them out loud to ourselves using mantras, or other verbal or written reminders. This will change our subconscious from thinking negatively about our flaws, to thinking positively about our potential.

We all have a negative internal monologue – the voice in our head that tells us something can't be done. Because we have a tendency to be a risk-averse species, it is easy to think that this voice is rational, but in truth it's hopelessly not the case, especially in the modern world we live in. We can become more positive by habitually pushing back against this negativity with rational, optimistic arguments; counterbalancing worst-case scenarios with best-case predictions, in order to identify more realistic middle-grounds.

Above all, we can completely reconfigure how we approach the concepts of disappointment and failure. Our inner pessimists make mountains out of molehills wherever setbacks are concerned, and perceive these shortcomings or blockers as fixed and permanent. But the reality is that very, very few things in life are beyond our control, and if we come to view setbacks as learning opportunities, then life immediately becomes more positive. We are always either succeeding, or learning.

One way that you can increase or better learn optimism is by practising gratitude. Think of a time in your life when you've felt or expressed extremely heartfelt thanks for something that someone else has done for you, or said to you. Of course, this feeling of thanks can also be directed to yourself, not just another. It's a powerful feeling. Every day, write down something that you're thankful to yourself for, and then another thing for which you're grateful that came from someone else. It doesn't have to be a physical item. Perhaps you are grateful for the kind ear that somebody gave you, or the conversation with a stranger on the train. It helps us to see the good qualities in others, adopting and picking up behaviour that we admire.

Studies show that more grateful people tend to have a stronger sense of belonging and are less likely to suffer from stress or depression. Practising gratitude breeds energy and enthusiasm, which an explorer would be lost without.

As in Chapter Three, where we looked at what scared us, the more we can push ourselves outside our own comfort zones, and face our fears, the more optimistic we will become. Fear is deeply rooted in the unfamiliar: it is when doing unusual things like flying in a plane that we tend to overestimate the dangers, compared to everyday things like travelling by car. Becoming familiar with the unusual, by expanding our comfort zones, will make us more optimistic over time. There is a compounding effect to it when we consistently show ourselves that we can come through situations that we perceived as difficult or dangerous.

Optimism in the face of adversity and uncertainty are the building blocks of good preparation. We can't control everything in our lives, and there will be times when things do go wrong, but what we can *always* control is the way that we react to those hardships. It is down to us, and us alone, to look for the possible over the probable. To see obstacles as opportunities. And to recognise that today's disaster is tomorrow's laughter with friends. With a positive mindset, you may still encounter setbacks in your life, but you will never lose.

A Polynesian Chief

5

Be Ready For Anything

By failing to prepare, you are preparing to fail – Benjamin Franklin

Public speaking

Like a lot of people, the thought of public speaking was something that crippled me with nerves. I'd had to stand up in front of people in the army, of course, but there is something about the uniform and rank that offers you protection. You're delivering a lesson or mission given to you by the army, not putting your own life on display for others to judge. Besides, it's not like my soldiers could choose to stand up and walk out if I was boring them!

My first offer to give a speech came out of the blue, but apparently setting up an adventure travel club and leading a few small expeditions warranted my invitation down to the local Rotary Club to speak to a handful of elderly gentlemen.

Before I went on stage, I was genuinely terrified. I got a flood of self-doubt and panic, convinced that the entire thing was going to be a mess. My heart beat faster in spite of my best efforts to slow it down. Comedians talk about 'dying on stage', and as much as my rational mind could tell my sweaty, shaking body to calm down, my flight reaction of feeling cornered, with all of those faces looking up at me, made my body involuntarily panic. My legs had a slight wobble, which I probably didn't manage to conceal successfully, and my hands were clammy. I was told once that this feeling of stage fright evolved from an ancestral tradition, whereby our forefathers were summoned in front of the tribal elders, usually in order to defend their actions when some wrongdoing had occurred.

I'd been fine for days beforehand, comfortable that I knew what I was going to say and that I was capable of communicating something coherent. Why then, when I was about to go on stage, did I suddenly feel that all of my lines were going to slip totally from my mind? Perhaps it was because I felt the stakes were higher here. These were my elders, and money was at stake – I was fundraising for a charity and some of the audience were local councillors and businessmen, and one was a former brigadier.

This is the part where I tell you that I overcame my fears, and delivered a Churchillian speech, right?

If only. The talk was a complete shambles. The projector stopped working, I forgot my lines, and nobody laughed at my jokes. It was a disaster, but when it was over, I realised that I was still standing and alive – despite what my body had been telling me. Just as I was consoling myself that hopefully they were all hard of hearing anyway, the chap who had invited me to talk came bowling over.

'Levison,' he said. I stood to attention, which probably says something about how detached my mind and body were; at that point I was working from muscle memory. 'That was fine as far as these things go, young man. An interesting story about Afghanistan, but you can definitely do better.'

He proceeded to provide a lengthy critique on how I might best improve. It was pretty embarrassing, but now I look back at it and laugh. In truth, I had probably not practised or prepared enough. I'd been too worried about what people thought, and not spent enough time simply rehearsing the content and making sure the projector worked.

Anyway, it was over and done with. The audience coughed up a couple of grand for the charity, and I escaped with nothing but a bruised ego and a few valuable lessons learned.

For me, stage fright has now pretty much abated. To be honest, I managed to overcome it by making one pretty straightforward change: I learnt to tell myself that I was excited, not nervous, and to see every potential moment of fear as an opportunity to grow and learn. To re-channel the feelings and tell myself that it was simply a healthy dose of anticipation and enthusiasm about going on stage.

As I got ready at the Rotary Club, I had been thinking about all the things that could possibly go wrong. In a disastrous downwards spiral of negative reinforcement, I thought to myself, *I'm just being realistic*. I hadn't practised enough, so this was a reasonable expectation, but if you are negative about something, I'd say it's doomed from the start.

Instead, if you adopt the mindset that you are ready for anything, and anticipate that anything can happen, then you'll never be taken on the back foot. That's not to say the fear will entirely disappear, but you remind yourself to keep things in perspective. Even if you don't feel that way, if you project it, others will buy into it, and this will reinforce your belief – 'fake it till you make it' – but nine years after my Rotary Club debacle, I found myself in another public speaking situation that was even more terrifying.

I am fortunate enough now to call myself a 'high profile supporter' for the charity UNICEF. I get to visit their amazing projects around the world and help promote a really important cause, for which I feel incredibly privileged. One of the perks of the job is to be invited to the occasional VIP reception. One such event was the England vs India World Cup cricket match at Edgbaston in the summer of 2019, for which UNICEF was the beneficiary charity. I was invited to watch the match from the press box alongside some of the cricket greats, including Sachin Tendulkar.

Over lunch, one of the UNICEF press team asked if I wouldn't mind appearing on a pre-recorded radio or TV interview to talk briefly about the great work being done by UNICEF, and of course, I agreed. After doing a couple of brief chats, which were very straightforward and about my own visits to UNICEF projects, I was asked if I would do one more.

'No problem.'

'It's live?'

'Sure, no problem.' I had done bits on TV before, so I wasn't worried.

I was led out of the press room and down the stairs; I figured to a position with a more interesting backdrop for television.

I was half-right.

Before I knew it, I was being led out in front of 25,000 people. There was a box in the centre of the pitch, and there might as well have been an executioner standing beside it – I felt sick, and all of a sudden my knees were wobbly. It turns out that you can be a para-trooper and go to war, but the eyes of a stadium upon you is far more daunting than Taliban bullets. If I had been hit on the battlefield, I'd be a hero. If I messed this up, I'd just be a prat.

As I was handed a microphone, I tried not to think about the millions of people watching my address around the world.

My saving grace was that for the last ten years I had been practising my public speaking, and that practice had bred confidence. It didn't take away the wave of fear, but it allowed me to see over it. And so, I puffed out my chest, took a deep breath and waffled something about what a great atmosphere it was, welcomed the Indian crowds, and told everyone to dig deep and support UNICEF. It was a roaring success and I walked off the box exhilarated.

There was more to come. As I was walking back up the stairs of the pavilion to the press box, I was rushed by Indian fans who wanted me to sign their bats and T-shirts, which of course I did heartily. It was only when one shamefaced boy asked me what team I played for that I realised not a single one of them had a clue who I was. While this was a little humbling, it was also a good reminder that if I *had* fluffed the whole thing up, nobody would have given a stuff but me. A significant moment in our own lives can be nothing more than a few seconds of distraction in someone else's – if that – and soon forgotten. It is us who will live with our performances, and us who must prepare.

Body Armour

According to traditional belief, the Tahitian god Ta'aroa, 'The Severer', created the world by separating it into two parts: the po, the world of darkness, night and death, and the ao, the world we know of light, daytime and life. This Tahitian view of the universe having come into being through an act of creative separation, or something like it, underpins the belief systems of native people across Polynesia, and continued to influence Polynesian culture even after Christianity spread throughout the region.

In this belief system, the two worlds are in perpetual threat of merging together once again, destroying the universe as we know it. Particularly vulnerable to this spiritual, supernatural threat are the backs of people – those parts of the body that we can't see – which represent an ever-present but invisible threat, like the po itself. That's why, in these cultures, it was forbidden to walk behind certain important, high-status individuals.

Men, especially adolescents on the verge of full manhood, were particularly vulnerable to the dangers of the po lurking unseen behind them, particularly where warfare and sex (because of the semi-sacred status of women) were concerned. In war especially, death in battle was viewed as a result of spiritual shortcomings as much as anything physical or martial; so before taking part in either love or war, adolescent Polynesian men needed to prepare themselves properly in order to gain spiritual protection.

Part of this protection took the form of tattoos. Tattooing in Polynesian culture creates a protective layer covering the body, warding off the spiritual dangers of the other-world. In Samoa and Tonga, this was typically represented by wrapping the body in a protective shell, emblematic of the natural armour of animals such as tortoises, or the cloaking wings of a flying fox.

In the Marquesas, tattoos often feature secondary faces, either representing protective Gods, or symbolic extra eyes to watch for the unseen cosmic dangers behind the wearer's back. These might often depict a skull, denoting the spirit of a dead chief thirsty for vengeance, protecting a warrior's back in battle.

Tattooing was an essential part of the Polynesian initiation into full manhood for young warriors, who would not even think about going into battle until they were properly prepared, physically and spiritually.

The same applies to your mind: success is an art form. Prepare yourself by polishing your own mental armour and victory will be yours.

There is no such thing as luck . . .

The motto of the Parachute Regiment is *Utrinque Paratus*, a Latin phrase that translates to 'Ready for Anything'. I learnt in the Paras that being prepared is the key to success, and it is something that has served me well both in my career in the army and beyond.

The Paras were formed in the Second World War to act as shock troops, light on their feet and ready to jump, literally, into any situation. They have been used in that same capacity since they were formed in 1942 and they are trained to the highest standard in fitness, navigation, close-quarter combat and survival in the harshest environments. But the main reason that Paratroopers have been used by conventional armies around the world over the last seventy-plus years is because of their exceptional resourcefulness – their ability to deal with rapidly changing circumstances, to fight on with limited kit and low ammunition, and find their way out of trouble.

Being 'ready for anything' is about having the right mindset; it's about preparing for the worst but hoping for the best. Paratroopers spend countless weeks and months on exercise in the pouring rain, going over the same weapon-handling drills, practising their marksmanship, getting their muscle memory in order, and making sure they are fitter than everyone else. That is because they stand by an old soldier's adage, often attributed to that most tenacious of Frenchmen, Napoleon Bonaparte: 'Train hard, fight easy.'

I also believe that you make your own luck in the world, and you do so by being ready for anything. Take the example of a professional boxer. In training, they constantly practise the same manoeuvre over and over again, to the point where their brain and body are so attuned to the process that it becomes second nature to them – even automatic – and once they have mastered that task, they can focus on more important things like winning the championship belt.

Similarly, when a soldier ducks down to avoid a bullet by mere inches, they may well be 'lucky', but perhaps that luck has been engendered by years of training, of becoming aware of their surroundings and in tune with their environment, and having the instinctiveness to know when to duck. As my sergeant explained to new recruits about how he had survived so many near-misses: 'The more I practise, the luckier I get!'

In my experience, lucky people are also busy people. They are doers, not pontificators. They are busy putting themselves out there, which helps them to create more opportunity for themselves through moving in new circles, or meeting new people. They are adept at networking and seeking out chances for success, and finding themselves in the right place at the right time. They tend to be great at observing the seed of an idea or an opportunity and seizing it; they are ready for anything.

There are two possible mindsets we can take to challenges or adversity; an internal locus of control, or an external locus of control. The latter thinks, *I am beholden to events, the world happens to me*; the former thinks, *I can shape events, I happen to the world*. People who adopt the former are the doers, the ones who believe you make your own luck and, simply by subscribing to this belief, they probably do.

We create success or failure through our thoughts. Unlucky people, on the other hand, know how to talk themselves out of an opportunity, to find a reason not to do something, as opposed to chancing their arm. They forget that, first and foremost, the prerequisite for luck is action, and making stuff happen.

As Tennessee Williams, the American playwright, put it: 'Luck is believing you're lucky.' Lucky people are convinced that their future will hold great things. Much like the power of positivity and optimism, these expectations can become self-fulfilling prophecies, where they believe that things will go well, and soon they do. This world-view is all part of the explorer's mindset, and as it gets repeatedly reinforced, it allows lucky people to persevere even when they are knocked back. Like a super power, they have a tendency to turn misfortune to their advantage.

It is all about mindset; those who have a resilient attitude to setbacks are inevitably stronger, more opportunistic and ultimately luckier. This subconscious psychological work allows them to reframe things − a set-back or a negative event is immediately construed as 'that could have gone worse', or 'at least this didn't happen'. What might be viewed by a pessimist as bad luck is reimagined as not so bad after all. Perhaps above all else, lucky people get good at listening to their instincts, and this ability to trust their intuition makes them effective decision makers.

Practice makes perfect, or if there's no such thing as perfect, at least it makes us fortunate. It changes our mindset from one where 'bad things happen to me' to one where 'I happen to bad things'. We become more resilient to adversity, because we believe that we can turn the tide in our favour if we keep working, practising and preparing ourselves for challenges. This is all part of the art of exploration: being tirelessly conscientious, and turning yourself into a lucky person through diligent, thorough preparation and practice.

The Six Ps

Expeditions rarely go to plan. You spend months preparing and lining everything up, but even with the most stringent contingencies in place, something will go the way you didn't expect. Of course, the thing to do in those situations is imagine just how badly it would or could have gone if you *hadn't* done all the legwork and prep beforehand. That's not to say it all has to be doom and gloom – you can hope for the best, as long as you prepare for the worst.

This is an adage that the army lives by, usually uttered in barracks by grizzled sergeants: 'Prior Planning Prevents Piss Poor Performance.' The importance of the Six Ps was a lesson I learned the hard way, time and time again.

The rain in Spain

In January 2005, as was often the case in my early twenties, I found myself eager for adventure but too poor to afford it. I had recently got back from a long trip hitchhiking to India, where I had spent all my meagre savings. I was staying at my parents' house in Stoke-on-Trent, waiting to join the army and go to Sandhurst to begin my military career, but that wasn't until May. I tried working for a bit, doing odd jobs, manual labour, and working as a hired hand filling up vending machines. It was enough to earn a few hundred quid to see me through the next months, and into the profession I had waited so long to join.

Stacking vending machines didn't give me quite the same thrill that travelling to India had done, and by the end of the first month I had itchy feet. Even though I had only a pittance to my name, I decided that I'd rather spend my time broke and on the road than being bored at home.

I've always had a love of maps, and I was soon poring over them. Given my limited resources, Europe would be my destination. I reckoned I could get away with a week-long trip somewhere if I camped out and lived on one or two meals a day. Outside the home in Stoke it was driving rain and windy, with temperatures hovering around freezing. I needed to go somewhere warm.

Spain suddenly jumped off the page. I had been reading *Don Quixote* in between work shifts, and fancied the romantic idea of exploring the Spanish countryside. I imagined its olive groves, crystalline beaches and sultry ladies. What's more, my friend Tim from university had invited me to visit him in Gibraltar. So, a trip to Iberia it was.

Now, how to get there? I checked flights to Madrid, and managed to get a very good deal on a low cost airline for the first week of February. I thought to myself, *what the heck?* I could make it from

Madrid to Gibraltar in four or five days easily enough if I relied on local help, but since I'd just finished a big hitchhiking trip I wanted something different, and I couldn't afford the trains and buses.

In a moment of inspiration, I decided that I would cycle. I didn't really have the money to rent one – and certainly not buy one – but I had one in the garage from when I was thirteen. That would do!

I packed a small bag, then pulled the bike apart and wrapped the whole thing in cardboard so that I could check it in as my luggage. I liked the idea of a spontaneous adventure, so I did absolutely no route planning. This was 2005, before Google Maps and TripAdvisor, so I would be entirely reliant on my trusty Lonely Planet guidebook and local directions.

The next week I touched down in Madrid, alone and excited. Unpacking my bike, I got it ready for its first road trip, and off we went, heading due south. For the next hundred miles or so, I weaved amongst and hill-top towns of the Spanish plains. I passed by Toledo, with its magnificent palace and dramatic bridges, and the lovely villages of Southern Castile. At first it was fun. A lot of fun. I was feeling pretty bloody proud of myself, to be honest.

And then it began to rain.

And rain.

And rain.

Whoever said 'The rain in Spain falls mainly on the plain' is a bloody liar. It turns out that the rain in Spain falls everywhere, especially in February. My grand plan to sleep rough fell at the first hurdle, and two nights of sleeping in a soaking wet bivvy bag at the side of the road was quite enough. The further south I got, the more miserable the situation became. I had massively underestimated the distances and even more overestimated my own cycling proficiency. In a bid to keep to schedule, I stayed mainly on the highways, which was both dull and dangerous, particularly when lorries flew by, beeping their horns as hailstones as large as bricks pounded the tarmac.

On the third day of cycling, I reached the industrial town of Ciudad Real late in the evening. I was hoping to find a hostel dorm bed for the night, even though I could barely afford to eat, but my guidebook advice on Ciudad Real was bleak: 'It's a gritty Spanish working town where tourists rarely venture, and there's not enough here to warrant a detour off the main highway.'

Brilliant.

But it was already dark, and I couldn't face another night in a ditch, so I peddled hard to reach the town centre, where I might at least be able to sleep on a bench in the train station.

I parked my bike outside, found a suitable dry corner and did exactly that. My sleeping bag was still damp from the night before, but it was better than being in the open. I took a whiff of myself, and I smelled pretty bad – it was probably for the best that I wasn't in a shared dorm room after all.

Just as I was falling asleep, I received a sharp dig to my ribs. Looking up, I saw a stern Spanish policeman, who was holding a baton and yelling loudly. I didn't know much Spanish then, but it definitely did not sound like he was asking me how my day was going.

I was at a loss as to how to reply, so I did the ridiculous hand motion that we associate with cycling. Maybe this means something very different in Spain, because a few seconds later I was bustled into handcuffs and dragged to the police car; my protestations about leaving my bicycle behind falling on deaf ears. Ten minutes later, I found myself at a strange building on the outskirts of town that didn't look like a police station apart from the bars on the windows.

Feeling rather sorry for myself, I was led down a dingy corridor to a room with a single bed, a washbasin in the corner, and a picture of Mary and the baby Jesus on the wall. I shrugged my shoulders as the copper pushed me into the room and locked the door behind me. I may have been locked up, but I did have a warm bed for the night.

The next morning I awoke at 6 a.m. to a knocking on the door, and a little lady beckoned me to follow her. I was led into a communal kitchen area with a large wooden dining table, still utterly confused, where the lady gestured that I sit, then a bowl of porridge was placed in front of me. I looked up from my breakfast as bearded, hairy men began to take their seats. Soon I was not the only one eating porridge, and then it hit me.

I was in a homeless shelter.

After breakfast, I was unceremoniously booted out and told to take my vagabonding elsewhere. It was a long, miserable walk back to the station to collect my bike. It was still there, but after that night I didn't do any more cycling, instead I hitched a lift to the south coast, and spent a few days in Gibraltar with my mate Tim. He found the whole episode very amusing, of course. For me, it was a lesson in humility, and the importance of preparation.

I also decided that cycling was not my thing.

Sir John Franklin

In May 1845, Sir John Franklin led a Royal Navy expedition to discover the Northwest Passage; a stretch of water north of Canada linking the Atlantic and Pacific oceans. He had two ships and 129 men under his command.

According to the subsequently maligned Arctic explorer John Rae, who later discovered the remains of the ill-fated expedition, this was Franklin's first mistake. The local Inuit peoples, who Rae spent many years living with and learning from in order to survive the harsh Polar conditions, never travelled in groups of more than ten or twelve, as the land can't support any more.

The ships were laden with useless, unnecessary burdens: a 1,200-book library, sophisticated cameras, silver cutlery and candlesticks, and even a piano with reams of accompanying sheet music. Also aboard were three years' worth of tinned food supplies — purchased short-notice from a cut-rate supplier, whose hasty soldering process allowed lead to seep into the food.

No one knows exactly what happened to the expedition, but Rae's conversations with Inuit groups near King William Island, as well as evidence on recovered bones, suggests that around forty of the crew died of starvation after resorting to cannibalism on the island. A combination of malnutrition, extreme conditions, lead poisoning and scurvy meant that none of the expedition's members survived. A note later found on Beechey Island revealed that Sir John Franklin had died there on 11 June 1847.

Bad luck contributed towards this tragedy, but poor preparation meant that the crew were especially unable to respond when misfortune struck. The mission was, in effect, doomed before it had even begun.

Hatch a plan

I loved my time in the army for the most part. It had its highs and lows of course, but after five years in the Paras I was getting a bit restless.

In the autumn of 2009, I decided to apply for Special Forces selection, but made the error of going horse riding in Mexico with my girlfriend's family the week before I was due to begin the notoriously difficult process. That was not a good idea, because I had as much luck horse riding in Mexico as I did cycling in Spain. I came off the horse, fracturing my ankle, and with my injuries, there was no way I was going to be able to run up and down the Welsh mountains with a rucksack on my back.

Unfortunately, all of the posts in my regiment were filled. I hadn't been assigned one, because I was due to go on selection, and the Parachute Regiment is not the kind of place where you hold something back for someone in case they fail. I went to speak with personnel to see what I might be able to do for the next year, and discovered to my surprise that my commission was nearly up. The Queen's commission gives an officer their authority to serve, and is, in effect, one's contract. I saw this as a sign, and rather than seeking to extend my commission, I secured myself a few weeks' gardening leave and mentally began to pack my bags.

Once I broke the news that I was leaving the army, the question everyone wanted to ask was, 'What are you going to do next?'

The truth was that I had no idea. Not a specific one, at least. I knew what I liked and I what I didn't, but rather than rush into a job that I might end up hating, I decided to take stock and make a plan instead – as you can see, my time in the army had taught me the value of preparation. Amazing how that lesson can be learned when you have an angry sergeant major to 'positively reinforce' it for you.

I was very fortunate that a lot had happened in my life up to this point, and I wanted to reflect on that so I could plan for the future. When the time came to do so, I sat down with a notebook and pen and used a technique called the combat estimate. In the military, whether you're a platoon commander leading thirty men to assault a bunker position, or Napoleon himself advancing on Moscow, you use this process. It's a plan, refined over centuries of warfare, designed to give commanders a clear picture of the options available to them.

There are many versions of this that leaders have used throughout history, but the British Army has simplified it to seven questions:

1. *What is the enemy doing and why?*
2. *What have I been told to do and why?*
3. *What effects do I want to have on the enemy and what direction must I give to develop my plan?*
4. *Where can I best accomplish each action/effect?*
5. *What resources do I need to accomplish each action/effect?*
6. *When and where do the actions take place in relation to each other?*
7. *What control measures do I need to impose?*

My days of planning operations were over, but what had worked in combat could work for me in life – after all, we're in a war against time, aren't we? A battle to fulfill our potential, to experience the world and to leave it a better place than we found it.

That being the case, I set about changing the terminology to fit my new goals, and adapted the formula into five questions for life planning. For each question, I gave myself a framework and method for how to answer it:

1. What is the current situation and how does it affect me?
   Method: Conduct a SWOT analysis. What are you good at? What do you enjoy? What will earn you enough cash to support your goals?

2. What do I want my mission to be and why? = mission statement, main effort, timeframe.
   Method: Write a mission statement, and set a REALISTIC timeframe.

3. What effects do I need to achieve and what direction must I give to develop the plan?
   Method: Write out my goals, and then the most important steps to achieving them – work backwards!

4. What resources do I need to accomplish what I want to do? = asset requirements.
   Method: List asset requirements – money, equipment, team members, skills, etc.

5. Where and when do the actions take place in relation to each other?
   Method: Synchronisation matrix – how do all these actions fit together, what are my options? A spreadsheet or a mind map.

If you want to find out more about the planning process, you can find templates online.

I can't recommend them enough, as the more questions I answered, the more the plan for the next stage of my life came together. I began to see a loose structure form on the paper in front of me. I made a list of all the things I was good at, and all the things I enjoyed, and suddenly these pie-in-the-sky ideas began to morph into a set of potential goals and challenges.

Thanks to that framework I knew what I wanted, and therefore my radar was set to picking up the right opportunities. I began talking about my ideas with a friend, Tom Bodkin, who was also in the process of leaving the Paras. He was keen on travel, loved winter sports and had a similar mindset to me. Because we'd both worked out what we wanted from the next stage of our lives, it was easy to make the decision to launch our own expedition company, and Secret Compass was born.

We were both experienced in leading expeditions, and more to the point, we both loved doing it. The idea was to run cool trips to far-flung destinations, but we weren't any more specific than that. Who our clients would be, and where we would take them, was something that we needed to determine, and so together we did a second combat estimate, but this time on Secret Compass as a business specifically.

I believe this is a very important step. It is not enough to conduct only one appraisal of your life and goals and be done with it. Keep refining. Keep honing down. By doing this, Tom and I decided that we'd use our military experience and take people to post-conflict zones, or areas that other companies were too scared to go. We pioneered a series of world-first expeditions, beginning with a horse-riding trek across the most remote valley in Afghanistan, and followed up with mountain climbing on the Iraq–Iran border. (We even took the first-ever bloke skiing in Kurdistan, which involved dodging a minefield – luckily, there was a lot of snow!)

It was all done with military precision to the highest standard of service and risk assessment, and the hard work and preparation paid off. In less than three years, Secret Compass became a global market leader.

I organised and led expeditions all around the world, from the jungles of Madagascar to the frozen forests of the Arctic. It wasn't long before I started getting phone calls from big news agencies and broadcasters asking if I would help them to get access to the places we were taking tourists. We became the experts in the field, and were described by many as 'an overnight success'. Tom and I laughed when we heard that, but we were far from the only people out there whose results of dogged preparation had been described that way.

Jonny Wilkinson

Ever since he kicked England to a win in the 2003 Rugby World Cup final, Jonny Wilkinson has become a household name in the UK. He is recognised as one of the greatest players of all time, and became one of rugby union's first millionaires.

What a lot of people don't know, or at least don't realise about 'Wilko', is that none of this came to him naturally. He wasn't born with an ability to play rugby. In fact, as a teenager he was rejected at county trials for the Surrey Under-15s team. More gifted athletes cruised onto the team, but where are they now?

Wilkinson did not have the natural gifts at that age, but the reason his name will be remembered is because of his near religious commitment to practice.

Throughout his career, he wouldn't leave a training session without having successfully kicked six drop-goals in a row, imagining each of them to be the deciding kick in a World Cup final. As he explained in an interview to ESPN, a few months before the 2003 World Cup:

'One afternoon it took me about an hour and a half . . . the balls

were blowing here and there in the wind. I got tired and angry that day too, because I know some days I can aim at a dot and actually hit it over and over again. I was constantly getting the fourth and fifth, but missing the sixth . . . Great players and kickers are great because they've done fantastic amounts of great practice. Everything you've done since you started is there in the bank to be drawn upon.'

When the big moment finally came for him, as he'd practised over and over again for years on end, Jonny was well-prepared. He had set his standards high, and whatever the external conditions, he'd held himself accountable for hitting them. As the saying goes – train hard, fight easy.

Being prepared

There is no such thing as an overnight success; it took diligent preparation for Tom and I to get Secret Compass up to where it was. Behind the scenes there had been a steady slog – hours and hours put in to get there.

Whatever it is you've got earmarked for your next venture in the world, however big or small, start by making a plan of action. This might involve something like the combat estimate, or if it's a more personal thing such as learning a new skill, make a plan of the resources you will need to do it. For sake of example, let's say you want to get better at cooking.

First among these resources is always time: when are you going to practise your cooking? Put space in your diary (if you don't use one, now's a great time to start – your phone will have one built in) on a weekly or daily recurring basis, and view that time as sacred. Thursday evening is cooking night – no ifs, no buts. Then, once you've secured yourself some time, think about the other things you'll need: materials, equipment, and instructions (i.e., ingredients, kitchen utensils and cookery books).

Identify any gaps, and get these filled before you start – this is really important, as the frustration of finding you're missing something crucial can kill the positive momentum that builds in the early stages of any new project. Plan what you're going to do in each session you've booked. This Thursday, Pad Thai; next week, chocolate brownies.

Of course, the bigger the project, the more planning will be needed. Think about each step of the process in detail, and question if there's anything you might have taken for granted that could cause problems if it goes wrong, or missing. This is especially helpful in working contexts. Big pitch to a client tomorrow? Read through your deck tonight – if you can, ask someone close to you to watch you rehearse. Whatever your chosen skill or area, practise and practise until you can do something in your sleep, and then you will not fail.

You must plan, but always remember to stay flexible; there is no use sticking stubbornly to a plan that is not serving you. Life is not neatly pre-packaged with clear instructions for use. You have to allow a space for possibility to flourish – you can't just live your life according to a five-year plan or a projection of what you want it to look like. By doing that, you will shut down true opportunity when it appears. Embrace those opportunities, anticipate them and pull them towards you. That's why it is important to set goals, and come up with options on how to get there.

By being goal oriented, you give yourself the best chance of understanding the bigger picture and not being distracted by easy wins; and by educating yourself in the different levels of detail required to succeed in any task, you can try your hand at a bit of everything, not only what you are good at.

On an expedition, preparation goes a long way in achieving the aim. The same goes if you are starting a business or writing a book: you may not have any experience or deep love of accountancy, but you – or someone you know – will have to do the job, so it makes sense at least to begin to understand what is required. Using positive thinking, figure out where your strengths lie.

Once you are prepared for anything, you can start focusing on the things that interest you the most, and then, for all the other stuff – DELEGATE. Even the most accomplished people cannot succeed alone. Expeditions, like all projects, need a solid team, and, as the next chapter explores, solid teamwork.

Buzz Aldrin on the moon, with Neil Armstrong

6

Build Your Tribe

*In order to achieve great things, you must surround
yourself with great people* – anonymous

Strength in diversity

In 2002, I was studying history at university in Nottingham. I was in
my second year and I'd made a good bunch of friends. There were
people from my halls of residence, my course and a few randoms I'd
met in the library. But the people I liked best were the crowd I met
at the University Officer Training Corps.

The UOTC was technically a branch of the army, aimed at
students to give them insight into military life. We were non-deploy-
able, so we couldn't be sent off to fight a war, but we did get to go
on exercises, shoot rifles and do training courses; everything from
parachuting to kayaking and hill-walking in Wales. I loved it, and I
ended up living with a bunch of fellow cadets in my final year at uni.

Every Wednesday night, after we'd finished our military training,
we'd have a few beers in the mess bar before going out into town to
go drinking. We'd usually end up in one of the regular student night-
clubs, but on one particular night our drunken foray happened to
coincide with the annual hustings for 'Mr and Miss Nottingham'.

It was a talent contest of sorts, where the applicants had put themselves forward a few weeks before and been selected on their looks,
banter and general extravagance. The entire student population then
gathered and crammed itself into the Palais nightclub to see the final
competition. The three male and female finalists were to parade
themselves on stage, show off whatever talent they had, and whoever
got the biggest cheers from the drunk crowds would be the winning
boy and girl.

The girls were up first, three stunners who gyrated to the music and downed shots of tequila. One of them did a cartwheel, while another did an impossibly low splits, much to all the boys' delight. The one with the biggest boobs won.

Then it was the boys' turn. One of them was a hulking rugby player, another a skinny but amusing comedian who wooed the girls with his acerbic wit, while the last one was a lad I recognised. He was one of my friend's housemates, a philosophy student who went by the name of Ash Bhardwaj. I remembered seeing him out and about, but had always found him too loud, too gregarious and brash. I hoped he wouldn't win.

The rugby player pranced around first, flexing his muscles and banging out hand-clap press-ups. The skinny lad couldn't compete with that, so he had his friend pass him a 'dirty yard' – a metre-long glass receptacle filled with two and a half pints of various alcoholic drinks, including an obscene amount of spirits – which he proceeded to down in one, before promptly vomiting the whole lot straight down into the faces of those unlucky enough to be in the front row. The crowds went wild.

Then it was Ash's turn. He pointed at the DJ and gave a thumbs up. The theme tune from *Baywatch* began, blaring out its familiar beats. Ash stood stone still at first, before ripping his shirt from his chest. Then he whipped off his shoes and jeans, whirling the lot around his head. Swiftly after that, off came his underpants. He was now fully naked in front of two thousand people. Finally, to top off the show, he lobbed his wardrobe straight into the crowd, with one of his shoes cracking me directly in the face.

What an idiot, I thought, but I was in the minority. The crowd burst into rip-roaring cheers, and he was crowned the new Mr Nottingham.

I didn't see Ash for six years after university and my enduring memory of him was of that night. In fact, I'd almost entirely forgotten he existed until the spring of 2011, when his profile popped up on Facebook with a friend request. I thought I might as well accept it, and when I viewed his profile, it appeared he'd been leading a rather interesting life.

There were photos of him riding horses in New Zealand, trekking in India and skiing all over the world. I knew he had studied philosophy, but surely he must have a job too? I had recently left the army and was doing a lot of travelling myself. I had not long got back from Africa, where I'd been volunteering for a charity, but now I was out of money and looking for my next project.

Most of my mates from university and the army were now settled down with wives or girlfriends and regular jobs, so I thought about messaging him and seeing what he was up to. He might still be the brash and loud character I remembered from uni, but he seemed to be doing well for himself and had carved out a niche that intrigued me.

A week later, we met for a coffee. He was still larger than life, but had mellowed somewhat and seemed to have his head screwed on. He chatted happily and enthusiastically about how he had worked in every conceivable job going, all around the world, from bartender to cowboy to ski instructor. 'In fact, Lev,' he said, 'are you free next week?'

I was.

'And you were in the army, so you're trained in fighting and all that stuff?'

I tried to explain that it was more nuanced that that, but before I went into any detail, he interrupted, 'Well, I'm just starting a new job running a billionaire's chalet in Verbier, Switzerland. Do you want to come and be the family bodyguard? It'll be good money.'

He didn't need to ask twice. 'Sure, why not?'

So that spring I managed all the security arrangements for a high-net-worth individual and his family. It was hardly what I aspired to, but I needed the cash, and as well as the time it allowed me to ski, it gave me an opportunity to develop the skills I needed to learn to become an explorer and writer. What's more, I got to know Ash properly. Far from the buffoon I had written him off as at university, I found him to be incredibly kind, intelligent and funny. He was polar opposites to me in respect to his outgoing character, but we shared an enthusiasm for travel and debate, and many an evening was engaged in thoughtful, philosophical conversation.

I was glad I had given him a chance and reconnected, and since then Ash and I have travelled together, helped each other out on projects, written articles together and gone on assignments all around the world. Ash was the person who first introduced me to the world of television, and he taught me how to pitch to media outlets. Ultimately, he was the person who inspired me to take a chance on focusing all my energies on writing a book and following my dreams.

Don't write people off simply because they aren't your 'type' on the face of it. Different people bring different things to the table, and it's this variety that gives teams an edge. At university I'd seen Ash as a bit of a showoff, but looking back now on that trip, I became friends with him because he embodies all of the traits of optimism: he does everything with bags of enthusiasm and energy and wears his heart on his sleeve.

The guy who stripped naked in a club and threw a shoe in my face would go on to become one of my most honest critics and one of my greatest friends.

Whānau

The Maori word whānau literally means to 'be born' or 'give birth', and it is often used to refer to the wider family unit. It is compared metaphorically to a spearhead, or a flock of birds flying in V formation. The implication is that, while everyone within the group is free to act as they please, the whole – the thrusting spearhead, the bird formation – is more effective if all its parts are pulling in the same direction.

One of the world's most successful sports teams of all time, the New Zealand rugby union team, aka the All Blacks, consciously adopted this philosophy and added the English short-hand, 'no dickheads'. No one in the All Blacks is bigger than the team, and however talented any given player, egos are not permitted to stand in the way of team cohesion and purpose.

For this reason, after any match or training session, senior players can be found sweeping the changing rooms and clearing away any mess – even after celebrating an important win. Part of their philosophy is: 'No one looks after the All Blacks, the All Blacks look after themselves.'

The most elite Special Forces selection processes around the world have a similar philosophy. It doesn't matter how strong or fast you are – if you think you're bigger than the team, you're out. In the army it doesn't

matter which regiment you are in, or what rank you hold, everyone
should be prepared and willing to get involved in even the most menial
tasks the situation requires – like on expedition. In Afghanistan, the best
officers were often to be found filling sandbags alongside the men, or
'stagging on', i.e. standing guard, in the sentry positions. It engendered
trust, respect, and cemented the team. If anyone was found slacking, then
you'd be considered selfish and ousted.

It takes only a few bad apples to undermine the morale of a team.
As the Maori saying goes: He iti wai kōwhao waka e tahuri te waka
('A little water seeping through a small hole may swamp a canoe'). If
just one individual doesn't pull his or her weight, then that negativity
will inevitably spread through the ranks causing a loss of faith: 'Why
should we work hard if they aren't?' Great teams require everyone to
unite fully behind the end goal, and work with singular focus towards
achieving it.

Attitude and energy

Once we have the self-awareness to confront our own strengths and
weaknesses, we can go forward armed with the knowledge of where
we are competent and capable, and where we are not. Then, if we
don't know what we are doing, we can bring in people who do. This
fundamentally underpins the explorer's attitude of mind; no person
is an island. There will always be things that you can't do and it will
always be better with two. No expeditions are accomplished alone;
even if the team is behind the scenes, or is informally made up of
friends and family who are fulfilling those roles, it is always a team
effort.

When I'm looking to build a team or choose a travelling companion, the first characteristic I consider is attitude. I don't mind if
someone doesn't have experience or skills in a particular field, or if
they don't know how to read a map. That can all be learned. But if
someone is negative or not up for an adventure, then they are not
welcome on my team. It's as simple as that. I also want to be around
people who are enthusiastic, fun and playful; bringing energy and

vitality to what they do. People who are passionate about what they do, without being too earnest or high and mighty.

There is an idea called the energy investment model, which suggests that people can be divided into four different types of behaviour, based on their typical feelings and reactions to events. It is measured by a combination of *attitude*, or how positive someone's mindset towards a certain situation may be, and the level of *effort* or energy someone puts in. The four categories are: spectator, player, deadwood and cynic.

Spectators are characterised by having a positive attitude towards a challenge, but a relatively low energy investment. They are the sort of people who see things through a positive lens and like the way things are; they are unlikely to take the initiative and release large amounts of energy reserves.

Cynics are the opposite, with high energy input but often a more sceptical or negative mental attitude towards the task at hand, often disillusioned about the things they are doing. This means that with their high energy and competence, they can be a distracting or troublesome element. Having said that, leaders do well to listen to cynics, and to take their views on board when their concerns are valid and constructive, because they can be the first people to spot problems in the way things are going. When cynics are given recognition, they can become players; if not, their disillusionment can grow and they can ultimately turn against the group.

Deadwoods have a bad attitude as well as low energy. They feel that things are done *to* them rather than *by* them and in a team they have usually been repeatedly undervalued or unsupported. Of course, these behaviour categories are not set in stone and don't necessarily mean that these members will always remain in this category. Whatever your circumstances, don't accept being deadwood, or a 'victim', as this category is sometimes called. Instead take responsibility for yourself; you are the person with the most power to change your own story. Leaders can also coax better attitude and more energy out of their deadwood teammates by encouraging and supporting them.

Which leads us to the final category, the players, who have a positive attitude and usually invest high energy into challenges and situations. These people tend to take the initiative and are capable of

investing the effort required to see things through. It is the responsibility of the enthusiastic, high-energy players to help empower those
who are feeling victimised. It's in everyone's power to bring something to the world, and to the people around you, even if it is only a
sense of enthusiasm and fun – and players know this. If you can bring
humour, warmth and a sense of fun to those around you, that is
worth more than any amount of money.

Get to know yourself and which category you tend towards.
Players are the sort of optimistic people who choose to get better
rather than getting bitter. This stuff is not in the hands of fate; this
choice belongs to you.

On all my expeditions, I have to select my local guides wisely.
Failure to do so could not only risk the success of the journey, but in
many places it could also mean life or death. Travelling across the
frontlines of Syria, I chose as my guide a lady called Nada, a straight-
talking grandmother, who got me through some of the most terrifying checkpoints I had ever seen. Why? Because as a hijab-wearing
woman of a certain age, she appeared non-threatening to the gun-
toting militiamen, who were immediately disarmed by her respectful
yet strong charisma.

In Central America, I was joined for five months by Alberto – a
photographer who had never walked anywhere in his life before. But
that didn't matter. I didn't need a guide as such – they are ten-a-
penny and I can read a map myself – what I needed was an enthusiastic companion; someone who would be good fun and positive, but
could also get us out of tricky situations if we came across them. His
natural charm certainly saved my skin on more than one occasion
when we bumped into drug runners and gangsters in the Guatemalan
badlands.

Team culture

With higher stakes and risk scenarios, team culture on an expedition
is apt to be more intense and arguably even more pivotal to success
than in everyday life. On expedition, there is total equality and
open-mindedness – there is no room for prejudice or intolerance.
There are usually all sorts of people involved, each with their own
roles: cameraman, director, security advisor, photographer, local

fixers, drivers, translators, and so on. Of course it's important that they are focused on their job, but at the same time each one needs to be prepared to get stuck into whatever task is at hand; whether that's helping to put up a tent, washing the dishes or fetching water. Nobody is excluded from these chores unless there's a very good reason.

I've learnt a lot from observing the team culture and team dynamics on expeditions, and teams undergo a process of developing a culture. When it first forms, everyone will busy themselves with defining the scope of the tasks – who will do what, when. Some of this gets discussed openly, and some of it falls into place without anyone having to say it. I've often been in teams where people didn't know each other before, so everyone is busy gathering first impressions and thoughts on each other too.

In these early stages, the group generally get started on tasks on their own, not yet fully comfortable in their relationships with the rest of the team. At this point, all but the most difficult or pig-headed of team members will avoid conflict; they want to be accepted into the group and be well-liked.

This is eventually followed by a period of hostility and conflict; a few frosty words or a row. People start sharing their ideas and their perspectives and this causes disruption or disagreement, and it's a distraction from the work the team is supposed to be doing. Those who naturally avoid conflict tend to find this uncomfortable and will shy away from the collective. Some groups are able to resolve this contention in no time, with good communication, but others will get stuck here, and a few teams never make it past this phase.

If we get the culture wrong, then individuals are forced to waste time on protecting themselves and their own interests from people within their own team. This defence is a waste of precious energy or resources; it causes splinters and factions, and weakens the team. When we feel safe and don't waste time on self-protection, we work together, combining forces to become stronger against the outside dangers, or towards the actual task at hand. Internal competition is perilous; it's hard to act as a team if you're inadvertently competing with your teammates. This is the stage when people start to wonder, *how would I do this differently*, or perhaps, *could I do this better alone?* If you're not careful, your Players can become Cynics.

If teams can get past this, they can get into a phase of cooperation. The team has a shared purpose and shared expectations and after the storms of sharing ideas on how to get things done, a consensus of sorts has been reached. There is a common goal that everyone has in sight. There is a strategy for how the team members might act if conflict rears its head again, so that time won't be wasted on disagreements and distractions. This gives a shared and structured understanding of how things are done, which streamlines and speeds things up enormously.

Only the very best of teams get beyond this into the magical sweet spot of trust and productivity. This is rare, but really rewarding to be part of. There is a synergy between team members, who naturally look out for each other, and the team is performing well with no friction. That's not to say that everyone miraculously gets along and agrees on everything, but group dynamics and interpersonal concerns tend to be aired and resolved quickly and without too much drama.

When this is at its very best, one team member can join or leave, or be absent, and the overall mission – the documentary or the expedition – doesn't suffer. This is a culture that a leader has to foster, but it is also characterised by the fact that team members are not totally over-reliant on the leader for everything.

If you're not all on the same page, your chances of success are severely limited. But if you share a purpose and there is an underlying yearning to serve something larger than the individuals, a team can become greater than the sum of its parts.

Neil Armstrong and NASA

The first step on the moon by a man was also the last of an eight-year odyssey by the largest expedition team in human history. On 20 July 1969, Neil Armstrong had travelled 384,000 kilometres (240,000 miles) in only four days to reach earth's moon and utter those immortal words, 'That's one small step for man; one giant leap for mankind.'

But the Apollo programme that put him and Buzz Aldrin there had employed the skills of 400,000 people for almost ten years. Over 200,000 companies and universities had supplied the equipment and *brainpower. The project cost $24 billion and was the longest, largest and most ambitious expedition ever conceived.*

It is also perhaps the greatest example of how teamwork is fundamental to success. Hundreds of the world's greatest scientific minds came together to solve seemingly impossible problems at breakneck speed to create a rocket and spacecraft that could transport a crew all the way to the moon and back; an astonishing achievement that inspired a whole generation, won the space race and changed the face of human potential forever.

It won't always be plain sailing . . .

Of course, teamwork isn't without its difficulties. Often teams get hamstrung by the personalities within them; egos obstruct and pride gets in the way of making the right decision – stuck in the stormy conflict phase. This is certainly something I've encountered in less formal hierarchies than the army, and on expeditions it can be a real problem, especially when you're tired or frightened, and even if you have the best company.

I'll never forget one particular night in Kashmir. I'd been walking for months along the length of the Himalayas, from Afghanistan into Pakistan and now I had reached the Indian side of the Kashmir line of control. I was with a local horse guide called Mehraj, and my friend Ash Bhardwaj (of Mr Nottingham fame) had flown out to come walking with me for a few weeks in India, the land of his father's ancestors.

We had followed a ridge for most of the day, before descending into a prehistoric forest with enormous ferns and oversized mushrooms. It was the kind of wild, primordial environment where you'd half expect to stumble upon a Stegosaurus at any moment. It had warmed up again and I chatted with Ash about how nice it was to be walking downhill after a debilitating climb the day before. We'd loaded our rucksacks onto the mules and carried only our cameras and water bottles to make things easier.

We had last seen Mehraj a couple of hours before. He was looking after the mules, so told Ash and me to go on ahead. We could wait for him at the top of the ridge above the village of Naranag, where we'd find an open meadow. Apparently it was so obvious we couldn't miss it.

I led the way, following a path that took us deeper into the forest. A thick layer of pine needles covered the track and lightning had felled several trees so that we kept losing the way. It looked as if no one had been here in months, if not years, so there was no way of knowing which of the myriad of trails was the right one. We tried to stay at the same height, but soon enough the path would diverge and then disappear altogether. We would go back and rejoin it and follow another one, but then the same thing would happen.

The afternoon wore on and both of us were getting frustrated. There was no phone signal to contact Mehraj and it was becoming more and more apparent that we were lost.

'For God's sake, Lev,' said Ash in a fit of exasperation. 'Do you know where you're going?'

I showed him my map. It was simple enough to work out where we were and where we needed to be. The only small problem was how to get there. To our left the hill fell away to an almost vertical drop into the valley, where a gushing river chiselled its way through a gorge. To the right the forest was thick and twelve-feet-high thorn bushes blocked our possible route. The village we were aiming for was only five miles away – as the crow flies – but it may as well have been on another planet. I looked at my watch; it was already 5 p.m. and Mehraj would have been waiting for us on the ridge for at least an hour.

'What do you reckon?' I said. 'Up or down?' Both looked equally appalling.

'Let's go down to the river and follow it round,' Ash said. I could tell he was exhausted and in no mood to climb again.

'You heard what Mehraj said. There are no bridges – what if we need to cross?'

I looked down into the valley. It must have been half a mile down, perhaps more. We had two options – a thorny scramble up, or a slippery descent.

I thought for a moment about the options. If I pushed to have my way and I was wrong, then I stood to lose Ash not only as my cameraman, but also potentially as a friend. He had volunteered to be here because of me, and had given up his spare time. Even if he was wrong, then I guess it didn't really matter.

'Okay,' I conceded. 'Let's go down.'

I guessed that it couldn't be too hard, and at least it would be easier than going up again, and so we slipped and slid on our backsides down through the Jurassic-sized ferns. A huge deer darted out of the bushes and seemed to fly into the pine forest below. I wished for a moment that I were an animal – unlike us, they never seemed to tire. We slid further and suddenly an adder slithered from under a rock, its diamond ridges flashing in the undergrowth. His life didn't look as nice as the deer's, and I reconsidered my aspirations for reincarnation.

We reached the bottom of the cliff and emerged onto a narrow beach. It was now almost 6.15 p.m. and my heart sank; we had less than an hour of daylight left. The river was a torrent of freezing glacial melt, crashing through the gorge like an icy bolt of lightning. There was absolutely no way of crossing, and on our side the cliffs up and down the river were sheer faces of crumbling rock. I was exhausted. I hadn't felt like this on the journey so far, but now I felt responsible for leading Ash down the wrong route. Fortunately, he seemed to get a second wind.

'Come on, get a grip,' he said. 'Let's get out of here.'

'But there's no way round,' I pointed out.

'We'll have to climb back up.'

So that's what we tried. Following a gulley, we tried to scramble out of the valley, but the soil was wet and the grass fell away in clumps in our hands. It was too dangerous; one false move and we would fall to certain death in the swirling eddies below. Suddenly a rock came loose above my head and tumbled out of the undergrowth, going straight for Ash's head!

'Watch out!' Somehow I stretched my hands out just in time; it was a miracle I didn't fall myself, but I managed to divert it between my legs and let it go safely past Ash before crashing down into the river. We clung to the cliff where we both shook with horror at the near miss.

'Let's climb back down!'

We had underestimated the power of nature in the mountains and taken them for granted, forgetting that the price of indescribable beauty from afar could mean terrible deadliness up close. It had taken us an hour to slide down half a mile to the river. There was no way we'd get back out before dark. I told Ash and the realisation set in.

'Shit.'

'Exactly.'

We both sat slumped in silence, side by side on a rock, wondering what to do. It was almost dark and the clouds were black. I was so physically done for that I began gasping for air and vomiting, although there was nothing to throw up – we hadn't eaten all day.

'We need shelter,' Ash said.

It was the first rule of survival – especially in the mountains where the weather could change at any moment, and I was grateful that Ash had done some basic army training himself – even if it was only a few weeks as a reservist. He helped me to my feet and we stumbled through the undergrowth, back along the narrow strip of rocks to the way we had come down. A hundred and fifty metres away, almost imperceptible were it not for one angular beam, was the frame of an old poacher's hut.

There is no such thing as a straight line in nature, and when you're in the forest, little things like that can stick out like a sore thumb. The roof had caved in and the whole building was overgrown with wild cannabis and vicious brambles, but it was the nearest thing to shelter we could see. Up close I could see that the only way in was through a gap in the bushes and so we pushed through, getting covered in scratches in the process.

'That was lucky,' said Ash.

'A miracle,' I agreed.

Just as we entered, there was a loud crack and a flash of light. An instant later the rain came down in sheets. 'Sod's law,' Ash looked at me. 'The one time we load the bloody bags onto the mules, you get us lost.'

'Me?' I shot back, annoyed that I'd let him have his way against my better judgement. 'It was your idea to come down the valley.'

'Piss off. You agreed.'

He was right, of course. I should have insisted we carry on climbing, instead of taking the easy road to appease him. After all, I was the leader and bore responsibility. I should have had the integrity to stick to my guns. Now we were stuck in a soaking ravine overnight with no sleeping bags, no food and no way of contacting Mehraj. We were cold, wet and hungry, but at least we had a collapsed roof over our heads and a lighter.

'Fine,' I said. 'Let's just forget it and make a fire.' For the next eight hours, we took it in turns to collect twigs and bits of moss to keep the camp fire alight. I was grateful we did have a lighter, because I didn't fancy my chances of doing a Bear Grylls impression in those conditions. The mere fact that we had a roof above our heads (however leaky) was probably the only reason we didn't die of hypothermia that night. We curled up, shivering around the embers, shifting in disgust as the forest's insects crawled over and around us.

I didn't know if I'd ever been more miserable . . .

Mutiny on the Bounty

Teamwork doesn't come automatically, and leaders can never take the obedience of their teams for granted. The consequences can be dire if, as a result of a leader's actions or their failure to consider the morale of their team, the group ceases to operate as a coherent unit.

Lieutenant William Bligh found this out to his cost during a bread-fruit-picking expedition aboard HMS Bounty in 1789. At the voyage's outset two years earlier, Bligh appeared to be a popular leader, raising his men's spirits with regular music and dancing sessions, and reporting that the crew were happy and in obedient order. Upon arrival at Tahiti, where the expedition stayed for five months cultivating breadfruit plants in exchange for gifts presented to the local chiefs, many of the Bounty's crew and officers got involved with Tahitian women. Bligh himself steered clear of this, but permitted his crew to do so for the sake of their morale, on the condition that they continued to go about their duties.

However, over time he became frustrated by their falling standards. He vented his frustration with harsh, often humiliating punishments, especially towards Fletcher Christian, to whom he had previously expressed his approval with a promotion to Acting Lieutenant early in the voyage. Floggings, rare early in the expedition, became routine.

Three crew members deserted, and were flogged themselves once they were recaptured.

When the Bounty left Tahiti, its crew were downbeat after five relaxed, hedonistic months on the island. Bligh himself was becoming paranoid, venting his fears with angry outbursts and disproportionate punishments of his officers, particularly Christian. On 28 April 1789, Christian and a small group of mutineers took over the ship and cast its captain and his supporters to sea in a lifeboat. Bligh and his followers eventually returned to Britain via Indonesia (then the Dutch East Indies). Their expedition had descended into failure thanks to the disorder of the crew and its officers, but Bligh was exonerated from blame.

Christian and his mutineers did not fare well; after capturing the Bounty, they tried to establish their own community on the island of Tubuai, but were forced to abandon this when Christian began to lose control of the team there in the face of skirmishes from local islanders. They split into two factions. One attempted to settle on Tahiti, but were eventually captured by British navy ships set on bringing the mutineers to justice. Christian and his supporters settled on the island of Pitcairn, along with around thirty Tahitian prisoners, mostly women.

Christian's group eventually succumbed to the forces of discord they had unleashed; infighting between the captured Tahitians and the mutineers led to the deaths of all but one of the latter. Christian was killed while tending his fields, but his son, Thursday October Christian, survived. The population that they founded still lives there to this day.

. . . but it's better as a team

Despite sharing the hut with some hairy spiders and millipedes the size of eels, Ash and I made it through till dawn. At last the rain abated and a chorus of birds heralded a new day; one in which we were alive. Weak with hunger, we climbed back out of the valley, following our trampled course from the day before, hoping to retrace our steps and find our guide, Mehraj.

Fortunately for us, our Kashmiri guide had the initiative to send out a search party. After just an hour, we heard shouts from the woods up above. I looked up to discover an old shepherd wielding an enormous axe and waiting for us on top of a boulder. I had never been so relieved to see anyone in my life.

I learned a lot of lessons from that experience. It was a mistake that cost us a miserable night, and yet if Ash hadn't been with me and I had got lost alone, things could have been far worse. I have always enjoyed travelling on my own. It gives you time to think, and some of my most useful journeys have been the ones that I completed alone. It forces you to interact with people in the place you are visiting, as you don't settle into the comfort of just chatting to your travel companions.

But there are perils, as evidenced by the sobering tale of Chris McCandless, who spent two years wandering, hitchhiking and hiking alone in North America. It was made famous by Jon Krakauer's retelling of Chris's diary entries in his book *Into the Wild*, which later became a film. Young Chris headed into the Alaskan wilderness without a map and in the hope of living in a peaceful solitude. But after four months alone in the forest, he finally succumbed to starvation. His diary entry sums up the dying man's final thoughts: 'Happiness is only real when shared.'

I was glad that I hadn't gone through that night in the forest alone. Sure it was a screw-up, but now Ash and I look back at it and laugh. So long as people have faith in the journey and believe in the team, sometimes the biggest mistakes can yield the best results. We remain the best of friends.

Choose wisely

I was once given some wise advice; that in order to achieve great things, you need to surround yourself with great people. Whatever it is you are setting out to accomplish, think carefully about the people that will be best placed to help you get there. Be honest with yourself about your own shortcomings, and think about the people you know who might be able to plug those gaps. In turn, work out what you can contribute that those people can't; it is a team game, which means it's not all about what you can get from other people, but how you can maximise your contribution to the whole, as well.

Above all, give your team time to establish its culture, and *listen* to the advice of the people you've brought on board. Far too many leaders, especially in the business world, ignore the words of Apple CEO Steve Jobs: 'It doesn't make sense to hire smart people and tell them what to do: we hire smart people so they can tell us what to do.'

Motivational speaker Jim Rohn has said that you are the average of the five people with whom you spend the most time. If that is the case, then choose your friends wisely and make sure you don't let your ego and pride dictate those that constitute your circle.

Teamwork is at the heart of great achievement, and fundamental to success. I've learned from my experiences in the army, in business and in the world of expeditions that getting the right people on board with your vision is the best chance you have of succeeding in any task, project or mission. Teamwork is about removing your pride, and working in harmony with others towards a common goal. Good teamwork is underpinned by the selfless actions of the individuals within the team, and this can be inspired through having a solid vision and a plan of how to enact it. It's about building mutual respect and trust and it is brought to fruition through making it fun and enjoyable. There is great joy to be found in being part of a team, particularly when on the road.

Remember that there's no such thing as a one-man expedition. Solo holidays are one thing, but if you are trekking to the North Pole, even if it's on your own, you will still need back-up in the form of a team at home tracking your progress, or providing emergency support. On all my big expeditions I've had to seek assistance in some form or another, whether that has come in the shape of resupply drops in the jungle, or getting local guides, fixers and translators to help navigate the complexities of travelling in difficult places. It becomes even more necessary to have a team of good people around you when you have a specific mission in mind, like making a film or documentary.

As part of a team, we can achieve great things – effective teams, pulling in the same direction, are more than the sum of their parts. Once we're able to operate as team players, we are able to take the next step towards our own individual goals, and we can have one of the most fulfilling and rewarding experiences that life has to offer – that of being a leader.

Mary Seacole

7

Lead From the Front

*I used to say of him that his presence on the field made
the difference of forty thousand men –* Arthur Wellesley,
1st Duke of Wellington, describing Napoleon

The secret of leadership

Helicopter blades slashed through the hot sky, the roar of engines
deafening as the pilot twisted and turned on our final approach.
Crammed into the back with my men, I tried to keep my balance by
tensing my legs, and focusing my gaze on the machine gun in the
helicopter's door. My kit was heavy on my shoulders, and sweat
poured into my eyes from under the rim of my helmet. My palms
were wet as they gripped the rifle. I pulled it closer to my chest, and
prepared myself for what was to come.

The airman behind the machine gun turned to me. His face was
covered by a scarf and the dark visor of his helmet, but I knew what
it meant when he held up his index finger.

I turned, and shouted to my men. 'One minute!'

One minute to landing, and whatever was waiting there for us.

Looking into the eyes of my young soldiers, I saw steely resolve
– the hardness of the paratrooper flying into battle. I was closest
to the rear door, which was now winching fully open. There was
no doubt in my mind that I had to be the first one down the
ramp. I had waited years for this moment, and now was my time.
I'd practised it over and over again, on grass fields, in mock-up
structures and on the real things during exercises all over the
world, but this was different. For the first time in my life, I was
flying into war.

Today, there would be an enemy waiting for us.

For the last eighteen months, I'd been training with the thirty men of my platoon for this moment. For eighteen months before that, I'd been schooled in the art of war and leadership at Sandhurst, and at the Infantry Training School in Brecon. I had three years of the best military training in the world to my name, but it would mean nothing if I wasn't the first down the ramp.

There was no way of knowing exactly what waited for us. It was the spring of 2008, and the fighting season was commencing in the deserts and valleys of southern Afghanistan. Since we'd arrived a month before, there had been the occasional patrol, and we'd seen mortars exploding in the far distance, but as a platoon we hadn't yet been 'in contact'. We hadn't seen with our own eyes the Taliban that we'd been sent to fight.

We were heading straight into the enemy heartland. A place called the Arghandab valley. It lay outside of Kandahar city, the birthplace of the Taliban, in the notorious *Dasht-i-Margo*, which is the Pashtun term for the 'Desert of Death'.

Our mission was a simple one – to kill or capture a Taliban bomb maker called Haji Mohammed, infamous for making the improvised bombs that were responsible for the deaths of dozens of British and allied soldiers.

We'd spent a week poring over maps and aerial photographs of Nalgham village, in which he was thought to live. My platoon – No. 8 Platoon, on attachment to A Company of the Third Battalion the Parachute Regiment – was given the honour of landing first, right in Haji Mohammed's back garden, and it was our task to surround his house.

It was a dangerous mission, but as the seconds counted down, and I looked out of the rear door of the helicopter towards the dusty plains below, I felt a tremendous sensation of both trepidation and sheer excitement. It was a lot of responsibility to shoulder, but I wanted to carry it.

The helicopter got closer to the ground, whipping the Afghan dust into the air until it was a thick cloud around us.

'Ten seconds!' shouted the airman, holding tightly to a rope. The door was now fully open. The ramp hit the floor with a clunk, and a shudder went through the airframe as the wheels touched down – everyone wobbled but kept their feet. They knew how important it was to stay upright, and get off the heli quickly. The Taliban had spies everywhere; scouts that reported the movement of helicopters. Every second that we delayed deplaning was a second for the enemy to train their weapons and kill those on the ramp.

Being on that ramp was my rightful place. There are times when an officer needs to step back to better control his men, but this wasn't one of them. I would be the first off this aircraft, and into whatever waited.

'Go, go, go!' the airman shouted, myself and my men picking up the call so that it rippled through the aircraft. And then we were running, gritting our teeth as though that would stop the bullets that may await us.

My feet touched down on the Afghan soil and I breathed in the dirt as I ran through the cloud that the helicopter's blade stirred up all around us. My rifle was up at eye level and I looked over my sights, ready to snap shoot at anyone that posed a threat to my men.

My soldiers followed me. I felt like a giant, leading them from a metal beast and into the jaws of death . . .

Except that when the helicopter lifted away, and the dust settled, we were quite alone.

Nobody home.

Shit.

I put some of my men into defensive positions and took others with me to search the house. This was still a dangerous time, as the Taliban were not above booby-trapping their own homes. Other than a few sacks of opium – the drug of choice in those parts – we found nothing.

I walked back outside and was shrugging off the disappointment of another quiet mission when a whip-like sound echoed across the fields, followed immediately by a crack. It wasn't the noise you hear in the films, it was altogether more visceral and unnerving.

'Incoming!' shouted my platoon sergeant.

I shouted at the men to jump into a nearby ditch and return fire. They looked at me, unbelieving. It was like being on an exercise on Salisbury plain, except the noises were not the dull simulations we'd become accustomed to. These were real and violent. Somebody was shooting with the evident intention of killing us.

Three hundred metres away, I saw the enemy moving in a line of trees. I took aim, and fired.

It was the start of a very long day.

Helen Sharman

*When I was thirteen, I went on a school trip to the Birmingham confer-
ence centre. Despite the dull sounding venue, this particular trip was very
exciting, not just because we were allowed to wear normal clothes and
potentially meet girls from another school, but because we were going to
hear a real-life astronaut speak to us about their experiences.*

*In 1991, Helen Sharman became the first Briton in space. Her
story is remarkable. Just a couple of years before, in November 1989,
this young woman was studying for a doctorate in food chemistry when
she heard an advert on the radio. It was calling for volunteers to go into
space – no prior experience needed – as part of a Soviet mission called
Project Juno. The idea was to improve relations between Britain and
her Cold War adversary.*

*Helen applied and had to undergo masses of physical and mental
tests, from being whizzed about in a centrifuge to aptitude tests and
problem-solving exams. Out of 13,000 applicants, she was one of two
who made it to Moscow for training. She had to learn Russian, of
course, so she could communicate with her fellow adventurers, and after
eighteen months she was picked to go on the mission.*

*So at just twenty-seven years old, the young Yorkshire woman became
the first British person to launch into space for an eight-day flight. Like
lots of youngsters, I was fascinated by space, curious more about the
mundane intricacies of daily life on a space mission than any great questions about the profundity of space travel. And that's what she described.
She told us about where they sleep, how they eat and what it is like to
float around in zero gravity. She explained the challenges she faced –
from space sickness to muscle wastage – and told us what it was like to
look out of the window and gaze down on our planet from afar.*

*In my mind, astronauts and cosmonauts were superheroes. Yet here
was this very normal woman, who seemed like one of my teachers, or
my mum, talking about how she had been into space. I was transfixed
by how ordinary she was – not in a rude way, but her stories were so*

relatable. It was a revelation to me; previously explorers had belonged to far-off distant lands or story books, but here was a nice lady from Sheffield right in front of me, who was also an astronaut. That was when I realised that there are no super-humans, everyone is capable of phenomenal and earth-shattering things; anyone is capable of being a pioneering leader – in any field.

In the questions afterwards, one little girl asked her if she had been afraid before the launch. She was very matter of fact: she said, there is no need to be afraid if you know what you're doing. She said the only astronauts she knew of who were scared or nervous before their space flight were the ones who didn't fully understand the procedure, or know what was going on, as they were usually passengers for the launch phase and part of the mission later on.

She knew she was well-trained and more than adequately equipped to handle it and so she wasn't afraid. That is a powerful lesson, in that with practice and hard work comes skill, and in that confidence is born the basis for strong leadership.

It's not a popularity contest

Leadership is one of those words that gets bandied around quite a lot, but what defines a good leader? They come in all shapes and sizes, and there isn't a simple formula to explain what makes a good leader.

Politicians, activists, generals, coaches and business tycoons have all written great books about the types and ingredients of leadership, and there isn't enough space to do it justice here. Leadership will mean different things to different people, and my understanding of what leadership means is heavily informed by my experiences in the army, as well as my experiences founding a business and leading teams in hostile environments.

What I can tell you for certain is that leadership is a crucial part of the explorer's mindset. Being trailblazers and boundary pushers, explorers are inherently leaders, and are looked up to. There is also the more practical matter of testing expeditions that require exemplary and proficient leadership in order to succeed and to get everyone home in one piece. For me, leadership is about setting an example to those I have the honour of leading. Ultimately, it's about inspiring people.

Of course, leadership is not limited to the battlefield. The same lessons apply in any situation. Whether you're in a sports team or a busy office, setting an example to your team is essential to engendering trust and respect; for without it, you're not a leader, you're a dictator.

When travelling, I've found myself in various circumstances that have required me to take a stance and demonstrate some leadership. Sometimes it was requested, and other times it was down to my own judgement. Often, it is hard to know when one must stand up to the plate, especially in a situation where there is no set hierarchy, and it's even more difficult when there is already a leader in place, but they aren't doing their job.

When you are in a team as part of an expedition, there will inevitably be times when you have to set an example, even if you aren't the designated boss. I've been on a number of expeditions where it might simply be a case of volunteering to tidy up the camp; to go and fetch water, or put up the tents. These are clearly the building blocks of what it takes to be a good team player, but being a good team player is also an attribute of a good leader. Others will look to your example and emulate it, which is ultimately the underlying aim. Let's not beat around the bush – leadership is about getting other people to do what you want them to do, and sometimes those things might not be pleasant.

In the business world, this might mean delegating a particular task, or asking an employee in your growing team to fire a colleague. In the army it's arguably more serious, in that people might be putting their lives on the line. Good leadership is not about likeability. There is a big difference between good leadership and popularity, though there is often some crossover, but it's important to understand that they are not the same thing. In fact, I'd say that a fixation on being liked can end up being to the detriment of respect; people can see through a desperate bid for approval and it can eclipse the real priorities. It is the difference between making decisions based on what will go down well with the group, compared to what is the right thing to do.

To take a less extreme example than the military, entrepreneurs are often said to have a reputation for being disagreeable; the sort of people who aren't reliant on the approval of their community and contemporaries. More likely to flout convention, they have to get used to saying or doing the unusual or non-conformist thing, and this takes a certain type of person; someone who is a natural pioneer, and does not seek approval from others telling them they are right.

Of course, different leaders have distinct ways of coming at this. Some people have a leadership style that is enormously charismatic and heavily dependent upon personality. The obvious advantage of such a leader is that those being led are imbued with energy and enthusiasm because, quite simply, they like that person. These leaders are motivational and followers want to listen to them, be around them, and importantly, follow them. But there's a major disadvantage to this reliance upon likeability; if the liked leader leaves, the group no longer has a figurehead. A group, a mission or an entire organisation could be pinned on the appeal and popularity of this one leader.

Additionally, any leader will sooner or later have to make an unpopular decision, or one where it's impossible to keep everybody happy. Leaders who rely on likeability for their authority will quickly crumble in these circumstances, as with our earlier story of Captain Bligh. Research shows that there is a gender bias here, too; success and likeability are positively correlated for men, while they are negatively correlated for women, which comes with its own set of unique complications and challenges.

One of the most liked entrepreneurs of our time is Elon Musk. Again and again he's made decisions that leave others aghast, but engender him to others. Smoking weed on the Joe Rogan podcast may have dropped Tesla's share prices the next day, but millions of people decided that they liked him based on that interview and action, and Musk knows how to turn that following into leadership capital, and business.

Musk is well known for asking the opinions of his staff at all levels. Many other leaders seek out popularity with their followers by adopting a far more devolved or participatory style of leadership, wherein the leader engages their followers in the decisions they are making. By getting people involved in the room, the leader is including followers in the broader mission, but it can be challenging and inefficient when trying to reach a consensus.

Others go so far as to be totally hands-off in their approach to leading, providing little or no guidance or supervision. This can make leaders popular – not meddling too much in the lives of their followers, or micro-managing and directing their actions – but what if those who are being led have little experience, or are seeking a figurehead? This approach would be untenable in the military, where leadership tends to be more hierarchical and commanding, in order to ensure efficiency where safety is tantamount.

This distinction is important. Very few entrepreneurs are likely to lead their employees through actual life-or-death scenarios, and certainly not in the split-second decision-making context that combat entails, so civilian leadership plays by a different rulebook from military leadership.

In the military there's no time for dissent; soldiers have to get used to following orders unquestioningly, especially under pressure. In business, it pays to have everyone challenging the consensus a little more, thinking outside the box and being prepared to voice opinions that go against what the CEO might be thinking – otherwise, boardrooms simply turn into groups of yes-men. Even in a military context, giving subordinates a degree of autonomy is beneficial. However, good leaders foster this level of dissent and autonomy for the creative ideation it facilitates, not for the popularity they think it gives them.

Live to lead another day

In October 2009, I led an expedition to climb Mera Peak in the Nepali Himalayas. At 6,476 metres (21,247 feet) it is one of the highest non-technical summits in the world, and we were a bunch of novice climbers. Only two of the team had ever worn crampons before, and they did not include me. That said, we were all paratroopers, imbued not only with some of the hardest training in the British military, but we had also recently returned from Afghanistan and were high on life, looking for the next adventure.

After a couple of days in Kathmandu, where we prepared our gear and bought last-minute supplies, we managed to get a flight to the tiny, high-altitude airstrip at Lukla, the gateway to Everest and the mighty Khumbu region. From there it was going to be a two-week round hike up the wildly remote Hinku valley, where we would camp amid the enormous boulders of the glacial moraine. Apart from me, only my senior NCO Geordie Taylor had been to Nepal before, and for the other seven soldiers, the sight of local children drinking directly from a yak's udder was bewildering, to say the least.

As the days progressed, the walking got harder with each metre of altitude gained, and even the fittest of the team found themselves out of breath. It was my job, as the sole commissioned officer and the expedition leader, to show them how it was done. Even when I was exhausted, I tried to flit between the front and the back, checking to make sure everyone else was okay, often when it was the last thing I wanted to do.

After more than ten days of hard trekking we finally reached the snow line, where temperatures plummeted to minus 27°C, and with gale-force winds making the setting-up of camp a dreadful prospect. At least three of the others and I were suffering from severe head-aches, dehydration and very cold feet, as we tried unsuccessfully to sleep at 5,000 metres.

On the summit day we were greeted with clear conditions, but two of the local Sherpas decided to remain with the tents in camp rather than ascend to the top. I led the way with Geordie, and our mountain guide, Jason. We plodded through the thick snow, tied together in case a crevasse opened up. It was punishing, slow going, and every step was hard-earned with short, gasping breaths. The summit came into view, a few hundred metres ahead, but there was no time to celebrate.

As we stopped for a short break, one of the soldiers approached me complaining that he couldn't feel his feet any more. His boots had been on the tight side, and as a result his toes were right up against the edge of the boot. As we'd been trained. I ordered him to remove his boots and socks, and I placed his bare toe inside my jacket right up in my armpit, where it would be able to warm up to body temperature naturally.

As we waited, I saw another soldier shifting about. He told me his feet too were numb, and so after a while I offered the same service to him, but before long my feet were also getting so cold they were excruciating. We needed to move, so once we'd taken a rest, we pushed on another hundred metres to a crag. But then, just before the final push to the summit, disaster struck. A howling wind flared up the valley, followed immediately by a white blanket of cloud. I knew instantly that even if it was short-lived, it would add time on to our exposure, which might mean the difference between someone keeping or losing their toes to frostbite.

We had trekked for days, and planned for months. No one wanted to give up

'Boss!' one the soldiers shouted. 'We can make it, it's not far to go. Two hundred metres more!'

I looked into the murky abyss of frozen air, and then back at the faces of the two shivering soldiers. I was torn. From the looks around me, it was clear the overwhelming urge of the group was to continue. These were all paratroopers, men proud of their own hardiness and expecting it above all from me, their leader. But I knew that if I decided to continue, I was putting all of our safety in danger, and the fault would be mine alone for any consequences.

'We turn back,' I shouted. 'Now!'

I hauled the youngest of the crew to his feet and pointed down the slope, back to the camp where the Sherpas waited for us. The most headstrong of the soldiers muttered and shook his head. I didn't say anything or blame him; I was as disappointed as he was. We all knew that our chance of conquering the mountain was gone, at least for this expedition. Months of anticipation, and weeks of physical training had gone to waste.

As we got back to the tents and packed up the camp, all were silent. It wasn't until hours later when we descended beyond the snow line, and to a sheltered gully where the sun had warmed up the rocks, that one of the senior soldiers approached me.

'You made the right call there, boss. Otherwise we might have died. Or at the very least, we'd all be missing a few toes.'

As we carried on down the trail, the disappointment that we all felt at not achieving our aim seemed to dissipate, and we were glad to have come down unscathed, having lived to fight another day.

I had not wanted to take the decision to turn back. It felt like failure, and I worried about the impact it would have on my soldiers' estimation of me. But as I discovered afterwards, even those who had wanted to continue at the time had a lot of respect for the decision in hindsight.

Moreover, that defeat instilled a wonderful attitude in those eight soldiers. After the expected banter and complaining that all soldiers are good at, every single one of them said that the trip was one of the highlights of their military career. What's more, many of them later became serious climbers and mountaineers, and went back again to summit Mera Peak.

If I had made the popular decision that day, rather than the right one, it could have been a very different story.

John Le Marchant

The British Army is rightly seen across the world as a bastion of exemplary leadership, but it wasn't always the case. In fact, if it weren't for the determination and vision of one particular military commander, it might never have been so.

John Le Marchant was a mid-ranking officer during Britain's calamitous Low Countries campaign of 1793–95. During the campaign, he was struck by the lack of leadership and equipment in the British Army, particularly its cavalry, which contributed to a significant defeat for Britain and its allies. He admired the horsemanship of the allied Austrians, but was aggrieved to hear one of their officers scoffing that British swordsmanship was 'most entertaining', but reminiscent of 'someone chopping wood'.

Le Marchant was clearly stung by these comments, and on returning home he set himself about lifting the standards of the British Army. To my mind, this is a defining trait of leaders; they don't settle for inadequacy, but are always looking for opportunities to improve things, and taking steps themselves to do so. He designed a new cavalry sabre – a heavy sword – with the help of cutler Henry Osborn, and published in 1796 a celebrated manual on cavalry swordsmanship; he then toured Britain and Ireland instructing cavalrymen on how to use it. However, his most enduring mark in the field of military leadership was yet to be made.

In 1801, despite initial resistance from parliament on the grounds of cost, Le Marchant established the British Army's first training school for officers that would lead foot soldiers – known as the infantry – and cavalry. This new establishment was titled the Royal Military College at Sandhurst, and 205 years later, I would stand on its parade square.

Le Marchant served as Sandhurst's governor for its first nine years, and was personally responsible for training many of the new and existing officers who would go on to serve under Wellington in Britain's much more successful part in the Peninsular War, which led to Napoleon's defeat in Spain and Portugal, and his imprisonment on the small island of Elba.

In 1947, Sandhurst merged with the Royal Military Academy, Woolwich, to form the Royal Military Academy, Sandhurst, whose mission is to be 'the national centre of excellence for leadership'.

Serve to Lead

Serve to Lead is the motto of the Royal Military Academy Sandhurst. The motto isn't mindless waffle – it underpins the mentality of the British officer class that has led soldiers on operations around the world for generations. Sandhurst teaches that service is fundamental to leadership and only by making sacrifice and leading by example can someone earn the trust, and right to command, of those under that leadership.

While some leaders are born, the academy also teaches that leadership can be learned by those willing to undergo rigorous training and preparation for the responsibility of command. It is the place that I learned how to be a leader too, and where I discovered both the joys and hardships of that duty, which I subsequently fulfilled on missions around the world and especially the battlefields of Afghanistan.

Before you can ask others to do your bidding, you must first be willing to do it yourself. My old brigade commander, and later Chief of the General Staff, Lt. Gen. Sir Mark Carleton-Smith, once gave all the junior officers in the Paras a fireside chat. He told us that the very best leaders should be able to do everything that their subordinates can do, and better.

That's obviously a big ask, and it isn't as clearly applicable in every walk of life. The CEO of a big tech company doesn't necessarily need to know how to code, for example, as long as he understands the business; and the conductor of an orchestra doesn't have to be able to play the cello. However, if they could, then the coder and the cellist would certainly be very impressed, and consequently would probably work that little bit harder.

Of course, teamwork and leadership are intertwined. You don't have to be a leader to be part of a team, but you do have to be part of a team to be a leader. One of the hardest parts of being a leader can be striking the right balance between the two roles. I have found, though, that the line can be walked so long as there is trust and loyalty.

Loyalty goes in many directions. In the army and in big organisations, there is loyalty to your superiors – those that give you orders; then there is loyalty to your peers – your friends, colleagues and acquaintances; and most importantly perhaps, there is loyalty to those under your command or in your team – because if you're not loyal to them, they will be the cause of your downfall. If people trust you, however, and they believe in your allegiance, then they will follow you to the ends of the earth.

Mission command

In the army there is a doctrine called mission command. It is all about the art of delegation and giving people responsibility for their own actions. It's based on the principle that when you manage a team, you should tell people *what* to do, but not *how* to do it. So long as they are qualified to do a job, you have to put your trust in their training and that they are capable of making their own decisions, which shows loyalty and engenders a real sense of ownership. That is how to build a team.

Once, on operations in Zabul province in southern Afghanistan, my platoon was given the mission to search a village for a known terrorist recruiter. For the most part, this involved being invited in by friendly women for tea, scanning their kitchens and gardens with metal detectors, and then being cursed and told the house belonged to an absent uncle as we dug up, and removed, caches of weapons.

After walking around all day, we were low on water and needed to get back to the helicopter pick-up point, which was five miles away across the desert. As we were leaving the village, I noticed a group of men huddled around under the shade of a mulberry tree. They looked shifty and stared at us as we walked past. One of them wore a white turban and had kohl around his eyes, looking like a Taliban leader. I got the translator to say hello and ask their names, which he duly noted.

I reported the names by radio to our intelligence cell and they said they were all clear, so we left the men and trekked back across the desert to where my boss was waiting. By now the whole platoon was exhausted and thirsty. We had not had time to eat all day and the temperature was over 50°C. One of the soldiers was beginning to wobble and I suspected it might be heat exhaustion.

Then, to make matters worse, my boss came over. 'Lev, you know that group of men in the village?'

'Yes?'

'Well, the one in the white turban, the Int cell now want him in for questioning.'

'What the hell? I reported his name on the radio and they said he was clear.'

'I know. They screwed up.'

'So what now?'

'Well, we've got two hours before your heli comes. Go and get him.'

I shook my head. I had two hours and it was 10 miles – a 16-kilometre round trip. In the Paras we have a well-known physical stamina test known as the Ten Miler, which is a punishing speed march while carrying kit. They can be hard work at home in the rain, but out in the desert and low on water, I knew that it might be deadly.

I looked at my men and could tell that half of them weren't up to it. They were exhausted, but orders were orders. I figured that I could do the job with ten or twelve men, so half the men could stay behind. I knew that in order to do so, I had to get them to buy into the vision and feel ownership, so instead of barking out an order, I gathered my section commanders around. I told them the situation and asked them what they thought were the best options.

A lesson I learned early on is that even if you already know the answer, ask the question – it makes people feel valued and part of the team and decision-making process. It doesn't matter who gets the credit for the decision, and when you take your own ego out of the equation, it's amazing what happens.

'Sir, I have an idea,' said the youngest corporal. 'Why don't we leave half the men behind, and take some of their water. I'm sure we can do the job with ten or twelve men.'

'That's a great idea,' I said, patting him on the back. He grinned from ear to ear, and I made him the point man.

'I need twelve volunteers to come with me.' I said. 'The rest of you can stay here.'

The men looked at each other. They knew it would be one of the hardest tabs of their life and that it would be dangerous, because the Taliban now knew our strength and would have time to prepare an attack as they saw us walking back across the desert.

Private Foster, one of the new soldiers, put his hand up. 'I'll come, sir. I need the exercise,' he joked. Sylvester was next, then another and another. Because we had a strong team, bonded with trust, I had no shortage of volunteers. Even some of the men whom I knew stood no chance of making it started to put up their hands, because they felt ashamed, but I already had enough. We redistributed the water, gritted our teeth and marched back across the desert to the village where we found the man in the white turban, arrested him, and marched all the way back again, being chased by an angry mob of Afghans.

It was a hard slog, but one of the most determined team efforts I'd seen in my career. To top it off, we later found out that the man in the white turban was at the top of the regional most-wanted list. That victory, and a shared hardship, cemented the bonds of the platoon even stronger – there was nothing that my men didn't think they could accomplish.

Mary Seacole

Born in 1805, Mary Seacole was a British-Jamaican nurse, healer and businesswoman, who became best known for her contribution to the Crimean War, where she established the 'British Hotel' behind the lines – a place Seacole described as 'a mess-table and comfortable quarters for sick and convalescent officers'.

Seacole did not have formal medical training, but she applied the healing skills that she had used in Jamaica, and was arguably the first nurse practitioner. She had originally been refused permission to travel to the Crimea as part of the war effort, but she was not one to take no for an answer, and made her own way there to offer her services to the injured soldiers. Mary became incredibly popular with the troops, because of her relentless, selfless commitment. So much so, that in 1857 crowds of 80,000 attended her fundraising galas in London.

Mary Seacole left a lasting impression on the medical world, and Britain's National Health Service has a leadership programme named in her honour. It teaches students valuable lessons in self-awareness and emotional intelligence; how to find a leadership style that suits your personality; how to wield authority and motivate a team; and how to transform emotion into an asset – all things that Mary learned on the battlefield and yet are applicable anywhere.

Mary Seacole is remembered to this day as one of the most formidable and yet caring leaders in the medical world.

Raising the stakes

Courage is at the heart of good leadership, and I don't mean solely in terms of taking measured risks. Whilst courage can come in many forms, it is mainly about accepting the truth, and being honest with yourself and others. The most frightening and yet rewarding place to be is when you are completely and brutally honest with yourself. It is both the hardest and best gift you can ever give to yourself – and others.

In being ruthless in your assessment of your own character, of your flaws and failings, and also your strengths, you are far better placed to accept the truth of the circumstances around you, and therefore how best to react to them. In doing so, you give yourself a greater chance of success in whatever it is you hope to achieve the first time around, rather than making mistakes through denial. What's more, when a leader is able to remove his or her ego from the decision-making process, it will engender trust among the team.

Whatever context you are leading in, you have a singular responsibility to those you are leading, and this may mean that speaking the truth is more important than receiving the praise. To be a good leader, you need to have the moral courage to tell people not only what they want to hear. For a military leader, your subordinates' lives are at stake, but for business leaders, the same is true of their livelihoods, and as far as their families are concerned, this verges on the existential as well. CEOs have a responsibility to their employees to make good decisions as opposed to popular ones; if they make bad decisions and the company goes bust, they are taking food off their followers' tables.

Above all else, remember that to be respected, leaders have to be *respectful*. Many leaders forget that although the objective is not to be liked, or likeable for its own sake, this isn't a green light for leaders to treat those below and around them without dignity. In fact, this is one of the quickest ways to turn your players into cynics. Remember always to understand, value and appreciate the distinct abilities and perspectives that each of your team members is bringing to the table, and respect the courage it takes for them to voice an opinion that goes against your own.

You need three things to bring people with you and compel others to understand and buy into your vision.

The first is all about you, the leader, as an individual. Be the person you pretend to be, and live up to the expectations you have of others. Of course, there is always a certain amount of 'branding' – what you decide to say and how you package yourself will define how others view you. It is important to consider what you will choose to share or amplify, and what will fall away because it doesn't serve the vision. Be honest, but you don't always need to let your team know everything; enigma can sometimes be a very powerful tool. What is most important is that however you choose to display your attributes, you can act on what you say. Style is nothing, unless it is underpinned by substance.

The second is about utilising your emotional intelligence to appeal to the collective and its shared purpose. This is about knowing your audience, and a good leader will always tailor and adjust what they say according to who is in the room. In some instances, it is ideal to pitch the tone as if you were chatting to a friend – it's amiable and warm and can build trust. In others, such as in the army, it would be inappropriate, and a more formal tone might be better suited. However you do it, this is about identifying and bringing out shared values and communicating them explicitly in your vision.

Finally, leadership is about getting things done. It is about pushing through your will and achieving the goal. A leader who can talk the talk but not walk the walk is not a leader, and so often the critical mindset is one of understanding urgency. If there is a deadline – meet it. Great leaders compel people to participate in their vision right away, so that the job gets done, come what may. It might not be the perfect solution, in fact it rarely is, but as we were always told in the army – an 80 per cent solution done on time, is better than a 100 per cent solution late.

It can be lonely as a leader. Sometimes the path might not be clear and you will question your own choices. But, if you truly want to be a pioneer, leading the way, exploring the world's hidden places, then it's a necessary path to take. How then, do leaders stay on course and navigate the perils ahead? The answer, as we'll find in the next chapter, relies on a well-calibrated moral compass.

Captain Lawrence Oates

8

Keep an Eye on the Compass

I am just going outside and may be some time
– Lawrence Oates, Antarctica, 1912

Watch your step

In Afghanistan we often came under attack from the Taliban. They would snipe at our patrols and launch mortars at our bases, but I think I speak for most soldiers when I say that the scariest aspect of being on operations was the prospect of hidden roadside bombs and landmines. In a firefight there is an element of control, and the ability to hit back with one's own weapon, artillery and air support, but for the professional modern foot soldier, the biggest terror is the unknown – any footstep could be your last.

In addition to the homemade bombs created by the likes of Mr Mohammed and his amateur engineer friends, the whole country was littered with landmines – a legacy of thirty years of war, where many were left behind by the Russians in the 1980s and never cleared up. Often, the minefields were never properly marked, and to make matters worse, over the decades the mines washed away in the rains and snow and moved from their original locations, so it's often impossible to predict where they might be.

Every patrol was a game of Russian roulette, so to speak, and we never knew if we would come back alive. One day, as we were setting up a temporary encampment on the outskirts of a lush valley, I got the call from my commanding officer that a vehicle had been blown up a couple of miles away and I was to take my platoon on a rescue mission.

Our armoured cars had special tracks, so that they could go over any kind of terrain. We drove them across the desert and up to the top of an escarpment, where the location of the explosion had been reported. As we got closer, I looked through the front windscreen and could see the remains of a Land Rover blown to smithereens. I was expecting the worst, as there should have been four soldiers inside. I called to the team medic and told him to be ready to treat any surviving casualties.

We stopped short by fifty metres in case there were any other bombs nearby, and when I got out of my vehicle, to my absolute surprise and joy, I saw that all the men were fine. When the mine exploded, it had sent a shockwave through the car, sending everyone in it flying out onto the ground – they were all alive, and seemingly unharmed. I asked them if they were okay, and apart from being a bit dizzy and shaken, they nodded and walked over to where I was standing. There was space in one of our three vehicles, so I put the men in the back of the car at the front, telling the lead vehicle that we should reverse back out of the danger area, because we might be in a minefield.

It seemed like the sensible option, so that's what we did, making sure that we stayed exactly in our own tracks until we were well clear of the flat plateau. At that point, my three vehicles needed to turn around so that we didn't get stuck in a bottleneck between two large cliffs, so the front vehicle did a three-point turn and pushed around the other two so that it was now facing forwards, again in the lead. We all did the same and drove off down a track back towards the encampment, and I was now in vehicle number two, where the commander should always be. Then just as we left the scraggy boulder field, there was an enormous explosion, and I felt the shockwaves hit my own car.

After a second of deafness and ringing in my ears, I looked through my windscreen to see a massive cloud of dust. As it cleared, I realised what had happened – the point vehicle had driven over another mine – and to make matters worse, it was the same four soldiers who had been in the first explosion. I shouted down the radio telling everyone to stop exactly where they were whilst I considered the situation.

I could see bodies lying in the dirt next to the car, which had the front end ripped off it. Now I knew I had to show some real leadership and there was only one thing for it. The metal detectors were in the car at the back and it would take them a good ten minutes to clear the path between the cars, let alone get to the front, where we might have heavy casualties. I got out of my car, pulled out my bayonet and began to crawl forwards, stabbing the sand in front of me to check for the mines. Luckily, the car in front wasn't too far and I was able to cover the distance quickly. I reached the car and to my relief, found that yet again, by some miracle everyone was alive, and what's more, uninjured.

One of the soldiers stood up, dusted himself off and looked at me stabbing around in the dirt.

'What are you doing sir?' he laughed. 'You won't find any Taliban down there!'

It was a lucky day, made even luckier as I was filling out the daily report back at camp, when I found out that my team and the remaining vehicle had been tasked with 'denying' the half-blown up cars; that meant going back to the site and blowing them up properly with explosives, so the Taliban couldn't make use of them in the future. It was a simple task and I was told that I should remain behind with the other platoon commanders, so that we could receive our orders for the next day. As the team were driving back, they too hit a landmine and the empty commander's seat, where I would normally have been sitting, was completely destroyed by the explosion.

You can't be a leader unless you're willing to put your team ahead of yourself when circumstances call for it. This requires moral courage and integrity, the building blocks not only of great leadership, but of a fulfilled, purposeful life.

Headhunters

In the isolated foothills of the north-eastern Indian border with Myanmar live a tribe who, up until relatively recently, had a very different moral compass and sense of integrity than our own. The Konyak warrior tribe is one of many Naga tribes in the region. However, what makes them different is that up until the 1960s, the Konyaks performed an important cultural practice – headhunting.

Any dispute over territory was settled with warfare and the Konyaks were famed and feared for taking the heads of their enemies. Taking a person's head in battle was understood as taking their power. The heads would be brought back to the villages as trophies, and presented on doorways or walls, or carried in specially made baskets. The warriors would also be tattooed after battle to mark them with their heroic deeds.

Since the 1960s, the Indian government has made headhunting illegal, but there are some people alive in the villages today who have the proud tattoos from battle. They still carry the long knives, passed down through generations, that were used for the violent act of removing the head from the body. Even now at festivals and rituals, members of the Konyaks will bring out their collected heads of the past to remind others of their strength and bravery.

In the West, we associate the act of beheading with criminal punishment in past years and, more lately, the work of terrorists. However, for some people, headhunting was until very recently a show of a man's worth and virtue. One man's barbarism is another's norm.

Moral courage and integrity

Moral courage is about doing the right thing even if it's the hard thing. Integrity is about doing the right thing even when nobody's looking. That being said, what those morals are can be difficult to define. This makes perfect sense, since these personal principles are so subjective, entirely shaped by our nature and our nurture. Each of us has a unique understanding of right and wrong, which has come about from every one of our experiences and interactions; an endless number of factors determining our current belief system. To a certain extent, our moral compass is a personalised construct; not that it feels that way when you see or hear something repulsive, or terrifying, that strikes you as evil and so obviously inhuman or 'wrong'.

On occasion, I have felt this when travelling, where different communities have their distinct cultures and entirely separate belief systems. If we could travel in time, no doubt we would be horrified by much of what supposedly upstanding individuals got up to. In my travels, I have visited people with very divergent customs to the ones with which I was brought up, and found their ideas and actions sometimes distasteful.

Different cultures have their own moral codes. Some US states consider the death penalty acceptable; Islam allows a man to have four wives, whereas in Bhutan a woman may marry two brothers if she chooses; across Africa, female circumcision is widely practised. In parts of China and Vietnam people eat dog meat; in France and Russia, they eat horses.

In Britain, any of the above would be considered not only illegal, but utterly immoral. Then again, some of the things that Brits do would be considered very disagreeable elsewhere. Getting boozed up on a Friday afternoon, whilst entirely appropriate on a bank holiday in London, would go down rather badly in Bangladesh or Saudi Arabia, as would our fondness for bacon sandwiches and pork scratchings.

I've had lunch with fighters from Hezbollah, a designated terrorist group; I've met plenty of men from cultures that embrace polygamy, and I've even met an Aghori monk who thought that cannibalism was perfectly acceptable. I didn't agree with their standards and would not condone their actions.

I do however believe in dialogue and communication, and I've found that by engaging with people whose views are diametrically different to your own, it can benefit both parties. You aren't necessarily going to change someone's mind over an issue, but by living according to your own values and by setting a good example, you might broaden their horizons a little. What's more, you will inevitably broaden your own. I never went on a journey with an agenda, or an intention to change or save the world. I have always tried to be an objective observer and refrain from judgement. By meeting those whose moral compass is oriented differently from your own, you simply develop a more sophisticated understanding of your personal moral code, and it may even swing your needle in one direction or another.

Good and evil

In the West, we've become used to thinking of Good and Evil as two opposing qualities, and the concepts are so second nature to us that sometimes we forget they need defining. It can seem self-evident what 'good' means and what is 'evil', until we remember how easily politicians can manipulate whole groups of fundamentally 'good' people into culture wars over issues that blur the boundaries. On top of this, that very notion of 'goodness' being opposed to 'badness' is the product of about 3,000 years of Old Testament influence on Western religious and moral thought.

The Genesis story of Satan tempting Eve with an apple, which God had forbidden her and Adam from eating, lays the foundations of a moral code in which Good (obedience, restraint, faith and humility) is diametrically opposed to and competes with Evil (disobedience, greed, deception, dishonesty and hubris).

Not all cultures see things the same way. Chinese Confucianism, for example, is more concerned with the proper rules of behaviour for educated or higher-class people. It's less about what we'd call Good and Evil, and more about Right and Wrong. Buddhists see Good and Evil as opposed to one another, but believe that both must be overcome and recognised as non-existent concepts, in order to achieve Sunyata or 'emptiness'.

There's a big difference, though, between morals and rules, and this is an important distinction to me. Our morals are often governed closely by rules and ethics, such as the justice system in the country we grew up in, and the laws to which we adhere, but they're not the same. The best leaders and people with the highest integrity stick unwaveringly to the former, their morals, but are often the first to break the accepted 'rules'. Indeed, someone once said that rules are for the guidance of the wise and the obedience of fools, and are often guilty of being outdated, throwbacks from moral codes of yesteryear.

However, I believe there are a few universal morals that are important to adopt in life, and particularly when exploring and travelling. One of these is respect for others. Many of the worst aspects of travel in the modern world stem from a lack of respect; people treat the countries of other people very differently from how they would treat their own home. It's pretty basic, but the tiny amount of forethought involved in bringing your own canteen and some water purifying tablets will stop you having to litter parts of the world without clean drinking water with endless plastic bottles.

Another is generosity. We need to remember that it's a privilege to be able to travel, or even explore outside the boundaries of our own upbringing, and that many of the world's population don't get this opportunity. We need to be thankful for it, and venture out with the openness of spirit that enables us to give back.

Whatever your moral values, though, sticking to them in the face of adversity is what really counts.

No shortcuts

In 2012, I led an expedition to walk across Madagascar. This was perhaps the most challenging of all the short-form expeditions that Tom and I ran with Secret Compass: a three-week trek from the east coast to the west coast of Madagascar, through some of the thickest rainforest I'd ever encountered.

The team consisted of eleven paying clients, me, the expedition assistant, Alastair, and a doctor, my friend Kate. I'd also employed the services of a local guide and a few porters to help carry our food and tents. It was an uncharted route over the highest mountains on the island. I'd chosen it deliberately because it looked like it would be tough, and also because it would enable us to see the remaining wilderness jungle on an island where 90 per cent of the original rainforest has been cut down.

After a crossing from the African mainland, endless red and umber hills poked out above the low-lying mist as we flew into Antananarivo. Snaking brown rivers weaved in between treeless valleys and only the rising smoke of village fires and dusty roads broke the mesmerising undulation. Flying over the stripped hillsides of the central highlands certainly gave us the impression that we may have been too late to see the original rainforest – and I admit that I was a little disappointed before the journey had even begun.

The plan was simple – to lead the first group on a walk across the northern part of the island from east to west, entirely on foot. It was a distance of almost 400 kilometres in the seemingly impossible timeframe of three weeks – a daunting task. All this in the company of strangers, many of whom had never travelled anywhere so remote.

'This is my first time anywhere near a jungle,' said Xaviar, with a nervous smile. The rest of the group looked at the 27-year-old French Canadian with sympathy.

Days passed by as we trekked west. As the settlements thinned out, the jungle grew closer. A high wall of black vegetation loomed ever nearer in the shape of an impenetrable mountain range. On the seventh day of the trek, the rainforest finally surrounded us. It had receded a full 20 kilometres since 1962 – the last time the region was properly mapped before Google Earth. Despite its foreboding appearance, it came as a relief to be amongst the trees.

This is what we had come to see, the Madagascar of our imagination. There were no people here. The tracks disappeared and off we went, hacking and traipsing our way through primary vegetation in one of the last remaining pieces of true forest on the island. For the next week, the group was entirely encased in green vines, hairy bamboo and wet ferns. Elusive lemurs stared curiously down from their canopy hideaways, as we ploughed on through marshes and rivers. It was one of the toughest treks I'd ever done, and that included most of the ones I'd accomplished in the army.

As we neared the western coast, villages sprung out of the cultivated valleys and the jungle at once became a hazy memory. All eyes were set on our goal – to reach the port of Ankify and make history. The final day turned into a true test of integrity, not to mention mental and physical endurance: there was still 93 kilometres to push, and we were a day behind schedule, having taken longer than expected to fight through the jungle. Delaying wasn't an option, as people had flights to catch back home and jobs that awaited them.

I studied the map: 93 kilometres is 58 miles. It was a long way, and everyone was already exhausted. I looked at the team. I knew there was a trailhead not too far away, where there would probably be a village with cars and motorbikes; from there we could scoot to the beach and enjoy a night out before flying home the next day. I wasn't about to make the suggestion first, though. Luckily, Simon, one of the other team members did.

'Look, why don't we just hitch a lift for the final day, we've almost done it anyway, and we don't have anything left to prove do we?' Almost everyone else nodded, glad that he had offered them a way out. He glanced at me as I remained silent.

Then I saw Xaviar shaking his head. 'We've come this far,' he said, 'and I paid to walk across Madagascar.'

He was right, of course, and I knew I had to demonstrate some leadership, despite the fact that every bone in my body wanted to jump in a car and get to the beach as soon as possible. I didn't have anything to prove. I'd done my time in the army and slogged through endless months of hardcore expeditions already. This was supposed to be fun!

And yet, something inside me knew the right thing to do.

'Those who want to carry on walking, come with me. Those that want to get to the road, go with Simon.' I looked around, my legs hoping that Xaviar would see the light and choose to follow the crowd.

'I'll walk,' said Kate, the doctor.

'Me too,' said Alastair.

The decision was made. I put on my most enthusiastic face. 'We're walking then.'

And that's what we did. As the rest of the group walked to the road and got a taxi to the beach, the four of us, and a couple of the local guides, set off at 2 a.m. to hike for 19 hours on what was one of the most punishing days of my life. By the end of it, when we finally reached the coast at almost 10 p.m., we were a bedraggled bunch with blisters atop of blisters. Alastair could barely walk and Xaviar was cramped up in agony.

But we'd made it.

Looking back, I didn't have to do that final day's walk, and I'm sure if I had suggested to Xaviar that we should all take a car to be on the safe side, then he would have followed. But deep down I knew what was right, and it was to attempt to finish the job, rather than taking the easy way out. What is more, everyone in that group looked up to me in some way, or was relying on me in some other way.

When you are a leader, you are letting more than yourself down if you don't adhere to your morals and act with integrity. Only by pushing myself, and the team, to their absolute limit were we able to achieve something that everyone else thought was impossible, and it is a lesson that I have often reminded myself of later in my career. It was a principle that got me through much bigger and more ambitious expeditions in due course.

This is why integrity is the cornerstone of leadership. When you lead, you are setting a tone and a culture. Not just for yourself, but for those around you who have been compelled to follow you in some way. This might be tiny in the grand scheme of things, or it could be far more substantial or influential; even the founder of a business transmits aspects of their own moral compass to a whole organisation.

In setting the tone, you have also taken up a mantle of sorts, a responsibility to those whom you are leading. It is your duty to do the best by yourself and by those people.

Captain 'Black Sam' Bellamy

Our moral compasses don't always equate to the law — though, by and large, they should! Someone who demonstrates this rather nicely is the famed pirate and explorer Captain 'Black Sam' Bellamy, who was born in Devon in the seventeenth century. There is no denying that pirates were the ultimate rulebreakers of the day, rebels who made a living from sailing the high seas and stealing from other ships.

But Black Sam was a slightly different sort of pirate, in that he had a pretty sturdy moral compass. He refused to wear the long, powdered wigs that were so fashionable and associated with the wealthy merchants he so despised, sticking instead to his natural long black hair, which is what earned him his name. He described the Navy and the establishment in his diaries: 'They vilify us, the scoundrels do, when there is only this difference: they rob the poor under the cover of law, forsooth, and we plunder the rich under the protection of our own courage.'

Sam wrote often of his conscience and was a charismatic captain, known for the mercy that he showed his victims; he and his men would often take ships without harming the crew, which was unheard of at the time. In fact, if they took a ship on the high seas and discovered that it did not suit their purpose, they would return it with crew and cargo intact. Captain Black Sam ran his ship as a republic, allowing his team to vote in important decisions, and he was known by his men as the Robin Hood of the seas.

He died very young in a storm, at only twenty-eight, on a ship with an almost 150-strong crew and an estimated four tonnes of loot, which now sits at the bottom of the ocean. Captain Black Sam Bellamy knew above all else that if you want to achieve greatness, you've got to stop asking permission.

Morals or rules

Sam Bellamy was a rule-breaker, but he had a sound moral compass. I'm not advocating breaking the rules for the sake of it here, despite the words of His Holiness the Dalai Lama: 'Know the rules well, so you can break them effectively.' But the lesson we can take from the story of Black Sam is that moral courage and integrity allow you to achieve more than you could without them.

As leaders, as explorers and as people, we are faced almost daily with challenges to which there is no clear answer. This is going to happen even more so in the future, as the work that humans, rather than machines, do will increasingly be that relating to other people – work that requires us not to be cold and calculating, but warm, considerate and creative. Without moral courage and integrity, this kind of ambiguity – dealing with people and their in-built unpredictability, or pursuing creative goals where something hasn't been done before – is impossible to navigate without some kind of guiding framework.

This is why we use the metaphor of a compass when we talk about morals. They guide us, helping us to navigate through previously unexplored territory. Without morals, we are rudderless. With them, even if it's impossible to see the way ahead, we have a set of values and actions to which we can commit, and trust that they will take us where we want to go.

And so we come onto integrity – doing the right thing when no one is looking, and when no one will know about it. My *moral values* determine who I am and what I stand for, and they give me a benchmark to understand right and wrong; *integrity* is whether I follow or practise those moral values. When a leader acts with integrity, they are adhering to their own moral code consistently, upholding the same principles in all situations and not wavering. They also follow it honestly and wholly, doing what they say they're going to do.

We are acting with integrity when our belief systems and our actions match up. It is often hard to ascertain the results of decisions, and we never know what might have been if different choices had been made. So, in the absence of a crystal ball to predict the future, one needs to establish one's own set of rules to live by, and then at least when it comes to decision-making you have a framework to go by – that's integrity.

You can choose which values and standards to abide by, as they are fundamentally a personal choice. Having integrity is about intentionally following your morals and choosing your own constraints. It will stop you from being pushed around by whatever forces happen to be strongest in your life and allow you to guide yourself. These should become a part of you and your personality; they are the sole things that ought to define who you are. Really, this should be the biggest lesson in life.

Doing the right thing can sometimes be hard. But you don't have to be faced with life or death situations to demonstrate moral courage. I've had my own integrity tested plenty of times on the road, and it is often in the moments when you think you can get away with things – those smaller, everyday incidents – that your integrity will be most tested. Of course, for others, one's integrity can become a matter of life or death.

I May Be Some Time

Some people seem born to a life of setbacks. Lawrence Oates was one of them. He lost his father when he was sixteen, and had to drop out of Eton College after only two years due to an illness. He was able to make enough of a recovery to join the British Army, and served as a young officer in the Boer War. When aged twenty-one he was shot in the thigh, and for the rest of his life his wounded leg would be an inch shorter than the other.

Even at a young age, Oates had an unshakable purpose. During one battle he was told twice to surrender, but replied simply, 'We came to fight, not surrender.' His actions that day brought him into consideration for the Victoria Cross, Britain's highest award for 'conspicuous bravery, or some daring or pre-eminent act of valour or self-sacrifice, or extreme devotion to duty in the presence of the enemy'.

Only four years after his near-death experiences at war, Oates applied to join the Terra Nova expedition to the South Pole. Referring back to our team-member types, we might describe Oates as the 'Cynic' on that journey; he was at times scathing about the expedition's leader, Robert Falcon Scott, especially his relative lack of knowledge about travelling with horses. However, he attributed much of his harshness to the challenges of the conditions they encountered, and was kept loyal to the expedition by a sense of duty, writing: *'Myself, I . . . would chuck the whole thing if it were not that we are a British expedition.'*

The expedition was successful in reaching its goal, but discovered to their dismay the remains of Norwegian Roald Amundsen's camp, the rival expedition having beaten the British to the South Pole by 35 days. Dejected, the party turned around and started retracing their 79-day journey. They were quickly beset by extreme weather conditions, disease and food shortages, and lost a team member – Edgar Evans – in a bad fall.

Oates was beginning to suffer from seriously frostbitten feet, and his old war wound had reopened due to scurvy. His rapidly deteriorating condition and pace of walking was putting the rest of the party increasingly behind schedule, which meant that they were falling short of the pace required to reach their predetermined food stops. The whole party faced the risk of starvation, because of their soldier's accelerating demise.

On 15 March 1912 – almost two months since they had turned around at the Norwegian camp at the South Pole – Oates told his team to leave him behind in his sleeping bag. He knew that he was putting them all in danger, but his companions refused to abandon him. Robert Scott's diary then records Oates famously taking matters into his own hands. During a severe blizzard, he announced, 'I am just going outside and may be some time.' Scott's diary records: 'We knew that poor Oates was walking to his death, but though we tried to dissuade him, we knew it was the act of a brave man and an English gentleman.'

Oates couldn't have known whether his companions would make it back without him, and tragically, they did not. All Oates knew for sure at the time was that, with him hindering their progress, none of them stood any chance of survival. His moral compass instilled in him a determination to give his teammates the best chance of survival he possibly could.

There is a memorial placed near where he is presumed to have died, his body having never been discovered. The inscription reads:

Hereabouts died a very gallant gentleman, Captain L.E.G. Oates, of the Inniskilling Dragoons. In March 1912, returning from the Pole, he walked willingly to his death in a blizzard to try and save his comrades, beset by hardships.

Staying true

Moral courage and integrity will help you in any walk of life. As a leader, they will inspire the respect of your team, and give you a framework to help you make difficult decisions. As an explorer, they will help you to make a positive impact wherever you go. But even in day-to-day life, outside the contexts of leadership or exploration, a few mindful practices that cultivate moral courage and integrity will have a really beneficial impact on your life.

For example, you might find your job frustrating and unfulfilling. It can help to take a step back and ask why this is, with particular reference to your moral code. Think about the values and principles that matter to you in life: do you want to help poorer people that you don't know, or to provide as much as you can for your family? Both of these are perfectly valid moral stances, but will probably take your career in very different directions, so it's important to be honest with yourself about which is more important to you.

You should also identify any moral red lines you're unwilling to cross. For example, you might decide that providing for your family is the most important thing to you, but not at the expense of exploiting less fortunate people elsewhere. This can help you identify why you find your work unfulfilling: are you being asked by your manager to do things that you think are morally dubious? Does the business you're in contradict your moral values?

If so, the answer is not to jump ship, at least not straight away: first, write down any beneficial changes that you or your business could make, and suggest these to your manager. This is the stuff that leaders are made from; they effect positive change from the inside. It can be challenging, but however unlikely it seems, your superiors will respect the fact that you've taken a moral stand. If they don't, this is a pretty good sign that their moral frameworks and yours are irreconcilable, in which case you can think about what you want to do instead.

Teams and individuals always perform best when they believe they are working towards a higher purpose. So don't compromise on your values; you will never achieve your potential unless you believe 100 per cent in the value of the task you have set yourself. Use the power of integrity to bring yourself towards your goal. If you want to become a better runner, commit to a certain distance of practice per week, and hold yourself accountable for it. Don't be swayed by the fact that no one will know if you skip one run; if you really want to accomplish something, what matters is how you behave when no one is looking.

Moral courage means the conviction and will to identify and stand up for what we believe in: integrity is the commitment to doing this day in, day out, even when no one is watching. This isn't easy: it takes motivation, tenacity and resilience. With these qualities, you can weather any storm.

Lt. Col. Sir David Stirling

9

Carry On and Grit Your Teeth

*Do not judge me by my success, judge me by how many times
I fell down and got back up again* – Nelson Mandela

You've got to be in it to win it

In the winter of 2006, the unit that I was about to join, 3 Para, had
recently returned from their first tour of Afghanistan. It was a deployment that will go down in history as the one that started a decade of
violent conflict, and was some of the heaviest fighting involving
British soldiers in a generation.

Along with the other new officers, I took over a platoon of battle-
hardened veterans, and suddenly being their boss was a daunting prospect. To give us young officers something useful to do, and to get the
men reintegrated back into 'normal life' in the UK, our commanding
officer, Stuart Tootal, ordered all the junior commanders to pick a
sport or activity and organise training sessions. I recall John Martin was
good at rugby, so he gathered up all the blokes who enjoyed that and
assembled a team. Matt Clamp helped to set up the football team.
Tom Bodkin, who was a proficient skier, led the ski team, and so on.

As for myself, I was an enthusiastic boxer, but the Paras already
had a boxing team that was regarded as the best in the army, so that
wasn't an option. I decided to try my hand at something entirely
new and told the CO that I would organise a Parachute Regiment
kayak and canoe team.

Colonel Tootal chuckled. 'You do know that Para's hate water,
don't you? Good luck.'

So, I started to beg, borrow and steal all the necessary equipment
– boats, life preservers, paddles, and all the rest. Luckily one of the
gym sergeants volunteered to help me out in the training, as he had

done it before. Getting volunteers was a rather trickier process. Most of the soldiers had already signed up to one of the other team sports and, as Tootal had advised, most Paras had no particular interest in getting cold and wet – especially given that it was the winter months, and our only available water was the Chelmsford canal system.

After some persuasion, I managed to get some less than willing soldiers to join up, but that was only because Tootal had ordered that every man must join one of the teams.

As an afterthought, the amused Colonel decreed that rather than doing the sport for a jolly, each of the teams must enter some sort of competition and – being the Paras – do a bloody good job of trying to win. Suddenly, what was until then a bit of a lark became serious. None of the young platoon commanders wanted to lose. We had all just arrived and needed to make an impression, but given the fact that the men had returned from a very hard tour of duty in Afghanistan, they weren't exactly enthusiastic about training in what was supposed to be their down time.

Anyway, the rugby lads all signed up for an international match against the Australian Army. The football team entered the tri-service annual competition, and Tom Bodkin took the guys off to ski in the brutal downhill army championships. Canoeing, as ever, proved to be a difficult proposition, not least because most of us had never really paddled before. Tootal told us that we had until the Easter holidays to complete training, enter whichever competition and come back having upheld the Regiment's long-standing reputation for being the best at everything.

I suddenly regretted choosing kayaking. For the next three months, I took our band of merry men into the icy, shopping-trolley filled canals of Essex to learn how to paddle, Eskimo roll and avoid drowning in the murky depths. Once, by way of sheer accident, one of the soldiers flipped his boat and emerged having caught a fish.

Needless to say, despite my best efforts, none of us was particularly good at the sport, let alone ready for a competition.

I searched high and low for something suitable to enter. The Devizes–Westminster race would have been the obvious choice – a hard slog along the length of the River Thames, attracting the best kayakers in the world to try and finish all 220 miles in under 24 hrs. But thankfully that wasn't until May, outside of the commanding officer's timeframe, as real soldiering was to begin in earnest after the spring. The only competition I could find advertised in the army adventurous training schedule was the Army Canoe Polo Championships, to be held at Aldershot swimming pool on Easter weekend.

It was make or break. So with that, I lobbed a football into the canal and we began to practise, much to the amusement of the Chelmsford homeless population, one of whom decided to take a piss off the town centre bridge and onto the heads of my heroes in training. That didn't end well, and neither did our training. It would be an exaggeration to say that the men were motivated. Not only had they been coerced into a sport they weren't interested in, after a long and gruelling tour of Afghanistan, what made matters worse was that the competition was slap bang in the middle of Easter leave.

I'm sure every single one of the 'volunteers' would rather have been at home with their families, or out boozing with their mates, but when I asked if anyone wanted to drop out, there was silence. Thankfully the sense of camaraderie that we had forged out of the ridiculous situation was strong enough to engender a competitive spirit.

So, on Easter Sunday we travelled by minibus to Aldershot, the spiritual home of the Parachute Regiment, and waited at the swimming pool for the competition to start. At this stage we stood no chance of winning anything, given that many regiments took this sport seriously and trained year round in actual swimming pools, but we readied ourselves to put our best paddles forward and at least try to retain a little dignity in defeat.

A sergeant of the Physical Training Corps arrived at the poolside with a whistle around his neck, looking bored. He seemed surprised to see us.

'I thought everyone had given up,' he said. 'All the other teams have called in sick. Lazy bastards didn't want to lose their leave.'

I was suddenly taken aback. 'Well, we are here and we are ready to play.'

The sergeant shrugged his shoulders. 'Okay,' he said, pointing at the pool, 'get in the boats.'

So we all got into the little sports kayaks and lined up at our side of the pool, waiting for another team to arrive.

The PT sergeant looked at his watch and blew his whistle.

'Well done, Paras. You can get out now.'

Perplexed, I watched as the sergeant came up to us one by one. He shook our hands and gave us all a gold medal – we had become the army canoe polo champions by default.

Not that anybody else had to know that . . .

We returned back to the barracks triumphant. I was the only one of the young officers to have led their team to victory: the commanding officer was over the moon with me, and my 'volunteers' went home early with their gold medals to brag to their girlfriends.

Never give up. It's not over till it's over.

Tenzing Norgay

To Sherpas, the world's highest mountain is known as Chomolungma or 'Holy Mother'. Westerners called it Everest, and in 1935 a young Sherpa called Tenzing Norgay was selected as part of Eric Shipton's reconnaissance expedition. His inclusion came from a bit of luck, as two of the expedition's first choices failed their medical tests, and Norgay's winning smile allegedly caught Shipton's eye.

Following this first venture onto the mountain, the young Sherpa would take part in five more unsuccessful attempts on the summit. Almost twenty years after his first climb on Everest, Norgay was selected to lead the twenty Sherpas who, in addition to nearly 400 porters, would accompany Colonel John Hunt's expedition in 1953.

By this time, Norgay had earned a formidable reputation for himself. George Band, the youngest climber on the expedition, described him as 'the best-known Sherpa climber and a mountaineer of world standing'. Norgay's previous assault on the mountain, a 1952 expedition with a Swiss team, had set a new altitude record for attempts on the peak. Edmund Hillary said of him in 1975: 'His success in the past had given him great physical confidence . . . Tenzing had substantially greater personal ambition than any Sherpa I had met.'

As well as being a determined and diligent climber, Norgay was a smart, outside-the-box thinker. In 1947, he managed to cross mid-partition India by train, unchallenged and without a ticket, by wearing one of his old employer's British Army uniforms. His ability to think on his feet served his mountaineering career brilliantly. Early in the 1953 expedition, he saved Hillary's life by attaching a rope to an ice pick after the latter fell into a ravine. This moment led Hillary to insist on him as his climbing partner for any future summit attempt.

On 29 May 1953 – which Norgay later came to celebrate as his birthday, knowing only that he'd been born in late May – he bore the weight of his fellow climber, Hillary, as the latter reached the summit of the world's highest mountain, the Sherpa soon following him up. As he described it in his autobiography Mountain Man, 'A little below the summit, Hillary and I stopped . . . I was not thinking of "first" and "second". I did not say to myself, "There is a golden apple up there. I will push Hillary aside and run for it." We went on slowly, steadily. And then we were there.'

Norgay described his life as a mountaineer as 'a long road . . . From a mountain coolie, a bearer of loads, to a wearer of a coat with rows of medals who is carried about in planes and worries about income tax.' His self-deprecation notwithstanding, his inspiring journey towards one of the world's most inaccessible points is a testament to the values of hard work, tenacity and diligence. He stuck to his task, always kept his end goal in sight, and was rewarded for it.

Grit

Albert Einstein once said, 'It's not that I'm so smart, it's just that I stay with problems longer.' Ask almost any successful person – in almost any field – what the secret to their accomplishment is, and you will likely receive the same answer again and again. Grit – determination, tenacity and diligence – is the deciding factor between winning and losing, more so than natural talent.

As Professor Angela Duckworth, who studies grit and self-control at the University of Pennsylvania, puts it, success 'entails diligently working towards challenges and being able to maintain effort and interest over long periods of time (years) despite setbacks and stagnation in progress.'

It impacts our happiness, too. A Harvard University study in 1940 asked 130 20-year-old men to run for up to five minutes on steep, fast treadmills. On average they only lasted four minutes, and some managed only a minute and a half. The participants were then interviewed every two years for the next six decades. Those who showed more determination on the treadmill at twenty years old were statistically more likely to have led fulfilling, happy and successful lives since then.

Duckworth and her colleagues developed a Grit Scale, which people can use to measure their own powers of determination. She studied the achievement of various groups of people in competitive circumstances, including the grades of Ivy League university students, the drop-out rates of West Point Military Academy cadets and the scores of National Spelling Bee candidates. Across all groups, grit and determination were better indicators of success than natural ability or IQ. Central to this, in Duckworth's opinion, is that grit equips people with the drive to 'stay the course' in the face of challenges and setbacks.

Resilience

Resilience is our ability to face crises or adversity, and remain calm and healthy in the process. There are countless factors that contribute towards resilience, most of them rooted in our childhood circumstances, but one of the most intriguing factors is positive emotions. Humour, optimism, goal-orientation and even forgiveness have all been shown, in scientific studies, to have a correlation with our resilience to stressful situations.

The field of cognitive behavioural therapy (CBT) aims at increasing people's resilience to stressful situations by building these kinds of positive emotions and thought patterns, replacing negative thoughts that reduce our resilience, such as *I can't do X*, with positive thoughts like *I can do X*. This small difference in our underlying outlook about the world can have big consequences for how ready we are to face adversity. Resilience is also built through coping skills, such as meditation, exercise and socialising. Keeping our minds and our bodies healthy and happy has a huge impact on our ability to overcome difficult challenges.

Socialisation is a massive part of this, particularly in military scenarios. A 2009 study by the US military into the reduction of stress factors for soldiers found that unit cohesion and morale were the best predictors of a unit's combat resiliency. Units that fostered effective peer support and cohesion were less likely to suffer stress-related breakdowns under pressure, and better able to respond adaptively to stressful circumstances.

Keeping standards

This ability to respond to stress calmly, effectively and adaptably is vital in the military, especially for officers and elite units like the Paras and Special Forces. Any decision made – even in training – can lead to the death of others, and so it is vital to 'keep your head when all about you are losing theirs', as Kipling put it.

To join the Parachute Regiment, candidates must undergo a tough selection process called Pre-Parachute Selection run by Pegasus Company, which is usually referred to as P Coy or P Company, based at the Infantry Training Centre in Catterick, North Yorkshire. After 21 weeks of training, candidates are put through eight tests designed to test their resilience and determination, including a 20 mile endurance march laden with a 16 kg pack and a rifle in under 4 hours and 10 minutes; an intimidating assault course 17 metres above the ground called the Trainasium; and 60 seconds of milling.

Milling, arguably the flagship event of parachute selection, is a boxing match between candidates of similar size and strength in which determination and aggression are rewarded, and dodging and blocking lose points. In short, it amounts to being punched hard in the head for a minute straight while trying to hit the other guy as much and as hard as possible. If either combatant sheds blood or is knocked to the floor, the clock is paused, blood wiped off and the bout resumes. It is forbidden to aim at any part of the opponent's body besides the head, and the winner is the most aggressive candidate.

Milling is designed specifically to replicate 'the conditions of stress and personal qualities required in a combat situation' and test the 'determination and raw fighting spirit' of P Company candidates. It is this raw spirit of controlled aggression that sets the Paras apart from the rest of the army.

Nothing worth having comes easily

Nothing worth having comes easy, and we will need to work hard to achieve the things we want most out of life. Whether this is learning a new skill or advancement in our professional careers, we need to be prepared to stay the course and keep working towards our goals, no matter which obstacles appear along the way.

When I was on my way into the Parachute Regiment, I bussed up to Catterick for my Pre-Parachute Selection. At that point, I had no idea what the next few weeks would look like for me; all I knew was that they would be the most stressful, demanding and challenging of my life so far. But I had a goal in mind; I was determined to earn that maroon beret at the end, the recognition of my achievement and my initiation into one of the world's elite fighting regiments.

That level of drive is absolutely crucial. We can't give our all to anything if we're not motivated by the end result. And if we're not giving our all, we've no chance of sticking things through when the going gets tough.

Over the first few weeks of Selection, it was pretty clear that a lot of people didn't have what it took. Some couldn't handle the rigours of training and fell behind; others decided that enough was enough and dropped out of their own accord midway through. I had my own moment when I thought my time on Selection was up. I came down with a shin injury that set me back behind the rest of my cohort for a few days. Unable to join in the rigorous drills and knowing that when I was back in action things would be exponentially tougher for the time I'd missed, I wondered whether this was all worth it.

I started thinking about what my life would be like if I failed Selection. Probably not all that bad; I could probably go and reapply to one of the army's other, more sedate regiments. Then what? Have a fairly average military career, perhaps go to some interesting places and do some interesting things. But nothing grabbed me about it. Even more so when I considered a life and career outside the army; having just passed out of Sandhurst, I couldn't for a moment contemplate the prospect of a civilian life.

All I wanted was that maroon beret. It kept appearing in front of me, every time I closed my eyes. In a way, it would have taken some motivation to present myself to one of the officers running Selection and tell them I wanted to drop out; that I couldn't do it. But I had no desire to do anything besides recover, get back to training and persevere through the rest of selection.

So that's what I did. I pushed myself harder than I'd previously thought possible, quickly making up the ground I'd lost on the rest of the cadets. I remember my fear of heights being pushed to the background when I tackled the Trainasium. My sixty seconds of milling passed in such a blur that I can't now remember them at all, besides an overwhelming need not to hurt the person I was paired with, but to prove to him and everyone looking on that I wasn't one for backing down, whatever the circumstances.

Perhaps I'm fortunate that I was born with this amount of grit and determination. It's not always a positive; I've been told many times that I am as stubborn as a mule. But up there in cold, wet, windy Catterick, these inner reserves of drive, vision, grit and resilience pulled me through and I got the beret I'd been dreaming about. It is hard to think how different my life would have been without it.

Who Dares Wins

Today, Special Forces are something that everyone is aware of. You hear about them on the news, and see veterans of their ranks on the television, but back in the Second World War the idea of 'SF' was the unpopular brain child of a man called David Stirling. Serving in North Africa, he was frustrated at the pace of action against the Germans and Italians, and the senior command's failure to embrace the concept of commando soldiers.

Stirling was of the view that his superiors were giving up on the idea too easily, and he conceived the SAS, a secret unit that could launch covert surprise attacks in the desert, by night. Stirling finally persuaded his seniors to buy into his vision by sneaking straight into HQ, and marching into the office of the person who was highest up the command chain – an action that was utterly forbidden in the rigid hierarchies of the day. Convinced, the command allowed Stirling to assemble his first team, and now the SAS is famed for its work in special operations and counter-terrorism.

Back then, Stirling set about handpicking a team that could create maximum damage for minimum cost, and these men came to be known as 'the originals'. Stirling targeted those who were frequently getting into trouble in the army for being naturally rebellious or free-spirited, approaching them personally and asking them to join his quirky band of brothers. True pirates, all of them had a thirst for action. Some of them naturally very calm and considered, and others explosively violent. It is thought that more than a couple were likely to be psychopaths.

Stirling managed to recruit a rugby player of enormous stature with a drinking problem, a very smart Oxford-educated Scotsman who invented a bomb they could attach to planes, a priest who came on missions but refused to carry a gun and a former diplomat with fluent Italian. They were all exceptionally brave, tough as nails and willing – come hell or high water – to commit with dogged determination to the mission. Without these traits, you weren't eligible.

Life expectancy was extremely low for the early recruits and the team's first mission was a disaster, losing almost half of its men. The weather had been appalling and the parachute jump risky, but they decided to take the risk; if they didn't, they feared their clandestine outfit would have been disbanded before it even truly got going. Thankfully the second mission was a huge success and the team went on to make a huge contribution to the war effort.

Stirling was eventually captured by the enemy in North Africa, but in little over a year the team had put hundreds of German and Italian aircraft and vehicles out of action from the ground, and had destroyed railway supply lines and communication networks that were crucial to the enemy.

Stirling, like the motley crew he assembled around him, was a maverick. There was little evidence to suggest that what he set out to do would be successful, and without his exceptional levels of tenacity and perseverance, he might never have got it off the ground. But he had a vision that inspired him and he committed to it; he worked hard and he did not allow any initial setbacks to put him off. The end result is one of the most feared and revered elite combat units in the world.

Touched by an angel

I mentioned my friend Ash in Chapter Six – he's the one who threw his shoe at me at university. Well, Ash once told me a theory that struck a chord with me. He said that most people he encountered would rather explain away other people's success with luck, rather than graft – he called it being 'touched by an angel'.

'Touched by an angel?' I asked him.

'Yes. You see, most people out there don't really *want* to acknowledge their potential. They don't want to risk following their dreams, because deep down they are scared of failure. But you know what's even worse? Most people are even more scared of success itself. I mean being *really* successful. Because when you become really successful, then the pressure is always on you to keep being even more successful – and that is terrifying.'

Ash explained, 'It is far easier to give up early on your dreams and blame outside circumstances on not getting there: that way you never have to face the truth. People say things like, "I couldn't do this job that I love because I have a mortgage to pay", or, "I couldn't be with this girl because she's out of my league", or, "I can't go to that country because I don't speak the language", or, "I've never had the opportunity". Or whatever . . .'

It is true. It's much easier to place the blame on something or someone else rather than accept that if you really do want something, and you're prepared to put in the hard work and make sacrifices, you really can do anything you want. It is a big pill to swallow.

So now when I am asked, 'How did you become an explorer?', there are two versions of the truth. The first, much shorter version – the one I tell people if I know that all they are after is a bit of entertainment or an autographed book – is that I was 'touched by an angel'. It goes something along the lines of: 'One day, when I happened to be working in Africa, I got a phone call from a friend of mine who worked in TV, who said, "Do you have any expedition ideas you'd like to pitch?" I told him I'd like to walk the Nile. The TV folks happened to be interested in commissioning an adventure series that year, and well, the rest is history . . .'

Basically, I had a stroke of luck, which meant that the big break I needed came along at the right time – I was 'touched by an angel' and lived happily ever after.

And you know what? People like that story, because it's an easy explanation. They also like it because it's an excuse as to why they haven't done the same things. They feel comfortable in the knowledge that they were not touched by an angel, and therefore they can carry on with their lives complaining about the opportunities they never received.

The much longer version, of course (and I'm not saying this to blow my own trumpet, but rather to demonstrate a point), is that I spent several years travelling around the world in my early twenties with no money, while I was preparing to get in the army. Then I passed the selection to get into the Paras, I fought in Afghanistan and then risked it all to set up an expedition company while sleeping on my mates' floors for three years. This in turn allowed me to establish myself as a photographer and writer, whilst earning enough money to save up to do the expedition I really wanted to do.

I sacrificed my house, my girlfriend and any form of stability to do the one thing that really made my heart sing; that I knew was going to enable me to succeed in what I wanted to do. Yes, of course there were some elements of good fortune and privilege that helped me along the way – it would be churlish to ignore those – but ultimately it was down to good, old-fashioned determination.

But people don't always like that version of events, because it reveals the uncomfortable truth – there are no shortcuts to success.

Resilience and rejection

My dream of becoming a published author was first realised with *Walking the Nile*, but this wasn't the first book I ever wrote, nor perhaps the one I learned the most from.

When I left the army in 2010, around the time that I was setting up Secret Compass, I began writing *Eastern Horizons*. It was the travelogue of a hitch-hiking trip I had done one university summer from England to India, and I wanted to immortalise it and make it the first book I published – all part of the five-year plan that I had worked out with the help of the 'combat estimate'.

I think that first manuscript would be almost unrecognisable to me now. I worked on it for so long, tweaking and editing along the way. I would show it to friends and trusted confidants whose opinion I valued, and I can't imagine how many hundreds of hours of work were poured into that particular book. Once I was happy with the first draft, I started to pitch the manuscript to agents, which is the first step in finding a publisher.

Needless to say, I got rejected by everyone, and to be honest it felt like shit. It's not as if you get all of the rejections in one day, or in one week. Rather, it is a drip feed of misery. A Chinese water torture, where each drip says, 'You're not good enough.'

Even worse than the 'no's are the ghosts. Utter silence – a very singular sort of rejection. What choice do you have, but to pick yourself up and with renewed enthusiasm, charge back into the arena with a load more pitches. No matter the amount of 'no's, I would not be deterred, and *Eastern Horizons* was finally published six years later in 2017. It felt very validating.

When you're up against that level of adversity, you have to dig deep into your reserves to find the tenacity and dogged determination to keep going. The truth is that challenge, adversity and even rejection can be really motivating. After being knocked back by the first few 'thanks but no thanks', I was spurred on by the rejections I was getting from agents. It's a combination of humility and self-belief; I took in the criticism, when any constructive feedback was offered, but I never lost the belief that my book was good enough to be published, to prove those agents wrong.

It's all a matter of perspective. It is the difference between finding out you didn't get a job after an interview, and telling yourself that it was the wrong fit, rather than you were not good enough. Instead of thinking that you will never find the right job, you tell yourself that the right job will come along soon. It is also having the presence of mind to recognise that not getting the job applies only to your work life – it is not an indictment of who you are as a person.

Of course, all of this stuff exists on a spectrum – you might have the ability to be confident and optimistic in one scenario, whilst another totally floors you, but if you can consciously reflect on this difference when you're faced with challenges, you can start to see the world through a more optimistic lens.

Isabella Bird

Isabella Bird was a British explorer, naturalist and writer. Born in 1831, Bird did not have an easy childhood, and suffered from a spinal complaint, insomnia and chronic headaches. Her doctor prescribed Bird an open-air life as her medicine – something that we seem to be coming back to almost two hundred years later.

Ailments aside, Bird became a prominent writer, having her first work published at only sixteen years old. After having a tumour removed from her spine, she later travelled to America, where her letters home formed the basis of more published works. Bird had a thirst for travel, and after America she explored Australia and Hawaii, climbing mountains, and documenting her tales for others. In 1872, she moved to Colorado, which was still very much an unsettled place as part of the new frontier – her close 'acquaintance', 'Rocky Mountain' Jim Nugent was an outlaw, who was shot and killed.

Bird travelled all over the world and became a renowned travel writer, and such was her exploration that she became the first woman to be elected Fellow of the Royal Geographical Society. Life had dealt her a tough hand with her medical conditions, but Bird turned it to her advantage, embracing the outdoors. Through her grit and determination not to be constrained, Isabella Bird blazed a trail for other authors and explorers to follow in her footsteps.

Work hard, work smart

Success doesn't come without sacrifice. I have learned this in so many different contexts in my life: in gruelling boxing sessions throughout my time at Sandhurst; constant drills and training with the Paras; the hard slog it took setting up Secret Compass; and the endless rewrites, edits, rejections and knock-backs it took to become a published author. It is not always obvious to onlookers, who can fail to see or understand the legwork that goes on behind the scenes. The same goes in business as it does on the battlefield. The winners are the ones that make sacrifices, train harder and spend time, energy and effort in preparing to succeed.

There is no way around it, you've got to be willing to put in the hours; diligence goes a very long way indeed. The vision and the dream will not become a reality unless you work for it.

Working hard alone is not good enough; it is also about working smart. Sometimes toil will be necessary, but other times if you take a step back, you can streamline the way you come at things. Discipline is crucial. When I write, I am extremely strict with myself – I plan the structure of the book thoroughly, mapping out how many thousands of words will be in each chapter, and so on. I am always working to a deadline from the publisher, so I have an end date in mind. This allows me to work out how much I will need to write in any given week, or on any given day.

I am often asked if I get writer's block. Of course I do, and unless you give yourself a word count or other requirement per day, it is very hard to overcome that when sitting on your own at a laptop. I always allow a little contingency grace period – a back-up plan of sorts – for those days where I am *really* struggling to express myself or communicate; but fundamentally, if you don't stick to the plan, you are never going to get the thing written. Are you really going to feel more inspired tomorrow, or do you need to be firm with yourself and get started? Getting the words on the page is more than half of the battle, and you can always inspect them with a careful editing eye a few days later.

All that said, spending hours staring at a screen can be debilitating and does not automatically lead to better focus. I delineate time that will be spent on writing, and I turn off the notifications on my computer and phone. I avoid all distractions. When I am really struggling, I go for a walk, or take thirty minutes off and read.

You can also work smart by finding out what your 'frog' is. Mark Twain once said that if you swallow a live frog first thing in the morning, you can go through the day with the satisfaction of knowing it is probably the worst thing that will happen to you all day long. Your 'frog' is your biggest, most important task – the one you are most likely to procrastinate over if you don't do something about it. Once you've done this, you've crossed the biggest hurdle and have achieved something that can launch you forwards through the rest of the day.

Far too many people get caught up in the weeds of detail, embroiling themselves in the minutiae of a plan while ignoring the bigger picture. It's usually because the little wins feel great, but nobody wants to address the elephant in the room. When it comes to expeditions, people start chasing after visas and booking flights before they've got the funding, or even checked to see if a route is viable. Plenty of my colleagues will wrap themselves up in the small joys of spending hours posting pictures on social media, or pontificating over which kind of boots to buy, without giving a thought to the political implications of a journey.

My advice is to think big and work backwards. Prioritise what is important, and what will lead to success. Set yourself goals against timelines and stick to them. Don't worry too much about how you'll get there, because there are many paths to success. Details are important, but they will come later: identify your frog first – then swallow it.

Say No more often

There's an almost cultish predilection these days that insists we must agree to everything. Say Yes! Go and do that 5K run! Go and spend a crazy weekend in Budapest! Go and take up lessons in ancient Sanskrit! . . . the list goes on.

But the truth is, we often go along out of peer pressure, or a misplaced sense that failure to do so will mean we are missing out. What we don't appreciate with this take on life is that by filling our time with stuff and nonsense that we will probably never utilise, or even enjoy, we are wasting precious opportunities to be doing the things that are useful, fun and genuinely fulfilling to us.

As I said at the start of this book, first we need to understand ourselves so that we know what we want, and how we wish to spend our time. The Say Yes More movement is childish and frankly rather patronising. What we should be doing is taking ownership of our lives, and saying No to all the bullshit, so that we can focus on exploring what really makes us happy.

That is not to say don't try new things – that would be entirely against what I talked about in the chapter on curiosity – but only say Yes to those things that make your heart sing, or otherwise might serve a useful purpose. Don't do stuff because everyone else is. If it's not a definite Yes, it's a No.

The key to all of this is discipline. It's about having self-control, and the willpower not to be distracted by all the white noise and temptation that surrounds us on a daily basis.

How is this relevant in the workplace? You can work smart by saying No more. You can't do everything, nor are you good at everything. I'm certainly not – I hate admin and I'm a bit of a Luddite, crap at anything that involves a Google Drive or an iCloud. Be discerning about what you commit to and then do it at full pelt, instead of spreading yourself too thinly and burning out.

Remember to factor in your body when you are trying to understand your own behaviour. Often our behaviour is dictated by physiology; say lack of sleep or low blood sugar. It is critical to be aware of your own energy levels and work out what is called your biological primetime; knowing what drains you and what energises you. Do you get your energy from being in your own company, or being around others? What boosts your mood and what drains you, and when are you at your most energetic? Are you a night owl or a morning person?

Knowing when you function best, your biological primetime, can be a great help. Record your personal energy throughout the day, noting what times and what things energise you. Once you've established this, you have greater potential for productivity and can plan your work and life around these ebbs and flows. If you're an extrovert, you may schedule meetings at a time when you're usually flagging, as they'll give you energy. If you're an introvert, this is more likely to be something that costs you energy. If you are able to concentrate all morning, but have an urge to snooze after lunch, schedule that time to do something mundane or non-creative, like replying to emails.

Discipline, graft and determination are critical to getting stuff done. Understanding your own needs, and what makes you tick, will make you more efficient, and finally accepting what is and isn't within your control will help you to navigate the complexities of any situation. What comes next is perhaps the hardest task of all – defeating your own ego and mastering yourself.

Palmyra, Syria

10

Admit When You Are Lost

Humility is not thinking less of yourself, but thinking of yourself less

Among the ruins

There are many treasures around the world. Many are natural and seemingly impervious to disasters, others man-made and artificial. Those, like the ancient city of Palmyra, have stood for thousands of years with no guarantee of their permanency. Palmyra, one of the best-preserved Roman sites in the world, resides in what is now the bloody battleground of Syria. I had always wanted to visit its ancient Semitic palaces, and now that I'd trekked around the Arabian peninsula all the way from Iraq, I had my chance.

The problem was that Palmyra was still very much on the frontline against ISIS. It was 2018, and they were on the back foot, but there was a genuine threat of attack and a grisly death. I couldn't help myself, though. I had to see it, and I was rewarded in this decision when the old town rose from the sandy plains like a mirage. Considering that it had twice been taken by ISIS, I didn't expect to see much more than a crumbled reminder of what once stood there, and a sense of relief washed over me when I saw how much of it still remained.

As I wandered between the ruins, I was overcome by a mixture of emotions. The damage was clear to see. Gone was the Triumphal Arch, the gateway to the Roman city. The Temple of Baalshamin lay in sad wreckage, along with much of the Great Colonnade. Though I was glad to see that many of the columns still stood strong, and that the Baths of Diocletian, and the Senate, were for the most part undamaged, I felt a strong sense of smallness, of the transitory, trivial nature of my problems in relation to the scale of these buildings, and of the world and time itself.

I looked up in wonder at the infamous Roman Theatre, which once held gladiatorial contests. In equally grim circumstances more recently, the executions of hundreds of men by Islamic State terrorists were held here. The Temple of Baal was utterly demolished, blown up by these modern-day philistines, and now only the central gateway remained. It was here, standing on top of the rubble of a temple to an ancient God, where I met Tarik Al-Assad.

'Tarik's father was the head of antiquities at Palmyra Museum,' Nada, my guide, introduced us. 'He has quite the story to tell.' He held out his hand for me to shake. I studied his face as we greeted one another, guessing him to be about my age. A sad look in his eyes betrayed an unknown tragedy.

'I work at the museum in Damascus,' he said, leading me through the piles of 2000-year-old masonry. 'My father was in charge here. His name was Khaled, please do not forget it.'

I nodded, willing the story to continue.

'My father loved this place, he worked here for forty years. He was a historian and a hero. It was because of him that Palmyra became a UNESCO world heritage site. When Daesh came here and took over, they arrested him, and me too. For weeks before, we had been taking the antiquities to a place in Damascus for safe keeping, because we knew that Daesh would steal them and sell them in Turkey. Before they came, my father told me to run away with my mother and brother, so we escaped one night and hid from them. But my father refused to leave.'

Daesh was what the locals called ISIS. I swallowed, knowing how this story would likely end.

Tarik paused as though steeling himself before continuing. 'He could have left with us, but he said his place was in Palmyra, and if that meant going down with it, so be it. Daesh were stupid and thought that my father was hiding gold in the ruins. They beat him and asked him where it was. They didn't believe that there was nothing, so they began blowing things up. When they realised it was just old stones, they demanded that he reveal the antiquities. My father refused to tell them anything.'

Tarik stuttered his words and I noticed a tear running down his cheek.

'Then one day, on the eighteenth of August 2015, they took him to the crossroads by the mosque, just over there.' He pointed beyond the gate to the shattered remnants of the modern town, where a bullet-strewn minaret jutted miserably into a grey sky.

'They forced him to kneel down on the pavement, and cut his head off with a sword.'

He fell silent and gazed off into the distance.

'He was eighty-three years old,' Nada added beside me.

'Look at this!' Tarik exclaimed suddenly, pulling his phone from his pocket and forcing it into my hand. I peered at the screen in disbelief, looking at an image so gruesome I could barely look for more than a couple of seconds. A body was hanging upside down from a traffic light, its decapitated head sat in a pool of blood below on the pavement, still wearing a pair of broken spectacles.

'It's my father,' whispered Tarik, forcing a smile. 'I still have his glasses.'

In a state of shock, I didn't know what to say. Tarik's father had been murdered and the criminals who had done it had sent this photo to him to torture the family even more. I asked Tarik what he would do if he ever met his father's killers.

He smiled. 'It'd not for me to punish them. That is God's decision. I must forgive them.'

Tarik had no anger and he had no urge for revenge, and he was putting his hand on my shoulder, as if *I* were the one in need of comfort. It was a reminder of the greatest of all virtues – *compassion*.

The Golden Temple

In the heart of Amritsar, in the Indian state of the Punjab, lies the Golden Temple, the most holy shrine in the Sikh religion. At its centre is a shining golden shrine surrounded by a placid square of water, in which the faithful bathe to purify their bodies and their souls.

Around this is a walkway on which Sikhs perambulate or prostrate themselves before the sacred temple, and the air shimmers with the soothing sounds of sermons broadcast in Punjabi through speakers at the four corners of the space. Its four surrounding walls face North, South, East and West as a symbol that its grounds are open for all races and religions of the world to enter, and its many kitchens serve food for free to ten thousand people, regardless of religion or status, every day.

To enter the temple complex, visitors must cover their heads as a sign of respect, and walk through small trickles of cleansing water to purify their bare feet. Then, they descend a small flight of stairs, a symbolic recognition of the humbleness of all people before God.

Guru Nanak, the founding father of Sikhism, taught that humility is key to fulfilment. Sikhism's holy book, the Sri Guru Granth Sahib, describes him as 'the companion of the lowest of the low and of the condemned lot. He has nothing in common with the high born'. According to Sikhism there is no place for Ego, or Haumain, in the sphere of Divine Love, and in the House of Guru Nanak Garibi, Nimrata, (Poverty, Alleviation) and Humility reign supreme. Because all people are equal before God, there should be no hierarchy, only humility.

Unlike some other religions that claim a monopoly over truth and wisdom, Sikhism recognises the ability of all other religions and faiths to enlighten their followers. In this sense, the quiet, reflective tranquility of the Golden Temple is one of the most humbling places on Earth.

Humility

Sikhism is not the only world religion to espouse the virtues of humility, though perhaps you could argue that it goes about it in one of the humblest ways (the gold sheet-covered temple at its heart notwithstanding). Philosophers and spiritual leaders across the world and throughout history have recognised the importance of humility in understanding our place in the world, and leading fulfilled and purposeful lives. Jesus taught 'Blessed are the meek', and the word Islam itself translates to 'Surrender (before God)'. Buddhism and Hinduism teach that humility and self-improvement are key steps on the path towards higher states of being.

What many religions teach is that humility is not the same thing as self-deprecation. Self-deprecation is a form of arrogance, a focus on yourself and a comparison between your own poor circumstances and an imagined better state, of which you are implicitly more deserving. Or in the words often wrongly attributed to C.S. Lewis, 'Humility is not thinking less of yourself, but thinking of yourself less.'

Humble leaders have been shown to have a huge impact on business performance. Researcher and consultant Jim C. Collins led a 1996 study that sought to identify the common factors between companies that went from a 'good' performance (i.e. broadly in line with market average for several years) to a 'great' performance (share price three or four times the market average for a sustained period).

The most significant factor that emerged from their four-year project was what Collins calls 'Level 5 Leadership' – and their definition of 'Level 5 Leadership' is counterintuitive, even by Collins' own admission. For all we've come to associate the vision of successful business leadership with big, flashy personalities like Alan Sugar and Richard Branson, the most effective leaders identified by this study were characterised by 'a paradoxical combination of personal humility plus professional will'.

These leaders themselves, when interviewed as part of the study, showed an unwillingness to credit their organisation's success to their own actions, downplaying their own contributions and up-selling the strength of their teams. One of the key criteria for a 'good to great' company in this study was sustained success. It wasn't enough to improve a company's fortunes temporarily; it had to show sustained, three-times-the-market results for fifteen years.

Collins points out that a lot of the companies that were discounted from their 'good-to-great' categorisation for this reason happened to have very arrogant, showy leaders. They might have temporarily turned a company's fortunes around, but soon became so absorbed in cultivating their own personal brand and self-promotion that company performance slumped.

To achieve anything great, it is important to recognise our own small, humble place in the world.

Inspiration all around

When I walked across the Sahara desert in 2014 as part of my expedition to walk the Nile, I found myself in a bit of quandary. I had reached my mental and physical limits, having already walked for more than six months over some of the harshest terrain in Africa, but nothing could have prepared me for what was to come. The searing heat of the desert, the empty barren wilderness and seeing nothing but sand for days on end. On top of that I'd got terrible blisters, and every inch of my body was in constant pain from the ceaseless walking.

I knew that I couldn't travel this part alone and would need some support. It came in the form of my Nubian guide Moez, and two Bedouin camel drivers, Ahmed and Ahmad, plus of course their three camels, which I acquired in Khartoum.

I worked out my progress and figured that we needed to reach the Egyptian border, some hundreds of miles to the north, within two months. The reason was that as soon as the Islamic month of Ramadan had begun, the border would be closed, and I would be stuck in Sudan for thirty days longer than I needed to be. Moez and the camel drivers agreed – in fact, the Bedouin said that we had sixty days and no more, because wherever we were then, they would turn back to make sure they had enough time to return to their families for Ramadan.

So that was it, decided. We trundled north into the Sahara, each day more arduous than the last. For weeks on end we would walk at least the distance of a marathon every day, sometimes up to fifty kilometres. It was the most punishing and demanding thing I had ever done. I couldn't have been good company: I was tired, lonely and fed up of the whole thing. I spent half my time trying to catch a mobile phone signal, so I could keep up with the outside world and contact my unresponsive girlfriend of the time. I was thoroughly miserable and wanted to get to the end as soon as possible.

To try to keep the logistics as simple as possible, I had planned to stay close to the River Nile, where it would be easy to obtain water, and when we passed by villages we could buy food and supplies.

The only problem was that Ahmed and Ahmad didn't like walking next to the river. 'We are Bedouin – people of the desert!' they shouted, theatrically. 'The camels prefer the sand.' As it turned out, my hardy camel men were simply scared of snakes and mosquitoes.

A bigger issue was keeping to the schedule when faced with overwhelming hospitality. Despite what I'd read in the media about Sudan, with its tribal violence, poverty and dictatorial government, its people are some of the most welcoming I have ever met. All along the famous river, I was greeted with a friendly smile and offers of endless tea, delicious flatbread and free meals of goat stew. It was hard to say no. The villagers never wanted anything in return, except the honour of hosting a foreign guest for the night.

For me, after the horrors of travelling through war-ravaged South Sudan, it came as a welcome break and soon helped me rise out of my depressed state of mind. However, it was less welcome for the other team mates, who were more concerned with making sure they got home in time for Ramadan. 'Ah, this is just normal here,' they said nonchalantly. 'We are used to it.'

For me, though, it was truly humbling. People often ask how I managed to stay motivated during the toughest times of my walks, and I often think of those Sudanese villagers. Even though they lived in abject poverty and had nothing of material worth, they would rather have died themselves than deny a drink of water to a guest. I reminded myself daily that no matter how lonely or demoralised or tired or hot I was, it was only temporary. These people lived their whole lives here in these desperate conditions. It was that incredible sense of generosity that got me through – those people with their kind smiles.

They would run after me laden with sweets or drinks, insisting that I stay a little while longer to enjoy their hospitality. Ahmed and Ahmad would always try to shoo them off and explain to me that we must hurry along. I even got to the point where they threatened to mutiny unless we avoided the villages entirely and followed the desert paths instead. In the end we reached a compromise, whereby every other day we would walk a mile or so away from the river to avoid the settlements, and thus risk being slowed down by the offers of lunch.

On many occasions it would prove fruitless anyway. Even a mile away from the villages, whenever we made camp and Moez lit the fire, dozens of villagers, intrigued as to why there would be a fire in the desert, would come wandering out to the dunes where we sat on rugs under the stars.

'What are you doing here?' they would shout.

Moez, or the camel men, would try to explain the situation, but the villagers were always upset that we would not accept their hospitality. One local man was so horrified that he stormed off into the night, and returned half an hour later, having carried his bed on his head.

'Here,' he huffed. 'If you will not come into my home . . . my home will come to you.' He slammed it down into the sand and bowed gracefully.

I wondered if I would ever be greeted with that sort of response back home in England. I seriously doubted it.

I swore I'd never complain about my lot again.

'The only thing we know for certain, is that we know nothing'

. . . so said Socrates. According to Ryan Holiday, author of the book *Ego is the Enemy*, many of our problems and challenges in life are not the fault of external factors, but are born of our own ego – an arrogant, 'self-centred belief in our own importance'. There are three phases we go through in which our ego plays a role, and our ability or otherwise to master it can determine success or failure, happiness or unhappiness.

Firstly, Aspiration, the desire to accomplish bigger and better things in life; secondly, Success, when we achieve these goals and receive praise for it; thirdly, Failure, when we don't achieve our aspirations and the consequences of this.

Aspiration is driven by our ego, and in that sense our ego serves a positive purpose. But when we start imagining and talking about our future accomplishments, it can trick our ego into imagining these things have already happened, and we can forget to put in the necessary work. It breeds the worst forms of arrogant behaviour. We focus more on the material perks of success, rather than the impacts that our actions have on the world. We become lazy, forgetting to put in the work. We convince ourselves that we have everything figured out, and stop learning from new experiences.

Success is one of the most dangerous threats to the ego. There are endless accounts of people who work extremely hard to achieve a position of power and influence, only to throw it away from their own hubris. It's an intoxicating drug that robs us of the sobriety required to sustain it. Failure hurts the ego. It's a direct challenge to our misplaced view of ourselves as the centre point of the universe. Our ego amplifies the negative aspects of failure, sending us into a downward spiral, where failure is seen as the end of the world, rather than an opportunity to learn and grow.

This all runs completely counter to the explorer's mindset. Our egos, if left unchecked, have the potential to stifle every aspect of our journey that makes the world worth living in. We lose sight of the self-knowledge and self-improvement that are key to a fulfilling existence; we succumb to fear because we lose our curiosity, and thereby our optimism, about the world around us. We alienate others, losing sight of the virtues and morals that have guided our decisions, and become poor leaders; we lose the capacity for diligence and hard work that are crucial to success. Without humility, we are unable to explore. Sometimes it's better to accept you are wrong, even if you think you are right, as difficult as that might sound.

The Darien Gap is one of the most remote and inaccessible jungles in the world. It is a stretch of rainforest in the lawless no-man's-land between Panama and Colombia that separates North and South America, and even now is a byword for danger amongst the hardiest of explorers. It is the kind of place where anything is possible.

I was trying to cross through the notorious jungle back in 2016, as part of an expedition to walk all of Central America. I'd left the highway behind and started upriver by dugout canoe, which for much of the time we had to push up cascades and around fallen trees. I had been to a lot of remote jungles in my time, but this was another level. The only way to navigate through this treacherous terrain was to enlist the help of the local tribe – the Embera-Wounan people – and so it was that I found myself in the company of a dozen or so of these men armed with machetes and bows.

After two days struggling upriver, we came to the final settlement before the mountains, and it was where most of the men came from. They insisted we spent the night in the village, where we were given a hut on stilts to protect against snakes and flooding.

As night fell, we were treated to a meal of roasted fish and rice by the chief's wife, who came and sat down next to me. Maria might have looked old and withered, but she had a twinkle in her eye that betrayed a lifetime of mischief, and she was most definitely the one who wore the trousers.

'Do you want to buy something?' she said in a conspiratorial tone.

'What?' I asked, expecting to be peddled some tribal beads or needlework, like we'd seen in the markets of Panama City.

Instead she pulled out of her apron a cloth, which she unwrapped to reveal a white thing the size of a thumb. It was a tooth.

'It's from a Jaguar,' she said.

I grimaced. *Poor thing*, I thought. *They've probably killed it to sell the teeth*.

'No thanks,' I said, explaining that I didn't want to encourage poaching.

She thought about it and shrugged her shoulders, wrapping it back up in the cloth.

'Okay, I have something else,' she said with a sigh. 'I've had it a very long time, but I want to sell it.'

From another pocket came another cloth, this time bigger. Before she unwrapped it, she looked me in the eye and stared.

'These are very rare,' she said in a whisper.

'Let me see.'

She placed the object into my hands and I felt the heavy coldness of something hard and triangular in shape. In the half-light of the room, I couldn't tell what it was. Two of the sides were razor-sharp and serrated, and it looked like some type of Stone Age spearhead made of flint. That must be what it was, evidence of a prehistoric society in Panama perhaps?

'No, it's not a spear,' said Maria. 'It's a *Una de Raya*.'

'She says it's a nail of lightning, like a fingernail,' said my guide. 'I think she means it's a thunderbolt.'

I laughed out loud. She frowned and grasped it out of my hand.

'It is, it is, that's what it is. My grandmother found one. They are only found in the Darien, nowhere else. We sometimes find them underneath trees that have been burned by the sky.'

I suppressed my chuckles and felt bad that I had laughed. Maria genuinely thought that it was the tip of some sort of supernatural thunderbolt, presumably petrified upon impact with the earth.

If it wasn't a spearhead (it was too big and irregular for that) and it wasn't a thunderbolt, there was only one thing left that it could be. It was a shark's tooth. But this was not any old shark's tooth, it was that of a prehistoric megalodon; a thirty-metre monster ten times bigger than your average Great White, which swam in the oceans over three million years ago. One thing was certain: this ancient fossil was formed at a time when Central America was nothing but a ridge of underwater volcanos, but then again, who was I to argue with this wise lady and her dreams of thunderbolts?

Even if I had a notion to correct her, what is a more likely story: a flash of lightning striking a tree and leaving a piece of stone in the shape of an arrow, or a giant sea monster leaving its teeth in the middle of a jungle? The old lady had never even seen the sea, nor had any concept that her piece of forest was once under it. Sometimes it is wise to hold your tongue, because what is true for one, might not be true for another. Choose your battles wisely.

So I told Maria that I'd love to buy her thunderbolt, even if it was a hundred dollars. I didn't barter.

Heinrich Harrer

Born in 1912 and raised in the Alps, explorer Heinrich Harrer grew up utterly obsessed with climbing and skiing. He was gung-ho about adventure, once surviving a 170-foot cliff fall. In the mountaineering world, he is famed for successfully scaling the almost vertical north face of the Eiger mountain in the Alps. But it is not his climbing exploits on which I wish to focus, but his unlikely friendship with a young boy.

In 1939, Harrer was in the Himalayas planning an ascent on Nanga Parbhat, when war broke out, and as an Austrian he was interned in British India in a prisoner-of-war camp. After several attempts, he and a companion escaped and hiked out across the mountains. They were looked after by nomads and treated with kindness and hospitality, and after almost two years of trekking in freezing conditions, and avoiding bears and roadside robbers, they made it to the city of Lhasa. Bear in mind, at this time, Tibet was resolutely closed, letting no one through its borders. But by some miracle of hardiness and persuasion, they got to the forbidden city.

It would turn out that, in reality, the Tibetans were curious and inquisitive about these two foreigners and, above all, they showed them compassion. Despite being ordered to leave, they sat tight and an aristo-crat took pity on them, letting them kip in his garden and feeding them. They got to work making themselves useful and soon the Tibetan government had given Harrer a job as a translator of foreign news and an engineer, and they gave him a home and servants. Part of his work also included cinematography, helping them with photography and film.

Here in Lhasa, they soon realised that the entire city revolved around a ten-year-old boy. His holiness had been discovered as the 14th Dalai Lama at just two years old, and as the human reincarnation of God was both Buddhist spiritual leader and Tibetan king. At his request Harrer was recruited to be the god king's tutor.

The young Dalai Lama clearly had a hunger for learning, and was diligent enough to do double the translation homework that Harrer would set him. He was curious about the mysteries of the outside world; he'd heard about aeroplanes and wanted to know how the engines worked. He would gobble up news and knowledge about the technical advancements happening in the Western world, even though they must have seemed utterly alien. He would ask about global politics and was particularly interested in geography and maps of the world, working out where Tibet fitted into it all. With twenty-three years between them, they were a rather unlikely pair, but this didn't stop them from talking for hours about Buddhist philosophy and Western science.

Ever resourceful, Harrer would keep the king entertained, running a cinema projector of a jeep engine – one of only a few cars in the whole region. I'm sure it made a welcome break from all the priests and reverence and rigmarole – underneath it all, of course, he was also a teenage boy. Besides, he had very few friends his own age, a strict study regime and was likely desperate for stimulation, variety and companionship.

Chinese troops invaded Tibet in 1951, forcing Harrer to flee to India. Not long later, and far more famously, the Dalai Lama was forced to flee himself. He has never been back and has lived a life in exile, having sought refuge in India. The Dalai Lama would go on to become a global leader, both as the spiritual head of Buddhism and as the political leader of 100,000 or so Tibetans in exile. I was lucky enough to meet him, getting a private audience with him in Mcleod

Ganj, his home in exile in the Indian Himalayas. Now eighty-four, he campaigns internationally for his exiled homeland and travels the world sharing Buddhist teachings and words of wisdom.

Harrer went on to write a book about his time in the Himalayas, *Seven Years in Tibet.* Published in the 1950s, it was the first time the Western world had heard any stories from this secretive kingdom. Even at a tender age, the Dalai Lama made a lasting impression on Harrer; the tutoring did not go only one way. Heinrich Harrer learned a huge amount from the boy.

He learnt the Buddhist philosophy of tolerance and about the belief of peaceful action; he was struck by the fact that Buddhism never sought to convert non-believers. He learnt about the idea that wealth is impermanent and will not grant you happiness, and the idea that we need to live each day as it comes, instead of dwelling in the past or focusing too much on the imagined future. He never carried a gun again, based on the non-violent Buddhist teachings he'd learnt from the Dalai Lama.

Despite all the trappings of power and wealth, Harrer described the young Dalai Lama as unspoilt and humble. He chose to fast and keep silence, keeping an ascetic way of life. There is a lot that we can learn and adopt from the Dalai Lama before he even grew into a man. In Tibet, Heinrich Harrer would find a sense of peace and self-awareness that he summed up thus: 'I have learned to contemplate the events of life with tranquillity and not let myself be flung to and fro by circumstances in a sea of doubt.'

Life of learning

For me, the most important thing about humility is that it reminds us of the limits of our own knowledge, which gives us curiosity and a desire to keep learning about the world. One of the most useful insights I have gained in life is that success is best measured against yourself. It's not profound, it makes perfect sense. But it's not something that we teach in schools, where we tend to pit children against each other, feeding the more negative sides of their egos, and creating the impression that success means doing better than other people.

It's not something that comes naturally to me either. I have quite a competitive streak and relished the rivalry as a boy. It can be a long time before we figure out that it doesn't matter what all of your peers are doing. What this revelation looks like for me, is a lifetime of learning and self-improvement. Like many children, I was hungry for learning and knowledge, but in our society this seems to dissipate and fall away as we get older. When school and university come to an end, we are sent out into the world, and for lots of us this stimulus and sense of constant personal development disappears.

In the early part of my career, in the army, I was lucky enough to be continually learning. But it was when I left and started out on my own that I understood the onus was on me to go out and learn new things. I had always read a lot and had a healthy curiosity, but this was the first time I'd really ventured into autodidacticism: self-education without the guidance of teaching or an institution.

Some of the most useful and important things that I know now, I had to learn on my own: from pension schemes and tax returns, to relationships and learning to communicate how you feel. More importantly now, because of the internet there is far too much knowledge for us to possibly absorb – and this is only getting harder. Everything that I learnt in Year 5 history, I could digest from one Wikipedia page. We are too focused on information.

One of the things that gives us the edge over animals is our ability to think collectively in large groups, but more and more we are becoming reliant upon the knowledge of others to create our understanding of the world. There are huge benefits to this collaboration, but there are also pitfalls. We think we know far more than we do. It's all an illusion. We treat knowledge in the minds of others as if it were our own, when we don't know how many of the simple things around us work. It's easy to think this comes from inside our own brains, when really it is drawn from the world around us and from our community.

Instead of our endless obsession with knowledge, we need to focus on teaching children the real-life skills of critical thinking, collaboration, communication and creativity. We also need to teach children the ability to embrace change, which is a lot harder than any chemical equation. This means giving kids a mindset that teaches them they can continually improve. In one study, children that pushed through their challenges were exclusively the ones who believed they could improve their own abilities; their trajectory was not fixed and they could grow. Those who pulled back, afraid of the challenges and not going for it, were the ones who held the belief that their ability was fixed.

It is the difference between the two outlooks, 'I didn't do very well in that maths test' and 'I'm bad at maths'. Some schools have even been giving kids the grade 'not yet'. This kind of thinking encourages young people to keep learning, to recognise that however much they already know, there is a lot more to learn out there, and it cuts out many of the dangers that can come from over-inflated egos.

Captain Tom Moore

By April 2020, you could argue that Captain Tom Moore had done his bit, his fighting days long behind him. A Second World War veteran, who had served with the Duke of Wellington's regiment in India, Sumatra and Myanmar, he was approaching his 100th birthday when the world was plunged into lockdown in response to the COVID-19 crisis.

'Captain Tom', as he has become known, could have been forgiven for sitting out the latest 'war' (as he described it), considering his age and relative frailty. Instead, he set about fundraising for the NHS Charities Together foundation, famously completing 100 laps of his garden with the assistance of a walking frame, ten 25-metre laps per day, before his centenary.

His initial fundraising target of £1,000 was smashed; the final total of £32,796,475 is a record for any JustGiving campaign. It captured hearts and minds across the world, and led to Moore being Number One in the UK charts for his birthday after recording a charity single with Michael Ball. It wasn't a desire for fame that had motivated Captain

Tom, but a view that however small a contribution he might make, it was worth trying to do, to make an impact on a cause bigger than himself.

Captain Tom's humility was a big part of the reason why he was successful in his goal, and why people across the world bought into his story. As the difference between his original target and the amount he finally raised shows, it is worth doing something for a worthy cause that's bigger than you, and we always underestimate the impact our actions can have when we put our ego aside in the face of a higher cause. Every time we do so, we're surprised and humbled by the results.

Everything in perspective

How can we learn to control our egos, and become humbler and more fulfilled in the process?

I could try to sum this up myself, but it would be a vain task indeed when Rudyard Kipling has already expressed it so eloquently in his poem, 'If':

> *If you can keep your head when all about you*
> *Are losing theirs and blaming it on you,*
> *If you can trust yourself when all men doubt you,*
> *But make allowance for their doubting too;*
> *If you can wait and not be tired by waiting,*
> *Or being lied about, don't deal in lies,*
> *Or being hated, don't give way to hating,*
> *And yet don't look too good, nor talk too wise:*
>
> *If you can dream – and not make dreams your master;*
> *If you can think – and not make thoughts your aim;*
> *If you can meet with Triumph and Disaster*
> *And treat those two impostors just the same;*
> *If you can bear to hear the truth you've spoken*
> *Twisted by knaves to make a trap for fools,*
> *Or watch the things you gave your life to, broken,*
> *And stoop and build 'em up with worn-out tools:*

If you can make one heap of all your winnings
And risk it on one turn of pitch-and-toss,
And lose, and start again at your beginnings
And never breathe a word about your loss;
If you can force your heart and nerve and sinew
To serve your turn long after they are gone,
And so hold on when there is nothing in you
Except the Will which says to them: 'Hold on!'

If you can talk with crowds and keep your virtue,
Or walk with Kings – nor lose the common touch,
If neither foes nor loving friends can hurt you,
If all men count with you, but none too much;
If you can fill the unforgiving minute
With sixty seconds' worth of distance run,
Yours is the Earth and everything that's in it,
And – which is more – you'll be a Man, my son!

Ultimately, we need to create a world in which we all recognise that what we currently know is not the extent of what is possible, and that we can continue to enrich ourselves and one another if we adopt the humility to listen and learn.

Our own egos can be the greatest demons we face. In this sense, they're a little like Mark Twain's frog – once we have overcome them, we are ready to find fulfilment within ourselves.

Jacques-Yves Cousteau

11

Conquer Your Own Everest

We shall not cease from exploration
And the end of all our exploring
Will be to arrive where we started
And know the place for the first time. – T.S. Eliot

Look after yourself

You know when they tell you on aeroplanes to always fit your own mask before helping others? The reason of course is that you can't be much use to anyone else if you're conked out unconscious. The same goes for happiness. If you're sad and miserable nobody is going to take lessons from you on how to live their lives. You can't go around preaching if you haven't got your own house in order first. That's why it's important to focus on yourself and your own internal journey first. Those in glass houses and all that.

That's not to say to ignore others, act selfishly and never extend a helping hand – of course not. But don't be a martyr either. When you feel fulfilled, you have a lot more to offer those around you, like a cup overflowing with water. Be a full, happy, overflowing vessel and you'll explore places you never imagined possible.

Take the time to learn your craft, become good at what you do, and do what you love. Life is way too short to be doing things that make you unhappy, so stop wasting time putting things off and focus on the task in hand. That's the first step to self-mastery and the first step to the art of exploration.

Enjoy the journey

In 2019, I decided I needed to be in one place in order to relax. I was feeling burnt out having been on the road pretty much constantly for a decade and I felt like all my recent travels had been for work, leaving little time to just appreciate what was going on around me. As I looked for somewhere to take a break from expeditions, Bali jumped out as an eminently sensible place to stay put for a few weeks. I had never been to Indonesia and I'd heard the food was good, it was relatively inexpensive, and I quite fancied getting into a routine that involved healthy eating and yoga.

As I touched down at Denpasar airport among throngs of Australian backpackers, I realised that Bali was the 100th country that I'd visited. I am not much into making bucket lists or counting where I've been, but it was a question I kept being asked, and one day I sat down with a map and figured it out. Bali was as good a place as any to celebrate half a lifetime on the road, so I was quite looking forward to a couple of days relaxing on the beach with a cocktail or two to get into the swing of things.

That being the case, I was rather disappointed when upon arrival at my little villa in the resort of Canggu, I was informed that the next day was Nyepi, a Balinese public holiday known as the Day of Silence.

Bugger.

Nyepi sees Hindus across the island practise fasting and meditation. Strict restrictions against working, entertainment and even leaving the house are in place. Electricity is typically turned off, and there is no internet or even phone signal. Nyepi is the Balinese New Year, the day when Hindus contemplate what has gone before and cleanse themselves of past sins. The silence and self-imposed exile is supposed to free the island of demons and devils, because when they come out at night to exercise their evil, they find nobody in the streets so they give up and leave, looking elsewhere for their victims. On a spiritual level, it's the equivalent of a reset button where people pray and look forward to a more hopeful future.

Locals don't work, make noise, play music or watch TV, and if you are doing it properly, you aren't even allowed to eat during Nyepi. It's a day where people simply stay at home and meditate. No one is exempt, not even tourists – who are forbidden from leaving their hotels or villas. Bear in mind this was in the days before the COVID pandemic, when all that became a norm . . .

Despite my initial reservations about a potential spoiled holiday, it turned out to be just what the doctor ordered. As I found out, it was rather nice being without the internet or electricity, and the fact that I couldn't leave the house meant that I sat around in silence, reading and thinking. It was actually pleasant that I couldn't do any work, and the fact that I was a prisoner to this cultural phenomenon meant that I felt an unspoken, yet incredibly powerful connection with all the other people who were having the same experience.

For days after, people asked each other how was their Nyepi. Did they feel okay? Did they feel renewed or reborn? I won't go so far as to say that I felt reborn after a day of no WhatsApp, but I could see the appeal of this communal purge. It also gave me time to grasp the value of enforced rest and contemplation.

It was the first time in any culture where I had been effectively 'forced' into joining in a religious practice. Even in strictest Afghanistan and Iran during Ramadan, I had been given sympathetic looks and the sly offering of a loaf of bread under the table. It's not often we are obliged to consider our beliefs under such duress, albeit in the tropical surroundings of a beautiful island where it's not such a drag. For most, it is tough to have to observe another person's customs, or even at times, one's own.

I imagined the uproar if this sort of spiritual incarceration was forced upon the people back home. There would be outrage. I asked the housekeeper, 'What if someone is ill or about to give birth and needs to go to hospital?'

'Of course, for that, we do make an exception for emergencies. But you must understand,' he went on with a smile, 'nobody gets ill or has babies on Nyepi, that would be inconsiderate.'

While I was in Bali, I spent every morning practising my downward dog yoga exercise and ate lentils. There is a sense of satisfaction that comes with gradually building your strength back up and getting fit again, and the bodily enrichment that comes with that; there is something very nourishing about getting into a slow, physical routine where choice is limited.

I had found that was beneficial on my long walking expeditions too. You go to sleep feeling physically exhausted, but deeply satisfied at the end of the day – you wake with the sun, sleep at dusk and eat whatever is presented to you. When there is no phone signal, or distractions from technology, the body will naturally relax into a more natural evolutionary pattern, refreshed and ready to make the most of another day.

I think we can all benefit from a little Nyepi in our lives. It might not go down well if you cut the power to your neighborhood, but maybe try at least a little time in your life where you turn off the devices, stay away from the screens and give yourself the silence to really *think* without the noise. I hope that you enjoy it as much as I did.

The Turning of the Bones

Philosophers have long recommended the ancient method of memento mori to focus the mind on the present. Memento mori means to keep a symbolic reminder of the inevitability of death as a way to encourage people to live while they can, and not to waste precious time on pointless worries. Usually it comes in the form of an emblem – a piece of art, a talisman or photograph. Christianity uses the crucifix, and Tibetan Buddhists used to keep images of skulls.

On the isolated island of Madagascar live a tribe known as the Malagasy, who have an unusual relationship with death. Every five to seven years, they dig up their ancestors. This unusual family reunion is known as Famadihana or The Turning of the Bones ceremony.

Family members carefully remove their loved ones from crypts and burial grounds. They take off the garments and cloth around the bodies. They carefully re-dress the bones in fresh linen before they begin to celebrate and pass around the bones for others to inspect. In their worldview, you haven't left the earth and died until you have completely decomposed. The family members make blessings and offerings and share stories of their deceased. Those who have died are seen as between the living and God, and have some power over the events and activities on earth.

The ceremony is seen as a joyful and happy time. It is more of a family gathering, with a feast and party atmosphere. But in this family reunion, the dead are also invited along. Guests can travel for two days to reach one of the ceremonies, bringing offerings of money and alcohol along with them. The bones are then returned to the tomb before sunset. The ceremonies act as a communication between families and ancestors and a reminder of death. This ceremony and celebration of death is a reminder to those still living to enjoy life and live in the moment while they can.

The only certainty in life is that it is a mortal game. We're all going to die eventually, and so what really matters is what happens in the meantime, and I'd like to think that we have at least some control over that. Being human is all about choice, and how you choose to live is ultimately up to you. Taking control of your own choices is perhaps one of life's greatest challenges, yet when we do, it can be our greatest reward.

Finding meaning

In an age where we seem to be more and more disconnected from our environment it's vitally important that we look after our minds and bodies. There are many ways in which we can do this, through physical fitness, mindfulness and meditation. One of the most useful things that I have learnt on my travels is to consciously foster a sense of empathy with those people that I meet, and it's something that I try to do at home and in my daily interactions too.

Empathy is what fuels connection, and human connection is what brings meaning to our lives. This ability to see things and understand things from someone else's point of view, without judgement, is what gives us purpose and creates a sense of belonging.

In her maiden speech to parliament in 2015, the late Jo Cox MP said, 'We have far more in common than that which divides us.' It is a good message to heed. Some people pray, others fast or read books on enlightenment, and yet more form communities or have children as a way of giving meaning to their lives.

I've visited myriad cultures around the world, from the cannibalistic Aghori monks of India to the polygamous Muslim tribes of Central Asia, and on the face of it they are all very different. Ostensibly, the long-neck Karen women of northern Thailand don't have a great deal in common with the Kuna tribe of southern Panama; nor do the cattle-herding Mundari have much similarity to their Nubian desert-dwelling neighbours of Sudan. The blue-eyed shepherds of Pakistan's Hunza valley couldn't appear more different to the black-skinned Nilotes of northern Uganda, and if you put a Yakutian bear hunter next to a Saudi Arabian mullah, they might struggle to chat.

And yet, wherever I have been in the world, I have discovered that people are more or less after the same thing. Despite surface differences in religion, faith, codes of practice and ethics, generally speaking people just want to have a sense of belonging: to love and be loved.

Trust the universe

It is also important to have a little faith. I don't necessarily mean religion, or spirituality, although the end goal is ultimately the same. Having faith in the universe, or if you will, faith in your own place within it, is the key to acceptance – after all, we're all part of the same spinning rock. Frank Lloyd Wright famously said, 'I believe in God, only I spell it nature.'

We're all in a constant battle with time. Some people worry about the past and get depressed because of bad decisions they might have made. Other people worry about the future and get anxious that it might not pan out the way they hope or expect. A lot of people get stressed about both sometimes (including myself). The thing is, and I know it's easy to say on paper, but both of those things are futile. The past has already gone and the future isn't yet decided, so why worry?

Faith is simply trusting that things will be okay, whatever happens. Faith is letting go of what isn't important and hoping that the best outcome will occur. Faith isn't naïve or lazy or fatalistic. Faith is being courageous, because it takes guts to believe in something that you can't see right in front of you. Faith is confidence in your own ability. You can grow faith with practice and experience by experimenting.

And of course, it's not only about ourselves, we must have faith in the good of other people; most humans are good after all. My last big expedition took me on a journey of over five thousand miles around the Arabian Peninsula through thirteen countries, including Iraq and Yemen and the Empty Quarter desert. I travelled on foot, camel and dhow, through some of the most hostile desert environments, warzones and waters on earth.

It is a region of which many people are afraid. In our collective imagination we hold so much fear about the Middle East, some of which has become distorted and grown and settled in as prejudice. Before I set off, everyone thought I was crazy. I wanted to pitch the project to the television people, but even with four successful documentaries under my belt, nobody would touch the idea.

'It's too dangerous,' they bleated. 'You'll be killed,' they warned. 'We're not paying your ransom,' they complained.

In fact, the only person who didn't think that I'd disappear and never be seen again was my mum, who simply shrugged and said, 'Have a lovely holiday.'

The point is, my journey was perceived by most as being far too dangerous, because they didn't have faith in the people of that part of the world. I'm not saying that I was being naïve or was looking at the people of the Middle East through rose-tinted spectacles, and I'm not saying that the commissioners were necessarily to blame; the media has been distorting the global view of this part of the world for decades and decades. Don't get me wrong, there are parts of the region that are a stinking mess – from hotbeds of terrorism to a deadly and futile civil war. But equally and far more importantly, large parts are not.

I often get asked if I travel armed. The truth is I'm sometimes obliged to take an armed escort or a policeman when travelling through dangerous areas in places like Syria or Iraq, but I never carry a weapon. If you go somewhere with a gun expecting trouble, you'll probably find it.

It's also worth adding that if you go somewhere with certain expectations, and they don't work out as you planned, then you'll be disappointed and unhappy. You'll come away with a negative perception.

Likewise, if you go somewhere thinking the people are bad, that negativity will rub off and you'll be treated poorly. Only if you take a punt will you ever discover if something is possible. What I have learned from my travels is that wherever you go in the world, people tend to look after each other so long as you go in peace, crush your ego and have a bit of faith in them.

So I set off on my journey around the Middle East hoping for the best. And guess what, the best happened (for the most part). I encountered incredible hospitality and warmth in the least likely places. In the midst of terrible poverty and tragic conflict, I encountered a kindness that I wouldn't have thought possible. I wanted to experience the very best of the Middle East, and I got exactly what I was looking for.

In Iraq, I was taken in by heavily armed militia forces and shown wonderful respect by people who had not so long ago been trying to kill British soldiers. In Yemen, I was looked after by refugees and rebels with nothing of material worth to their name, and in Jordan I spent weeks with the Bedouin in the simplicity of the desert.

In Syria, I was taken in by a lady whose son was a soldier in Assad's army and had been killed by rebel fighters a couple of years previously. She invited me into her bullet-strafed apartment on the front line in Homs and insisted I stay in her son's bedroom, all this in the knowledge that 'her side' was technically the 'enemy'. Never once did I feel endangered by the people who had taken me in, but often I felt incredibly grateful to have met such generous and humble people.

Heroes of our own journey

Travel has long been romanticised and portrayed as a challenge or quest. This is nothing new. Homer's *Odyssey* was the first in a very long line of heroic depictions of travellers going off in search of something. In these stories, our hero must leave behind the world of the familiar and venture into an alien world full of dangers and obstacles. He must overcome them in a series of tests, before meeting his ultimate challenge in whatever form that may come.

Whether you're Saint George needing to slay a dragon, or Frodo Baggins and you must throw the ring into the volcano of Mordor, the hero always has to come face to face with his greatest fear, which of course he does before winning the battle, the girl or whatever the prize may be, before going home a better person to share his spoils with his countrymen.

Think of any Hollywood movie script, Disney film, or the plot of any adventure novel, and they're all basically the same. There's a reason that Paolo Coelho's *The Alchemist* sold 65 million copies. It is utterly predictable with a basic plot that is so formulaic, it is almost as if you know exactly what's coming next. The reason being that you *do know* what is coming next – you've read and watched it a hundred times, even if you didn't realise it. It's called the monomyth, or the twelve phases of the hero's journey, and forms the basis of every story ever told. There isn't enough space to go into the detail here, but Google it, and you'll never watch a film in the same way again.

We have become so enamoured with the concept that travel gives us the opportunity for adventure and glory, that we see ourselves as the hero in our own stories. That's what adventure is all about – living out a fantasy in an alien realm. We get to experience our childhood dreams. Even the most placid beach holiday is an opportunity to go away, try a new cocktail, hear a little of a new language and go home to boast about how tough the airport transfer was.

For those who travel independently and avoid the crowds, this takes us one step further into the realms of adventure. We can play out a role, and be whoever we want to be – especially if we travel alone. There's no one to tell you what to do, and who to be. Strangers never knew the 'you' back home, and it gives anyone the opportunity to start again, or at the very least try out a new way of being, away from the constraints and expectations of home.

But there is a danger in thinking that travelling is the solution to all our problems. Without a focus on empathy and faith, it won't bring us contentment or fulfilment. The point of the stories we tell, to and about ourselves and other people, is that they have a narrative, an overarching meaning that takes us to an end point, having learned something along the way. It's not enough to travel the world; we must do so in a spirit of openness, empathy and good faith, or we are only moving our discontent from one place to another.

Underlying every Hero's Journey narrative is a question of character. Ultimately, the story takes the hero from a situation of relative safety, where their character flaws hold them back but don't get directly tested, to one where they find themselves in mortal peril. At this point, every character faces a choice. They can identify whatever it was that was holding them back, overcome it and save the world or themselves. This is a story we recognise as one with a happy ending – the ancient Greeks called this 'comedy', though the word means something different nowadays.

But there are also tragedies, where the hero (or better, the protagonist) doesn't recognise or admit this character flaw. They persist with whatever vice it was that held them back in the beginning of the story, and this leads inexorably to their downfall.

We can all be the hero of our own journey, but what kind of journey this will be is a choice that lies with us. It ties back to self-knowledge, where we began this particular journey, and requires us to explore the world with faith, empathy, gratitude and ultimately courage. Be the master of your own destiny. You can do this with both confidence and humility, with compassion, bravery and flair all at the same time, without the need for one-upmanship, false modesty or deceit. Ultimately that's the job of the modern explorer: to master oneself and to share one's learnings for the benefit of others.

Share Your Findings

Jacques-Yves Cousteau is the father of marine exploration. His pioneering aquatic discoveries in the 1940s led to the development of modern diving techniques and underwater filming equipment that enabled a new understanding of the world's oceans.

Born in France in 1910, he was a naval officer who assisted the allies in the Second World War, conducting anti-espionage operations against the Italians. After the war, he led teams of marine scientists to push the boundaries of breathing apparatus, so that divers could spend more time underwater and conduct marine surveys and archaeological excavations around the world. He co-invented the aqualung, advanced underwater photography, discovered oil beneath the ocean floor in the Persian Gulf and built undersea stations and small submarines for oceanographic research. He even tried to build an underwater city.

He soon became famous for his explorations and daring discoveries. He was involved in more than 120 television documentaries and contributed to some eighty books, receiving countless medals and accolades in the process.

More importantly, Cousteau was an ardent conservationist and a leader in the movement to protect the world's oceans, and his legacy is a huge body of work that educated an entire generation about the global need to address climate change – inspiring millions of people to take environmentalism seriously.

He used to describe himself as a humble oceanographic technician, but he was no shy boffin. He redefined the notion of exploration in the twentieth century, and demonstrated that an individual could indeed leave a lasting, positive change by sharing his findings with others.

Jacques Cousteau summed up his solid self-confidence and aversion to false modesty rather well: 'When one man, for whatever reason, has the opportunity to lead an extraordinary life, he has no right to keep it to himself.'

Be grateful to be alive

In 2015, I was in Nepal as part of a journey to walk the length of the Himalayas, some 2,000 miles from the Wakhan corridor in Afghanistan to the mountainous kingdom of Bhutan. I was with my guide, Binod, and my brother, Pete, who had taken some valuable holiday from his job in the UK and flown out to join me for a few weeks. It had been a tricky time; the monsoon had struck with a vengeance making many of the roads impassable, or at the very least slippery and dangerous. What is more, the Maoists were on strike, which meant that the majority of restaurants and tea houses, where we might be able to eat or sleep, were closed.

We were trekking in the rain, day in day out, and it was pretty demoralising. One evening we made it to a tiny remote village high in the mountains and Binod set about trying to find us a place to stay. It was getting late and we were soaked through, but no one was able to house us and there was no place for us to camp. Due to the strike, all driving was banned, but he managed to persuade a taxi to take us at dusk up to the nearby town of Musikot, where we would be able to find somewhere safe and dry to sleep.

It wasn't the most reassuring thought; I knew the roads in the mountains were lethal and many of the drivers seemed to be verging on suicidal. I had witnessed accidents and the wet weather was going to make it even more risky, but it was getting dark and it was not safe to walk any further in the darkness. I tried to ignore my nerves as we clambered into the battered 4x4, and I noticed that like most cars in that part of the world there were no seatbelts.

So we drove into the pitch black, spluttering and winding up the narrow roads with thick forest on either side of us. We had not gone far and I was beginning to relax, lulled into a false sense of security as we crested the top of the mountain pass. Suddenly I felt the car lurch and then fly forwards. I immediately recognised that the brake cable had snapped.

The driver was panicked and hadn't managed to get down through the gears quickly enough to slow us down, or to steer us into the cliff. I remember yelling at him to hit the wall, begging him to drive into the cliff. While that might sound mad and totally counterintuitive, in the mountains it's not. The alternative, on the other side of the road, was much, much worse. I knew that at some stage we'd have to come off the road, and that's exactly what happened.

As we gathered speed, I steeled myself.

'Hit the wall!' I shouted, 'Turn the wheel right and hit the wall!'

I begged in vain as I felt the car lurch out of control. I gripped at the dashboard and instantly froze, not daring to even look at the man supposedly in control to my right. He was too busy battling with the gears to see the logic in my cry. We were now rocketing straight down the road and all I could see were flashes of rock and low-lying branches as the headlights flashed into what lay before us. If only he had turned into the wall when I first shouted, we'd have crashed, but at least we'd all have survived unscathed.

That was no longer an option. We'd missed the window of opportunity and as we flew aimlessly in the darkness of the night, my body crippled under the terror of what could only happen next. The car jerked sideways as the front tyre clipped an invisible drainage ditch, the impact causing the vehicle to veer left until it was almost on two wheels, the momentum careering us faster and closer to the inevitable; plunging straight off the edge of a vertical cliff, hundreds of feet into a jungle ravine in the dead of night.

The next thing I can clearly recall was thinking the word 'No'. It echoed through my body. I didn't want it to end like this and certainly not with my brother and Binod in the car too. They couldn't die.

We went over, we went down, and somehow, we lived. I remember coming to an abrupt stop; I was upside down and with searing pain coursing through my upper body. That was reassuring at least, because it meant I was alive. As I realised this, my survival instinct kicked in. I yelled for Pete and Binod, desperately calling out their names to see if they were there. I remember willing Pete to respond; I was bellowing for help into the darkness. I couldn't focus. I was paralysed by dread at the thought of my brother being gone, and I wanted the nightmare to be over. I used all my energy to yell into the night.

'Pete, are you alive?'

'Lev!' Pete shouted. 'I'm here.'

I've never been so glad in all my life to hear someone's voice. The relief gave me renewed energy. Miraculously, Pete was in better shape than I was, with the fewest injuries, and he was able to find a torch in the car and he started flashing it into the dark. Suddenly Pete spotted lights, there was a chance of hope.

I was hallucinating by this point, determined that we weren't really alive, and that this was hell. I tried to convince Pete that there was no use, they were too far away and they would never find us; we were going to stay in that valley forever. Thankfully, Pete had the presence of mind to ignore my pain-induced ramblings and he screamed and screamed in the direction of their lights. They must have heard the crash or my yells of pain, or seen the lights. Either way, after a while – I couldn't tell you how long – dozens of villagers appeared.

Only then did I believe that we had been saved. I have a blurry recollection of being scooped up on a very makeshift stretcher and dragged out of the jungle. I remember thinking about my Paras training, where we'd have to learn how to carry the weight of an injured man off a battlefield, and here were these diminutive Nepali men, doing it for real – through dense jungle and crossing streams up to their waists. It was agony, bumping and crashing through the thick forest, and they dropped me more than once. But it didn't matter. We had been rescued.

I came round a day or so later, hazy from the painkillers, to find myself in a filthy, dirty, ramshackle clinic high in the mountains. We were nursed here for three days, because the monsoon and the heavy rains meant that it was impossible to be evacuated either by road, due to landslides, or by helicopter, due to the low visibility. It was only a week later that I was able to get surgery to fix my broken bones and fully comprehend what had happened.

Of course, it was a disaster. I had broken my arm badly and was unlikely ever to get full and proper use of my shoulder again; the expedition had ground to a halt and my guide Binod, as well as my brother, had both sustained physical and emotional injuries that might have untold consequences. There were times as I lay in agony, with my arm twisted and shattered, when I contemplated giving it all up, the world of exploring and expeditions. I questioned my own sanity; what on earth was I doing taking these risks anyway?

I would later learn that we had rolled and bounced almost 200 feet down the side of a cliff into the valley below. I was shocked into self doubt and mortal fear. What was the point of it all? I thought about packing it all in and getting a regular 9–5 job. It was that serious, but then I was reminded of a quote by J.R.R. Tolkien: 'Faithless is he that says farewell when the road darkens.'

I knew deep down that I couldn't just give up, no matter how hard it was to contemplate carrying on. I counted my blessings instead; I knew I was extremely fortunate to be alive. Looking back now, this was the clearest moment in my life where having a sense of hope for the future was essential to my inward happiness. That could only be engendered by positivity towards myself and my own worth. We can choose our own destiny, in effect, if only we have the courage to take a leap of faith. Even in the most trying of circumstances, hope can prevail, and that for me has been one of the most astounding discoveries on any of my travels.

So I persevered (albeit accompanied by a forgivable and deep-seated fear of travelling in the back of cars on mountain roads, which I still cannot shake) and I journeyed on. After a few weeks off to let my arm heal, I returned to Nepal to continue the expedition.

Skip forward three and a half years to 2019 and I am back in Nepal. I have arranged for Pete, Binod and I to return to the site of the crash. We go by helicopter this time, instead of driving, and as we soar over the lush foothills of the Himalayas, I start to contemplate properly what is happening.

What is the point of this trip? What am I trying to achieve? I know it was hard for both Pete and Binod to get to grips with the accident. I can only imagine how terrifying it must have been for Pete, as the one who was the least injured; he must have felt a huge responsibility to get us out of there. He then had to watch us both drugged up and out of it in that clinic, while he had to go through the stress of trying to get us airlifted out.

What about me? I have had no nightmares or flashbacks about the accident, which might be considered a bit odd. But trauma can present itself in strange ways. I think that night's experience came for me in other ways. I have always been restless, but for a long time after I became even more so. I would go off on long expeditions, spending more and more time away from friends and family, and burying my head in my work. I was holding onto a lot of guilt, I resented myself for putting my brother and friends in mortal danger and of course my poor family who I knew must worry about me every day.

As we swoop down to land on the remote, dusty airstrip, I try to stop overthinking it all. We are nearly here now and I want to take in the experience for what it is; I will never come back here again. We clamber out of the helicopter into the dust and set off towards the crash site, trailed by a troupe of children and adults curious to see what we're up to. We traipse along the road, in a rather sombre and reflective silence, until on rounding a corner, we see the car.

It is mangled, completely destroyed, sitting there rotting on the side of the road, unceremonious. We are quiet, filled with disbelief that we are still here. We stare at the remains of the crumbling 4x4 that nearly cut our lives short, but also saved them. Our silence is punctuated by a group of nearby villagers, as quite a crowd has gathered, clearly wondering why we are paying homage to a rusting hulk of metal. Suddenly, looking around at the curious, friendly faces, I feel a warm rush of gratitude. Any negativity I feel about the whole affair is dissipated.

Standing there that day, I realised there was no use pointing fingers of blame at anyone – even myself. I felt a huge amount of gratitude to the people who had saved my life. How had they found us and why had they come out to look for us? My mind raced with alternate endings. What if they hadn't heard us – or if they had heard our cries and ignored us?

I wondered for a second what would happen in other parts of the world. Here in Nepal I had been looked after as a brother on many occasions, fed to bursting and given a place to sleep by perfect strangers. Binod himself had done that for me when I first met him as a young traveller all those years before, and looking into his eyes now, I saw nothing but humble compassion.

I was grateful too for everything that I've had the chance to do since then. I think that accident changed me for the better in so many ways. It gave me a newfound respect for my life and a deep sense of gratitude that I had never felt before; it also gave me a fortitude that I'd not had either. After the accident I could have given up, but I would never have forgiven myself. I had two choices; I could admit defeat and go home, or I could see it as a blessing in disguise and crack on. That was entirely up to me. Everything in life is a choice, including how we react to the things that happen to us. That even goes for our emotions: we can choose to be happy as much as we can choose to be sad.

Standing there that day, staring at the wreck of the car, I also felt a huge amount of gratitude towards my brother, not only for saving my life, but for his friendship. I am extremely lucky to be alive. It's a funny thing to say that and for it to be factually correct, when usually it's such a throwaway line, but I seriously am. It took me falling off a 200-foot cliff to really appreciate what that truly means.

Not all of our challenges will involve climbing mountains, or crossing deserts. A lot of our greatest battles are with our mind, and by returning to the crash with the people I loved, I felt the same flood of emotions as I had at the end of some of my most arduous explorations.

More often that not our own Everest is resting within us, simply waiting to be conquered.

Nims Purja

Nirmal Purja, or Nims, as he goes by, grew up in a small village in the lowlands of Nepal. At eighteen, he passed the gruelling selection process to join the Gurkhas in the British Army. Nims went on to serve in the Special Forces, but in 2019, after sixteen years of service, he dedicated himself to a new goal – a world record climbing attempt, which he named Project Possible.

Nims's mission was to summit the fourteen highest mountains on the planet, all of which are over 8,000 metres tall in the Himalayas. The last person to succeed took almost eight years, but Nims planned to pull it off in just seven months. Nims only came to climbing in his late twenties, when he got fed up with telling people that he had never seen Everest – his home village was miles away from the region and no more than 500 metres above sea level.

So, determined to clap eyes on Everest, he decided to trek to base camp and it was while winding his way up the narrow pathways that he saw the distinctive shape of a mountain called Ama Dablam. At 6,812 metres, it is certainly no beginner's climb, but Nims persuaded his guide to let him do it – learning how to use crampons in only a few days – and the pair successfully reached the peak.

Project Possible was another beast altogether. Above 8,000 metres, in what is known as the Death Zone, your body starts to shut down. With no oxygen you are slowed to a snail's pace, expending no spare energy and focusing overwhelmingly on keeping the extremities warm. It takes incredible mental fortitude to keep on going up, instead of turning around and going down. Physical risks aside, expeditions like this are phenomenally pricey; faced by a shortfall of funding, Nims left his job, forgoing his army pension, and remortgaged his house.

Nims achieved his goal of climbing the world's fourteen tallest peaks in the record time of six months and six days. In doing so, he bagged a further six world records along the way. If that wasn't incredible enough, Nims risked not only his record attempts but also his own life on *multiple occasions, to aid in the rescue missions of other climbers. That is the sign of a real hero. Even with all those things at stake, he put the lives of others ahead of his own goals.*

Nims's attitude is remarkable. His positive mindset combined with a steely determination allowed him to achieve the impossible, and yet despite it all he remained humble. Nims is a man who embodies the Art of Exploration; keeping the destination in sight, but always remembering to enjoy the journey.

Happiness or fulfilment?

Learning and understanding what makes us happy is no easy feat. If we can observe when we are expressing ourselves most purely, contentedly, and being honest, then we are a long way towards satisfaction. But there is no magic recipe for contentment, and it is hard to assess, because hindsight can alter our perception significantly. On my walking expeditions, I have covered somewhere in the region of ten thousand miles on foot. I have often looked back and pondered how much of that time spent plodding I was actually happy.

Even now it's hard to judge, because we tend to forget the bad bits, and we are only reminded on our Facebook memories of the moments we shared those years ago, which were inevitably the good ones. I do recall that there were plenty of low times, and I've still got the scars to prove it, but they have given me food for thought as to what keeps me going during the toughest times. I now realise how much I appreciate companionship, and it is important to me that I share these journeys with my friends and loved ones. As Mark Twain said, 'to get the full value of joy you must have somebody to divide it with.'

I have also learnt the crucial difference between happiness and fulfilment: one is fleeting, but the other is long-lasting. Happiness is euphoric and makes your heart race, while fulfilment is serene and makes your heart sing. Casting off expectation is the key to fulfilment; it is about peace, not quick hits or immediate fixes. I would say that happiness is a byproduct of fulfilment.

One-off events or incidents can make you feel happy, but

fulfilment is deeper; it's about finding your purpose and a sense of meaning. I am unlikely to come out of a meeting and say, that went well, I feel really fulfilled; but I might get into bed at night thinking, that was a good day, I feel really fulfilled.

Happiness is also often artificial, and fulfilment is natural. Fulfilment is about achievement and about satisfaction; something bigger that you can achieve through time and effort, whilst happiness is something that you might feel along the way.

Think of happiness as short, sharp bursts of energy and excitement to keep you going, dopamine and endorphins flooding through your body; but this is temporary. We can seldom call upon the feeling of happiness from something that happened to us a few years ago. It is intense, but it fades.

Fulfilment on the other hand is far more enduring, far deeper and more all-encompassing. Happiness is a mood, while fulfilment is a life goal. It requires a lot more dedication, too. In my experience, it requires two things if you want to achieve it.

Purpose and compassion. Firstly, find out what it is that drives you, discover your higher calling and believe in it. Stick at it through the tough times. It won't always be easy, or fun, but it will be worth it. By following your dreams there is a good chance you will discover true fulfilment, because you are being your true self.

The second requirement is compassion, for it is only by letting go of our egos and giving of ourselves that we can truly feel fulfilment. Compassion is born out of empathy and it is the human emotion that instils peace of mind, and helps us in sticking up for and protecting those in suffering. A compassionate person is able to use their empathy to be accepting of themselves, and accepting of others.

The Dalai Lama says that the more compassionate our mind, the better it will function. The opposite of this is letting in fear and anger, and as we all know, that never leads to anything good. And he is right, compassion acts as a buffer against stress and anxiety; it gives us confidence in our own abilities and imbues us with an inner strength, as well as keeping us calm. As His Holiness once said to me, in the glistening courtyard of his Himalayan retreat, 'Helping others is the best way to help yourself, the best way to promote your own happiness. It is you, yourself, who will receive the benefit.'

Who knows, maybe there is no such thing as a truly selfless act, and that all charity is done to serve yourself in some way. Perhaps this is true, but does it really matter if you are doing a kind deed? Whatever the motivation, true exploration is to know that you have had a positive impact on the world around you; that you have done more good than harm. When you adopt this attitude and accept that true discovery is inside us, then the explorer within you will never tire, never fade and never give up.

The Art of Exploration is simple really. It is in realising that world is a far better place than others would have you believe. So go out and see it with your own eyes and rediscover your own childlike sense of wonder, because it is in that joy that you will find true happiness. While you are on the path to discovery, tread lightly and leave the world a better place than you found it. Inspire and help others to achieve their dreams. Judge people less and focus on improving yourself more.

We can all do better. Live a life that you are proud of and remember that it is never too late to start over again. Face your fears and have the courage to choose the hard path; by embracing the unknown, the universe rewards you with hidden treasures. Magic is everywhere, if only you will open your eyes to see it.

The essence of the art of exploration is already inside you.

Explore, Dream, Discover.

The author in Afghanistan, 2008

CIVILIZATION, SOCIETY AND RELIGION:

GROUP PSYCHOLOGY, CIVILIZATION AND ITS DISCONTENTS AND OTHER WORKS

Sigmund Freud

•

Translated from the German
under the general editorship of James Strachey

The present volume
edited by Albert Dickson

Penguin Books Ltd, Harmondsworth, Middlesex, England
Viking Penguin Inc., 40 West 23rd Street, New York, New York 10010, U.S.A.
Penguin Books Australia Ltd, Ringwood, Victoria, Australia
Penguin Books Canada Ltd, 2801 John Street, Markham, Ontario, Canada L3R 1B4
Penguin Books (N.Z.) Ltd, 182–190 Wairau Road, Auckland 10, New Zealand

Group Psychology,
Civilization and its Discontents
and other works

Present English translations first published in *The Standard Edition of the Complete
Psychological Works of Sigmund Freud* by the Hogarth Press and the Institute of
Psycho-Analysis, London, as follows:

' "Civilized" Sexual Morality and Modern Nervous Illness', Volume IX
(1959); 'Thoughts for the Times on War and Death', Volume XIV (1957);
Group Psychology and the Analysis of the Ego, Volume XVIII (1955); *The
Future of an Illusion, Civilization and its Discontents*, Volume XXI (1961);
Why War?, Volume XXII (1964).

'Sigmund Freud: A Sketch of his Life and Ideas' first published in *Two Short
Accounts of Psycho-Analysis* in Pelican Books 1962

This collection, *Civilization, Society and Religion*, first published in Pelican Books 1985
Reprinted 1985, 1987

Translation and Editorial Matter copyright © Angela Richards and
The Institute of Psycho-Analysis, 1955, 1957, 1959, 1961, 1962, 1964

Additional Editorial Matter copyright © Angela Richards, 1985
All rights reserved

Grateful acknowledgement is made to the Hebrew University of Jerusalem
for permission to reprint Einstein's letter on pages 345–8

Made and printed in Great Britain by
Richard Clay Ltd, Bungay, Suffolk
Filmset in Monophoto Bembo

Except in the United States of America,
this book is sold subject to the condition
that it shall not, by way of trade or otherwise,
be lent, re-sold, hired out, or otherwise circulated
without the publisher's prior consent in any form of
binding or cover other than that in which it is
published and without a similar condition
including this condition being imposed
on the subsequent purchaser

CONTENTS

VOLUME 12
CIVILIZATION, SOCIETY AND RELIGION

CONTENTS

INTRODUCTION TO THE PELICAN
FREUD LIBRARY

The Pelican Freud Library is intended to meet the needs of the
general reader by providing all Freud's major writings in translation together with an appropriate linking commentary. It is
the first time that such an edition has been produced in paperback in the English language. It does not supplant *The Standard
Edition of the Complete Psychological Works of Sigmund Freud*,
translated from the German under the general editorship of
James Strachey in collaboration with Anna Freud, assisted by
Alix Strachey and Alan Tyson, editorial assistant Angela Richards (Hogarth Press, 24 volumes, 1953–74). The *Standard Edition*
remains the fullest and most authoritative collection published
in any language. It does, however, provide a large enough
selection to meet the requirements of all but the most specialist
reader – in particular it aims to cater for students of sociology,
anthropology, criminology, medicine, aesthetics and education, all of them fields in which Freud's ideas have established
their relevance.

The texts are reprinted unabridged, with corrections, from
the *Standard Edition*. The editorial commentary – introductions,
footnotes, internal cross-references, bibliographies and indexes
– is also based upon the *Standard Edition*, but it has been abridged
and where necessary adapted to suit the less specialized scope
and purposes of the *Pelican Freud Library*. Some corrections have
been made and some new material added.

Selection of Material

This is not a complete edition of Freud's psychological works
– still less of his works as a whole, which included important

contributions to neurology and neuropathology dating from the early part of his professional life. Of the psychological writings, virtually all the major works have been included. The arrangement is by subject-matter, so that the main contributions to any particular theme will be found in one volume. Within each volume the works are, for the main part, in chronological sequence. The aim has been to cover the whole field of Freud's observations and his theory of psychoanalysis: that is to say, in the first place, the structure and dynamics of human mental activity; secondly, psychopathology and the mechanism of mental disorder; and thirdly, the application of psychoanalytic theory to wider spheres than the disorders of individuals which Freud originally, and indeed for the greater part of his life, investigated – to the psychology of groups, to social institutions and to religion, art and literature.

In his 'Sigmund Freud: A Sketch of his Life and Ideas' (p. 11 ff. below), James Strachey includes an account of Freud's discoveries as well as defining his principal theories and tracing their development.

Writings excluded from the Edition

The works that have been excluded are: (1) The neurological writings and most of those very early works from the period before the idea of psychoanalysis had taken form. (2) Writings on the actual technique of treatment. These were written specifically for practitioners of psychoanalysis and for analysts in training and their interest is correspondingly specialized. Freud never in fact produced a complete text on psychoanalytic treatment and the papers on technique only deal with selected points of difficulty or theoretical interest. (3) Writings which cover the same ground as other major works which have been included; for example, since the *Library* includes the *Introductory Lectures on Psychoanalysis* and the *New Lectures*, it was decided to leave out several of the shorter expository works in which Freud surveys the whole subject. Similarly, because the *Interpretation of Dreams* is included, the shorter writings on this topic have been omitted. (4) Freud's private correspondence, much of which has now been published in translation.[1] This is not to imply that such letters are without interest or importance though they have not yet received full critical treatment. (5) The numerous short writings such as reviews of books, prefaces to other authors' works, obituary notices and little *pièces d'occasion* – all of which lose interest to a large extent when separated from the books or occasions to which they refer and which would often demand long editorial explanations to make them comprehensible.

All of these excluded writings (with the exception of the works on neurology and the private letters) can be found in the *Standard Edition*.

Editorial Commentary

The bibliographical information, included at the beginning of the Editor's Note or Introduction to each work, gives the title of the German (or other) original, the date and place of its first publication and the position, where applicable, of the work in Freud's *Gesammelte Werke*, the most complete edition at present available of the works in German (published by S. Fischer Verlag, Frankfurt am Main). Details of the first translation of each work into English are also included, together with the *Standard Edition* reference. Other editions are listed only if they contain significant changes. (Full details of all German editions published in Freud's lifetime and of all English editions prior to the *Standard Edition* are included in the *Standard Edition*.)

The date of original publication of each work has been added to the half-title page, with the date of composition included in square brackets wherever it is different from the former date.

Further background information is given in introductory notes and in footnotes to the text. Apart from dealing with the time and circumstances of composition, these notes aim to make it possible to follow the inception and development

1. [See the list, p. 23 *n*. below, and the details in the Bibliography, p. 363 ff.]

of important psychoanalytic concepts by means of systematic cross-references. Most of these references are to other works included in the *Pelican Freud Library*. A secondary purpose is to date additions and alterations made by Freud in successive revisions of the text and in certain cases to provide the earlier versions. No attempt has been made to do this as comprehensively as in the *Standard Edition*, but variants are given whenever they indicate a definite change of view. Square brackets are used throughout to distinguish editorial additions from Freud's text and his own footnotes.

It will be clear from this account that an overwhelming debt is due to the late James Strachey, the general editor and chief translator of the *Standard Edition*. He indeed was mainly responsible for the idea of a *Pelican Freud Library*, and for the original plan of contents. Miss Anna Freud and Mrs Alix Strachey, both now deceased, gave advice of the greatest value. The late Mr Ernst Freud and the Publications Committee of the Institute of Psycho-Analysis also helped in the preparations for this edition.

SIGMUND FREUD

A SKETCH OF HIS LIFE AND IDEAS

SIGMUND FREUD was born on 6 May 1856 in Freiberg, a small town in Moravia, which was at that time a part of Austria-Hungary. In an external sense the eighty-three years of his life were on the whole uneventful and call for no lengthy history.

He came of a middle-class Jewish family and was the eldest child of his father's second wife. His position in the family was a little unusual, for there were already two grown-up sons by his father's first wife. These were more than twenty years older than he was and one of them was already married, with a little boy; so that Freud was in fact born an uncle. This nephew played at least as important a part in his very earliest years as his own younger brothers and sisters, of whom seven were born after him.

His father was a wool-merchant and soon after Freud's birth found himself in increasing commercial difficulties. He therefore decided, when Freud was just three years old, to leave Freiberg, and a year later the whole family settled in Vienna, with the exception of the two elder half-brothers and their children, who established themselves instead in Manchester. At more than one stage in his life Freud played with the idea of joining them in England, but nothing was to come of this for nearly eighty years.

In Vienna during the whole of Freud's childhood the family lived in the most straitened conditions; but it is much to his father's credit that he gave invariable priority to the charge of Freud's education, for the boy was obviously intelligent and was a hard worker as well. The result was that he won a place in the 'Gymnasium' at the early age of nine, and for the last six of the eight years he spent at the school he was regularly top of his class. When at the age of seventeen he passed out of school his career was still undecided; his education so far had been of the most general kind, and, though he seemed in any case destined for the University, several faculties lay open to him.

Freud insisted more than once that at no time in his life did he feel 'any particular predilection for the career of a doctor. I was moved, rather,' he says, 'by a sort of curiosity, which was, however, directed more towards human concerns than towards natural objects.'[1] Elsewhere he writes: 'I have no knowledge of having had any craving in my early childhood to help suffering humanity ... In my youth I felt an over-powering need to understand something of the riddles of the world in which we live and perhaps even to contribute something to their solution.'[2] And in yet another passage in which he was discussing the sociological studies of his last years: 'My interest, after making a lifelong *détour* through the natural sciences, medicine, and psychotherapy, returned to the cultural problems which had fascinated me long before, when I was a youth scarcely old enough for thinking.'[3]

What immediately determined Freud's choice of a scientific career was, so he tells us, being present just when he was leaving school at a public reading of an extremely flowery essay on 'Nature', attributed (wrongly, it seems) to Goethe. But if it was to be science, practical considerations narrowed the choice to medicine. And it was as a medical student that Freud enrolled himself at the University in the autumn of 1873 at the age of seventeen. Even so, however, he was in no hurry to obtain a medical degree. For his first year or two he attended lectures on a variety of subjects, but gradually concentrated first on biology and then on physiology. His very first piece of research was in his third year at the University, when he was deputed by the Professor of Comparative Anatomy to investigate a detail in the anatomy of the eel, which involved the dissection

1. [*An Autobiographical Study* (1925*d*), near the opening of the work.]
2. ['Postscript to *The Question of Lay Analysis*' (1927*a*).]
3. ['Postscript (1935) to *An Autobiographical Study*' (1935*a*).]

of some four hundred specimens. Soon afterwards he entered the Physiological Laboratory under Brücke, and worked there happily for six years. It was no doubt from him that he acquired the main outlines of his attitude to physical science in general. During these years Freud worked chiefly on the anatomy of the central nervous system and was already beginning to produce publications. But it was becoming obvious that no livelihood which would be sufficient to meet the needs of the large family at home was to be picked up from these laboratory studies. So at last, in 1881, he decided to take his medical degree, and a year later, most unwillingly, gave up his position under Brücke and began work in the Vienna General Hospital.

What finally determined this change in his life was something more urgent than family considerations: in June 1882 he became engaged to be married, and thenceforward all his efforts were directed towards making marriage possible. His fiancée, Martha Bernays, came of a well-known Jewish family in Hamburg, and though for the moment she was living in Vienna she was very soon obliged to return to her remote North-German home. During the four years that followed, it was only for brief visits that he could have glimpses of her, and the two lovers had to content themselves with an almost daily interchange of letters. Freud now set himself to establishing a position and a reputation in the medical world. He worked in various departments of the hospital, but soon came to concentrate on neuroanatomy and neuropathology. During this period, too, he published the first inquiry into the possible medical uses of cocaine; and it was this that suggested to Koller the drug's employment as a local anaesthetic. He soon formed two immediate plans: one of these was to obtain an appointment as *Privatdozent*, a post not unlike that of a university lecturer in England, the other was to gain a travelling bursary which would enable him to spend some time in Paris, where the reigning figure was the great Charcot. Both of these aims, if they were realized, would, he felt, bring him real advantages, and in 1885, after a hard struggle, he achieved them both.

The months which Freud spent under Charcot at the Salpêtrière (the famous Paris hospital for nervous diseases) brought another change in the course of his life and this time a revolutionary one. So far his work had been concerned entirely with physical science and he was still carrying out histological studies on the brain while he was in Paris. Charcot's interests were at that period concentrated mainly on hysteria and hypnotism. In the world from which Freud came these subjects were regarded as barely respectable, but he became absorbed in them, and, though Charcot himself looked at them purely as branches of neuropathology, for Freud they meant the first beginnings of the investigation of the mind.

On his return to Vienna in the spring of 1886 Freud set up in private practice as a consultant in nervous diseases, and his long-delayed marriage followed soon afterwards. He did not, however, at once abandon all his neuropathological work: for several more years he studied in particular the cerebral palsies of children, on which he became a leading authority. At this period, too, he produced an important monograph on aphasia. But he was becoming more and more engaged in the treatment of the neuroses. After experimenting in vain with electrotherapy, he turned to hypnotic suggestion, and in 1888 visited Nancy to learn the technique used with such apparent success there by Liébeault and Bernheim. This still proved unsatisfactory and he was driven to yet another line of approach. He knew that a friend of his, Dr Josef Breuer, a Vienna consultant considerably his senior, had some ten years earlier cured a girl suffering from hysteria by a quite new procedure. He now persuaded Breuer to take up the method once more, and he himself applied it to several fresh cases with promising results. The method was based on the assumption that hysteria was the product of a psychical trauma which had been forgotten by the patient; and the treatment consisted in inducing her in a hypnotic state to recall the forgotten trauma to the accompaniment of appropriate emotions. Before very long Freud began to make changes both in the procedure and in the underlying theory; this led eventually to a breach with Breuer, and to the ultimate development by Freud of the whole system of ideas to which he soon gave the name of psychoanalysis.

From this moment onwards – from 1895, perhaps – to the very end of his life, the whole of Freud's intellectual existence revolved around this development, its far-reaching implications, and its theoretical and practical repercussions. It would, of course, be impossible to give in a few sentences any consecutive account of Freud's discoveries and ideas, but an attempt will be made presently to indicate in a disconnected fashion some of the main changes he has brought about in our habits of thought. Meanwhile we may continue to follow the course of his external life.

His domestic existence in Vienna was essentially devoid of episode: his home and his consulting rooms were in the same house from 1891 till his departure for London forty-seven years later. His happy marriage and his growing family – three sons and three daughters – provided a solid counterweight to the difficulties which, to begin with at least, surrounded his professional career. It was not only the nature of his discoveries that created prejudice against him in medical circles; just as great, perhaps, was the effect of the intense anti-semitic feeling which dominated the official world of Vienna: his appointment to a university professorship was constantly held back by political influence.

One particular feature of these early years calls for mention on account of its consequences. This was Freud's friendship with Wilhelm Fliess, a brilliant but unbalanced Berlin physician, who specialized in the ear and throat, but whose wider interests extended over human biology and the effects of periodic phenomena in vital processes. For fifteen years, from 1887 to 1902, Freud corresponded with him regularly, reported the development of his ideas, forwarded him long drafts outlining his future writings, and, most important of all, sent him an essay of some forty thousand words which has been given the name of a 'Project for a Scientific Psychology'. This essay was composed in 1895, at what might be described as the watershed of Freud's career, when he was reluctantly moving from physiology to psychology; it is an attempt to state the facts of psychology in purely neurological terms. This paper and all the rest of Freud's communications to Fliess have, by a lucky chance, survived: they throw a fascinating light on the development of Freud's ideas and show how much of the later findings of psychoanalysis were already present in his mind at this early stage.

Apart from his relations with Fliess, Freud had little outside support to begin with. He gradually gathered a few pupils round him in Vienna, but it was only after some ten years, in about 1906, that a change was inaugurated by the adhesion of a number of Swiss psychiatrists to his views. Chief among these were Bleuler, the head of the Zurich mental hospital, and his assistant Jung. This proved to be the beginning of the first spread of psychoanalysis. An international meeting of psycho-analysts gathered at Salzburg in 1908, and in 1909 Freud and Jung were invited to give a number of lectures in the United States. Freud's writings began to be translated into many languages, and groups of practising analysts sprang up all over the world. But the progress of psychoanalysis was not without its set-backs: the currents which its subject-matter stirred up in the mind ran too deep for its easy acceptance. In 1911 one of Freud's prominent Viennese supporters, Alfred Adler, broke away from him, and two or three years later Jung's differences from Freud led to their separation. Almost immediately after this came the First World War and an interruption of the international spread of psychoanalysis. Soon afterwards, too, came the gravest personal tragedies – the death of a daughter and of a favourite grandchild, and the onset of the malignant illness which was to pursue him relentlessly for the last sixteen years of his life. None of these troubles, however, brought any interruption to the development of Freud's observations and inferences. The structure of his ideas continued to expand and to find ever wider applications – particularly in the sociological field. By now he had become generally recognized as a figure of world celebrity, and no honour pleased him more than his election in 1936, the year of his eightieth birthday, as a

Corresponding Member of the Royal Society. It was no doubt this fame, supported by the efforts of influential admirers, including, it is said, President Roosevelt, that protected him from the worst excesses of the National Socialists when Hitler invaded Austria in 1938, though they seized and destroyed his publications. Freud's departure from Vienna was nevertheless essential, and in June of that year, accompanied by some of his family, he made the journey to London, and it was there, a year later, on 23 September 1939, that he died.

It has become a journalistic cliché to speak of Freud as one of the revolutionary founders of modern thought and to couple his name with that of Einstein. Most people would however find it almost as hard to summarize the changes introduced by the one as by the other.

Freud's discoveries may be grouped under three headings – an instrument of research, the findings produced by the instrument, and the theoretical hypotheses inferred from the findings – though the three groups were of course mutually interrelated. Behind all of Freud's work, however, we should posit his belief in the universal validity of the law of determinism. As regards physical phenomena this belief was perhaps derived from his experience in Brücke's laboratory and so, ultimately, from the school of Helmholtz; but Freud extended the belief uncompromisingly to the field of mental phenomena, and here he may have been influenced by his teacher, the psychiatrist Meynert, and indirectly by the philosophy of Herbart.

First and foremost, Freud was the discoverer of the first instrument for the scientific examination of the human mind. Creative writers of genius had had fragmentary insight into mental processes, but no systematic method of investigation existed before Freud. It was only gradually that he perfected the instrument, since it was only gradually that the difficulties in the way of such an investigation became apparent. The forgotten trauma in Breuer's explanation of hysteria provided the earliest problem and perhaps the most fundamental of all, for it showed conclusively that there were active parts of the mind not immediately open to inspection either by an onlooker or by the subject himself. These parts of the mind were described by Freud, without regard for metaphysical or terminological disputes, as the unconscious. Their existence was equally demonstrated by the fact of post-hypnotic suggestion, where a person in a fully waking state performs an action which had been suggested to him some time earlier, though he had totally forgotten the suggestion itself. No examination of the mind could thus be considered complete unless it included this unconscious part of it in its scope. How was this to be accomplished? The obvious answer seemed to be: by means of hypnotic suggestion; and this was the instrument used by Breuer and, to begin with, by Freud. But it soon turned out to be an imperfect one, acting irregularly and uncertainly and sometimes not at all. Little by little, accordingly, Freud abandoned the use of suggestion and replaced it by an entirely fresh instrument, which was later known as 'free association'. He adopted the unheard-of plan of simply asking the person whose mind he was investigating to say whatever came into his head. This crucial decision led at once to the most startling results; even in this primitive form Freud's instrument produced fresh insight. For, though things went along swimmingly for a while, sooner or later the flow of associations dried up: the subject would not or could not think of anything more to say. There thus came to light the fact of 'resistance', of a force, separate from the subject's conscious will, which was refusing to collaborate with the investigation. Here was one basis for a very fundamental piece of theory, for a hypothesis of the mind as something dynamic, as consisting in a number of mental forces, some conscious and some unconscious, operating now in harmony now in opposition with one another.

Though these phenomena eventually turned out to be of universal occurrence, they were first observed and studied in neurotic patients, and the earlier years of Freud's work were largely concerned with discovering means by which the 're-sistance' of these patients could be overcome and what lay behind it could be brought to light. The solution was only made possible by an extraordinary piece of self-observation on Freud's part – what we should now describe as his self-analysis. We are fortunate in having a contemporary first-hand description of this event in his letters to Fliess which have already been mentioned. This analysis enabled him to discover the nature of the unconscious processes at work in the mind and to understand why there is such a strong resistance to their becoming conscious; it enabled him to devise techniques for overcoming or evading the resistance in his patients; and, most important of all, it enabled him to realize the very great difference between the mode of functioning of these unconscious processes and that of our familiar conscious ones. A word may be said on each of these three points, for in fact they constitute the core of Freud's contributions to our knowledge of the mind.

The unconscious contents of the mind were found to consist wholly in the activity of conative trends – desires or wishes – which derive their energy directly from the primary physical instincts. They function quite regardless of any consideration other than that of obtaining immediate satisfaction, and are thus liable to be out of step with those more conscious elements in the mind which are concerned with adaptation to reality and the avoidance of external dangers. Since, moreover, these primitive trends are to a great extent of a sexual or of a destructive nature, they are bound to come in conflict with the more social and civilized mental forces. Investigations along this path were what led Freud to his discoveries of the long-disguised secrets of the sexual life of children and of the Oedipus complex.

In the second place, his self-analysis led him to an inquiry into the nature of dreams. These turned out to be, like neurotic symptoms, the product of a conflict and a compromise between the primary unconscious impulses and the secondary conscious ones. By analysing them into their elements it was therefore possible to infer their hidden unconscious contents; and, since dreams are common phenomena of almost universal occurrence, their interpretation turned out to be one of the most useful technical contrivances for penetrating the resistances of neurotic patients.

Finally, the painstaking examination of dreams enabled Freud to classify the remarkable differences between what he termed the primary and secondary processes of thought, between events in the unconscious and conscious regions of the mind. In the unconscious, it was found, there is no sort of organization or coordination: each separate impulse seeks satisfaction independently of all the rest; they proceed un-influenced by one another; contradictions are completely in-operative, and the most opposite impulses flourish side by side. So, too, in the unconscious, associations of ideas proceed along lines without any regard to logic: similarities are treated as identities, negatives are equated with positives. Again, the objects to which the conative trends are attached in the un-conscious are extraordinarily changeable – one may be replaced by another along a whole chain of associations that have no rational basis. Freud perceived that the intrusion into conscious thinking of mechanisms that belong properly to the primary process accounts for the oddity not only of dreams but of many other normal and pathological mental events.

It is not much of an exaggeration to say that all the later part of Freud's work lay in an immense extension and elaboration of these early ideas. They were applied to an elucidation of the mechanisms not only of the psychoneuroses and psychoses but also of such normal processes as slips of the tongue, making jokes, artistic creation, political institutions, and religions; they played a part in throwing fresh light on many applied sciences – archaeology, anthropology, criminology, education; they also served to account for the effectiveness of psychoanalytic therapy. Lastly, too, Freud erected on the basis of these elementary observations a theoretical superstructure, what he named a 'metapsychology', of more general concepts. These, however, fascinating as many people will find them, he always insisted were in the nature of provisional hypotheses. Quite late in his life, indeed, influenced by the ambiguity of the term 'unconscious' and its many conflicting uses, he proposed a new structural account of the mind in which the uncoordinated instinctual trends were called the 'id', the organized realistic part the 'ego', and the critical and moralizing function the 'super-ego' – a new account which has certainly made for a clarification of many issues.

This, then, will have given the reader an outline of the external events of Freud's life and some notion of the scope of his discoveries. Is it legitimate to ask for more? to try to penetrate a little further and to inquire what sort of person Freud was? Possibly not. But human curiosity about great men is insatiable, and if it is not gratified with true accounts it will inevitably clutch at mythological ones. In two of Freud's early books (*The Interpretation of Dreams* and *The Psychopathology of Everyday Life*) the presentation of his thesis had forced on him the necessity of bringing up an unusual amount of personal material. Nevertheless, or perhaps for that very reason, he intensely objected to any intrusion into his private life, and he was correspondingly the subject of a wealth of myths. According to the first and most naïve rumours, for instance, he was an abandoned profligate, devoted to the corruption of public morals. Later fantasies have tended in the opposite direction: he has been represented as a harsh moralist, a ruthless disciplinarian, an autocrat, egocentric and unsmiling, and an essentially unhappy man. To anyone who was acquainted with him, even slightly, both these pictures must seem equally preposterous. The second of them was no doubt partly derived from a knowledge of his physical sufferings during his last years; but partly too it may have been due to the unfortunate impression produced by some of his most widespread portraits. He disliked being photographed, at least by professional photographers, and his features on occasion expressed the fact; artists too seem always to have been overwhelmed by the necessity for representing the inventor of psychoanalysis as a ferocious and terrifying figure. Fortunately, however, alternative versions exist of a more amiable and truer kind – snapshots, for instance, taken on a

holiday or with his children, such as will be found in his eldest
son's memoir of his father (*Glory Reflected*, by Martin Freud
[1957]). In many ways, indeed, this delightful and amusing
book serves to redress the balance from more official bio-
graphies, invaluable as they are, and reveals something of Freud
as he was in ordinary life. Some of these portraits show us
that in his earlier days he had well-filled features, but in later
life, at any rate after the First World War and even before
his illness, this was no longer so, and his features, as well as
his whole figure (which was of medium height), were chiefly
remarkable for the impression they gave of tense energy and
alert observation. He was serious but kindly and considerate
in his more formal manners, but in other circumstances could
be an entertaining talker with a pleasantly ironical sense of
humour. It was easy to discover his devoted fondness for his
family and to recognize a man who would inspire affection.
He had many miscellaneous interests – he was fond of travelling
abroad, of country holidays, of mountain walks – and there
were other, more engrossing subjects, art, archaeology, literature. Freud was a very well read man in many languages, not
only in German. He read English and French fluently, besides
having a fair knowledge of Spanish and Italian. It must be
remembered, too, that though the later phases of his education
were chiefly scientific (it is true that at the University he studied
philosophy for a short time) at school he had learnt the classics
and never lost his affection for them. We happen to have a
letter written by him at the age of seventeen to a school friend.[1]
In it he describes his varying success in the different papers
of his school-leaving examination: in Latin a passage from
Virgil, and in Greek thirty-three lines from, of all things,
Oedipus Rex.

In short, we might regard Freud as what in England we should
consider the best kind of product of a Victorian upbringing. His
tastes in literature and art would obviously differ from ours, his
views on ethics, though decidedly liberal, would not belong to

1. [Emil Fluss. The letter is included in the volume of Freud's correspondence (1960*a*).]

the post-Freudian age. But we should see in him a man who lived a life of full emotion and of much suffering without embitterment. Complete honesty and directness were qualities that stood out in him, and so too did his intellectual readiness to take in and consider any fact, however new or extraordinary, that was presented to him. It was perhaps an inevitable corollary and extension of these qualities, combined with a general benevolence which a surface misanthropy failed to disguise, that led to some features of a surprising kind. In spite of his subtlety of mind he was essentially unsophisticated, and there were sometimes unexpected lapses in his critical faculty – a failure, for instance, to perceive an untrustworthy authority in some subject that was off his own beat such as Egyptology or philology, and, strangest of all in someone whose powers of perception had to be experienced to be believed, an occasional blindness to defects in his acquaintances. But though it may flatter our vanity to declare that Freud was a human being of a kind like our own, that satisfaction can easily be carried too far. There must in fact have been something very extraordinary in the man who was first able to recognize a whole field of mental facts which had hitherto been excluded from normal consciousness, the man who first interpreted dreams, who first accepted the facts of infantile sexuality, who first made the distinction between the primary and secondary processes of thinking – the man who first made the unconscious mind real to us.

JAMES STRACHEY

[Those in search of further information will find it in the three-volume biography of Freud by Ernest Jones, an abridged version of which was published in Pelican in 1964 (reissued 1974), in the important volume of Freud's letters edited by his son and daughter-in-law, Ernst and Lucie Freud (1960*a*), in several further volumes of his correspondence, with Wilhelm Fliess (1950*a*), Karl Abraham (1965*a*), C. G. Jung (1974*a*), Oskar Pfister (1963*a*), Lou Andreas-Salomé (1966*a*), Edoardo Weiss (1970*a*) and Arnold Zweig (1968*a*), and above all in the many volumes of Freud's own works.]

CHRONOLOGICAL TABLE

This table traces very roughly some of the main turning-points in Freud's intellectual development and opinions. A few of the chief events in his external life are also included in it.

1856. 6 May. Birth at Freiberg in Moravia.
1860. Family settles in Vienna.
1865. Enters Gymnasium (secondary school).
1873. Enters Vienna University as medical student.
1876–82. Works under Brücke at the Institute of Physiology in Vienna.
1877. First publications: papers on anatomy and physiology.
1881. Graduates as Doctor of Medicine.
1882. Engagement to Martha Bernays.
1882–5. Works in Vienna General Hospital, concentrating on cerebral anatomy: numerous publications.
1884–7. Researches into the clinical uses of cocaine.
1885. Appointed *Privatdozent* (University Lecturer) in Neuropathology.
1885 (October)–1886 (February). Studies under Charcot at the Salpêtrière (hospital for nervous diseases) in Paris. Interest first turns to hysteria and hypnosis.
1886. Marriage to Martha Bernays. Sets up private practice in nervous diseases in Vienna.
1886–93. Continues work on neurology, especially on the cerebral palsies of children at the Kassowitz Institute in Vienna, with numerous publications. Gradual shift of interest from neurology to psychopathology.
1887. Birth of eldest child (Mathilde).
1887–1902. Friendship and correspondence with Wilhelm Fliess in Berlin. Freud's letters to him during this period, published posthumously in 1950, throw much light on the development of his views.
1887. Begins the use of hypnotic suggestion in his practice.
c. 1888. Begins to follow Breuer in using hypnosis for cathartic treatment of hysteria. Gradually drops hypnosis and substitutes free association.
1889. Visits Bernheim at Nancy to study his suggestion technique.
1889. Birth of eldest son (Martin).
1891. Monograph on Aphasia.
Birth of second son (Oliver).

1892. Birth of youngest son (Ernst).

1893. Publication of Breuer and Freud 'Preliminary Communication': exposition of trauma theory of hysteria and of cathartic treatment.
Birth of second daughter (Sophie).

1893–8. Researches and short papers on hysteria, obsessions, and anxiety.

1895. Jointly with Breuer, *Studies on Hysteria*: case histories and description by Freud of his technique, including first account of transference.

1893–6. Gradual divergence of views between Freud and Breuer. Freud introduces concepts of defence and repression and of neurosis being a result of a conflict between the ego and the libido.

1895. *Project for a Scientific Psychology*: included in Freud's letters to Fliess and first published in 1950. An abortive attempt to state psychology in neurological terms; but foreshadows much of Freud's later theories.
Birth of youngest child (Anna).

1896. Introduces the term 'psychoanalysis'.
Death of father (aged eighty).

1897. Freud's self-analysis, leading to the abandonment of the trauma theory and the recognition of infantile sexuality and the Oedipus complex.

1900. *The Interpretation of Dreams*, with final chapter giving first full account of Freud's dynamic view of mental processes, of the unconscious, and of the dominance of the 'pleasure principle'.

1901. *The Psychopathology of Everyday Life*. This, together with the book on dreams, made it plain that Freud's theories applied not only to pathological states but also to normal mental life.

1902. Appointed Professor Extraordinarius.

1905. *Three Essays on the Theory of Sexuality*: tracing for the first time the course of development of the sexual instinct in human beings from infancy to maturity.

c. 1906. Jung becomes an adherent of psychoanalysis.

1908. First international meeting of psychoanalysts (at Salzburg).

1909. Freud and Jung invited to the USA to lecture.
Case history of the first analysis of a child (Little Hans, aged five): confirming inferences previously made from adult analyses, especially as to infantile sexuality and the Oedipus and castration complexes.

c. 1910. First emergence of the theory of 'narcissism'.

1911–15. Papers on the technique of psychoanalysis.

1911. Secession of Adler.
Application of psychoanalytic theories to a psychotic case: the autobiography of Dr Schreber.

1912–13. *Totem and Taboo*: application of psychoanalysis to anthropological material.

1914. Secession of Jung.
'On the History of the Psycho-Analytic Movement'. Includes a polemical section on Adler and Jung.

Writes his last major case history, of the 'Wolf Man' (not published till 1918).

1915. Writes a series of twelve 'metapsychological' papers on basic theoretical questions, of which only five have survived.

1915–17. *Introductory Lectures*: giving an extensive general account of the state of Freud's views up to the time of the First World War.

1919. Application of the theory of narcissism to the war neuroses.

1920. Death of second daughter.

Beyond the Pleasure Principle: the first explicit introduction of the concept of the 'compulsion to repeat' and of the theory of the 'death instinct'.

1921. *Group Psychology*. Beginnings of a systematic analytic study of the ego.

1923. *The Ego and the Id*. Largely revised account of the structure and functioning of the mind with the division into an id, an ego, and a super-ego.

1923. First onset of cancer.

1925. Revised views on the sexual development of women.

1926. *Inhibitions, Symptoms, and Anxiety*. Revised views on the problem of anxiety.

1927. *The Future of an Illusion*. A discussion of religion: the first of a number of sociological works to which Freud devoted most of his remaining years.

1930. *Civilization and its Discontents*. This includes Freud's first extensive study of the destructive instinct (regarded as a manifestation of the 'death instinct').

Freud awarded the Goethe Prize by the City of Frankfurt.

Death of mother (aged ninety-five).

1933. Hitler seizes power in Germany: Freud's books publicly burned in Berlin.

1934–8. *Moses and Monotheism*: the last of Freud's works to appear during his lifetime.

1936. Eightieth birthday. Election as Corresponding Member of Royal Society.

1938. Hitler's invasion of Austria. Freud leaves Vienna for London.

An Outline of Psycho-Analysis. A final, unfinished, but profound exposition of psychoanalysis.

1939. 23 September. Death in London.

JAMES STRACHEY

'CIVILIZED' SEXUAL MORALITY
AND MODERN NERVOUS ILLNESS
(1908)

EDITOR'S NOTE

DIE 'KULTURELLE' SEXUALMORAL UND DIE MODERNE NERVOSITÄT

(A) GERMAN EDITIONS:

1908 *Sexual-Probleme*, **4** (3) [March], 107–29.
1909 *S.K.S.N.*, **2**, 175–96. (1912, 2nd ed.; 1921, 3rd ed.)
1941 *Gesammelte Werke*, **7**, 143–67.

(B) ENGLISH TRANSLATIONS:
'Modern Sexual Morality and Modern Nervousness'

1915 *American Journal of Urology*, **11**, 391–405. (Incomplete.)

'"Civilized" Sexual Morality and Modern Nervousness'

1924 *Collected Papers*, **2**, 76–99. (Tr. E. B. Herford and E. C. Mayne.)
1959 *Standard Edition*, **9**, 177–204. (Based on the translation of 1924, with a modified title.)

The present edition is a corrected reprint of the *Standard Edition* version, with a few editorial modifications.

A reprint of the 1915 translation appeared as a pamphlet (edited by W. J. Robinson) published by Eugenics Publications, New York, 1931. Both omit the first ten paragraphs.

Sexual-Probleme, the periodical in which this paper appeared, was a continuation of the journal *Mutterschutz*, under which title it is sometimes catalogued. The numbering of the volumes continued unbroken in spite of the change of title.

*

Though this was the earliest of Freud's full-length discussions of the antagonism between civilization and instinctual life, his convictions on the subject went back much further. For instance, in a memorandum sent to Fliess on 31 May 1897, he wrote that 'incest is anti-social and civilization consists in a progressive renunciation of it'. (Freud, 1950a, Draft N.) He expressed similar views in the paper on 'Sexuality in the Aetiology of the Neuroses' (1898a), concluding that 'we may with justice regard civilization, too, as responsible for the spread of neurasthenia'; his discussion there of the problem of contraception foreshadows the remarks on p. 46 below. But, indeed, this antagonism was implied in his whole theory of the impact of the latency period on the development of human sexuality, and in the last pages of his *Three Essays* (1905d) he spoke of 'the inverse relation holding between civilization and the free development of sexuality' (*P.F.L.*, **7**, 168). Much of the present paper, it may be remarked, summarizes the findings of this last-mentioned work, which had first appeared only three years previously.

The sociological aspects of that antagonism form the main subject of the present paper, and Freud often recurred to it in the course of his later writings. Thus, leaving out of account the many passing allusions to it, we may mention in particular the last two sections of the second of his papers on the psychology of love (1912d), *P.F.L.*, **7**, 252 ff., and similar places in the following works: a long passage in 'Thoughts for the Times on War and Death' (1915b), pp. 69–74, the opening pages of *The Future of an Illusion* (1927c), p. 183 ff., and the closing paragraphs of *Why War?* (1933b), pp. 361–2. But his longest and most elaborate discussion of the subject was, of course, in *Civilization and its Discontents* (1930a).

Two further important topics discussed in the last-mentioned work – the assumption of an 'organic repression' which paved the way to civilization, and of the aggressive or destructive instincts – are not touched on in the present paper. This does not analyse the deeper, internal origins of civilization, and gives the impression of the restrictions of civilization as something imposed from without. The only instincts considered here in relation to conflict with civilization are the sexual instincts.

In the problem of whether the German word *'Kultur'* is to be translated 'culture' or 'civilization', the translators have been given a free hand by Freud's remark in *The Future of an Illusion*: 'I scorn to distinguish between culture and civilization.'

'CIVILIZED' SEXUAL MORALITY
AND MODERN NERVOUS ILLNESS

In his recently published book, *Sexual Ethics*, Von Ehrenfels[1] (1907) dwells on the difference between 'natural' and 'civilized' sexual morality. By natural sexual morality we are to understand, according to him, a sexual morality under whose dominance a human stock is able to remain in lasting possession of health and efficiency, while civilized sexual morality is a sexual morality obedience to which, on the other hand, spurs men on to intense and productive cultural activity. This contrast, he thinks, is best illustrated by comparing the innate character of a people with their cultural attainments. I may refer the reader to Von Ehrenfels's own work for a more extensive consideration of this significant line of thought, and I shall extract from it here only as much as I need as a starting-point for my own contribution to the subject.

It is not difficult to suppose that under the domination of a civilized sexual morality the health and efficiency of single individuals may be liable to impairment and that ultimately this injury to them, caused by the sacrifices imposed on them, may reach such a pitch that, by this indirect path, the cultural aim in view will be endangered as well. And Von Ehrenfels does in fact attribute a number of ill-effects to the sexual morality which dominates our Western society to-day, ill-effects for which he is obliged to make that morality responsible; and, although he fully acknowledges its high aptitude for the furtherance of civilization, he is led to convict it of standing in need of reform. In his view, what is

1. [Christian von Ehrenfels (1859–1932), Professor of Philosophy at Prague, is praised by Freud for his courageous criticisms of the institution of marriage in his book on jokes (1905*c*), *P.F.L.*, **6**, 156.]

characteristic of the civilized sexual morality that dominates us is that the demands made on women are carried over to the sexual life of men and that all sexual intercourse is prohibited except in monogamous marriage. Nevertheless, consideration of the natural difference between the sexes makes it necessary to visit men's lapses with less severity and thus in fact to admit a *double* morality for them. But a society which accepts this double morality cannot carry 'the love of truth, honesty and humanity' (Von Ehrenfels, ibid., 32 ff.) beyond a definite and narrow limit, and is bound to induce in its members conceal-ment of the truth, false optimism, self-deception and deception of others. And civilized sexual morality has still worse effects, for, by glorifying monogamy, it cripples the factor of *selection by virility* – the factor whose influence alone can bring about an improvement of the individual's innate constitution, since in civilized peoples *selection by vitality* has been reduced to a minimum by humanity and hygiene (ibid., 35).

Among the damaging effects which are here laid at the door of civilized sexual morality, the physician will miss a particular one whose significance will be discussed in detail in the present paper. I refer to the increase traceable to it of modern nervous illness – of the nervous illness, that is, which is rapidly spreading in our present-day society. Occasionally a nervous patient will himself draw the doctor's attention to the part played in the causation of his complaint by the opposition between his constitution and the demands of civilization and will say: 'In our family we've all become neurotic because we wanted to be something better than what, with our origin, we are capable of being.' Often, too, the physician finds food for thought in observing that those who succumb to nervous illness are precisely the offspring of fathers who, having been born of rough but vigorous families, living in simple, healthy, country conditions, had successfully established themselves in the metropolis, and in a short space of time had brought their children to a high level of culture. But, above all, nerve specialists themselves have loudly proclaimed the connection between 'increasing nervous illness' and modern civilized life.

The grounds to which they attribute this connection will be shown by a few extracts from statements that have been made by some eminent observers.

W. Erb (1893): 'The original question, then, is whether the causes of nervous illness that have been put before you are present in modern life to such a heightened degree as to account for a marked increase in that form of illness. The question can be answered without hesitation in the affirmative, as a cursory glance at our present-day existence and its features will show.

'This is already clearly demonstrated by a number of general facts. The extraordinary achievements of modern times, the discoveries and inventions in every sphere, the maintenance of progress in the face of increasing competition – these things have only been gained, and can only be held, by great mental effort. The demands made on the efficiency of the individual in the struggle for existence have greatly increased and it is only by putting out all his mental powers that he can meet them. At the same time, the individual's needs and his demands for the enjoyments of life have increased in all classes; unprecedented luxury has spread to strata of the population who were formerly quite untouched by it; irreligion, discontent and covetousness have grown up in wide social spheres. The immense extension of communications which has been brought about by the network of telegraphs and telephones that encircle the world has completely altered the conditions of trade and commerce. All is hurry and agitation; night is used for travel, day for business, even 'holiday trips' have become a strain on the nervous system. Important political, industrial and financial crises carry excitement into far wider circles of people than they used to do; political life is engaged in quite generally; political, religious and social struggles, party-politics, electioneering, and the enormous spread of trade-unionism inflame tempers, place an ever greater strain on the mind, and encroach upon the hours for recreation, sleep and rest. City life is constantly becoming more sophisticated and more restless. The exhausted nerves seek recuperation in increased stimulation and in highly-spiced pleasures, only to become more exhausted than

35

before. Modern literature is predominantly concerned with the most questionable problems which stir up all the passions, and which encourage sensuality and a craving for pleasure, and contempt for every fundamental ethical principle and every ideal. It brings before the reader's mind pathological figures and problems concerned with psychopathic sexuality, and revolutionary and other subjects. Our ears are excited and over-stimulated by large doses of noisy and insistent music. The theatres captivate all our senses with their exciting performances. The plastic arts, too, turn by preference to what is repellent, ugly and suggestive, and do not hesitate to set before our eyes with revolting fidelity the most horrible sights that reality has to offer.

'This general description is already enough to indicate a number of dangers presented by the evolution of our modern civilization. Let me now fill in the picture with a few details.'

Binswanger (1896): 'Neurasthenia in particular has been described as an essentially modern disorder, and Beard, to whom we are indebted for a first comprehensive account of it,[1] believed that he had discovered a new nervous disease which had developed specifically on American soil. This supposition was of course a mistaken one; nevertheless, the fact that it was an *American* physician who was first able to grasp and describe the peculiar features of this illness, as the fruit of a wide experience, indicates, no doubt, the close connections which exist between it and modern life, with its unbridled pursuit of money and possessions, and its immense advances in the field of technology which have rendered illusory every obstacle, whether temporal or spatial, to our means of intercommunication.'

Von Krafft-Ebing (1895): 'The mode of life of countless civilized people exhibits nowadays an abundance of anti-hygienic factors which make it easy to understand the fateful

1. [Cf. Beard (1881, 1884). G. M. Beard (1839–83), the American neurologist, was regarded as the principal authority on neurasthenia. Freud mentioned his work in some of his earlier discussions of the disease, e.g. Freud (1895b), *P.F.L.*, **10**, 35.]

increase of nervous illness; for those injurious factors take effect first and foremost on the brain. In the course of the last decades changes have taken place in the political and social – and especially in the mercantile, industrial and agricultural – conditions of civilized nations which have brought about great changes in people's occupations, social position and property, and this at the cost of the nervous system, which is called upon to meet the increased social and economic demands by a greater expenditure of energy, often with quite inadequate opportunity for recuperation.'

The fault I have to find with these and many other similarly-worded opinions is not that they are mistaken but that they prove insufficient to explain the details in the picture of nervous disturbances and that they leave out of account precisely the most important of the aetiological factors involved. If we disregard the vaguer ways of being 'nervous' and consider the specific forms of nervous illness, we shall find that the injurious influence of civilization reduces itself in the main to the harmful suppression of the sexual life of civilized peoples (or classes) through the 'civilized' sexual morality prevalent in them.

I have tried to bring forward the evidence for this assertion in a number of technical papers.[1] I cannot repeat it here. I will, however, quote the most important of the arguments arising from my investigations.

Careful clinical observation allows us to distinguish two groups of nervous disorders: the *neuroses* proper and the *psychoneuroses*. In the former the disturbances (the symptoms), whether they show their effects in somatic or mental functioning, appear to be of a *toxic* nature. They behave exactly like the phenomena accompanying an excess or a deprivation of certain nerve poisons. These neuroses – which are commonly grouped together as 'neurasthenia' – can be induced by certain

1. See the collection of my shorter papers on the theory of the neuroses published in 1906. [*Sammlung kleiner Schriften zur Neurosenlehre*, Vienna, 1906. – The volume contains fourteen papers published between 1893 and 1906, three of which are included in the present series: Freud (1893*a*), P.F.L., **3**, 51; (1895*b*), ibid., **10**, 31; and (1906*a*), ibid., **10**, 67.]

injurious influences in sexual life, without any hereditary taint being necessarily present; indeed, the form taken by the disease corresponds to the nature of these noxae, so that often enough the particular sexual aetiology can at once be deduced from the clinical picture. There is a total absence, on the other hand, of any such regular correspondence between the form of a nervous illness and the other injurious influences of civilization which are blamed by the authorities. We may, therefore, regard the sexual factor as the essential one in the causation of the neuroses proper.

With the psychoneuroses, the influence of heredity is more marked and the causation less transparent. A peculiar method of investigation known as psychoanalysis has, however, enabled us to recognize that the symptoms of these disorders (hysteria, obsessional neurosis, etc.) are *psychogenic* and depend upon the operation of unconscious (repressed) ideational complexes. This same method has also taught us what those unconscious complexes are and has shown that, quite generally speaking, they have a sexual content. They spring from the sexual needs of people who are unsatisfied and represent for them a kind of substitutive satisfaction. We must therefore view all factors which impair sexual life, suppress its activity or distort its aims as being pathogenic factors in the psychoneuroses as well.

The value of a theoretical distinction between toxic and psychogenic neuroses is, of course, not diminished by the fact that, in most people suffering from nervous illness, disturbances arising from both sources are to be observed.

The reader who is prepared to agree with me in looking for the aetiology of nervous illness pre-eminently in influences which damage sexual life, will also be ready to follow the further discussion, which is intended to set the theme of increasing nervous illness in a wider context.

Generally speaking, our civilization is built up on the suppression of instincts. Each individual has surrendered some part of his assets – some part of the sense of omnipotence or of the aggressive or vindictive inclinations in his personality. From these contributions has grown civilization's common assets in material and ideal wealth. Besides the exigencies of life, no doubt it has been family feelings, derived from erotism, that have induced the separate individuals to make this renunciation. The renunciation has been a progressive one in the course of the evolution of civilization. The single steps in it were sanctioned by religion; the piece of instinctual satisfaction which each person had renounced was offered to the Deity as a sacrifice, and the communal property thus acquired was declared 'holy'. The man who, in consequence of his unyielding constitution, cannot fall in with this suppression of instinct, becomes a 'criminal', an 'outlaw',[1] in the face of society – unless his social position or his exceptional capacities enable him to impose himself upon it as a great man, a 'hero'.

The sexual instinct – or, more correctly, the sexual instincts, for analytic investigation teaches us that the sexual instinct is made up of many separate constituents or component instincts – is probably more strongly developed in man than in most of the higher animals; it is certainly more constant, since it has almost entirely overcome the periodicity to which it is tied in animals. It places extraordinarily large amounts of force at the disposal of civilized activity, and it does this in virtue of its especially marked characteristic of being able to displace its aim without materially diminishing in intensity. This capacity to exchange its originally sexual aim for another one, which is no longer sexual but which is psychically related to the first aim, is called the capacity for *sublimation*. In contrast to this displaceability, in which its value for civilization lies, the sexual instinct may also exhibit a particularly obstinate fixation which renders it unserviceable and which sometimes causes it to degenerate into what are described as abnormalities. The original strength of the sexual instinct probably varies in each individual; certainly the proportion of it which is suitable for sublimation varies. It seems to us that it is the innate constitution

1. [In English in the original. – The gist of this paragraph, including the definition of 'holy' ('*heilig*'), will be found in a note to Fliess of 31 May 1897 (Freud, 1950a, Draft N). The word is again discussed in Essay III, Part II (D) of *Moses and Monotheism* (1939a), *P.F.L.*, **13**, 367.]

of each individual which decides in the first instance how large a part of his sexual instinct it will be possible to sublimate and make use of. In addition to this, the effects of experience and the intellectual influences upon his mental apparatus succeed in bringing about the sublimation of a further portion of it. To extend this process of displacement indefinitely is, however, certainly not possible, any more than is the case with the transformation of heat into mechanical energy in our machines. A certain amount of direct sexual satisfaction seems to be indispensable for most organizations, and a deficiency[1] in this amount, which varies from individual to individual, is visited by phenomena which, on account of their detrimental effects on functioning and their subjective quality of unpleasure, must be regarded as an illness.

Further prospects are opened up when we take into consideration the fact that in man the sexual instinct does not originally serve the purposes of reproduction at all, but has as its aim the gaining of particular kinds of pleasure.[2] It manifests itself in this way in human infancy, during which it attains its aim of gaining pleasure not only from the genitals but from other parts of the body (the erotogenic zones), and can therefore disregard any objects other than these convenient ones. We call this stage the stage of *auto-erotism*, and the child's upbringing has, in our view, the task of restricting it, because to linger in it would make the sexual instinct uncontrollable and unserviceable later on. The development of the sexual instinct then proceeds from auto-erotism to object-love and from the autonomy of the erotogenic zones to their subordination under the primacy of the genitals, which are put at the service of reproduction. During this development a part of the sexual excitation which is provided by the subject's own

1. [The German word here is *'Versagung'*. Freud later used this term, in a wider sense, to describe the principal factor in bringing about the onset of neurosis. In this sense it is rendered by the English 'frustration'. See the Editor's Note to the paper on 'Types of Onset of Neurosis' (1912c), *P.F.L.*, 10, 117.]

2. Cf. my *Three Essays on the Theory of Sexuality* (1905d) [*P.F.L.*, 7, 116].

body is inhibited as being unserviceable for the reproductive function and in favourable cases is brought to sublimation. The forces that can be employed for cultural activities are thus to a great extent obtained through the suppression of what are known as the *perverse* elements of sexual excitation.

If this evolution of the sexual instinct is borne in mind, three stages of civilization can be distinguished: a first one, in which the sexual instinct may be freely exercised without regard to the aims of reproduction; a second, in which all of the sexual instinct is suppressed except what serves the aims of reproduction; and a third, in which only *legitimate* reproduction is allowed as a sexual aim. This third stage is reflected in our present-day 'civilized' sexual morality.

If we take the second of these stages as an average, we must point out that a number of people are, on account of their organization, not equal to meeting its demands. In whole classes of individuals the development of the sexual instinct, as we have described it above, from auto-erotism to object-love with its aim of uniting the genitals, has not been carried out correctly and sufficiently fully. As a result of these disturbances of development two kinds of harmful deviation from normal sexuality – that is, sexuality which is serviceable to civilization – come about; and the relation between these two is almost that of positive and negative.[1]

In the first place (disregarding people whose sexual instinct is altogether excessive and uninhibitable) there are the different varieties of *perverts*, in whom an infantile fixation to a preliminary sexual aim has prevented the primacy of the reproductive function from being established, and the *homosexuals* or *inverts*, in whom, in a manner that is not yet quite understood, the sexual aim has been deflected away from the opposite sex. If the injurious effects of these two kinds of developmental disturbance are less than might be expected, this mitigation can be ascribed precisely to the complex way in which the sexual instinct is put together, which makes it possible

1. [See below, p. 43.]

for a person's sexual life to reach a serviceable final form even if one or more components of the instinct have been shut off from development. The constitution of people suffering from inversion – the homosexuals – is, indeed, often distinguished by their sexual instinct's possessing a special aptitude for cultural sublimation.

More pronounced forms of the perversions and of homosexuality, especially if they are exclusive, do, it is true, make those subject to them socially useless and unhappy, so that it must be recognized that the cultural requirements even of the second stage are a source of suffering for a certain proportion of mankind. The fate of these people who differ constitutionally from the rest varies, and depends on whether they have been born with a sexual instinct which by absolute standards is strong or comparatively weak. In the latter case – where the sexual instinct is in general weak – perverts succeed in totally suppressing the inclinations which bring them into conflict with the moral demands of their stage of civilization. But this, from the ideal point of view, is also the only thing they succeed in achieving; for, in order to effect this suppression of their sexual instinct, they use up the forces which they would otherwise employ in cultural activities. They are, as it were, inwardly inhibited and outwardly paralysed. What we shall be saying again later on about the abstinence demanded of men and women in the third stage of civilization applies to them too.

Where the sexual instinct is fairly intense, but perverse, there are two possible outcomes. The first, which we shall not discuss further, is that the person affected remains a pervert and has to put up with the consequences of his deviation from the standard of civilization. The second is far more interesting. It is that, under the influence of education and social demands, a suppression of the perverse instincts is indeed achieved, but it is a kind of suppression which is really no suppression at all. It can better be described as a suppression that has failed. The inhibited sexual instincts are, it is true, no longer expressed as such – and this constitutes the success of the process – but they find expression in other ways, which are quite as injurious to the subject and make him quite as useless for society as satisfaction of the suppressed instincts in an unmodified form would have done. This constitutes the failure of the process, which in the long run more than counterbalances its success. The substitutive phenomena which emerge in consequence of the suppression of the instinct amount to what we call nervous illness, or, more precisely, the psychoneuroses.[1] Neurotics are the class of people who, since they possess a recalcitrant organization, only succeed, under the influence of cultural requirements, in achieving a suppression of their instincts which is *apparent* and which becomes increasingly unsuccessful. They therefore only carry on their collaboration with cultural activities by a great expenditure of force and at the cost of an internal impoverishment, or are obliged at times to interrupt it and fall ill. I have described the neuroses as the 'negative' of the perversions [p. 41 above] because in the neuroses the perverse impulses, after being repressed, manifest themselves from the unconscious part of the mind – because the neuroses contain the same tendencies, though in a state of 'repression', as do the positive perversions.[2]

Experience teaches us that for most people there is a limit beyond which their constitution cannot comply with the demands of civilization. All who wish to be more noble-minded than their constitution allows fall victims to neurosis; they would have been more healthy if it could have been possible for them to be less good. The discovery that perversions and neuroses stand in the relation of positive and negative is often unmistakably confirmed by observations made on the members of one generation of a family. Quite frequently a brother is a sexual pervert, while his sister, who, being a woman, possesses a weaker sexual instinct, is a neurotic whose symptoms express the same inclinations as the perversions of her sexually more active brother. And correspondingly, in many families the men are healthy, but from a social point

1. Cf. my introductory remarks above [p. 38].

2. [Freud's first published statement to this effect occurs in the *Three Essays* (1905*d*), P.F.L., **7**, 80.]

of view immoral to an undesirable degree, while the women are high-minded and over-refined, but severely neurotic.

It is one of the obvious social injustices that the standard of civilization should demand from everyone the same conduct of sexual life – conduct which can be followed without any difficulty by some people, thanks to their organization, but which imposes the heaviest psychical sacrifices on others; though, indeed, the injustice is as a rule wiped out by dis-obedience to the injunctions of morality.

These considerations have been based so far on the require-ment laid down by the second of the stages of civilization which we have postulated [p. 41], the requirement that every sexual activity of the kind described as perverse is prohibited, while what is called normal sexual intercourse is freely permitted. We have found that even when the line between sexual freedom and restriction is drawn at this point, a number of individuals are ruled out as perverts, and a number of others, who make efforts not to be perverts whilst constitutionally they should be so, are forced into nervous illness. It is easy to predict the result that will follow if sexual freedom is still further circum-scribed and the requirements of civilization are raised to the level of the third stage, which bans all sexual activity outside legal marriage. The number of strong natures who openly oppose the demands of civilization will increase enormously, and so will the number of weaker ones who, faced with the conflict between the pressure of cultural influences and the resistance of their constitution, take flight into neurotic illness.[1]

Let us now try to answer three questions that arise here:

(1) What is the task that is set to the individual by the re-quirements of the third stage of civilization?

(2) Can the legitimate sexual satisfaction that is permissible offer acceptable compensation for the renunciation of all other satisfactions?

(3) In what relation do the possible injurious effects of this renunciation stand to its exploitation in the cultural field?

1. [This anticipates the concept 'flight into illness', introduced in the paper on hysterical attacks (Freud, 1909a; *P.F.L.*, **10**, 100 *n*. 1.]

The answer to the first question touches on a problem which has often been discussed and cannot be exhaustively treated here – that of sexual abstinence. Our third stage of civilization demands of individuals of both sexes that they shall practise abstinence until they are married and that all who do not contract a legal marriage shall remain abstinent throughout their lives. The position, agreeable to all the authorities, that sexual abstinence is not harmful and not difficult to maintain, has also been widely supported by the medical profession. It may be asserted, however, that the task of mastering such a powerful impulse as that of the sexual instinct by any other means than satisfying it is one which can call for the whole of a man's forces. Mastering it by sublimation, by deflecting the sexual instinctual forces away from their sexual aim to higher cultural aims, can be achieved by a minority and then only intermittently, and least easily during the period of ardent and vigorous youth. Most of the rest become neurotic or are harmed in one way or another. Experience shows that the majority of the people who make up our society are constitutionally unfit to face the task of abstinence. Those who would have fallen ill under milder sexual restrictions fall ill all the more readily and more severely before the demands of our cultural sexual morality of to-day; for we know no better safeguard against the threat to normal sexual life offered by defective innate dispositions or disturbances of development than sexual satisfaction itself. The more a person is disposed to neurosis, the less can he tolerate abstinence; instincts which have been withdrawn from normal development, in the sense in which it has been described above, become at the same time all the more uninhibitable. But even those people who would have retained their health under the requirements of the second stage of civilization will now succumb to neurosis in great numbers. For the psychical value of sexual satisfaction increases with its frustration. The dammed-up libido is now put in a position to detect one or other of the weaker spots which are seldom absent in the structure of sexual life, and there to break through and obtain substitutive satisfaction of a neurotic kind in the form of pathological symptoms. Anyone who is able to penetrate the determinants of nervous illness will soon become convinced that its increase in our society arises from the intensification of sexual restrictions.

This brings us to the question whether sexual intercourse in legal marriage can offer full compensation for the restrictions imposed before marriage. There is such an abundance of material supporting a reply in the negative that we can give only the briefest summary of it. It must above all be borne in mind that our cultural sexual morality restricts sexual intercourse even in marriage itself, since it imposes on married couples the necessity of contenting themselves, as a rule, with a very few procreative acts. As a consequence of this considera-tion, satisfying sexual intercourse in marriage takes place only for a few years; and we must subtract from this, of course, the intervals of abstention necessitated by regard for the wife's health. After these three, four or five years, the marriage becomes a failure in so far as it has promised the satisfaction of sexual needs. For all the devices hitherto invented for preventing conception impair sexual enjoyment, hurt the fine susceptibilities of both partners and even actually cause illness.[1] Fear of the consequences of sexual intercourse first brings the married couple's physical affection to an end; and then, as a remoter result, it usually puts a stop as well to the mental sympathy between them, which should have been the successor to their original passionate love. The spiritual disillusionment and bodily deprivation to which most marriages are thus doomed puts both partners back in the state they were in before their marriage, except for being the poorer by the loss of an illusion, and they must once more have recourse to their fortitude in mastering and deflecting their sexual instinct. We need not inquire how far men, by then in their maturer years, succeed in this task. Experience shows that they very frequently avail themselves of the degree of sexual freedom which is allowed them – although only with reluctance and under a

1. [The subject of contraception was discussed in Freud's earlier paper 'Sexuality in the Aetiology of the Neuroses' (1898*a*).]

veil of silence – by even the strictest sexual code. The 'double' sexual morality which is valid for men in our society is the plainest admission that society itself does not believe in the possibility of enforcing the precepts which it itself has laid down. But experience shows as well that women, who, as being the actual vehicle of the sexual interests of mankind, are only endowed in a small measure with the gift of sublimating their instincts, and who, though they may find a sufficient substitute for the sexual object in an infant at the breast, do not find one in a growing child – experience shows, I repeat, that women, when they are subjected to the disillusionments of marriage, fall ill of severe neuroses which permanently darken their lives. Under the cultural conditions of to-day, marriage has long ceased to be a panacea for the nervous troubles of women; and if we doctors still advise marriage in such cases, we are nevertheless aware that, on the contrary, a girl must be very healthy if she is to be able to tolerate it, and we urgently advise our male patients not to marry any girl who has had nervous trouble before marriage. On the contrary, the cure for nervous illness arising from marriage would be marital unfaithfulness. But the more strictly a woman has been brought up and the more sternly she has submitted to the demands of civilization, the more she is afraid of taking this way out; and in the conflict between her desires and her sense of duty, she once more seeks refuge in a neurosis. Nothing protects her virtue as securely as an illness. Thus the married state, which is held out as a consolation to the sexual instinct of the civilized person in his youth, proves to be inadequate even to the demands of the actual period of life covered by it. There is no question of its being able to compensate for the deprivation which precedes it.

But even if the damage done by civilized sexual morality is admitted, it may be argued in reply to our third question [p. 44] that the cultural gain derived from such an extensive restriction of sexuality probably more than balances these sufferings, which, after all, only affect a minority in any severe form. I must confess that I am unable to balance gain against loss correctly on this point, but I could advance a great many more considerations on the side of the loss. Going back to the subject of abstinence, which I have already touched on, I must insist that it brings in its train other noxae besides those involved in the neuroses and that the importance of the neuroses has for the most part not been fully appreciated.

The retardation of sexual development and sexual activity at which our education and civilization aim is certainly not injurious to begin with. It is seen to be a necessity, when one considers the late age at which young people of the educated classes reach independence and are able to earn a living. (This reminds one, incidentally, of the intimate interconnection between all our cultural institutions and of the difficulty of altering any part of them without regard to the whole.)[1] But abstinence continued long after the age of twenty is no longer unobjectionable for a young man; and it leads to other damage even when it does not lead to neurosis. People say, to be sure, that the struggle against such a powerful instinct, and the strengthening of all the ethical and aesthetic forces which are necessary for this struggle, 'steel' the character; and this is true for a few specially favourably organized natures. It must also be admitted that the differentiation of individual character, which is so marked in our day, has only become possible with the existence of sexual restriction. But in the vast majority of cases the struggle against sexuality eats up the energy available in a character and this at the very time when a young man is in need of all his forces in order to win his share and place in society. The relationship between the amount of sublimation possible and the amount of sexual activity necessary naturally varies very much from person to person and even from one calling to another. An abstinent artist is hardly conceivable; but an abstinent young *savant* is certainly no rarity. The latter can, by his self-restraint, liberate forces for his studies; while the former probably finds his artistic achievements powerfully stimulated by his sexual experience. In general I have not gained

1. [Freud makes the same point, in connection with education, in 'The Sexual Enlightenment of Children' (1907c), *P.F.L.*, **7**, 181.]

the impression that sexual abstinence helps to bring about energetic and self-reliant men of action or original thinkers or bold emancipators and reformers. Far more often it goes to produce well-behaved weaklings who later become lost in the great mass of people that tends to follow, unwillingly, the leads given by strong individuals.

The fact that the sexual instinct behaves in general in a self-willed and inflexible fashion is also seen in the results produced by efforts at abstinence. Civilized education may only attempt to suppress the instinct temporarily, till marriage, intending to give it free rein afterwards with the idea of then making use of it. But extreme measures are more successful against it than attempts at moderating it; thus the suppression often goes too far, with the unwished-for result that when the instinct is set free it turns out to be permanently impaired. For this reason complete abstinence in youth is often not the best preparation for marriage for a young man. Women sense this, and prefer among their suitors those who have already proved their masculinity with other women. The harmful results which the strict demand for abstinence before marriage produces in women's natures are quite especially apparent. It is clear that education is far from underestimating the task of suppressing a girl's sensuality till her marriage, for it makes use of the most drastic measures. Not only does it forbid sexual intercourse and set a high premium on the preservation of female chastity, but it also protects the young woman from temptation as she grows up, by keeping her ignorant of all the facts of the part she is to play and by not tolerating any impulse of love in her which cannot lead to marriage. The result is that when the girl's parental authorities suddenly allow her to fall in love, she is unequal to this psychical achievement and enters marriage uncertain of her own feelings. In consequence of this artificial retardation in her function of love, she has nothing but disappointments to offer the man who has saved up all his desire for her. In her mental feelings she is still attached to her parents, whose authority has brought about the suppression of her sexuality; and in her physical behaviour she shows herself frigid, which deprives the man of any high degree of sexual enjoyment. I do not know whether the anaesthetic type of woman exists apart from civilized education, though I consider it probable. But in any case such education actually breeds it, and these women who conceive without pleasure show little willingness afterwards to face the pains of frequent childbirth. In this way, the preparation for marriage frustrates the aims of marriage itself. When later on the retardation in the wife's development has been overcome and her capacity to love is awakened at the climax of her life as a woman, her relations to her husband have long since been ruined; and, as a reward for her previous docility, she is left with the choice between unappeased desire, unfaithfulness or a neurosis.

The sexual behaviour of a human being often *lays down the pattern* for all his other modes of reacting to life. If a man is energetic in winning the object of his love, we are confident that he will pursue his other aims with an equally unswerving energy; but if, for all sorts of reasons, he refrains from satisfying his strong sexual instincts, his behaviour will be conciliatory and resigned rather than vigorous in other spheres of life as well. A special application of this proposition that sexual life lays down the pattern for the exercise of other functions can easily be recognized in the female sex as a whole. Their up-bringing forbids their concerning themselves intellectually with sexual problems though they nevertheless feel extremely curious about them, and frightens them by condemning such curiosity as unwomanly and a sign of a sinful disposition. In this way they are scared away from *any* form of thinking, and knowledge loses its value for them. The prohibition of thought extends beyond the sexual field, partly through unavoidable association, partly automatically, like the prohibition of thought about religion among men, or the prohibition of thought about loyalty among faithful subjects. I do not believe that women's 'physiological feeble-mindedness' is to be explained by a biological opposition between intellectual work and sexual activity, as Moebius has asserted in a work[1] which

1. [Cf. Moebius (1903) and p. 231 below.]

has been widely disputed. I think that the undoubted intellectual inferiority of so many women can rather be traced back to the inhibition of thought necessitated by sexual suppression.

In considering the question of abstinence, the distinction is not nearly strictly enough made between two forms of it – namely abstention from any sexual activity whatever and abstention from sexual intercourse with the opposite sex. Many people who boast of succeeding in being abstinent have only been able to do so with the help of masturbation and similar satisfactions which are linked with the auto-erotic sexual activities of early childhood. But precisely because of this connection such substitutive means of sexual satisfaction are by no means harmless; they predispose to the numerous varieties of neuroses and psychoses which are conditional on an involution of sexual life to its infantile forms. Masturbation, moreover, is far from meeting the ideal demands of civilized sexual morality, and consequently drives young people into the same conflicts with the ideals of education which they hoped to escape by abstinence. Furthermore, it vitiates the character through *indulgence*, and this in more than one way. In the first place, it teaches people to achieve important aims without taking trouble and by easy paths instead of through an energetic exertion of force – that is, it follows the principle that *sexuality lays down the pattern* of behaviour [see above, p. 50]; secondly, in the phantasies that accompany satisfaction the sexual object is raised to a degree of excellence which is not easily found again in reality. A witty writer (Karl Kraus in the Vienna paper *Die Fackel*[1]) once expressed this truth in reverse by cynically remarking: 'Copulation is no more than an unsatisfying substitute for masturbation.'

The sternness of the demands of civilization and the difficulty of the task of abstinence have combined to make avoidance of the union of the genitals of the two opposite sexes into the

---

1. [Karl Kraus (1874–1936), the Austrian journalist and poet, was celebrated for his pugnacious and scathing wit. An anecdote about him is quoted by Freud in his book on jokes (1905c), *P.F.L.*, **6**, 118, and is repeated in the 'Rat Man' case history (1909d), ibid., **9**, 107 *n*. 1.]

central point of abstinence and to favour other kinds of sexual activity, which, it might be said, are equivalent to semi-obedience. Since normal intercourse has been so relentlessly persecuted by morality – and also, on account of the possibilities of infection, by hygiene – what are known as the perverse forms of intercourse between the two sexes, in which other parts of the body take over the role of the genitals, have undoubtedly increased in social importance. These activities cannot, however, be regarded as being as harmless as analogous extensions [of the sexual aim] in love-relationships. They are ethically objectionable, for they degrade the relationships of love between two human beings from a serious matter to a convenient game, attended by no risk and no spiritual participation. A further consequence of the aggravation of the difficulties of normal sexual life is to be found in the spread of homosexual satisfaction; in addition to all those who are homosexuals in virtue of their organization, or who became so in their childhood, there must be reckoned the great number of those in whom, in their maturer years, a blocking of the main stream of their libido has caused a widening in the side-channel of homosexuality.

All these unavoidable and unintended consequences of the requirement for abstinence converge in the one common result of completely ruining the preparation for marriage – marriage, which civilized sexual morality thinks should be the sole heir to the sexual impulsions. Every man whose libido, as a result of masturbatory or perverse sexual practices, has become habituated to situations and conditions of satisfaction which are not normal, develops diminished potency in marriage. Women, too, who have been able to preserve their virginity with the help of similar measures, show themselves anaesthetic to normal intercourse in marriage. A marriage begun with a reduced capacity to love on both sides succumbs to the process of dissolution even more quickly than others. As a result of the man's weak potency, the woman is not satisfied, and she remains anaesthetic even in cases where her disposition to frigidity, derived from her education, could have been overcome by a powerful sexual experience. A couple like this finds more difficulties, too, in the prevention of children than a healthy one, since the husband's diminished potency tolerates the use of contraceptives badly. In this perplexity, sexual intercourse, as being the source of all their embarrassments, is soon given up, and with this the basis of married life is abandoned.

I ask any well-informed person to bear witness to the fact that I am not exaggerating but that I am describing a state of affairs of which equally bad instances can be observed over and over again. To the uninitiated it is hardly credible how seldom normal potency is to be found in a husband and how often a wife is frigid among married couples who live under the dominance of our civilized sexual morality, what a degree of renunciation, often on both sides, is entailed by marriage, and to what narrow limits married life – the happiness that is so ardently desired – is narrowed down. I have already explained that in these circumstances the most obvious outcome is nervous illness; but I must further point out the way in which a marriage of this kind continues to exercise its influence on the few children, or the only child born of it. At a first glance, it seems to be a case of transmission by inheritance; but closer inspection shows that it is really a question of the effect of powerful infantile impressions. A neurotic wife who is unsatisfied with her husband is, as a mother, over-tender and over-anxious towards her child, on to whom she transfers her need for love; and she awakens it to sexual precocity. The bad relations between its parents, moreover, excite its emotional life and cause it to feel love and hatred to an intense degree while it is still at a very tender age. Its strict upbringing, which tolerates no activity of the sexual life that has been aroused so early, lends support to the suppressing force and this conflict at such an age contains everything necessary for bringing about lifelong nervous illness.

I return now to my earlier assertion [p. 48] that, in judging the neuroses, their full importance is not as a rule taken into account. I do not mean by this the undervaluation of these states shown in their frivolous dismissal by relatives and in the boasting assurances by doctors that a few weeks of cold water treatment or a few months of rest and convalescence will cure the condition. These are merely the opinions of quite ignorant doctors and laymen and are mostly no more than words intended to give the sufferer a short-lived consolation. It is, on the contrary, a well-known fact that a chronic neurosis, even if it does not totally put an end to the subject's capacity for existence, represents a severe handicap in his life, of the same order, perhaps, as tuberculosis or a cardiac defect. The situation would even be tolerable if neurotic illness were to exclude from civilized activities only a number of individuals who were in any case of the weaker sort, and allowed the rest to play their part in it at the cost of troubles that were merely subjective. But, far from this being so, I must insist upon the view that neuroses, whatever their extent and wherever they occur, always succeed in frustrating the purposes of civilization, and in that way actually perform the work of the suppressed mental forces that are hostile to civilization. Thus, when society pays for obedience to its far-reaching regulations by an increase in nervous illness, it cannot claim to have purchased a gain at the price of sacrifices; it cannot claim a gain at all. Let us, for instance, consider the very common case of a woman who does not love her husband, because, owing to the conditions under which she entered marriage, she has no reason to love him, but who very much wants to love him, because that alone corresponds to the ideal of marriage to which she has been brought up. She will in that case suppress every impulse which would express the truth and contradict her endeavours to fulfil her ideal, and she will make special efforts to play the part of a loving, affectionate and attentive wife. The outcome of this self-suppression will be a neurotic illness; and this neurosis will in a short time have taken revenge on the unloved husband and have caused him just as much lack of satisfaction and worry as would have resulted from an acknowledgement of the true state of affairs. This example is completely typical of what a neurosis achieves. A similar failure to obtain compensation is to be seen after the suppression of impulses inimical to civilization which are not directly sexual. If a man, for example, has become over-kind as a result of a violent suppression of a constitutional inclination to harshness and cruelty, he often loses so much energy in doing this that he fails to carry out all that his compensatory impulses require, and he may, after all, do less good on the whole than he would have done without the suppression.

Let us add that a restriction of sexual activity in a community is quite generally accompanied by an increase of anxiety about life and of fear of death with interferes with the individual's capacity for enjoyment and does away with his readiness to face death for any purpose. A diminished inclination to beget children is the result, and the community or group of people in question is thus excluded from any share in the future. In view of this, we may well raise the question whether our 'civilized' sexual morality is worth the sacrifice which it imposes on us, especially if we are still so much enslaved to hedonism as to include among the aims of our cultural development a certain amount of satisfaction of individual happiness. It is certainly not a physician's business to come forward with proposals for reform; but it seemed to me that I might support the urgency of such proposals if I were to amplify Von Ehrenfels's description of the injurious effects of our 'civilized' sexual morality by pointing to the important bearing of that morality upon the spread of modern nervous illness.

THOUGHTS FOR THE TIMES ON WAR AND DEATH
(1915)

ZEITGEMÄSSES ÜBER KRIEG UND TOD

(A) German Editions:

1915   *Imago*, **4** (1), 1–21.
1918   *S.K.S.N.*, **4**, 486–520. (1922, 2nd ed.)
1924   Leipzig, Vienna and Zurich: Internationaler Psycho-
       analytischer Verlag.
1946   *Gesammelte Werke*, **10**, 324–55.

(B) English Translations:

Reflections on War and Death

1918   New York: Moffat, Yard. (Tr. A. A. Brill and A. B.
       Kuttner.)

'Thoughts for the Times on War and Death'

1925   *Collected Papers*, **4**, 288–317. (Tr. E. C. Mayne.)
1957   *Standard Edition*, **14**, 273–300. (Based on the translation
       of 1925.)

The present edition is a corrected reprint of the *Standard Edition* version.

These two essays were written round about March and April 1915, some six months after the outbreak of the First World War, and express some of Freud's considered views on it. His more personal reactions will be found described in Chapter VII of Ernest Jones's second volume (1955). Towards the end of 1915, Freud wrote an essay on an analogous theme, 'On

Transcience' (1916*a*, *P.F.L.*, **14**). Many years later he returned to the subject once more in his open letter to Einstein, *Why War?* (1933*b*; p. 349 below). The first of these essays considers again the effects of the antagonism between civilization and instinctual life that were discussed in the paper on 'civilized' sexual morality (p. 29 above). The second essay – on death – seems to have been first read by Freud at a meeting, early in April 1915, of the B'nai B'rith, the Jewish club in Vienna to which he belonged for a large part of his life. This essay is, of course, to a great extent based on the same material as Essay II of *Totem and Taboo* (1912–13; *P.F.L.*, **13**).

THOUGHTS FOR THE TIMES ON WAR AND DEATH

I

THE DISILLUSIONMENT OF THE WAR

IN the confusion of wartime in which we are caught up, relying as we must on one-sided information, standing too close to the great changes that have already taken place or are beginning to, and without a glimmering of the future that is being shaped, we ourselves are at a loss as to the significance of the impressions which press in upon us and as to the value of the judgements which we form. We cannot but feel that no event has ever destroyed so much that is precious in the common possessions of humanity, confused so many of the clearest intelligences, or so thoroughly debased what is highest. Science herself has lost her passionless impartiality; her deeply embittered servants seek for weapons from her with which to contribute towards the struggle with the enemy. Anthropologists feel driven to declare him inferior and degenerate, psychiatrists issue a diagnosis of his disease of mind or spirit. Probably, however, our sense of these immediate evils is disproportionately strong, and we are not entitled to compare them with the evils of other times which we have not experienced.

The individual who is not himself a combatant – and so a cog in the gigantic machine of war – feels bewildered in his orientation, and inhibited in his powers and activities. I believe that he will welcome any indication, however slight, which will make it easier for him to find his bearings within himself at least. I propose to pick out two among the factors which are responsible for the mental distress felt by non-combatants, against which it is such a heavy task to struggle, and to treat of them here: the disillusionment which this war has evoked, and the altered attitude towards death which this – like every other war – forces upon us.

When I speak of disillusionment, everyone will know at once what I mean. One need not be a sentimentalist; one may perceive the biological and psychological necessity for suffering in the economy of human life, and yet condemn war both in its means and ends and long for the cessation of all wars. We have told ourselves, no doubt, that wars can never cease so long as nations live under such widely differing conditions, so long as the value of individual life is so variously assessed among them, and so long as the animosities which divide them represent such powerful motive forces in the mind. We were prepared to find that wars between the primitive and the civilized peoples, between the races who are divided by the colour of their skin – wars, even, against and among the nationalities of Europe whose civilization is little developed or has been lost – would occupy mankind for some time to come. But we permitted ourselves to have other hopes. We had expected the great world-dominating nations of white race upon whom the leadership of the human species has fallen, who were known to have world-wide interests as their concern, to whose creative powers were due not only our technical advances towards the control of nature but the artistic and scientific standards of civilization – we had expected these peoples to succeed in discovering another way of settling misunderstandings and conflicts of interest. Within each of these nations high norms of moral conduct were laid down for the individual, to which his manner of life was bound to conform if he desired to take part in a civilized community. These ordinances, often too stringent, demanded a great deal of him – much self-restraint, much renunciation of instinctual satisfaction. He was above all forbidden to make use of the immense advantages to be gained by the practice of lying and deception in the competition with his fellow-men. The civilized states regarded these moral standards as the basis of their existence. They took serious steps if anyone ventured to tamper with them, and often declared it improper even to subject them to examination by a critical intelligence. It was to be assumed, therefore, that the state itself would respect them, and would not think of undertaking anything against them which would contradict the basis of its own existence. Observation showed, to be sure, that embedded in these civilized states there were remnants of certain other peoples, which were universally unpopular and had therefore been only reluctantly, and even so not fully, admitted to participation in the common work of civilization, for which they had shown themselves suitable enough. But the great nations themselves, it might have been supposed, would have acquired so much comprehension of what they had in common, and so much tolerance for their differences, that 'foreigner' and 'enemy' could no longer be merged, as they still were in classical antiquity, into a single concept.

Relying on this unity among the civilized peoples, countless men and women have exchanged their native home for a foreign one, and made their existence dependent on the intercommunications between friendly nations. Moreover anyone who was not by stress of circumstance confined to one spot could create for himself out of all the advantages and attractions of these civilized countries a new and wider fatherland, in which he could move about without hindrance or suspicion. In this way he enjoyed the blue sea and the grey; the beauty of snow-covered mountains and of green meadow lands; the magic of northern forests and the splendour of southern vegetation; the mood evoked by landscapes that recall great historical events, and the silence of untouched nature. This new fatherland was a museum for him, too, filled with all the treasures which the artists of civilized humanity had in the successive centuries created and left behind. As he wandered from one gallery to another in this museum, he could recognize with impartial appreciation what varied types of perfection a mixture of blood, the course of history, and the special quality of their mother-earth had produced among his compatriots in this wider sense.

Here he would find cool inflexible energy developed to the highest point; there, the graceful art of beautifying existence; elsewhere, the feeling for orderliness and law, or others among the qualities which have made mankind the lords of the earth.

Nor must we forget that each of these citizens of the civilized world had created for himself a 'Parnassus' and a 'School of Athens' of his own.[1] From among the great thinkers, writers and artists of all nations he had chosen those to whom he considered he owed the best of what he had been able to achieve in enjoyment and understanding of life, and he had venerated them along with the immortal ancients as well as with the familiar masters of his own tongue. None of these great men had seemed to him foreign because they spoke another language – neither the incomparable explorer of human passions, nor the intoxicated worshipper of beauty, nor the powerful and menacing prophet, nor the subtle satirist; and he never reproached himself on that account for being a renegade towards his own nation and his beloved mother-tongue.

The enjoyment of this common civilization was disturbed from time to time by warning voices, which declared that old traditional differences made wars inevitable, even among the members of a community such as this. We refused to believe it; but if such a war were to happen, how did we picture it? We saw it as an opportunity for demonstrating the progress of comity among men since the era when the Greek Amphictyonic Council proclaimed that no city of the league might be destroyed, nor its olive-groves cut down, nor its water-supply stopped; we pictured it as a chivalrous passage of arms, which would limit itself to establishing the superiority of one side in the struggle, while as far as possible avoiding acute suffering that could contribute nothing to the decision, and granting complete immunity for the wounded who had

1. [Two of the famous frescoes by Raphael in the Papal Apartments of the Vatican. One of them represents a group of the world's great poets and the other a similar group of scholars. In *The Interpretation of Dreams* (1900a), *P.F.L.*, **4**, 424–5, Freud uses the same two paintings as a parallel to one of the techniques employed by the dream-work.]

to withdraw from the contest, as well as for the doctors and nurses who devoted themselves to their recovery. There would, of course, be the utmost consideration for the non-combatant classes of the population – for women who take no part in war-work, and for the children who, when they are grown up, should become on both sides one another's friends and helpers. And again, all the international undertakings and institutions in which the common civilization of peace-time had been embodied would be maintained.

Even a war like this would have produced enough horror and suffering; but it would not have interrupted the development of ethical relations between the collective individuals of mankind – the peoples and states.

Then the war in which we had refused to believe broke out, and it brought – disillusionment. Not only is it more bloody and more destructive than any war of other days, because of the enormously increased perfection of weapons of attack and defence; it is at least as cruel, as embittered, as implacable as any that has preceded it. It disregards all the restrictions known as International Law, which in peace-time the states had bound themselves to observe; it ignores the prerogatives of the wounded and the medical service, the distinction between civil and military sections of the population, the claims of private property. It tramples in blind fury on all that comes in its way, as though there were to be no future and no peace among men after it is over. It cuts all the common bonds between the contending peoples, and threatens to leave a legacy of embitterment that will make any renewal of those bonds impossible for a long time to come.

Moreover, it has brought to light an almost incredible phenomenon: the civilized nations know and understand one another so little that one can turn against the other with hate and loathing. Indeed, one of the great civilized nations is so universally unpopular that the attempt can actually be made to exclude it from the civilized community as 'barbaric', although it has long proved its fitness by the magnificent contributions to that community which it has made. We live in hopes that the pages of an impartial history will prove that that nation, in whose language we write and for whose victory our dear ones are fighting, has been precisely the one which has least transgressed the laws of civilization. But at such a time who dares to set himself up as judge in his own cause?

Peoples are more or less represented by the states which they form, and these states by the governments which rule them. The individual citizen can with horror convince himself in this war of what would occasionally cross his mind in peace-time – that the state has forbidden to the individual the practice of wrong-doing, not because it desires to abolish it, but because it desires to monopolize it, like salt and tobacco. A belligerent state permits itself every such misdeed, every such act of violence, as would disgrace the individual. It makes use against the enemy not only of the accepted *ruses de guerre*, but of deliberate lying and deception as well – and to a degree which seems to exceed the usage of former wars. The state exacts the utmost degree of obedience and sacrifice from its citizens, but at the same time it treats them like children by an excess of secrecy and a censorship upon news and expressions of opinion which leaves the spirits of those whose intellects it thus suppresses defenceless against every unfavourable turn of events and every sinister rumour. It absolves itself from the guarantees and treaties by which it was bound to other states, and confesses shamelessly to its own rapacity and lust for power, which the private individual has then to sanction in the name of patriotism.

It should not be objected that the state cannot refrain from wrong-doing, since that would place it at a disadvantage. It is no less disadvantageous, as a general rule, for the individual man to conform to the standards of morality and refrain from brutal and arbitrary conduct; and the state seldom proves able to indemnify him for the sacrifices it exacts. Nor should it be a matter for surprise that this relaxation of all the moral ties between the collective individuals of mankind should have had repercussions on the morality of individuals; for our conscience is not the inflexible judge that ethical teachers declare it, but in its origin is 'social anxiety' and nothing else.[1] When the community no longer raises objections, there is an end, too, to the suppression of evil passions, and men perpetrate deeds of cruelty, fraud, treachery and barbarity so incompatible with their level of civilization that one would have thought them impossible.

Well may the citizen of the civilized world of whom I have spoken stand helpless in a world that has grown strange to him – his great fatherland disintegrated, its common estates laid waste, his fellow-citizens divided and debased!

There is something to be said, however, in criticism of his disappointment. Strictly speaking it is not justified, for it consists in the destruction of an illusion. We welcome illusions because they spare us unpleasurable feelings, and enable us to enjoy satisfactions instead. We must not complain, then, if now and again they come into collision with some portion of reality, and are shattered against it.

Two things in this war have aroused our sense of disillusionment: the low morality shown externally by states which in their internal relations pose as the guardians of moral standards, and the brutality shown by individuals whom, as participants in the highest human civilization, one would not have thought capable of such behaviour.

Let us begin with the second point and try to formulate, in a few brief words, the point of view that we wish to criticize. How, in point of fact, do we imagine the process by which an individual rises to a comparatively high plane of morality? The first answer will no doubt simply be that he is virtuous and noble from birth – from the very start. We shall not consider this view any further here. A second answer will suggest that we are concerned with a developmental process, and will probably assume that the development consists in eradicating his evil human tendencies and, under the influence of education and a civilized environment, replacing them by good ones. If so, it is nevertheless surprising that evil should

1. [A more detailed view of the nature of conscience is given in *Civilization and its Discontents* (1930a), pp. 315–26 and 328–9 below.]

re-emerge with such force in anyone who has been brought up in this way.

But this answer also contains the thesis which we propose to contradict. In reality, there is no such thing as 'eradicating' evil. Psychological – or, more strictly speaking, psychoanalytic – investigation shows instead that the deepest essence of human nature consists of instinctual impulses which are of an elementary nature, which are similar in all men and which aim at the satisfaction of certain primal needs. These impulses in themselves are neither good nor bad. We classify them and their expressions in that way, according to their relation to the needs and demands of the human community. It must be granted that all the impulses which society condemns as evil – let us take as representative the selfish and the cruel ones – are of this primitive kind.

These primitive impulses undergo a lengthy process of development before they are allowed to become active in the adult. They are inhibited, directed towards other aims and fields, become commingled, alter their objects, and are to some extent turned back upon their possessor. Reaction-formations against certain instincts take the deceptive form of a change in their content, as though egoism had changed into altruism, or cruelty into pity.[1] These reaction-formations are facilitated by the circumstance that some instinctual impulses make their appearance almost from the first in pairs of opposites – a very remarkable phenomenon, and one strange to the lay public, which is termed 'ambivalence of feeling'. The most easily observed and comprehensible instance of this is the fact that intense love and intense hatred are so often to be found together in the same person. Psychoanalysis adds that the two opposed feelings not infrequently have the same person for their object.

It is not until all these 'instinctual vicissitudes' have been surmounted that what we call a person's character is formed, and

1. [As Freud states elsewhere, reaction-formation and sublimation must be regarded as two quite different processes. Cf. a footnote added in 1915 (when Freud wrote the present paper) to the *Three Essays* (1905*d*), *P.F.L.*, **7**, 94 *n*. 2.]

this, as we know, can only very inadequately be classified as 'good' or 'bad'. A human being is seldom altogether good or bad; he is usually 'good' in one relation and 'bad' in another, or 'good' in certain external circumstances and in others decidedly 'bad'. It is interesting to find that the pre-existence of strong 'bad' impulses in infancy is often the actual condition for an unmistakable inclination towards 'good' in the adult. Those who as children have been the most pronounced egoists may well become the most helpful and self-sacrificing members of the community; most of our sentimentalists, friends of humanity and protectors of animals have been evolved from little sadists and animal-tormentors.

The transformation of 'bad' instincts is brought about by two factors working in the same direction, an internal and an external one. The internal factor consists in the influence exercised on the bad (let us say, the egoistic) instincts by erotism – that is, by the human need for love, taken in its widest sense. By the admixture of *erotic* components the egoistic instincts are transformed into *social* ones. We learn to value being loved as an advantage for which we are willing to sacrifice other advantages. The external factor is the force exercised by upbringing, which represents the claims of our cultural environment, and this is continued later by the direct pressure of that environment. Civilization has been attained through the renunciation of instinctual satisfaction, and it demands the same renunciation from each newcomer in turn. Throughout an individual's life there is a constant replacement of external by internal compulsion. The influences of civilization cause an ever-increasing transformation of egoistic trends into altruistic and social ones by an admixture of erotic elements. In the last resort it may be assumed that every internal compulsion which makes itself felt in the development of human beings was originally – that is, in the *history of mankind* – only an external one. Those who are born to-day bring with them as an inherited organization some degree of tendency (disposition) towards the transformation of egoistic into social instincts, and this disposition is easily stimulated into bringing about that result. A further portion of this instinctual transformation has to be accomplished during the life of the individual himself. So the human being is subject not only to the pressure of his immediate cultural environment, but also to the influence of the cultural history of his ancestors.

If we give the name of 'susceptibility to culture'[1] to a man's personal capacity for the transformation of the egoistic impulses under the influence of erotism, we may further affirm that this susceptibility is made up of two parts, one innate and the other acquired in the course of life, and that the relation of the two to each other and to that portion of the instinctual life which remains untransformed is a very variable one.

Generally speaking, we are apt to attach too much importance to the innate part, and in addition to this we run the risk of over-estimating the total susceptibility to culture in comparison with the portion of instinctual life which has remained primitive – that is, we are misled into regarding men as 'better' than they actually are. For there is yet another element which obscures our judgement and falsifies the issue in a favourable sense.

The instinctual impulses of other people are of course hidden from our observation. We infer them from their actions and behaviour, which we trace back to *motives* arising from their instinctual life. Such an inference is bound to be erroneous in many cases. This or that action which is 'good' from the cultural point of view may in one instance originate from a 'noble' motive, in another not. Ethical theorists class as 'good' actions only those which are the outcome of good impulses; to the others they refuse recognition. But society, which is practical in its aims, is not on the whole troubled by this distinction; it is content if a man regulates his behaviour and actions by the precepts of civilization, and is little concerned with his motives.

We have learned that the *external compulsion* exercised on a human being by his upbringing and environment produces

1. [See also p. 220 below.]

a further transformation towards good in his instinctual life – a further turning from egoism towards altruism. But this is not the regular or necessary effect of the external compulsion. Upbringing and environment not only offer benefits in the way of love, but also employ other kinds of incentive, namely, rewards and punishments. In this way their effect may turn out to be that a person who is subjected to their influence will choose to behave well in the cultural sense of the phrase, although no ennoblement of instinct, no transformation of egoistic into altruistic inclinations, has taken place in him. The result will, roughly speaking, be the same; only a particular concatenation of circumstances will reveal that one man always acts in a good way because his instinctual inclinations compel him to, and the other is good only in so far and for so long as such cultural behaviour is advantageous for his own selfish purposes. But superficial acquaintance with an individual will not enable us to distinguish between the two cases, and we are certainly misled by our optimism into grossly exaggerating the number of human beings who have been transformed in a cultural sense.

Civilized society, which demands good conduct and does not trouble itself about the instinctual basis of this conduct, has thus won over to obedience a great many people who are not in this following their own natures. Encouraged by this success, society has allowed itself to be misled into tightening the moral standard to the greatest possible degree, and it has thus forced its members into a yet greater estrangement from their instinctual disposition. They are consequently subject to an unceasing suppression of instinct, and the resulting tension betrays itself in the most remarkable phenomena of reaction and compensation. In the domain of sexuality, where such suppression is most difficult to carry out, the result is seen in the reactive phenomena of neurotic disorders. Elsewhere the pressure of civilization brings in its train no pathological results, it is true, but is shown in malformations of character, and in the perpetual readiness of the inhibited instincts to break through to satisfaction at any suitable opportunity. Anyone thus compelled to act continually in accordance with precepts which are not the expression of his instinctual inclinations, is living, psychologically speaking, beyond his means, and may objectively be described as a hypocrite, whether he is clearly aware of the incongruity or not. It is undeniable that our contemporary civilization favours the production of this form of hypocrisy to an extraordinary extent. One might venture to say that it is built up on such hypocrisy, and that it would have to submit to far-reaching modifications if people were to undertake to live in accordance with psychological truth. Thus there are very many more cultural hypocrites than truly civilized men – indeed, it is a debatable point whether a certain degree of cultural hypocrisy is not indispensable for the maintenance of civilization, because the susceptibility to culture which has hitherto been organized in the minds of present-day men would perhaps not prove sufficient for the task. On the other hand, the maintenance of civilization even on so dubious a basis offers the prospect of paving the way in each new generation for a more far-reaching transformation of instinct which shall be the vehicle of a better civilization.

We may already derive one consolation from this discussion: our mortification and our painful disillusionment on account of the uncivilized behaviour of our fellow-citizens of the world during this war were unjustified. They were based on an illusion to which we had given way. In reality our fellow-citizens have not sunk so low as we feared, because they had never risen so high as we believed. The fact that the collective individuals of mankind, the peoples and states, mutually abrogated their moral restraints naturally prompted these individual citizens to withdraw for a while from the constant pressure of civilization and to grant a temporary satisfaction to the instincts which they had been holding in check. This probably involved no breach in their relative morality within their own nations.

We may, however, obtain a deeper insight than this into the change brought about by the war in our former compatriots, and at the same time receive a warning against doing them an injustice. For the development of the mind shows a peculiarity which is present in no other developmental process. When a village grows into a town or a child into a man, the village and the child become lost in the town and the man. Memory alone can trace the old features in the new picture; and in fact the old materials or forms have been got rid of and replaced by new ones. It is otherwise with the development of the mind. Here one can describe the state of affairs, which has nothing to compare with it, only by saying that in this case every earlier stage of development persists alongside the later stage which has arisen from it; here succession also involves co-existence, although it is to the same materials that the whole series of transformations has applied. The earlier mental state may not have manifested itself for years, but none the less it is so far present that it may at any time again become the mode of expression of the forces in the mind, and indeed the only one, as though all later developments had been annulled or undone. This extraordinary plasticity of mental developments is not unrestricted as regards direction; it may be described as a special capacity for involution – for regression – since it may well happen that a later and higher stage of development, once abandoned, cannot be reached again. But the primitive stages can always be re-established; the primitive mind is, in the fullest meaning of the word, imperishable.

What are called mental diseases inevitably produce an impression in the layman that intellectual and mental life have been destroyed. In reality, the destruction only applies to later acquisitions and developments. The essence of mental disease lies in a return to earlier states of affective life and of functioning. An excellent example of the plasticity of mental life is afforded by the state of sleep, which is our goal every night. Since we have learnt to interpret even absurd and confused dreams, we know that whenever we go to sleep we throw off our hard-won morality like a garment, and put it on again next morning. This stripping of ourselves is not, of course, dangerous, because we are paralysed, condemned to inactivity, by the state of sleep. It is only dreams that can tell us about the regression of our emotional life to one of the earliest stages of development. For instance, it is noteworthy that all our dreams are governed by purely egoistic motives.[1] One of my English friends put forward this thesis at a scientific meeting in America, whereupon a lady who was present remarked that that might be the case in Austria, but she could assert as regards herself and her friends that *they* were altruistic even in their dreams. My friend, although himself of English race, was obliged to contradict the lady emphatically on the ground of his personal experience in dream-analysis, and to declare that in their dreams high-minded American ladies were quite as egoistic as the Austrians.

Thus the transformation of instinct, on which our susceptibility to culture is based, may also be permanently or temporarily undone by the impacts of life. The influences of war are undoubtedly among the forces that can bring about such involution; so we need not deny susceptibility to culture to all who are at the present time behaving in an uncivilized way, and we may anticipate that the ennoblement of their instincts will be restored in more peaceful times.

There is, however, another symptom in our fellow-citizens of the world which has perhaps astonished and shocked us no less than the descent from their ethical heights which has given us so much pain. What I have in mind is the want of insight shown by the best intellects, their obduracy, their inaccessibility to the most forcible arguments and their uncritical credulity towards the most disputable assertions. This indeed presents a lamentable picture, and I wish to say emphatically that in this I am by no means a blind partisan who finds all the intellectual shortcomings on one side. But this phenomenon is much easier to account for and much less disquieting than the one we have just considered. Students of human nature and philosophers have long taught us that we are mistaken in regarding our intelligence as an independent force and in overlooking its dependence on emotional life. Our intellect, they

1. [Freud later qualified this view in an addition made in 1925 to a footnote to *The Interpretation of Dreams* (*P.F.L.*, **4**, 374 *n.*), where he also tells the anecdote which follows. The 'English friend', as is there made plain, was Dr Ernest Jones.]

teach us, can function reliably only when it is removed from the influences of strong emotional impulses; otherwise it behaves merely as an instrument of the will and delivers the inference which the will requires. Thus, in their view, logical arguments are impotent against affective interests, and that is why disputes backed by reasons, which in Falstaff's phrase are 'as plenty as blackberries',[1] are so unfruitful in the world of interests. Psychoanalytic experience has, if possible, further confirmed this statement. It can show every day that the shrewdest people will all of a sudden behave without insight, like imbeciles, as soon as the necessary insight is confronted by an emotional resistance, but that they will completely regain their understanding once that resistance has been overcome. The logical bedazzlement which this war has conjured up in our fellow-citizens, many of them the best of their kind, is therefore a secondary phenomenon, a consequence of emotional excitement, and is bound, we may hope, to disappear with it.

Having in this way once more come to understand our fellow-citizens who are now alienated from us, we shall much more easily endure the disappointment which the nations, the collective individuals of mankind, have caused us, for the demands we make upon these should be far more modest. Perhaps they are recapitulating the course of individual development, and to-day still represent very primitive phases in organization and in the formation of higher unities. It is in agreement with this that the educative factor of an external compulsion towards morality, which we found was so effective in individuals, is as yet barely discernible in them. We had hoped, certainly, that the extensive community of interests established by commerce and production would constitute the germ of such a compulsion, but it would seem that nations still obey their passions far more readily than their interests. Their interests serve them, at most, as *rationalizations* for their passions; they put forward their interests in order to be able to give reasons for satisfying their passions. It is, to be sure,

1. [*I Henry IV*, Act II, Scene 4.]

a mystery why the collective individuals should in fact despise, hate and detest one another – every nation against every other – and even in times of peace. I cannot tell why that is so. It is just as though when it becomes a question of a number of people, not to say millions, all individual moral acquisitions are obliterated, and only the most primitive, the oldest, the crudest mental attitudes are left. It may be that only later stages in development will be able to make some change in this regrettable state of affairs. But a little more truthfulness and honesty on all sides – in the relations of men to one another and between them and their rulers – should also smooth the way for this transformation.

II

OUR ATTITUDE TOWARDS DEATH

THE second factor to which I attribute our present sense of estrangement in this once lovely and congenial world is the disturbance that has taken place in the attitude which we have hitherto adopted towards death.

That attitude was far from straightforward. To anyone who listened to us we were of course prepared to maintain that death was the necessary outcome of life, that everyone owes nature a death[1] and must expect to pay the debt – in short, that death was natural, undeniable and unavoidable. In reality, however, we were accustomed to behave as if it were otherwise. We showed an unmistakable tendency to put death on one side, to eliminate it from life. We tried to hush it up; indeed we even have a saying [in German]: 'to think of something as though it were death'.[2] That is, as though it were our own death, of course. It is indeed impossible to imagine our own death; and whenever we attempt to do so we can perceive that we are in fact still present as spectators. Hence the psychoanalytic school could venture on the assertion that at bottom no one believes in his own death, or, to put the same thing another way, that in the unconscious every one of us is convinced of his own immortality.

When it comes to someone else's death, the civilized man will carefully avoid speaking of such a possibility in the hearing of the person under sentence. Children alone disregard this restriction; they unashamedly threaten one another with the possibility of dying, and even go so far as to do the same thing

1. [A reminiscence of Prince Hal's remark to Falstaff in *I Henry IV* (Act V, Scene 1): 'Thou owest God a death.']
2. [I.e. to think something unlikely or incredible.]

to someone whom they love, as, for instance: 'Dear Mummy, when you're dead I'll do this or that.' The civilized adult can hardly even entertain the thought of another person's death without seeming to himself hard-hearted or wicked; unless, of course, as a doctor or lawyer or something of the kind, he has to deal with death professionally. Least of all will he allow himself to think of the other person's death if some gain to himself in freedom, property or position is bound up with it. This sensitiveness of ours does not, of course, prevent the occurrence of deaths; when one does happen, we are always deeply affected, and it is as though we were badly shaken in our expectations. Our habit is to lay stress on the fortuitous causation of the death – accident, disease, infection, advanced age; in this way we betray an effort to reduce death from a necessity to a chance event. A number of simultaneous deaths strikes us as something extremely terrible. Towards the actual person who has died we adopt a special attitude – something almost like admiration for someone who has accomplished a very difficult task. We suspend criticism of him, overlook his possible misdeeds, declare that 'de mortuis nil nisi bonum', and think it justifiable to set out all that is most favourable to his memory in the funeral oration and upon the tombstone. Consideration for the dead, who, after all, no longer need it, is more important to us than the truth, and certainly, for most of us, than consideration for the living.

The complement to this cultural and conventional attitude towards death is provided by our complete collapse when death has struck down someone whom we love – a parent or a partner in marriage, a brother or sister, a child or a close friend. Our hopes, our desires and our pleasures lie in the grave with him, we will not be consoled, we will not fill the lost one's place. We behave as if we were a kind of Asra, who die when those they love die.[1]

But this attitude of ours towards death has a powerful effect on our lives. Life is impoverished, it loses in interest, when

1. [The Asra in Heine's poem ('Der Asra', in *Romanzero*, based on a passage in Stendhal's *De l'amour*) were a tribe of Arabs who 'die when they love'.]

78

the highest stake in the game of living, life itself, may not be risked. It becomes as shallow and empty as, let us say, an American flirtation, in which it is understood from the first that nothing is to happen, as contrasted with a Continental love-affair in which both partners must constantly bear its serious consequences in mind. Our emotional ties, the unbearable intensity of our grief, make us disinclined to court danger for ourselves and for those who belong to us. We dare not contemplate a great many undertakings which are dangerous but in fact indispensable, such as attempts at artificial flight, expeditions to distant countries or experiments with explosive substances. We are paralysed by the thought of who is to take the son's place with his mother, the husband's with his wife, the father's with his children, if a disaster should occur. Thus the tendency to exclude death from our calculations in life brings in its train many other renunciations and exclusions. Yet the motto of the Hanseatic League ran: *'Navigare necesse est, vivere non necesse.'* ('It is necessary to sail the seas, it is not necessary to live.')

It is an inevitable result of all this that we should seek in the world of fiction, in literature and in the theatre compensation for what has been lost in life. There we still find people who know how to die – who, indeed, even manage to kill someone else. There alone too the condition can be fulfilled which makes it possible for us to reconcile ourselves with death: namely, that behind all the vicissitudes of life we should still be able to preserve a life intact. For it is really too sad that in life it should be as it is in chess, where one false move may force us to resign the game, but with the difference that we can start no second game, no return-match. In the realm of fiction we find the plurality of lives which we need. We die with the hero with whom we have identified ourselves; yet we survive him, and are ready to die again just as safely with another hero.

It is evident that war is bound to sweep away this conventional treatment of death. Death will no longer be denied; we are forced to believe in it. People really die; and no longer one by one, but many, often tens of thousands, in a single day. And death is no longer a chance event. To be sure, it still seems a matter of chance whether a bullet hits this man or that; but a second bullet may well hit the survivor; and the accumulation of deaths puts an end to the impression of chance. Life has, indeed, become interesting again; it has recovered its full content.

Here a distinction should be made between two groups – those who themselves risk their lives in battle, and those who have stayed at home and have only to wait for the loss of one of their dear ones by wounds, disease or infection. It would be most interesting, no doubt, to study the changes in the psychology of the combatants, but I know too little about it. We must restrict ourselves to the second group, to which we ourselves belong. I have said already that in my opinion the bewilderment and the paralysis of capacity, from which we suffer, are essentially determined among other things by the circumstance that we are unable to maintain our former attitude towards death, and have not yet found a new one. It may assist us to do this if we direct our psychological inquiry towards two other relations to death – the one which we may ascribe to primaeval, prehistoric men, and the one which still exists in every one of us, but which conceals itself, invisible to consciousness, in the deeper strata of our mental life.

What the attitude of prehistoric man was towards death is, of course, only known to us by inferences and constructions, but I believe that these methods have furnished us with fairly trustworthy conclusions.

Primaeval man took up a very remarkable attitude towards death. It was far from consistent; it was indeed most contradictory. On the one hand, he took death seriously, recognized it as the termination of life and made use of it in that sense; on the other hand, he also denied death and reduced it to nothing. This contradiction arose from the fact that he took up radically different attitudes towards the death of other people, of strangers, of enemies, and towards his own. He had no objection to someone else's death; it meant the annihilation of someone he hated, and primitive man had no scruples against bringing it about. He was no doubt a very passionate creature and more cruel and more malignant than other animals. He liked to kill, and killed as a matter of course. The instinct which is said to restrain other animals from killing and devouring their own species need not be attributed to him.

Hence the primaeval history of mankind is filled with murder. Even to-day, the history of the world which our children learn at school is essentially a series of murders of peoples. The obscure sense of guilt to which mankind has been subject since prehistoric times, and which in some religions has been condensed into the doctrine of primal guilt, of original sin, is probably the outcome of a blood-guilt incurred by pre-historic man. In my book *Totem and Taboo* (1912–13)[1] I have, following clues given by Robertson Smith, Atkinson and Charles Darwin, tried to guess the nature of this primal guilt, and I believe, too, that the Christian doctrine of to-day enables us to deduce it. If the Son of God was obliged to sacrifice his life to redeem mankind from original sin, then by the law of talion, the requital of like by like, that sin must have been a killing, a murder. Nothing else could call for the sacrifice of a life for its expiation. And the original sin was an offence against God the Father, the primal crime of mankind must have been a parricide, the killing of the primal father of the primitive human horde, whose mnemic image was later transfigured into a deity.[2]

His own death was certainly just as unimaginable and unreal for primaeval man as it is for any one of us to-day. But there was for him one case in which the two opposite attitudes towards death collided and came into conflict with each other; and this case became highly important and productive of far-reaching consequences. It occurred when primaeval man saw someone who belonged to him die – his wife, his child, his friend – whom he undoubtedly loved as we love ours, for love cannot be much younger than the lust to kill. Then, in his

1. [*P.F.L.*, **13**.]
2. Cf. *Totem and Taboo*, Essay IV [*P.F.L.*, **13**].

pain, he was forced to learn that one can die, too, oneself, and his whole being revolted against the admission; for each of these loved ones was, after all, a part of his own beloved ego. But, on the other hand, deaths such as these pleased him as well, since in each of the loved ones there was also something of the stranger. The law of ambivalence of feeling, which to this day governs our emotional relations with those whom we love most, certainly had a very much wider validity in primaeval times. Thus these beloved dead had also been enemies and strangers who had aroused in him some degree of hostile feeling.[1]

Philosophers have declared that the intellectual enigma presented to primaeval man by the picture of death forced him to reflection, and thus became the starting-point of all speculation. I believe that here the philosophers are thinking too philosophically, and giving too little consideration to the motives that were primarily operative. I should like therefore to limit and correct their assertion. In my view, primaeval man must have triumphed beside the body of his slain enemy, without being led to rack his brains about the enigma of life and death. What released the spirit of inquiry in man was not the intellectual enigma, and not every death, but the conflict of feeling at the death of loved yet alien and hated persons. Of this conflict of feeling psychology was the first offspring. Man could no longer keep death at a distance, for he had tasted it in his pain about the dead; but he was nevertheless unwilling to acknowledge it, for he could not conceive of himself as dead. So he devised a compromise: he conceded the fact of his own death as well, but denied it the significance of annihilation – a significance which he had had no motive for denying where the death of his enemy was concerned. It was beside the dead body of someone he loved that he invented spirits, and his sense of guilt at the satisfaction mingled with his sorrow turned these new-born spirits into evil demons that had to be dreaded. The [physical] changes brought about by death suggested to him

1. Ibid., Essay II.

the division of the individual into a body and a soul – originally several souls. In this way his train of thought ran parallel with the process of disintegration which sets in with death. His persisting memory of the dead became the basis for assuming other forms of existence and gave him the conception of a life continuing after apparent death.

These subsequent existences were at first no more than appendages to the existence which death had brought to a close – shadowy, empty of content, and valued at little until later times; they still bore the character of wretched makeshifts. We may recall the answer made to Odysseus by the soul of Achilles:

'For of old, when thou wast alive, we Argives honoured thee even as the gods, and now that thou art here, thou rulest mightily over the dead. Wherefore grieve not at all that thou art dead, Achilles.'

So I spoke, and he straightaway made answer and said: 'Nay, seek not to speak soothingly to me of death, glorious Odysseus. I should choose, so I might live on earth, to serve as the hireling of another, of some portionless man whose livelihood was but small, rather than to be lord over all the dead that have perished.'[1]

Or in Heine's powerful and bitter parody:

> Der kleinste lebendige Philister
> Zu Stuckert am Neckar
> Viel glücklicher ist er
> Als ich, der Pelide, der tote Held,
> Der Schattenfürst in der Unterwelt.[2]

It was only later that religions succeeded in representing this after-life as the more desirable, the truly valid one, and in reducing the life which is ended by death to a mere preparation. After this, it was no more than consistent to extend life backwards into the past, to form the notion of earlier existences, of the transmigration of souls and of reincarnation, all with

1. *Odyssey* XI, 484–91. [Trans. A. T. Murray.]

2. [Literally: 'The smallest living Philistine at Stuckert-am-Neckar is far happier than I, the son of Peleus, the dead hero, the shadow-prince in the underworld.' The closing lines of 'Der Scheidende', one of the very last of Heine's poems.]

the purpose of depriving death of its meaning as the termination of life. So early did the denial of death, which we have described [p. 78] as a 'conventional and cultural attitude', have its origin.

What came into existence beside the dead body of the loved one was not only the doctrine of the soul, the belief in immortality and a powerful source of man's sense of guilt, but also the earliest ethical commandments. The first and most important prohibition made by the awakening conscience was: 'Thou shalt not kill.' It was acquired in relation to dead people who were loved, as a reaction against the satisfaction of the hatred hidden behind the grief for them; and it was gradually extended to strangers who were not loved, and finally even to enemies.

This final extension of the commandment is no longer experienced by civilized man. When the furious struggle of the present war has been decided, each one of the victorious fighters will return home joyfully to his wife and children, unchecked and undisturbed by thoughts of the enemies he has killed whether at close quarters or at long range. It is worthy of note that the primitive races which still survive in the world, and are undoubtedly closer than we are to primaeval man, act differently in this respect, or did until they came under the influence of our civilization. Savages – Australians, Bushmen, Tierra del Fuegans – are far from being remorseless murderers; when they return victorious from the war-path they may not set foot in their village or touch their wives till they have atoned for the murders they committed in war by penances which are often long and tedious. It is easy, of course, to attribute this to their superstition: the savage still goes in fear of the avenging spirits of the slain. But the spirits of his slain enemy are nothing but the expression of his bad conscience about his blood-guilt; behind this superstition there lies concealed a vein of ethical sensitiveness which has been lost by us civilized men.[1]

Pious souls, no doubt, who would like to believe that our nature is remote from any contact with what is evil and base,

1. Cf. *Totem and Taboo* (1912–13) [Essay II (4); *P.F.L.*, **13**].

will not fail to use the early appearance and the urgency of the prohibition against murder as the basis for gratifying conclusions as to the strength of the ethical impulses which must have been implanted in us. Unfortunately this argument proves even more for the opposite view. So powerful a prohibition can only be directed against an equally powerful impulse. What no human soul desires stands in no need of prohibition;[1] it is excluded automatically. The very emphasis laid on the commandment 'Thou shalt not kill' makes it certain that we spring from an endless series of generations of murderers, who had the lust for killing in their blood, as, perhaps, we ourselves have to-day. Mankind's ethical strivings, whose strength and significance we need not in the least depreciate, were acquired in the course of man's history; since then they have become, though unfortunately only in a very variable amount, the inherited property of contemporary men.

Let us now leave primaeval man, and turn to the unconscious in our own mental life. Here we depend entirely upon the psychoanalytic method of investigation, the only one which reaches to such depths. What, we ask, is the attitude of our unconscious towards the problem of death? The answer must be: almost exactly the same as that of primaeval man. In this respect, as in many others, the man of prehistoric times survives unchanged in our unconscious. Our unconscious, then, does not believe in its own death; it behaves as if it were immortal. What we call our 'unconscious' – the deepest strata of our minds, made up of instinctual impulses – knows nothing that is negative, and no negation; in it contradictories coincide. For that reason it does not know its own death, for to that we can give only a negative content. Thus there is nothing instinctual in us which responds to a belief in death. This may even be the secret of heroism. The rational grounds for heroism rest on a judgement that the subject's own life cannot be so precious as certain abstract and general goods. But more frequent, in my view, is the instinctive and impulsive heroism

1. Cf. Frazer's brilliant argument quoted in *Totem and Taboo* [in Essay IV; *P.F.L.*, **13**, 183–4].

which knows no such reasons, and flouts danger in the spirit of Anzengruber's *Steinklopferhans*: 'Nothing can happen to *me*'.[1] Or else those reasons only serve to clear away the hesitations which might hold back the heroic reaction that corresponds to the unconscious. The fear of death, which dominates us oftener than we know, is on the other hand something secondary, and is usually the outcome of a sense of guilt.[2]

On the other hand, for strangers and for enemies we do acknowledge death, and consign them to it quite as readily and unhesitatingly as did primaeval man. There is, it is true, a distinction here which will be pronounced decisive so far as real life is concerned. Our unconscious does not carry out the killing; it merely thinks it and wishes it. But it would be wrong so completely to undervalue this psychical reality as compared with factual reality. It is significant and momentous enough. In our unconscious impulses we daily and hourly get rid of anyone who stands in our way, of anyone who has offended or injured us. The expression 'Devil take him!', which so often comes to people's lips in joking anger and which really means 'Death take him!', is in our unconscious a serious and powerful death wish. Indeed, our unconscious will murder even for trifles; like the ancient Athenian code of Draco, it knows no other punishment for crime than death. And this has a certain consistency, for every injury to our almighty and autocratic ego is at bottom a crime of *lèse-majesté*.

And so, if we are to be judged by our unconscious wishful impulses, we ourselves are, like primaeval man, a gang of murderers. It is fortunate that all these wishes do not possess the potency that was attributed to them in primaeval times;[3] in the cross-fire of mutual curses mankind would long since have perished, the best and wisest of men and the loveliest and fairest of women with the rest.

1. ['Hans the Stone-Breaker' – a character in a comedy by the Viennese dramatist Ludwig Anzengruber (1839–89).]

2. [The fear of death is discussed more fully in *The Ego and the Id* (1923*b*), *P.F.L.*, **11**, and in *Inhibitions, Symptoms and Anxiety* (1926*d*), ibid., **10**, 284–7.]

3. See *Totem and Taboo*, Essay III (3). [*P.F.L.*, **13**, 143.]

Psychoanalysis finds as a rule no credence among laymen for assertions such as these. They reject them as calumnies which are confuted by conscious experience, and they adroitly overlook the faint indications by which even the unconscious is apt to betray itself to consciousness. It is therefore relevant to point out that many thinkers who could not have been influenced by psychoanalysis have quite definitely accused our unspoken thoughts of being ready, heedless of the prohibition against murder, to get rid of anything which stands in our way. From many examples of this I will choose one that has become famous:

In *Le Père Goriot*, Balzac alludes to a passage in the works of J. J. Rousseau where that author asks the reader what he would do if – without leaving Paris and of course without being discovered – he could kill, with great profit to himself, an old mandarin in Peking by a mere act of will. Rousseau implies that he would not give much for the life of that dignitary. '*Tuer son mandarin*' has become a proverbial phrase for this secret readiness, present even in modern man.

There are also a whole number of cynical jokes and anecdotes which reveal the same tendency – such, for instance, as the words attributed to a husband: 'If one of us two dies, I shall move to Paris.' Such cynical jokes would not be possible unless they contained an unacknowledged truth which could not be admitted if it were expressed seriously and without disguise. In jest – it is well known – one may even tell the truth.

Just as for primaeval man, so also for our unconscious, there is one case in which the two opposing attitudes towards death, the one which acknowledges it as the annihilation of life and the other which denies it as unreal, collide and come into conflict. This case is the same as in primal ages: the death, or the risk of death, of someone we love, a parent or a partner in marriage, a brother or sister, a child or a dear friend. These loved ones are on the one hand an inner possession, components of our own ego; but on the other hand they are partly strangers, even enemies. With the exception of only a very few situations, there adheres to the tenderest and most intimate of our love-relations a small portion of hostility which can excite an unconscious death-wish. But this conflict due to ambivalence does not now, as it did then, lead to the doctrine of the soul and to ethics, but to neurosis, which affords us deep insight into normal mental life as well. How often have physicians who practise psychoanalysis had to deal with the symptom of an exaggerated worry over the well-being of relatives, or with entirely unfounded self-reproaches after the death of a loved person. The study of such phenomena has left them in no doubt about the extent and importance of unconscious death-wishes.

The layman feels an extraordinary horror at the possibility of such feelings, and takes this aversion as a legitimate ground for disbelief in the assertions of psychoanalysis. Mistakenly, I think. No depreciation of feelings of love is intended, and there is in fact none. It is indeed foreign to our intelligence as well as to our feelings thus to couple love and hate; but Nature, by making use of this pair of opposites, contrives to keep love ever vigilant and fresh, so as to guard it against the hate which lurks behind it. It might be said that we owe the fairest flowerings of our love to the reaction against the hostile impulse which we sense within us.

To sum up: our unconscious is just as inaccessible to the idea of our own death, just as murderously inclined towards strangers, just as divided (that is, ambivalent) towards those we love, as was primaeval man. But how far we have moved from this primal state in our conventional and cultural attitude towards death!

It is easy to see how war impinges on this dichotomy. It strips us of the later accretions of civilization, and lays bare the primal man in each of us. It compels us once more to be heroes who cannot believe in their own death; it stamps strangers as enemies, whose death is to be brought about or desired; it tells us to disregard the death of those we love. But war cannot be abolished; so long as the conditions of existence among nations are so different and their mutual repulsion so violent, there are bound to be wars. The question then arises: Is it not we who should give in, who should adapt ourselves to war? Should we not confess that in our civilized attitude towards death we are once again living psychologically beyond our means, and should we not rather turn back and recognize the truth? Would it not be better to give death the place in reality and in our thoughts which is its due, and to give a little more prominence to the unconscious attitude towards death which we have hitherto so carefully suppressed? This hardly seems an advance to higher achievement, but rather in some respects a backward step – a regression; but it has the advantage of taking the truth more into account, and of making life more tolerable for us once again. To tolerate life remains, after all, the first duty of all living beings. Illusion becomes valueless if it makes this harder for us.

We recall the old saying: *Si vis pacem, para bellum*. If you want to preserve peace, arm for war.

It would be in keeping with the times to alter it: *Si vis vitam, para mortem*. If you want to endure life, prepare yourself for death.

GROUP PSYCHOLOGY AND THE ANALYSIS OF THE EGO
(1921)

EDITOR'S NOTE

MASSENPSYCHOLOGIE UND ICH-ANALYSE

(A) German Editions:

1921   Leipzig, Vienna and Zurich: Internationaler Psycho-
        analytischer Verlag. (2nd ed., 1923.)
1940   *Gesammelte Werke*, **13**, 71–161.

(B) English Translation:

Group Psychology and the Analysis of the Ego

1922   London and Vienna: International Psycho-Analytical
        Press. (Tr. J. Strachey.)
1940   London: Hogarth Press and Institute of Psycho-
        Analysis; New York: Liveright. (Re-issue of above.)
1955   *Standard Edition*, **18**, 65–143. (Considerably altered
        version of the 1922 translation.)

The present edition is a reprint of the *Standard Edition* version,
with slight editorial changes.

In the first German edition some of the paragraphs in the text
were printed in small type. The English translator was
instructed by Freud at the time to transfer these paragraphs
to footnotes. The same transposition was carried out in all the
later German editions except in the case mentioned on p. 124
below. Freud made some slight changes and additions in the
later editions of the work.

Freud's letters showed that the first 'simple idea' of an
explanation of group psychology occurred to him during the

spring of 1919. Nothing came of this at the time, but in February 1920, he was working at the subject and he had written a first draft in August of the same year. It was not until February 1921, however, that he began giving it its final form. The book was finished before the end of March 1921, and published some three or four months later.

There is little direct connection between the present work and its close predecessor, *Beyond the Pleasure Principle* (1920g). The trains of thought which Freud here takes up are more especially derived from the fourth essay in *Totem and Taboo* (1912–13) and his papers on narcissism (1914c) (the last paragraph of which raises in a highly condensed form many of the points discussed in the present work) and 'Mourning and Melancholia' (1917e). Freud also returns here to his early interest in hypnotism and suggestion, which dated from his studies with Charcot in 1885–6.

As is indicated by its title, the work is important in two different directions. On the one hand it explains the psychology of groups on the basis of changes in the psychology of the individual mind. And on the other hand it carries a stage further Freud's investigation of the anatomical structure of the mind which was already foreshadowed in *Beyond the Pleasure Principle* (1920g) and was to be more completely worked out in *The Ego and the Id* (1923b).

GROUP PSYCHOLOGY AND THE ANALYSIS OF THE EGO

I

INTRODUCTION

THE contrast between individual psychology and social or group[1] psychology, which at a first glance may seem to be full of significance, loses a great deal of its sharpness when it is examined more closely. It is true that individual psychology is concerned with the individual man and explores the paths by which he seeks to find satisfaction for his instinctual impulses; but only rarely and under certain exceptional conditions is individual psychology in a position to disregard the relations of this individual to others. In the individual's mental life someone else is invariably involved, as a model, as an object, as a helper, as an opponent; and so from the very first individual psychology, in this extended but entirely justifiable sense of the words, is at the same time social psychology as well.

The relations of an individual to his parents and to his brothers and sisters, to the object of his love, and to his physician – in fact all the relations which have hitherto been the chief subject of psychoanalytic research – may claim to be considered

---

1. ['Group' is used throughout the translation of this work as equivalent to the rather more comprehensive German '*Masse*'. The author uses this latter word to render both McDougall's 'group', and also Le Bon's '*foule*', which would more naturally be translated 'crowd' in English. For the sake of uniformity, however, 'group' has been preferred in this case as well, and has been substituted for 'crowd' even in the extracts from the English translation of Le Bon.]

as social phenomena; and in this respect they may be contrasted with certain other processes, described by us as 'narcissistic', in which the satisfaction of the instincts is partially or totally withdrawn from the influence of other people. The contrast between social and narcissistic – Bleuler [1912] would perhaps call them 'autistic' – mental acts therefore falls wholly within the domain of individual psychology, and is not well calculated to differentiate it from a social or group psychology.

The individual in the relations which have already been mentioned – to his parents and to his brothers and sisters, to the person he is in love with, to his friend, and to his physician – comes under the influence of only a single person, or of a very small number of persons, each one of whom has become enormously important to him. Now in speaking of social or group psychology it has become usual to leave these relations on one side and to isolate as the subject of inquiry the influencing of an individual by a large number of people simultaneously, people with whom he is connected by something, though otherwise they may in many respects be strangers to him. Group psychology is therefore concerned with the individual man as a member of a race, of a nation, of a caste, of a profession, of an institution, or as a component part of a crowd of people who have been organized into a group at some particular time for some definite purpose. When once natural continuity has been severed in this way, if a breach is thus made between things which are by nature interconnected, it is easy to regard the phenomena that appear under these special conditions as being expressions of a special instinct that is not further reducible – the social instinct ('herd instinct', 'group mind'),[1] which does not come to light in any other situations. But we may perhaps venture to object that it seems difficult to attribute to the factor of number a significance so great as to make it capable by itself of arousing in our mental life a new instinct that is otherwise not brought into play. Our expectation is therefore directed towards two other possibilities:

1. [These terms are in English in the original.]

that the social instinct may not be a primitive one and insusceptible of dissection, and that it may be possible to discover the beginnings of its development in a narrower circle, such as that of the family.

Although group psychology is only in its infancy, it embraces an immense number of separate issues and offers to investigators countless problems which have hitherto not even been properly distinguished from one another. The mere classification of the different forms of group formation and the description of the mental phenomena produced by them require a great expenditure of observation and exposition, and have already given rise to a copious literature. Anyone who compares the narrow dimensions of this little book with the wide extent of group psychology will at once be able to guess that only a few points chosen from the whole material are to be dealt with here. And they will in fact only be a few questions with which the depth-psychology of psychoanalysis is specially concerned.

II

LE BON'S DESCRIPTION OF THE GROUP MIND

INSTEAD of starting from a definition, it seems more useful to begin with some indication of the range of the phenomena under review, and to select from among them a few specially striking and characteristic facts to which our inquiry can be attached. We can achieve both of these aims by means of quotation from Le Bon's deservedly famous work *Psychologie des foules* [1895].

Let us make the matter clear once again. If a psychology, concerned with exploring the predispositions, the instinctual impulses, the motives and the aims of an individual man down to his actions and his relations with those who are nearest to him, had completely achieved its task, and had cleared up the whole of these matters with their interconnections, it would then suddenly find itself confronted by a new task which would lie before it unachieved. It would be obliged to explain the surprising fact that under a certain condition this individual, whom it had come to understand, thought, felt and acted in quite a different way from what would have been expected. And this condition is his insertion into a collection of people which has acquired the characteristic of a 'psychological group'. What, then, is a 'group'? How does it acquire the capacity for exercising such a decisive influence over the mental life of the individual? And what is the nature of the mental change which it forces upon the individual?

It is the task of a theoretical group psychology to answer these three questions. The best way of approaching them is evidently to start with the third. Observation of the changes in the individual's reactions is what provides group psychology with its material; for every attempt at an explanation must be preceded by a description of the thing that is to be explained.

I will now let Le Bon speak for himself. He says: 'The most striking peculiarity presented by a psychological group[1] is the following. Whoever be the individuals that compose it, however like or unlike be their mode of life, their occupations, their character, or their intelligence, the fact that they have been transformed into a group puts them in possession of a sort of collective mind which makes them feel, think, and act in a manner quite different from that in which each individual of them would feel, think, and act were he in a state of isolation. There are certain ideas and feelings which do not come into being, or do not transform themselves into acts except in the case of individuals forming a group. The psychological group is a provisional being formed of heterogeneous elements, which for a moment are combined, exactly as the cells which constitute a living body form by their reunion a new being which displays characteristics very different from those possessed by each of the cells singly.' (Trans. 1920, 29.)

We shall take the liberty of interrupting Le Bon's exposition with glosses of our own, and shall accordingly insert an observation at this point. If the individuals in the group are combined into a unity, there must surely be something to unite them, and this bond might be precisely the thing that is characteristic of a group. But Le Bon does not answer this question; he goes on to consider the alteration which the individual undergoes when in a group and describes it in terms which harmonize well with the fundamental postulates of our own depth-psychology.

'It is easy to prove how much the individual forming part of a group differs from the isolated individual, but it is less easy to discover the causes of this difference.

'To obtain at any rate a glimpse of them it is necessary in the first place to call to mind the truth established by modern psychology, that unconscious phenomena play an altogether preponderating part not only in organic life, but also in the

1. [See footnote p. 95. – This and the following quotations are from the English translation.]

operations of the intelligence. The conscious life of the mind is of small importance in comparison with its unconscious life. The most subtle analyst, the most acute observer, is scarcely successful in discovering more than a very small number of the conscious[1] motives that determine his conduct. Our conscious acts are the outcome of an unconscious substratum created in the mind mainly by hereditary influences. This substratum consists of the innumerable common characteristics handed down from generation to generation, which constitute the genius of a race. Behind the avowed causes of our acts there undoubtedly lie secret causes that we do not avow, but behind these secret causes there are many others more secret still, of which we ourselves are ignorant.[2] The greater part of our daily actions are the result of hidden motives which escape our observation.' (Ibid., 30.)

Le Bon thinks that the particular acquirements of individuals become obliterated in a group, and that in this way their distinctiveness vanishes. The racial unconscious emerges; what is heterogeneous is submerged in what is homogeneous. As we should say, the mental superstructure, the development of which in individuals shows such dissimilarities, is removed, and the unconscious foundations, which are similar in everyone, stand exposed to view.

In this way individuals in a group would come to show an average character. But Le Bon believes that they also display new characteristics which they have not previously possessed, and he seeks the reason for this in three different factors.

'The first is that the individual forming part of a group acquires, solely from numerical considerations, a sentiment of invincible power which allows him to yield to instincts which, had he been alone, he would perforce have kept under restraint.

1. [As was pointed out in a footnote in the German edition of 1940, the original French text reads '*inconscients*'. The English translation of Le Bon has 'unconscious', but the German version, quoted by Freud, has '*bewusster*' ('conscious').]

2. [The English translation reads 'which we ourselves ignore' – a misunderstanding of the French word '*ignorées*'.]

He will be the less disposed to check himself, from the consideration that, a group being anonymous and in consequence irresponsible, the sentiment of responsibility which always controls individuals disappears entirely.' (Ibid., 33.)

From our point of view we need not attribute so much importance to the appearance of new characteristics. For us it would be enough to say that in a group the individual is brought under conditions which allow him to throw off the repressions of his unconscious instinctual impulses. The apparently new characteristics which he then displays are in fact the manifestations of this unconscious, in which all that is evil in the human mind is contained as a predisposition. We can find no difficulty in understanding the disappearance of conscience or of a sense of responsibility in these circumstances. It has long been our contention that 'social anxiety' is the essence of what is called conscience.[1]

'The second cause, which is contagion, also intervenes to determine the manifestation in groups of their special characteristics, and at the same time the trend they are to take. Contagion is a phenomenon of which it is easy to establish the presence, but which it is not easy to explain. It must be classed among those phenomena of a hypnotic order, which we shall shortly study. In a group every sentiment and act is contagious, and contagious to such a degree that an individual readily sacrifices his personal interest to the collective interest. This is an aptitude very contrary to his nature, and of which a

---

1. There is some difference between Le Bon's view and ours owing to his concept of the unconscious not quite coinciding with the one adopted by psychoanalysis. Le Bon's unconscious more especially contains the most deeply buried features of the racial mind, which as a matter of fact lies outside the scope of psychoanalysis. We do not fail to recognize, indeed, that the ego's nucleus, which comprises the 'archaic heritage' of the human mind, is unconscious; but in addition to this we distinguish the 'unconscious repressed', which arose from a portion of that heritage. This concept of the repressed is not to be found in Le Bon. [On the relation of conscience to 'social anxiety', see a similar remark in the paper on 'war and death', p. 67 and *n*. I above.]

man is scarcely capable, except when he makes part of a group.'
(Ibid., 33.)

We shall later on base an important conjecture upon this
last statement.

'A third cause, and by far the most important, determines
in the individuals of a group special characteristics which are
quite contrary at times to those presented by the isolated individual. I allude to that suggestibility of which, moreover, the
contagion mentioned above is only an effect.

'To understand this phenomenon it is necessary to bear in
mind certain recent physiological discoveries. We know to-day
that by various processes an individual may be brought into
such a condition that, having entirely lost his conscious personality, he obeys all the suggestions of the operator who has
deprived him of it, and commits acts in utter contradiction
with his character and habits. The most careful investigations
seem to prove that an individual immersed for some length
of time in a group in action soon finds himself – either in
consequence of the magnetic influence given out by the group,
or from some other cause of which we are ignorant – in a
special state, which much resembles the state of "fascination"
in which the hypnotized individual finds himself in the hands
of the hypnotizer ... The conscious personality has entirely
vanished; will and discernment are lost. All feelings and
thoughts are bent in the direction determined by the hypnotizer.

'Such also is approximately the state of the individual forming part of a psychological group. He is no longer conscious
of his acts. In his case, as in the case of the hypnotized subject,
at the same time that certain faculties are destroyed, others
may be brought to a high degree of exaltation. Under the
influence of a suggestion, he will undertake the accomplishment
of certain acts with irresistible impetuosity. This impetuosity
is the more irresistible in the case of groups than in that of
the hypnotized subject, from the fact that, the suggestion being
the same for all the individuals in the group, it gains in strength
by reciprocity.' (Ibid., 34.)

'We see, then, that the disappearance of the conscious personality, the predominance of the unconscious personality, the turning by means of suggestion and contagion of feelings and ideas in an identical direction, the tendency to immediately transform the suggested ideas into acts; these, we see, are the principal characteristics of the individual forming part of a group. He is no longer himself, but has become an automaton who has ceased to be guided by his will.' (Ibid., 35.)

I have quoted this passage so fully in order to make it quite clear that Le Bon explains the condition of an individual in a group as being actually hypnotic, and does not merely make a comparison between the two states. We have no intention of raising any objection at this point, but wish only to emphasize the fact that the two last causes of an individual becoming altered in a group (the contagion and the heightened suggestibility) are evidently not on a par, since the contagion seems actually to be a manifestation of the suggestibility. Moreover the effects of the two factors do not seem to be sharply differentiated in the text of Le Bon's remarks. We may perhaps best interpret his statement if we connect the contagion with the effects of the individual members of the group on one another, while we point to another source for those manifestations of suggestion in the group which he regards as similar to the phenomena of hypnotic influence. But to what source? We cannot avoid being struck with a sense of deficiency when we notice that one of the chief elements of the comparison, namely the person who is to replace the hypnotist in the case of the group, is not mentioned in Le Bon's exposition. But he nevertheless distinguishes between this influence of 'fascination' which remains plunged in obscurity and the contagious effect which the individuals exercise upon one another and by which the original suggestion is strengthened.

Here is yet another important consideration for helping us to understand the individual in a group: 'Moreover, by the mere fact that he forms part of an organized group, a man descends several rungs in the ladder of civilization. Isolated, he may be a cultivated individual; in a crowd, he is a barbarian

– that is, a creature acting by instinct. He possesses the spontaneity, the violence, the ferocity, and also the enthusiasm and heroism of primitive beings.' (Ibid., 36.) Le Bon then dwells especially upon the lowering in intellectual ability which an individual experiences when he becomes merged in a group.[1]

Let us now leave the individual, and turn to the group mind, as it has been outlined by Le Bon. It shows not a single feature which a psychoanalyst would find any difficulty in placing or in deriving from its source. Le Bon himself shows us the way by pointing to its similarity with the mental life of primitive people and of children (ibid., 40).

A group is impulsive, changeable and irritable. It is led almost exclusively by the unconscious.[2] The impulses which a group obeys may according to circumstances be generous or cruel, heroic or cowardly, but they are always so imperious that no personal interest, not even that of self-preservation, can make itself felt (ibid., 41). Nothing about it is premeditated. Though it may desire things passionately, yet this is never so for long, for it is incapable of perseverance. It cannot tolerate any delay between its desire and the fulfilment of what it desires. It has a sense of omnipotence; the notion of impossibility disappears for the individual in a group.[3]

A group is extraordinarily credulous and open to influence, it has no critical faculty, and the improbable does not exist for it. It thinks in images, which call one another up by association (just as they arise with individuals in states of free imagination), and whose agreement with reality is never checked by any reasonable agency. The feelings of a group are always

---

1. Compare Schiller's couplet ['G.G.', one of the 'Aphorisms']:
   Jeder, sieht man ihn einzeln, ist leidlich klug und verständig;
     Sind sie in corpore, gleich wird euch ein Dummkopf daraus.

   [Everyone, looked at alone, is passably shrewd and discerning;
     When they're *in corpore*, then straightway you'll find he's an ass.]
2. 'Unconscious' is used here correctly by Le Bon in the descriptive sense, where it does not mean only the 'repressed'.
3. Compare the third essay in my *Totem and Taboo* (1912–13) [*P.F.L.*, **13**].

very simple and very exaggerated. So that a group knows neither doubt nor uncertainty.[1]

It goes directly to extremes; if a suspicion is expressed, it is instantly changed into an incontrovertible certainty; a trace of antipathy is turned into furious hatred (ibid., 56).[2]

Inclined as it itself is to all extremes, a group can only be excited by an excessive stimulus. Anyone who wishes to produce an effect upon it needs no logical adjustment in his arguments; he must paint in the most forcible colours, he must exaggerate, and he must repeat the same thing again and again.

Since a group is in no doubt as to what constitutes truth or error, and is conscious, moreover, of its own great strength, it is as intolerant as it is obedient to authority. It respects force and can only be slightly influenced by kindness, which it regards merely as a form of weakness. What it demands of its heroes is strength, or even violence. It wants to be ruled and oppressed and to fear its masters. Fundamentally it is

1. In the interpretation of dreams, to which, indeed, we owe our best knowledge of unconscious mental life, we follow a technical rule of disregarding doubt and uncertainty in the narrative of the dream, and of treating every element of the manifest dream as being quite certain. We attribute doubt and uncertainty to the influence of the censorship to which the dreamwork is subjected, and we assume that the primary dream-thoughts are not acquainted with doubt and uncertainty as critical processes. They may of course be present, like anything else, as part of the content of the day's residues which lead to the dream. (See *The Interpretation of Dreams* (1900a) [*P.F.L.*, 4, 660–61].)

2. The same extreme and unmeasured intensification of every emotion is also a feature of the affective life of children, and it is present as well in dream life. Thanks to the isolation of the single emotions in the unconscious, a slight annoyance during the day will express itself in a dream as a wish for the offending person's death, or a breath of temptation may give the impetus to the portrayal in the dream of a criminal action. Hanns Sachs [1912, 569] has made an appropriate remark on this point: 'If we look in our consciousness at something that has been told us by a dream about a contemporary (real) situation, we ought not to be surprised to find that the monster which we saw under the magnifying glass of analysis turns out to be a tiny infusorian.' (*The Interpretation of Dreams* (1900a) [*P.F.L.*, 4, 782].)

entirely conservative, and it has a deep aversion to all innovations and advances and an unbounded respect for tradition (ibid., 62).

In order to make a correct judgement upon the morals of groups, one must take into consideration the fact that when individuals come together in a group all their individual inhibitions fall away and all the cruel, brutal and destructive instincts, which lie dormant in individuals as relics of a primitive epoch, are stirred up to find free gratification. But under the influence of suggestion groups are also capable of high achievements in the shape of abnegation, unselfishness, and devotion to an ideal. While with isolated individuals personal interest is almost the only motive force, with groups it is very rarely prominent. It is possible to speak of an individual having his moral standards raised by a group (ibid., 65). Whereas the intellectual capacity of a group is always far below that of an individual, its ethical conduct may rise as high above his as it may sink deep below it.

Some other features in Le Bon's description show in a clear light how well justified is the identification of the group mind with the mind of primitive people. In groups the most contradictory ideas can exist side by side and tolerate each other, without any conflict arising from the logical contradiction between them. But this is also the case in the unconscious mental life of individuals, of children and of neurotics, as psychoanalysis has long pointed out.[1]

1. In young children, for instance, ambivalent emotional attitudes towards those who are nearest to them exist side by side for a long time, without either of them interfering with the expression of the other and opposite one. If eventually a conflict breaks out between the two, it is often settled by the child making a change of object and displacing one of the ambivalent emotions on to a substitute. The history of the development of a neurosis in an adult will also show that a suppressed emotion may frequently persist for a long time in unconscious or even in conscious phantasies, the content of which naturally runs directly counter to some predominant tendency, and yet that this opposition does not result in any proceedings on the part of the ego against what it has repudiated. The phantasy is tolerated for quite a long time, until suddenly one day, usually as a result of an increase

A group, further, is subject to the truly magical power of words; they can evoke the most formidable tempests in the group mind, and are also capable of stilling them (ibid., 117). 'Reason and arguments are incapable of combating certain words and formulas. They are uttered with solemnity in the presence of groups, and as soon as they have been pronounced an expression of respect is visible on every countenance, and all heads are bowed. By many they are considered as natural forces or as supernatural powers.' (Ibid., 117.) It is only necessary in this connection to remember the taboo upon names among primitive people and the magical powers which they ascribe to names and words.[1]

And, finally, groups have never thirsted after truth. They demand illusions, and cannot do without them. They constantly give what is unreal precedence over what is real; they are almost as strongly influenced by what is untrue as by what is true. They have an evident tendency not to distinguish between the two (ibid., 77).

We have pointed out that this predominance of the life of phantasy and of the illusion born of an unfulfilled wish is the ruling factor in the psychology of neuroses. We have found that what neurotics are guided by is not ordinary objective reality but psychological reality. A hysterical symptom is based upon phantasy instead of upon the repetition of real

---

in the affective cathexis of the phantasy, a conflict breaks out between it and the ego with all the usual consequences. In the process of a child's development into a mature adult there is a more and more extensive integration of his personality, a co-ordination of the separate instinctual impulses and purposive trends which have grown up in him independently of one another. The analogous process in the domain of sexual life has long been known to us as the co-ordination of all the sexual instincts into a definitive genital organization. (*Three Essays on the Theory of Sexuality*, 1905*d* [*P.F.L.*, **7**, 127].) Moreover, that the unification of the ego is liable to the same interferences as that of the libido is shown by numerous familiar instances, such as that of men of science who have preserved their faith in the Bible, and other similar cases. – [*Added* 1923:] The various possible ways in which the ego can later disintegrate form a special chapter in psychopathology.

1. See *Totem and Taboo* (1912–13) [Essay II 3 (*c*); *P.F.L.*, **13**, 110–13].

experience, and the sense of guilt in an obsessional neurosis is based upon the fact of an evil intention which was never carried out. Indeed, just as in dreams and in hypnosis, in the mental operations of a group the function for testing the reality of things falls into the background in comparison with the strength of wishful impulses with their affective cathexis.

What Le Bon says on the subject of leaders of groups is less exhaustive, and does not enable us to make out an underlying principle so clearly. He thinks that as soon as living beings are gathered together in certain numbers, no matter whether they are a herd of animals or a collection of human beings, they place themselves instinctively under the authority of a chief (ibid., 134). A group is an obedient herd, which could never live without a master. It has such a thirst for obedience that it submits instinctively to anyone who appoints himself its master.

Although in this way the needs of a group carry it half-way to meet the leader, yet he too must fit in with it in his personal qualities. He must himself be held in fascination by a strong faith (in an idea) in order to awaken the group's faith; he must possess a strong and imposing will, which the group, which has no will of its own, can accept from him. Le Bon then discusses the different kinds of leaders, and the means by which they work upon the group. On the whole he believes that the leaders make themselves felt by means of the ideas in which they themselves are fanatical believers.

Moreover, he ascribes both to the ideas and to the leaders a mysterious and irresistible power, which he calls 'prestige'. Prestige is a sort of domination exercised over us by an individual, a work or an idea. It entirely paralyses our critical faculty, and fills us with wonderment and respect. It would seem to arouse a feeling like that of 'fascination' in hypnosis (ibid., 148). He distinguishes between acquired or artificial and personal prestige. The former is attached to persons in virtue of their name, fortune and reputation, and to opinions, works of art, etc., in virtue of tradition. Since in every case it harks back to the past, it cannot be of much help to us in understanding this puzzling influence. Personal prestige is attached to a few people, who become leaders by means of it, and it has the effect of making everyone obey them as though by the operation of some magnetic magic. All prestige, however, is also dependent upon success, and is lost in the event of failure (ibid., 159).

Le Bon does not give the impression of having succeeded in bringing the function of the leader and the importance of prestige completely into harmony with his brilliantly executed picture of the group mind.

III

OTHER ACCOUNTS OF COLLECTIVE
MENTAL LIFE

WE have made use of Le Bon's description by way of introduction, because it fits in so well with our own psychology
in the emphasis which it lays upon unconscious mental life.
But we must now add that as a matter of fact none of that
author's statements bring forward anything new. Everything
that he says to the detriment and depreciation of the manifestations of the group mind had already been said by others before
him with equal distinctness and equal hostility, and has been
repeated in unison by thinkers, statesmen and writers since
the earliest periods of literature.[1] The two theses which com-
prise the most important of Le Bon's opinions, those touching
upon the collective inhibition of intellectual functioning and
the heightening of affectivity in groups, had been formulated
shortly before by Sighele.[2] At bottom, all that is left over
as being peculiar to Le Bon are the two notions of the unconscious and of the comparison with the mental life of primitive people, and even these had naturally often been alluded
to before him.

But, what is more, the description and estimate of the group
mind as they have been given by Le Bon and the rest have
not by any means been left undisputed. There is no doubt
that all the phenomena of the group mind which have just
been mentioned have been correctly observed, but it is also
possible to distinguish other manifestations of group formation,
which operate in a precisely opposite sense, and from which
a much higher opinion of the group mind must necessarily
follow.

1. See Kraškovič (1915), particularly the bibliography.
2. See Moede (1915).

Le Bon himself was prepared to admit that in certain circumstances the morals of a group can be higher than those of the individuals that compose it, and that only collectivities are capable of a high degree of unselfishness and devotion. 'While with isolated individuals personal interest is almost the only motive force, with groups it is very rarely prominent.' (Le Bon, trans. 1920, 65.) Other writers adduce the fact that it is only society which prescribes any ethical standards at all for the individual, while he as a rule fails in one way or another to come up to its high demands. Or they point out that in exceptional circumstances there may arise in communities the phenomenon of enthusiasm, which has made the most splendid group achievements possible.

As regards intellectual work it remains a fact, indeed, that great decisions in the realm of thought and momentous discoveries and solutions of problems are only possible to an individual working in solitude. But even the group mind is capable of creative genius in the field of intelligence, as is shown above all by language itself, as well as by folk-song, folklore and the like. It remains an open question, moreover, how much the individual thinker or writer owes to the stimulation of the group in which he lives, and whether he does more than perfect a mental work in which the others have had a simultaneous share.

In face of these completely contradictory accounts, it looks as though the work of group psychology were bound to come to an ineffectual end. But it is easy to find a more hopeful escape from the dilemma. A number of very different structures have probably been merged under the term 'group' and may require to be distinguished. The assertions of Sighele, Le Bon and the rest relate to groups of a short-lived character, which some passing interest has hastily agglomerated out of various sorts of individuals. The characteristics of revolutionary groups, and especially those of the great French Revolution, have unmistakably influenced their descriptions. The opposite opinions owe their origin to the consideration of those stable groups or associations in which mankind pass their lives, and which are embodied in the institutions of society. Groups of the first kind stand in the same sort of relation to those of the second as a high but choppy sea to a ground swell.

McDougall, in his book on *The Group Mind* (1920a), starts out from the same contradiction that has just been mentioned, and finds a solution for it in the factor of organization. In the simplest case, he says, the 'group' possesses no organization at all or one scarcely deserving the name. He describes a group of this kind as a 'crowd'. But he admits that a crowd of human beings can hardly come together without possessing at all events the rudiments of an organization, and that precisely in these simple groups some fundamental facts of collective psychology can be observed with special ease (McDougall, 1920a, 22). Before the members of a random crowd of people can constitute something like a group in the psychological sense, a condition has to be fulfilled: these individuals must have something in common with one another, a common interest in an object, a similar emotional bias in some situation or other, and ('consequently', I should like to interpolate) 'some degree of reciprocal influence' (ibid., 23). The higher the degree of 'this mental homogeneity', the more readily do the individuals form a psychological group, and the more striking are the manifestations of a group mind.

The most remarkable and also the most important result of the formation of a group is the 'exaltation or intensification of emotion' produced in every member of it (ibid., 24). In McDougall's opinion men's emotions are stirred in a group to a pitch that they seldom or never attain under other conditions; and it is a pleasurable experience for those who are concerned, to surrender themselves so unreservedly to their passions and thus to become merged in the group and to lose the sense of the limits of their individuality. The manner in which individuals are thus carried away by a common impulse is explained by McDougall by means of what he calls the 'principle of direct induction of emotion by way of the primitive sympathetic response' (ibid., 25), that is, by means of the emotional contagion with which we are already familiar. The fact is that the perception of the signs of an affective state is calculated automatically to arouse the same affect in the person who perceives them. The greater the number of people in whom the same affect can be simultaneously observed, the stronger does this automatic compulsion grow. The individual loses his power of criticism, and lets himself slip into the same affect. But in so doing he increases the excitement of the other people, who had produced this result in him, and thus the affective charge of the individuals becomes intensified by mutual interaction. Something is unmistakably at work in the nature of a compulsion to do the same as the others, to remain in harmony with the many. The cruder and simpler emotional impulses are the more apt to spread through a group in this way (ibid., 39).

This mechanism for the intensification of affect is favoured by some other influences which emanate from groups. A group impresses the individual as being an unlimited power and an insurmountable peril. For the moment it replaces the whole of human society, which is the wielder of authority, whose punishments the individual fears, and for whose sake he has submitted to so many inhibitions. It is clearly perilous for him to put himself in opposition to it, and it will be safer to follow the example of those around him and perhaps even 'hunt with the pack'. In obedience to the new authority he may put his former 'conscience' out of action, and so surrender to the attraction of the increased pleasure that is certainly obtained from the removal of inhibitions. On the whole, therefore, it is not so remarkable that we should see an individual in a group doing or approving things which he would have avoided in the normal conditions of life; and in this way we may even hope to clear up a little of the obscurity which is so often covered by the enigmatic word 'suggestion'.

McDougall does not dispute the thesis as to the collective inhibition of intelligence in groups (ibid., 41). He says that the minds of lower intelligence bring down those of a higher order to their own level. The latter are obstructed in their activity, because in general an intensification of affect creates unfavourable conditions for sound intellectual work, and further because the individuals are intimidated by the group and their mental activity is not free, and because there is a lowering in each individual of his sense of responsibility for his own performances.

The judgement with which McDougall sums up the psychological behaviour of a simple 'unorganized' group is no more friendly than that of Le Bon. Such a group 'is excessively emotional, impulsive, violent, fickle, inconsistent, irresolute and extreme in action, displaying only the coarser emotions and the less refined sentiments; extremely suggestible, careless in deliberation, hasty in judgement, incapable of any but the simpler and imperfect forms of reasoning; easily swayed and led, lacking in self-consciousness, devoid of self-respect and of sense of responsibility, and apt to be carried away by the consciousness of its own force, so that it tends to produce all the manifestations we have learnt to expect of any irresponsible and absolute power. Hence its behaviour is like that of an unruly child or an untutored passionate savage in a strange situation, rather than like that of its average member; and in the worst cases it is like that of a wild beast, rather than like that of human beings.' (Ibid., 45.)

Since McDougall contrasts the behaviour of a highly organized group with what has just been described, we shall be particularly interested to learn in what this organization consists, and by what factors it is produced. The author enumerates five 'principal conditions' for raising collective mental life to a higher level.

The first and fundamental condition is that there should be some degree of continuity of existence in the group. This may be either material or formal: material, if the same individuals persist in the group for some time; and formal, if there is developed within the group a system of fixed positions which are occupied by a succession of individuals.

The second condition is that in the individual member of the group some definite idea should be formed of the nature, composition, functions and capacities of the group, so that from this he may develop an emotional relation to the group as a whole.

The third is that the group should be brought into interaction (perhaps in the form of rivalry) with other groups similar to it but differing from it in many respects.

The fourth is that the group should possess traditions, customs and habits, and especially such as determine the relations of its members to one another.

The fifth is that the group should have a definite structure, expressed in the specialization and differentiation of the functions of its constituents.

According to McDougall, if these conditions are fulfilled, the psychological disadvantages of group formations are removed. The collective lowering of intellectual ability is avoided by withdrawing the performance of intellectual tasks from the group and reserving them for individual members of it.

It seems to us that the condition which McDougall designates as the 'organization' of a group can with more justification be described in another way. The problem consists in how to procure for the group precisely those features which were characteristic of the individual and which are extinguished in him by the formation of the group. For the individual, outside the primitive group, possessed his own continuity, his self-consciousness, his traditions and customs, his own particular functions and position, and he kept apart from his rivals. Owing to his entry into an 'unorganized' group he had lost this distinctiveness for a time. If we thus recognize that the aim is to equip the group with the attributes of the individual, we shall be reminded of a valuable remark of Trotter's,[1] to the effect that the tendency towards the formation of groups is biologically a continuation of the multicellular character of all the higher organisms.[2]

1. *Instincts of the Herd in Peace and War* (1916). [See below, p. 149 ff.]

2. [*Footnote added* 1923:] I differ from what is in other respects an understanding and shrewd criticism by Hans Kelsen (1922) [of the present work] when he says that to provide the 'group mind' with an organization of this kind signifies a hypostasis of it – that is to say, implies an attribution to it of independence of the mental processes in the individual.

IV

SUGGESTION AND LIBIDO

WE started from the fundamental fact that an individual in a group is subjected through its influence to what is often a profound alteration in his mental activity. His liability to affect becomes extraordinarily intensified, while his intellectual ability is markedly reduced, both processes being evidently in the direction of an approximation to the other individuals in the group; and this result can only be reached by the removal of those inhibitions upon his instincts which are peculiar to each individual, and by his resigning those expressions of his inclinations which are especially his own. We have heard that these often unwelcome consequences are to some extent at least prevented by a higher 'organization' of the group; but this does not contradict the fundamental fact of group psychology – the two theses as to the intensification of the affects and the inhibition of the intellect in primitive groups. Our interest is now directed to discovering the psychological explanation of this mental change which is experienced by the individual in a group.

It is clear that rational factors (such as the intimidation of the individual which has already been mentioned, that is, the action of his instinct of self-preservation) do not cover the observable phenomena. Beyond this what we are offered as an explanation by authorities on sociology and group psychology is always the same, even though it is given various names, and that is – the magic word 'suggestion'. Tarde [1890] calls it 'imitation'; but we cannot help agreeing with a writer who protests that imitation comes under the concept of suggestion, and is in fact one of its results (Brugeilles, 1913).

Le Bon traces back all the puzzling features of social phenomena to two factors: the mutual suggestion of individuals and the prestige of leaders. But prestige, again, is only recognizable by its capacity for evoking suggestion. McDougall for a moment gives us an impression that his principle of 'primitive induction of emotion' might enable us to do without the assumption of suggestion. But on further consideration we are forced to perceive that this principle makes no more than the familiar assertions about 'imitation' or 'contagion', except for a decided stress upon the emotional factor. There is no doubt that something exists in us which, when we become aware of signs of an emotion in someone else, tends to make us fall into the same emotion; but how often do we not success-fully oppose it, resist the emotion, and react in quite an opposite way? Why, therefore, do we invariably give way to this con-tagion when we are in a group? Once more we should have to say that what compels us to obey this tendency is imitation, and what induces the emotion in us is the group's suggestive influence. Moreover, quite apart from this, McDougall does not enable us to evade suggestion; we hear from him as well as from other writers that groups are distinguished by their special suggestibility.

We shall therefore be prepared for the statement that sugges-tion (or more correctly suggestibility) is actually an irreducible, primitive phenomenon, a fundamental fact in the mental life of man. Such, too, was the opinion of Bernheim, of whose astonishing arts I was a witness in the year 1889. But I can remember even then feeling a muffled hostility to this tyranny of suggestion. When a patient who showed himself un-amenable was met with the shout: 'What are you doing? *Vous vous contre-suggestionnez!*', I said to myself that this was an evident injustice and an act of violence. For the man certainly had a right to counter-suggestions if people were trying to subdue him with suggestions. Later on my resist-ance took the direction of protesting against the view that suggestion, which explained everything, was itself to be exempt from explanation. Thinking of it, I repeated the old conundrum:[1]

> Christoph trug Christum,
> Christus trug die ganze Welt,
> Sag' wo hat Christoph
> Damals hin den Fuss gestellt?

> Christophorus Christum, sed Christus sustulit orbem:
> Constiterit pedibus dic ubi Christophorus?[2]

Now that I once more approach the riddle of suggestion after having kept away from it for some thirty years, I find there is no change in the situation. (There is one exception to be made to this statement, and one which bears witness precisely to the influence of psychoanalysis.) I notice that particular efforts are being made to formulate the concept of suggestion correctly, that is, to fix the conventional use of the name (e.g. McDougall, 1920*b*). And this is by no means superfluous, for the word is acquiring a more and more extended use and a looser and looser meaning [in German], and will soon come to designate any sort of influence whatever, just as it does in English, where 'to suggest' and 'suggestion' correspond to our *nahelegen* and *Anregung*. But there has been no explanation of the nature of suggestion, that is, of the conditions under which influence without adequate logical foundation takes place. I should not avoid the task of supporting this statement by an analysis of the literature of the last thirty years, if I were not aware that an exhaustive inquiry is being undertaken close at hand which has in view the fulfilment of this very task.[3]

Instead of this I shall make an attempt at using the concept

---

1. Konrad Richter, 'Der deutsche S. Christoph.' [Berlin, 1896. *Acta Germanica*, V, 1.]

2. [Literally: 'Christopher bore Christ; Christ bore the whole world; Say, where did Christopher then put his foot?']

3. [*Footnote added* 1925:] This work has unfortunately not materialized.

of *libido* for the purpose of throwing light upon group psychology, a concept which has done us such good service in the study of psychoneuroses.

Libido is an expression taken from the theory of the emotions. We call by that name the energy, regarded as a quantitative magnitude (though not at present actually measurable), of those instincts which have to do with all that may be comprised under the word 'love'. The nucleus of what we mean by love naturally consists (and this is what is commonly called love, and what the poets sing of) in sexual love with sexual union as its aim. But we do not separate from this – what in any case has a share in the name 'love' – on the one hand, self-love, and on the other, love for parents and children, friendship and love for humanity in general, and also devotion to concrete objects and to abstract ideas. Our justification lies in the fact that psychoanalytic research has taught us that all these tendencies are an expression of the same instinctual impulses; in relations between the sexes these impulses force their way towards sexual union, but in other circumstances they are diverted from this aim or are prevented from reaching it, though always preserving enough of their original nature to keep their identity recognizable (as in such features as the longing for proximity, and self-sacrifice).

We are of opinion, then, that language has carried out an entirely justifiable piece of unification in creating the word 'love' with its numerous uses, and that we cannot do better than take it as the basis of our scientific discussions and expositions as well. By coming to this decision, psychoanalysis has let loose a storm of indignation, as though it had been guilty of an act of outrageous innovation. Yet it has done nothing original in taking love in this 'wider' sense. In its origin, function, and relation to sexual love, the 'Eros' of the philosopher Plato coincides exactly with the love-force, the libido of psychoanalysis, as has been shown in detail by Nachmansohn (1915) and Pfister (1921); and when the apostle Paul, in his famous epistle to the Corinthians, praises love above all else, he certainly understands it in the same 'wider' sense.[1] But this only shows that men do not always take their great thinkers seriously, even when they profess most to admire them.

Psychoanalysis, then, gives these love instincts the name of sexual instincts, *a potiori* and by reason of their origin. The majority of 'educated' people have regarded this nomenclature as an insult, and have taken their revenge by retorting upon psychoanalysis with the reproach of 'pan-sexualism'. Anyone who considers sex as something mortifying and humiliating to human nature is at liberty to make use of the more genteel expressions 'Eros' and 'erotic'. I might have done so myself from the first and thus have spared myself much opposition. But I did not want to, for I like to avoid concessions to faint-heartedness. One can never tell where that road may lead one; one gives way first in words, and then little by little in substance too. I cannot see any merit in being ashamed of sex; the Greek word 'Eros', which is to soften the affront, is in the end nothing more than a translation of our German word *Liebe* [love]; and finally, he who knows how to wait need make no concessions.

We will try our fortune, then, with the supposition that love relationships (or, to use a more neutral expression, emotional ties) also constitute the essence of the group mind. Let us remember that the authorities make no mention of any such relations. What would correspond to them is evidently concealed behind the shelter, the screen, of suggestion. Our hypothesis finds support in the first instance from two passing thoughts. First, that a group is clearly held together by a power of some kind: and to what power could this feat be better ascribed than to Eros, which holds together everything in the world? Secondly, that if an individual gives up his distinctiveness in a group and lets its other members influence him by suggestion, it gives one the impression that he does it because

1. 'Though I speak with the tongues of men and of angels, and have not charity [love], I am become as sounding brass, or a tinkling cymbal.' [I *Corinthians*, xiii, 1.]

he feels the need of being in harmony with them rather than in opposition to them – so that perhaps after all he does it 'ihnen zu Liebe'.[1]

1. [An idiom meaning 'for their sake'. Literally: 'for love of them'. – A line of thought similar to that expressed in the last three paragraphs will be found in the almost contemporary preface to the fourth edition of Freud's *Three Essays* (1905d), *P.F.L.*, **7**, 42–3.]

V

TWO ARTIFICIAL GROUPS: THE CHURCH AND THE ARMY

WE may recall from what we know of the morphology of groups that it is possible to distinguish very different kinds of groups and opposing lines in their development. There are very fleeting groups and extremely lasting ones; homogeneous ones, made up of the same sorts of individuals, and unhomogeneous ones; natural groups, and artificial ones, requiring an external force to keep them together; primitive groups, and highly organized ones with a definite structure. But for reasons which remain to be explained we should like to lay particular stress upon a distinction to which writers on the subject have been inclined to give too little attention; I refer to that between leaderless groups and those with leaders. And, in complete opposition to the usual practice, we shall not choose a relatively simple group formation as our point of departure, but shall begin with highly organized, lasting and artificial groups. The most interesting example of such structures are Churches – communities of believers – and armies.

A Church and an army are artificial groups – that is, a certain external force is employed to prevent them from dis-integrating[1] and to check alterations in their structure. As a rule a person is not consulted, or is given no choice, as to whether he wants to enter such a group; any attempt at leaving it is usually met with persecution or with severe punishment, or has quite definite conditions attached to it. It is quite outside our present interest to inquire why these associations need such special safeguards. We are only attracted by one circumstance, namely that certain facts, which are far more concealed

1. [*Footnote added* 1923:] In groups, the attributes 'stable' and 'artificial' seem to coincide or at least to be intimately connected.

in other cases, can be observed very clearly in those highly organized groups which are protected from dissolution in the manner that has been mentioned.

In a Church (and we may with advantage take the Catholic Church as a type) as well as in an army, however different the two may be in other respects, the same illusion holds good of there being a head – in the Catholic Church Christ, in an army its Commander-in-Chief – who loves all the individuals in the group with an equal love. Everything depends upon this illusion; if it were to be dropped, then both Church and army would dissolve, so far as the external force permitted them to. This equal love was expressly enunciated by Christ: 'Inasmuch as ye have done it unto one of the least of these my brethren, ye have done it unto me.' He stands to the individual members of the group of believers in the relation of a kind elder brother; he is their substitute father. All the demands that are made upon the individual are derived from this love of Christ's. A democratic strain runs through the Church, for the very reason that before Christ everyone is equal, and that everyone has an equal share in his love. It is not without a deep reason that the similarity between the Christian community and a family is invoked, and that believers call themselves brothers in Christ, that is, brothers through the love which Christ has for them. There is no doubt that the tie which unites each individual with Christ is also the cause of the tie which unites them with one another. The like holds good of an army. The Commander-in-Chief is a father who loves all soldiers equally, and for that reason they are comrades among themselves. The army differs structurally from the Church in being built up of a series of such groups. Every captain is, as it were, the Commander-in-Chief and the father of his company, and so is every non-commissioned officer of his section. It is true that a similar hierarchy has been constructed in the Church, but it does not play the same part in it economically;[1] for more knowledge and care about

1. [I.e. in the quantitative distribution of the psychical forces involved.]

individuals may be attributed to Christ than to a human Commander-in-Chief.

An objection will justly be raised against this conception of the libidinal structure of an army on the ground that no place has been found in it for such ideas as those of one's country, of national glory, etc., which are of such importance in holding an army together. The answer is that that is a different instance of a group tie, and no longer such a simple one; for the examples of great generals, like Caesar, Wallenstein, or Napoleon, show that such ideas are not indispensable to the existence of an army. We shall presently touch upon the possibility of a leading idea being substituted for a leader and upon the relations between the two. The neglect of this libidinal factor in an army, even when it is not the only factor operative, seems to be not merely a theoretical omission but also a practical danger. Prussian militarism, which was just as unpsychological as German science, may have had to suffer the consequences of this in the [First] World War. We know that the war neuroses which ravaged the German army have been recognized as being a protest of the individual against the part he was expected to play in the army; and according to the communication of Simmel (1918), the hard treatment of the men by their superiors may be considered as foremost among the motive forces of the disease. If the importance of the libido's claims on this score had been better appreciated, the fantastic promises of the American President's Fourteen Points[1] would probably not have been believed so easily, and the splendid instrument would not have broken in the hands of the German leaders.[2]

It is to be noticed that in these two artificial groups each individual is bound by libidinal ties on the one hand to the

1. [The Fourteen Points proposed in January 1918 by President Woodrow Wilson to safeguard future peace, although greatly modified, formed the basis of the armistice and Versailles peace agreements which ended World War I.]

2. [By Freud's wish this paragraph was printed as a footnote in the English translation of 1922. It appears in the text in all the German editions, however, both before and after that date. See Editor's Note, p. 93.]

leader (Christ, the Commander-in-Chief) and on the other hand to the other members of the group. How these two ties are related to each other, whether they are of the same kind and the same value, and how they are to be described psychologically – these questions must be reserved for subsequent inquiry. But we shall venture even now upon a mild reproach against earlier writers for not having sufficiently appreciated the importance of the leader in the psychology of the group, while our own choice of this as a first subject for investigation has brought us into a more favourable position. It would appear as though we were on the right road towards an explanation of the principal phenomenon of group psychology – the individual's lack of freedom in a group. If each individual is bound in two directions by such an intense emotional tie, we shall find no difficulty in attributing to that circumstance the alteration and limitation which have been observed in his personality.

A hint to the same effect, that the essence of a group lies in the libidinal ties existing in it, is also to be found in the phenomenon of panic, which is best studied in military groups. A panic arises if a group of that kind becomes disintegrated. Its characteristics are that none of the orders given by superiors are any longer listened to, and that each individual is only solicitous on his own account, and without any consideration for the rest. The mutual ties have ceased to exist, and a gigantic and senseless fear is set free. At this point, again, the objection will naturally be made that it is rather the other way round; and that the fear has grown so great as to be able to disregard all ties and all feelings of consideration for others. McDougall (1920a, 24) has even made use of panic (though not of military panic) as a typical instance of that intensification of emotion by contagion ('primary induction') on which he lays so much emphasis. But nevertheless this rational method of explanation is here quite inadequate. The very question that needs explanation is why the fear has become so gigantic. The greatness of the danger cannot be responsible, for the same army which now falls a victim to panic may previously have faced equally great or greater danger with complete success; it is of the very essence of panic that it bears no relation to the danger that threatens, and often breaks out on the most trivial occasions. If an individual in panic fear begins to be solicitous only on his own account, he bears witness in so doing to the fact that the emotional ties, which have hitherto made the danger seem small to him, have ceased to exist. Now that he is by himself in facing the danger, he may surely think it greater. The fact is, therefore, that panic fear presupposes a relaxation in the libidinal structure of the group and reacts to that relaxation in a justifiable manner, and the contrary view – that the libidinal ties of the group are destroyed owing to fear in the face of the danger – can be refuted.

The contention that fear in a group is increased to enormous proportions through induction (contagion) is not in the least contradicted by these remarks. McDougall's view meets the case entirely when the danger is a really great one and when the group has no strong emotional ties – conditions which are fulfilled, for instance, when a fire breaks out in a theatre or a place of amusement. But the truly instructive case and the one which can be best employed for our purposes is that mentioned above, in which a body of troops breaks into a panic although the danger has not increased beyond a degree that is usual and has often been previously faced. It is not to be expected that the usage of the word 'panic' should be clearly and unambiguously determined. Sometimes it is used to describe any collective fear, sometimes even fear in an individual when it exceeds all bounds, and often the name seems to be reserved for cases in which the outbreak of fear is not warranted by the occasion. If we take the word 'panic' in the sense of collective fear, we can establish a far-reaching analogy. Fear in an individual is provoked either by the greatness of a danger or by the cessation of emotional ties (libidinal cathexes); the latter is the case of neurotic fear or anxiety.[1]

1. See Lecture 25 of my *Introductory Lectures* (1916–17). [*P.F.L.*, **1**, 440 ff. See, however, a modification of this view in *Inhibitions, Symptoms and Anxiety* (1926*d*), ibid., **10**, 320–22.]

In just the same way panic arises either owing to an increase of the common danger or owing to the disappearance of the emotional ties which hold the group together; and the latter case is analogous to that of neurotic anxiety.[1]

Anyone who, like McDougall (1920a), describes a panic as one of the plainest functions of the 'group mind', arrives at the paradoxical position that this group mind does away with itself in one of its most striking manifestations. It is impossible to doubt that panic means the disintegration of a group; it involves the cessation of all the feelings of consideration which the members of the group otherwise show one another.

The typical occasion of the outbreak of a panic is very much as it is represented in Nestroy's parody of Hebbel's play about Judith and Holofernes. A soldier cries out: 'The general has lost his head!' and thereupon all the Assyrians take to flight. The loss of the leader in some sense or other, the birth of misgivings about him, brings on the outbreak of panic, though the danger remains the same; the mutual ties between the members of the group disappear, as a rule, at the same time as the tie with their leader. The group vanishes in dust, like a Prince Rupert's drop when its tail is broken off.

The dissolution of a religious group is not so easy to observe. A short time ago there came into my hands an English novel of Catholic origin, recommended by the Bishop of London, with the title *When It Was Dark*.[2] It gave a clever and, as it seems to me, a convincing picture of such a possibility and its consequences. The novel, which is supposed to relate to the present day, tells how a conspiracy of enemies of the person of Christ and of the Christian faith succeed in arranging for a sepulchre to be discovered in Jerusalem. In this sepulchre is an inscription, in which Joseph of Arimathaea confesses that for reasons of piety he secretly removed the body of Christ from its grave on the third day after its entombment and

1. Cf. Béla von Felszeghy's interesting though somewhat over-imaginative paper 'Panik und Pankomplex' (1920).

2. [A book by 'Guy Thorne' (pseudonym of C. Ranger Gull) which enjoyed extremely large sales at the time of its publication in 1903.]

buried it in this spot. The resurrection of Christ and his divine nature are by this means disproved, and the result of this archaeological discovery is a convulsion in European civilization and an extraordinary increase in all crimes and acts of violence, which only ceases when the forgers' plot has been revealed.

The phenomenon which accompanies the dissolution that is here supposed to overtake a religious group is not fear, for which the occasion is wanting. Instead of it ruthless and hostile impulses towards other people make their appearance, which, owing to the equal love of Christ, they had previously been unable to do.[1] But even during the kingdom of Christ those people who do not belong to the community of believers, who do not love him, and whom he does not love, stand outside this tie. Therefore a religion, even if it calls itself the religion of love, must be hard and unloving to those who do not belong to it. Fundamentally indeed every religion is in this same way a religion of love for all those whom it embraces; while cruelty and intolerance towards those who do not belong to it are natural to every religion. However difficult we may find it personally, we ought not to reproach believers too severely on this account; people who are un-believing or indifferent are much better off psychologically in this matter [of cruelty and intolerance]. If to-day that in-tolerance no longer shows itself so violent and cruel as in former centuries, we can scarcely conclude that there has been a softening in human manners. The cause is rather to be found in the undeniable weakening of religious feelings and the libidinal ties which depend upon them. If another group tie takes the place of the religious one – and the socialistic tie seems to be succeeding in doing so – then there will be the same intolerance towards outsiders as in the age of the Wars of Religion; and if differences between scientific opinions could ever attain a similar significance for groups, the same result would again be repeated with this new motivation.

1. Compare the explanation of similar phenomena after the abolition of the paternal authority of the sovereign given in Federn's *Die vaterlose Gesellschaft* (1919).

FURTHER PROBLEMS AND LINES OF WORK

WE have hitherto considered two artificial groups and have found that both are dominated by emotional ties of two kinds. One of these, the tie with the leader, seems (at all events for these cases) to be more of a ruling factor than the other, which holds between the members of the group.

Now much else remains to be examined and described in the morphology of groups. We should have to start from the ascertained fact that a mere collection of people is not a group, so long as these ties have not been established in it; but we should have to admit that in any collection of people the tendency to form a psychological group may very easily come to the fore. We should have to give our attention to the different kinds of groups, more or less stable, that arise spontaneously, and to study the conditions of their origin and of their dissolution. We should above all be concerned with the distinction between groups which have a leader and leaderless groups. We should consider whether groups with leaders may not be the more primitive and complete, whether in the others an idea, an abstraction, may not take the place of the leader (a state of things to which religious groups, with their invisible head, form a transitional stage), and whether a common tendency, a wish in which a number of people can have a share, may not in the same way serve as a substitute. This abstraction, again, might be more or less completely embodied in the figure of what we might call a secondary leader, and interesting varieties would arise from the relation between the idea and the leader. The leader or the leading idea might also, so to speak, be negative; hatred against a particular person or institution might operate in just the same unifying way, and might call up the same kind of emotional ties as positive attachment. Then the question would also arise whether a leader is really indispensable to the essence of a group – and other questions besides.

But all these questions, which may, moreover, have been dealt with in part in the literature of group psychology, will not succeed in diverting our interest from the fundamental psychological problems that confront us in the structure of a group. And our attention will first be attracted by a consideration which promises to bring us in the most direct way to a proof that libidinal ties are what characterize a group.

Let us keep before our eyes ᴉe nature of the emotional relations which hold between men in general. According to Schopenhauer's famous simile of the freezing porcupines no one can tolerate a too intimate approach to his neighbour.[1]

The evidence of psychoanalysis shows that almost every intimate emotional relation between two people which lasts for some time – marriage, friendship, the relations between parents and children[2] – contains a sediment of feelings of aversion and hostility, which only escapes perception as a result of repression.[3] This is less disguised in the common wrangles between business partners or in the grumbles of a subordinate at his superior. The same thing happens when men come together in larger units. Every time two families become

1. 'A company of porcupines crowded themselves very close together one cold winter's day so as to profit by one another's warmth and so save themselves from being frozen to death. But soon they felt one another's quills, which induced them to separate again. And now, when the need for warmth brought them nearer together again, the second evil arose once more. So that they were driven backwards and forwards from one trouble to the other, until they had discovered a mean distance at which they could most tolerably exist.' (*Parerga und Paralipomena*, Part II, 31, 'Gleichnisse und Parabeln'.)

2. Perhaps with the solitary exception of the relation of a mother to her son, which is based on narcissism, is not disturbed by subsequent rivalry, and is reinforced by a rudimentary attempt at sexual object-choice. [Cf. p. 304 and *n*. 2 below.]

3. [In the 1921 edition only this read 'leaves a sediment . . .' and the last clause read 'which has first to be eliminated by repression'.]

connected by a marriage, each of them thinks itself superior to or of better birth than the other. Of two neighbouring towns each is the other's most jealous rival; every little canton looks down upon the others with contempt. Closely related races keep one another at arm's length; the South German cannot endure the North German, the Englishman casts every kind of aspersion upon the Scot, the Spaniard despises the Portuguese.[1] We are no longer astonished that greater differences should lead to an almost insuperable repugnance, such as the Gallic people feel for the German, the Aryan for the Semite, and the white races for the coloured.

When this hostility is directed against people who are otherwise loved we describe it as ambivalence of feeling; and we explain the fact, in what is probably far too rational a manner, by means of the numerous occasions for conflicts of interest which arise precisely in such intimate relations. In the undisguised antipathies and aversions which people feel towards strangers with whom they have to do we may recognize the expression of self-love – of narcissism. This self-love works for the preservation of the individual, and behaves as though the occurrence of any divergence from his own particular lines of development involved a criticism of them and a demand for their alteration. We do not know why such sensitiveness should have been directed to just these details of differentiation; but it is unmistakable that in this whole connection men give evidence of a readiness for hatred, an aggressiveness, the source of which is unknown, and to which one is tempted to ascribe an elementary character.[2]

But when a group is formed the whole of this intolerance vanishes, temporarily or permanently, within the group. So long as a group formation persists or so far as it extends, indi-

1. ['The narcissism of minor differences'; cf. p. 305 and *n.* 1 below.]

2. In a recently published study, *Beyond the Pleasure Principle* [1920*g*; *P.F.L.*, **11**, 327], I have attempted to connect the polarity of love and hatred with a hypothetical opposition between instincts of life and death, and to establish the sexual instincts as the purest examples of the former, the instincts of life.

viduals in the group behave as though they were uniform, tolerate the peculiarities of its other members, equate themselves with them, and have no feeling of aversion towards them. Such a limitation of narcissism can, according to our theoretical views, only be produced by one factor, a libidinal tie with other people. Love for oneself knows only one barrier – love for others, love for objects.[1] The question will at once be raised whether community of interest in itself, without any addition of libido, must not necessarily lead to the toleration of other people and to considerateness for them. This objection may be met by the reply that nevertheless no lasting limitation of narcissism is effected in this way, since this tolerance does not persist longer than the immediate advantage gained from the other people's collaboration. But the practical importance of this discussion is less than might be supposed, for experience has shown that in cases of collaboration libidinal ties are regularly formed between the fellow-workers which prolong and solidify the relation between them to a point beyond what is merely profitable. The same thing occurs in men's social relations as has become familiar to psychoanalytic research in the course of the development of the individual libido. The libido attaches itself to the satisfaction of the great vital needs, and chooses as its first objects the people who have a share in that process.[2] And in the development of mankind as a whole, just as in individuals, love alone acts as the civilizing factor in the sense that it brings a change from egoism to altruism. And this is true both of sexual love for women, with all the obligations which it involves of not harming the things that are dear to women, and also of desexualized, sublimated homosexual love for other men, which springs from work in common.

If therefore in groups narcissistic self-love is subject to limitations which do not operate outside them, that is cogent evidence that the essence of a group formation consists in new kinds of libidinal ties among the members of the group.

1. See my paper on narcissism (1914c) [P.F.L., 11].
2. [See Freud's *Three Essays* (1905d), P.F.L., 7, 144–5.]

Our interest now leads us on to the pressing question as to what may be the nature of these ties which exist in groups. In the psychoanalytic study of neuroses we have hitherto been occupied almost exclusively with ties with objects made by love instincts which still pursue directly sexual aims. In groups there can evidently be no question of sexual aims of that kind. We are concerned here with love instincts which have been diverted from their original aims, though they do not operate with less energy on that account. Now, within the range of the usual sexual object-cathexis, we have already observed phenomena which represent a diversion of the instinct from its sexual aim. We have described them as degrees of being in love, and have recognized that they involve a certain encroachment upon the ego. We shall now turn our attention more closely to these phenomena of being in love, in the firm expectation of finding in them conditions which can be transferred to the ties that exist in groups. But we should also like to know whether this kind of object-cathexis, as we know it in sexual life, represents the only manner of emotional tie with other people, or whether we must take other mechanisms of the sort into account. As a matter of fact we learn from psychoanalysis that there do exist other mechanisms for emotional ties, the so-called *identifications*, insufficiently known processes and hard to describe, the investigation of which will for some time keep us away from the subject of group psychology.

VII

IDENTIFICATION

IDENTIFICATION is known to psychoanalysis as the earliest expression of an emotional tie with another person. It plays a part in the early history of the Oedipus complex. A little boy will exhibit a special interest in his father; he would like to grow like him and be like him, and take his place everywhere. We may say simply that he takes his father as his ideal. This behaviour has nothing to do with a passive or feminine attitude towards his father (and towards males in general); it is on the contrary typically masculine. It fits in very well with the Oedipus complex, for which it helps to prepare the way.

At the same time as this identification with his father, or a little later, the boy has begun to develop a true object-cathexis towards his mother according to the attachment [anaclitic] type.[1] He then exhibits, therefore, two psychologically distinct ties: a straightforward sexual object-cathexis towards his mother and an identification with his father which takes him as his model. The two subsist side by side for a time without any mutual influence or interference. In consequence of the irresistible advance towards a unification of mental life, they come together at last; and the normal Oedipus complex originates from their confluence. The little boy notices that his father stands in his way with his mother. His identification with his father then takes on a hostile colouring and becomes identical with the wish to replace his father in regard to his mother as well. Identification, in fact, is ambivalent from the very first; it can turn into an expression of tenderness as easily as into a wish for someone's removal. It behaves like a derivative

1. [See Section II of Freud's paper on narcissism (1914c), *P.F.L.*, **11**, 81–4; see also p. 204 and *n*. 1 below.]

of the first, *oral* phase of the organization of the libido, in which the object that we long for and prize is assimilated by eating and is in that way annihilated as such. The cannibal, as we know, has remained at this standpoint; he has a devouring affection for his enemies and only devours people of whom he is fond.[1]

The subsequent history of this identification with the father may easily be lost sight of. It may happen that the Oedipus complex becomes inverted, and that the father is taken as the object of a feminine attitude, an object from which the directly sexual instincts look for satisfaction; in that event the identification with the father has become the precursor of an object-tie with the father. The same holds good, with the necessary substitutions, of the baby daughter as well.[2]

It is easy to state in a formula the distinction between an identification with the father and the choice of the father as an object. In the first case one's father is what one would like to *be*, and in the second he is what one would like to *have*. The distinction, that is, depends upon whether the tie attaches to the subject or to the object of the ego. The former kind of tie is therefore already possible before any sexual object-choice has been made. It is much more difficult to give a clear metapsychological representation of the distinction. We can only see that identification endeavours to mould a person's own ego after the fashion of the one that has been taken as a model.

Let us disentangle identification as it occurs in the structure of a neurotic symptom from its rather complicated connections. Supposing that a little girl (and we will keep to her for the present) develops the same painful symptom as her mother – for instance, the same tormenting cough. This may come about in various ways. The identification may come from the Oedipus complex; in that case it signifies a hostile desire

1. See my *Three Essays* (1905*d*) [*P.F.L.*, **7**, 117] and Abraham (1916).

2. [The 'complete' Oedipus complex, comprising both its positive and negative forms, is discussed in Chapter III of *The Ego and the Id* (1923*b*), *P.F.L.*, **11**, 371–4.]

on the girl's part to take her mother's place, and the symptom expresses her object-love towards her father, and brings about a realization, under the influence of a sense of guilt, of her desire to take her mother's place: 'You wanted to be your mother, and now you *are* – anyhow so far as your sufferings are concerned.' This is the complete mechanism of the structure of a hysterical symptom. Or, on the other hand, the symptom may be the same as that of the person who is loved; so, for instance, Dora[1] imitated her father's cough. In that case we can only describe the state of things by saying *that identification has appeared instead of object-choice, and that object-choice has regressed to identification*. We have heard that identification is the earliest and original form of emotional tie; it often happens that under the conditions in which symptoms are constructed, that is, where there is repression and where the mechanisms of the unconscious are dominant, object-choice is turned back into identification – the ego assumes the characteristics of the object. It is noticeable that in these identifications the ego sometimes copies the person who is not loved and sometimes the one who is loved. It must also strike us that in both cases the identification is a partial and extremely limited one and only borrows a single trait from the person who is its object.

There is a third particularly frequent and important case of symptom formation, in which the identification leaves entirely out of account any object-relation to the person who is being copied. Supposing, for instance, that one of the girls in a boarding school has had a letter from someone with whom she is secretly in love which arouses her jealousy, and that she reacts to it with a fit of hysterics; then some of her friends who know about it will catch the fit, as we say, by mental infection. The mechanism is that of identification based upon the possibility or desire of putting oneself in the same situation. The other girls would like to have a secret love affair too, and under the influence of a sense of guilt they also accept the suffering involved in it. It would be wrong

1. In my 'Fragment of an Analysis of a Case of Hysteria' (1905*e*) [*P.F.L.*, **8**, 119–20].

to suppose that they take on the symptom out of sympathy. On the contrary, the sympathy only arises out of the identification, and this is proved by the fact that infection or imitation of this kind takes place in circumstances where even less pre-existing sympathy is to be assumed than usually exists between friends in a girls' school. One ego has perceived a significant analogy with another upon one point – in our example upon openness to a similar emotion; an identification is thereupon constructed on this point, and, under the influence of the pathogenic situation, is displaced on to the symptom which the one ego has produced. The identification by means of the symptom has thus become the mark of a point of coincidence between the two egos which has to be kept repressed.

What we have learned from these three sources may be summarized as follows. First, identification is the original form of emotional tie with an object; secondly, in a regressive way it becomes a substitute for a libidinal object-tie, as it were by means of introjection of the object into the ego; and thirdly, it may arise with any new perception of a common quality shared with some other person who is not an object of the sexual instinct. The more important this common quality is, the more successful may this partial identification become, and it may thus represent the beginning of a new tie.

We already begin to divine that the mutual tie between members of a group is in the nature of an identification of this kind, based upon an important emotional common quality; and we may suspect that this common quality lies in the nature of the tie with the leader. Another suspicion may tell us that we are far from having exhausted the problem of identification, and that we are faced by the process which psychology calls 'empathy [*Einfühlung*]' and which plays the largest part in our understanding of what is inherently foreign to our ego in other people. But we shall here limit ourselves to the immediate emotional effects of identification, and shall leave on one side its significance for our intellectual life.

Psychoanalytic research, which has already occasionally attacked the more difficult problems of the psychoses, has also been able to exhibit identification to us in some other cases which are not immediately comprehensible. I shall treat two of these cases in detail as material for our further consideration.

The genesis of male homosexuality in a large class of cases is as follows.[1] A young man has been unusually long and intensely fixated upon his mother in the sense of the Oedipus complex. But at last, after the end of puberty, the time comes for exchanging his mother for some other sexual object. Things take a sudden turn: the young man does not abandon his mother, but identifies himself with her; he transforms himself into her, and now looks about for objects which can replace his ego for him, and on which he can bestow such love and care as he has experienced from his mother. This is a frequent process, which can be confirmed as often as one likes, and which is naturally quite independent of any hypothesis that may be made as to the organic driving force and the motives of the sudden transformation. A striking thing about this identification is its ample scale; it remoulds the ego in one of its important features – in its sexual character – upon the model of what has hitherto been the object. In this process the object itself is renounced – whether entirely or in the sense of being preserved only in the unconscious is a question outside the present discussion. Identification with an object that is renounced or lost, as a substitute for that object – introjection of it into the ego – is indeed no longer a novelty to us. A process of the kind may sometimes be directly observed in small children. A short time ago an observation of this sort was published in the *Internationale Zeitschrift für Psychoanalyse*. A child who was unhappy over the loss of a kitten declared straight out that now he himself was the kitten, and accordingly crawled about on all fours, would not eat at table, etc.[2]

Another such instance of introjection of the object has been

---

1. [See Chapter III of Freud's study on Leonardo (1910c), *P.F.L.*, **14**. For other mechanisms of the genesis of homosexuality, see Freud (1920a), ibid., **9**, 384–6, and (1922b), ibid., **10**, 206–8.]

2. Marcuszewicz (1920).

provided by the analysis of melancholia,[1] an affection which counts among the most notable of its exciting causes the real or emotional loss of a loved object. A leading characteristic of these cases is a cruel self-depreciation of the ego combined with relentless self-criticism and bitter self-reproaches. Analyses have shown that this disparagement and these reproaches apply at bottom to the object and represent the ego's revenge upon it. The shadow of the object has fallen upon the ego, as I have said elsewhere.[2] The introjection of the object is here unmistakably clear.

But these melancholias also show us something else, which may be of importance for our later discussions. They show us the ego divided, fallen apart into two pieces, one of which rages against the second. This second piece is the one which has been altered by introjection and which contains the lost object. But the piece which behaves so cruelly is not unknown to us either. It comprises the conscience, a critical agency within the ego, which even in normal times takes up a critical attitude towards the ego, though never so relentlessly and so unjustifiably. On previous occasions[3] we have been driven to the hypothesis that some such agency develops in our ego which may cut itself off from the rest of the ego and come into conflict with it. We have called it the 'ego ideal', and by way of functions we have ascribed to it self-observation, the moral conscience, the censorship of dreams, and the chief influence in repression. We have said that it is the heir to the original narcissism in which the childish ego enjoyed self-sufficiency; it gradually gathers up from the influences of the environment the demands which that environment makes upon the ego and which the ego cannot always rise to; so that a man, when he cannot be satisfied with his ego itself, may nevertheless be able to find satisfaction in the ego ideal which

1. [Freud habitually uses the term 'melancholia' for conditions which would now be described as 'depression'.]

2. See 'Mourning and Melancholia' (1917e) [P.F.L., 11, 258].

3. In my paper on narcissism (1914c) [P.F.L., 11, 89–90] and in 'Mourning and Melancholia' (1917e) [ibid., 11, 256].

has been differentiated out of the ego. In delusions of observation, as we have further shown, the disintegration of this agency has become patent, and has thus revealed its origin in the influence of superior powers, and above all of parents.[1] But we have not forgotten to add that the amount of distance between this ego ideal and the real ego is very variable from one individual to another, and that with many people this differentiation within the ego does not go further than with children.

But before we can employ this material for understanding the libidinal organization of groups, we must take into account some other examples of the mutual relations between the object and the ego.[2]

---

1. Section III of my paper on narcissism [(1914c), *P.F.L.*, **11**].

2. We are very well aware that we have not exhausted the nature of identification with these examples taken from pathology, and that we have consequently left part of the riddle of group formations untouched. A far more fundamental and comprehensive psychological analysis would have to intervene at this point. A path leads from identification by way of imitation to empathy, that is, to the comprehension of the mechanism by means of which we are enabled to take up any attitude at all towards another mental life. Moreover there is still much to be explained in the manifestations of existing identifications. These result among other things in a person limiting his aggressiveness towards those with whom he has identified himself, and in his sparing them and giving them help. The study of such identifications, like those, for instance, which lie at the root of clan feeling, led Robertson Smith (*Kinship and Marriage*, 1885) to the surprising discovery that they rest upon the acknowledgement of the possession of a common substance [by the members of the clan], and may even therefore be created by a meal eaten in common. This feature makes it possible to connect this kind of identification with the early history of the human family which I constructed in *Totem and Taboo* [(1912–13), *P.F.L.*, **13**].

VIII

BEING IN LOVE AND HYPNOSIS

EVEN in its caprices the usage of language remains true to some kind of reality. Thus it gives the name of 'love' to a great many kinds of emotional relationship which we too group together theoretically as love; but then again it feels a doubt whether this love is real, true, actual love, and so hints at a whole scale of possibilities within the range of the phenomena of love. We shall have no difficulty in making the same discovery from our own observations.

In one class of cases being in love is nothing more than object-cathexis on the part of the sexual instincts with a view to directly sexual satisfaction, a cathexis which expires, moreover, when this aim has been reached; this is what is called common, sensual love. But, as we know, the libidinal situation rarely remains so simple. It was possible to calculate with certainty upon the revival of the need which had just expired; and this must no doubt have been the first motive for directing a lasting cathexis upon the sexual object and for 'loving' it in the passionless intervals as well.

To this must be added another factor derived from the very remarkable course of development which is pursued by the erotic life of man. In its first phase, which has usually come to an end by the time a child is five years old, he has found the first object for his love in one or other of his parents, and all of his sexual instincts with their demand for satisfaction have been united upon this object. The repression which then sets in compels him to renounce the greater number of these infantile sexual aims, and leaves behind a profound modification in his relation to his parents. The child still remains tied to his parents, but by instincts which must be described as being 'inhibited in their aim'. The emotions which he feels henceforward towards these objects of his love are characterized as 'affectionate'. It is well known that the earlier 'sensual' tendencies remain more or less strongly preserved in the unconscious, so that in a certain sense the whole of the original current continues to exist.[1]

At puberty, as we know, there set in new and very strong impulses towards directly sexual aims. In unfavourable cases they remain separate, in the form of a sensual current, from the 'affectionate' trends of feeling which persist. We then have before us a picture whose two aspects are typified with such delight by certain schools of literature. A man will show a sentimental enthusiasm for women whom he deeply respects but who do not excite him to sexual activities, and he will only be potent with other women whom he does not 'love' and thinks little of or even despises.[2] More often, however, the adolescent succeeds in bringing about a certain degree of synthesis between the unsensual, heavenly love and the sensual, earthly love, and his relation to his sexual object is characterized by the interaction of uninhibited instincts and of instincts inhibited in their aim. The depth to which anyone is in love, as contrasted with his purely sensual desire, may be measured by the size of the share taken by the aim-inhibited instincts of affection.

In connection with this question of being in love we have always been struck by the phenomenon of sexual overvaluation – the fact that the loved object enjoys a certain amount of freedom from criticism, and that all its characteristics are valued more highly than those of people who are not loved, or than its own were at a time when it itself was not loved. If the sensual impulses are more or less effectively repressed or set aside, the illusion is produced that the object has come to be sensually loved on account of its spiritual merits, whereas

1. See my *Three Essays* (1905*d*) [*P.F.L.*, **7**, 119].

2. 'On the Universal Tendency to Debasement in the Sphere of Love' (1912*d*) [*P.F.L.*, **7**, 251].

on the contrary these merits may really only have been lent to it by its sensual charm.

The tendency which falsifies judgement in this respect is that of *idealization*. But now it is easier for us to find our bearings. We see that the object is being treated in the same way as our own ego, so that when we are in love a considerable amount of narcissistic libido overflows on to the object.[1] It is even obvious, in many forms of love-choice, that the object serves as a substitute for some unattained ego ideal of our own. We love it on account of the perfections which we have striven to reach for our own ego, and which we should now like to procure in this roundabout way as a means of satisfying our narcissism.

If the sexual overvaluation and the being in love increase even further, then the interpretation of the picture becomes still more unmistakable. The impulsions whose trend is towards directly sexual satisfaction may now be pushed into the background entirely, as regularly happens, for instance, with a young man's sentimental passion; the ego becomes more and more unassuming and modest, and the object more and more sublime and precious, until at last it gets possession of the entire self-love of the ego, whose self-sacrifice thus follows as a natural consequence. The object has, so to speak, consumed the ego. Traits of humility, of the limitation of narcissism, and of self-injury occur in every case of being in love; in the extreme case they are merely intensified, and as a result of the withdrawal of the sensual claims they remain in solitary supremacy.

This happens especially easily with love that is unhappy and cannot be satisfied; for in spite of everything each sexual satisfaction always involves a reduction in sexual overvaluation. Contemporaneously with this 'devotion' of the ego to the object, which is no longer to be distinguished from a sublimated devotion to an abstract idea, the functions allotted to the ego ideal entirely cease to operate. The criticism exercised by that

1. [Cf. Part III of Freud's paper on narcissism (1914c), P.F.L., **11**, 88–9.]

agency is silent; everything that the object does and asks for is right and blameless. Conscience has no application to anything that is done for the sake of the object; in the blindness of love remorselessness is carried to the pitch of crime. The whole situation can be completely summarized in a formula: *The object has been put in the place of the ego ideal.*

It is now easy to define the difference between identification and such extreme developments of being in love as may be described as 'fascination' or 'bondage'.[1] In the former case the ego has enriched itself with the properties of the object, it has 'introjected' the object into itself, as Ferenczi [1909] expresses it. In the second case it is impoverished, it has surrendered itself to the object, it has substituted the object for its own most important constituent. Closer consideration soon makes it plain, however, that this kind of account creates an illusion of contradistinctions that have no real existence. Economically there is no question of impoverishment or enrichment; it is even possible to describe an extreme case of being in love as a state in which the ego has introjected the object into itself. Another distinction is perhaps better calculated to meet the essence of the matter. In the case of identification the object has been lost or given up; it is then set up again inside the ego, and the ego makes a partial alteration in itself after the model of the lost object. In the other case the object is retained, and there is a hypercathexis of it by the ego and at the ego's expense. But here again a difficulty presents itself. Is it quite certain that identification presupposes that object-cathexis has been given up? Can there be no identification while the object is retained? And before we embark upon a discussion of this delicate question, the perception may already be beginning to dawn on us that yet another alternative embraces the real essence of the matter, namely, *whether the object is put in the place of the ego or of the ego ideal.*

From being in love to hypnosis is evidently only a short step. The respects in which the two agree are obvious. There

1. [The 'bondage' of love had been discussed by Freud in his paper on 'The Taboo of Virginity' (1918*a*), *P.F.L.*, **7**, 265–6.]

is the same humble subjection, the same compliance, the same
absence of criticism, towards the hypnotist as towards the loved
object. There is the same sapping of the subject's own initiative;
no one can doubt that the hypnotist has stepped into the place
of the ego ideal. It is only that everything is even clearer
and more intense in hypnosis, so that it would be more to
the point to explain being in love by means of hypnosis than
the other way round. The hypnotist is the sole object, and
no attention is paid to any but him. The fact that the ego
experiences in a dreamlike way whatever he may request or
assert reminds us that we omitted to mention among the
functions of the ego ideal the business of testing the reality
of things.[1] No wonder that the ego takes a perception for
real if its reality is vouched for by the mental agency which
ordinarily discharges the duty of testing the reality of things.
The complete absence of impulsions which are uninhibited
in their sexual aims contributes further towards the extreme
purity of the phenomena. The hypnotic relation is the unlimited
devotion of someone in love, but with sexual satisfaction excluded; whereas in the actual case of being in love this kind
of satisfaction is only temporarily kept back, and remains in
the background as a possible aim at some later time.

But on the other hand we may also say that the hypnotic
relation is (if the expression is permissible) a group formation
with two members. Hypnosis is not a good object for comparison with a group formation, because it is truer to say
that it is identical with it. Out of the complicated fabric of
the group it isolates one element for us – the behaviour of
the individual to the leader. Hypnosis is distinguished from
a group formation by this limitation of number, just as it
is distinguished from being in love by the absence of directly

1. Cf. 'A Metapsychological Supplement to the Theory of Dreams' (Freud,
1917d) [P.F.L., 11, 239] – [Added 1923:] There seems, however, to be some
doubt whether the attribution of this function to the ego ideal is justified. The
point requires thorough discussion. [See Chapter III of The Ego and the Id
(1923b), P.F.L., 11, 367 n. 2, where the function is definitely attributed to the
ego.]

sexual trends. In this respect it occupies a middle position between the two.

It is interesting to see that it is precisely those sexual impulsions that are inhibited in their aims which achieve such lasting ties between people. But this can easily be understood from the fact that they are not capable of complete satisfaction, while sexual impulsions which are uninhibited in their aims suffer an extraordinary reduction through the discharge of energy every time the sexual aim is attained. It is the fate of sensual love to become extinguished when it is satisfied; for it to be able to last, it must from the beginning be mixed with purely affectionate components – with such, that is, as are inhibited in their aims – or it must itself undergo a transformation of this kind.

Hypnosis would solve the riddle of the libidinal constitution of groups for us straight away, if it were not that it itself exhibits some features which are not met by the rational explanation we have hitherto given of it as a state of being in love with the directly sexual trends excluded. There is still a great deal in it which we must recognize as unexplained and mysterious. It contains an additional element of paralysis derived from the relation between someone with superior power and someone who is without power and helpless – which may afford a transition to the hypnosis of fright which occurs in animals. The manner in which it is produced and its relationship to sleep are not clear; and the puzzling way in which some people are subject to it, while others resist it completely, points to some factor still unknown which is realized in it and which perhaps alone makes possible the purity of the attitudes of the libido which it exhibits. It is noticeable that, even when there is complete suggestive compliance in other respects, the moral conscience of the person hypnotized may show resistance. But this may be due to the fact that in hypnosis as it is usually practised some knowledge may be retained that what is happening is only a game, an untrue reproduction of another situation of far more importance to life.

But after the preceding discussions we are quite in a position to give the formula for the libidinal constitution of groups, or at least of such groups as we have hitherto considered – namely, those that have a leader and have not been able by means of too much 'organization' to acquire secondarily the characteristics of an individual. *A primary group of this kind is a number of individuals who have put one and the same object in the place of their ego ideal and have consequently identified themselves with one another in their ego.* This condition admits of graphic representation:

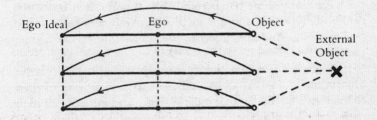

IX

THE HERD INSTINCT

WE cannot for long enjoy the illusion that we have solved the riddle of the group with this formula. It is impossible to escape the immediate and disturbing recollection that all we have really done has been to shift the question on to the riddle of hypnosis, about which so many points have yet to be cleared up. And now another objection shows us our further path.

It might be said that the intense emotional ties which we observe in groups are quite sufficient to explain one of their characteristics – the lack of independence and initiative in their members, the similarity in the reactions of all of them, their reduction, so to speak, to the level of group individuals. But if we look at it as a whole, a group shows us more than this. Some of its features – the weakness of intellectual ability, the lack of emotional restraint, the incapacity for moderation and delay, the inclination to exceed every limit in the expression of emotion and to work it off completely in the form of action – these and similar features, which we find so impressively described in Le Bon, show an unmistakable picture of a regression of mental activity to an earlier stage such as we are not surprised to find among savages or children. A regression of this sort is in particular an essential characteristic of common groups, while, as we have heard, in organized and artificial groups it can to a large extent be checked.

We thus have an impression of a state in which an individual's private emotional impulses and intellectual acts are too weak to come to anything by themselves and are entirely dependent for this on being reinforced by being repeated in a similar way in the other members of the group. We are reminded of how many of these phenomena of dependence are part of the normal constitution of human society, of how little originality and personal courage are to be found in it, of how much every individual is ruled by those attitudes of the group mind which exhibit themselves in such forms as racial characteristics, class prejudices, public opinion, etc. The influence of suggestion becomes a greater riddle for us when we admit that it is not exercised only by the leader, but by every individual upon every other individual; and we must reproach ourselves with having unfairly emphasized the relation to the leader and with having kept the other factor of mutual suggestion too much in the background.

After this encouragement to modesty, we shall be inclined to listen to another voice, which promises us an explanation based upon simpler grounds. Such a one is to be found in Trotter's thoughtful book on the herd instinct (1916), concerning which my only regret is that it does not entirely escape the antipathies that were set loose by the recent great war.

Trotter derives the mental phenomena that are described as occurring in groups from a herd instinct ('gregariousness'[1]), which is innate in human beings just as in other species of animals. Biologically, he says, this gregariousness is an analogy to multicellularity and as it were a continuation of it. (In terms of the libido theory it is a further manifestation of the tendency which proceeds from the libido and which is felt by all living beings of the same kind, to combine in more and more comprehensive units.[2]) The individual feels incomplete if he is alone. The fear shown by small children would seem already to be an expression of this herd instinct. Opposition to the herd is as good as separation from it, and is therefore anxiously avoided. But the herd turns away from anything that is new or unusual. The herd instinct would appear to be something primary, something which cannot be split up.[3]

Trotter gives as the list of instincts which he considers as

---

1. [This word is in English in the original.]
2. See *Beyond the Pleasure Principle* [(1920g), *P.F.L.*, **11**, 323].
3. [The last five words are in English in the original.]

primary those of self-preservation, of nutrition, of sex, and of the herd. The last often comes into opposition with the others. The feelings of guilt and of duty are the peculiar possessions of a gregarious animal. Trotter also derives from the herd instinct the repressive forces which psychoanalysis has shown to exist in the ego, and from the same source accordingly the resistances which the physician comes up against in psychoanalytic treatment. Speech owes its importance to its aptitude for mutual understanding in the herd, and upon it the identification of the individuals with one another largely rests.

While Le Bon is principally concerned with typical transient group formations, and McDougall with stable associations, Trotter has chosen as the centre of his interest the most generalized form of assemblage in which man, that $ζῷον$ $πολιτικόν$,[1] passes his life, and he gives us its psychological basis. But Trotter is under no necessity of tracing back the herd instinct, for he characterizes it as primary and not further reducible. Boris Sidis's attempt, to which he refers, at tracing the herd instinct back to suggestibility is fortunately superfluous as far as he is concerned; it is an explanation of a familiar and unsatisfactory type, and the converse proposition – that suggestibility is a derivative of the herd instinct – would seem to me to throw far more light on the subject.

But Trotter's exposition is open, with even more justice than the others, to the objection that it takes too little account of the leader's part in a group, while we incline rather to the opposite judgement, that it is impossible to grasp the nature of a group if the leader is disregarded. The herd instinct leaves no room at all for the leader; he is merely thrown in along with the herd, almost by chance; it follows, too, that no path leads from this instinct to the need for a God; the herd is without a herdsman. But besides this, Trotter's exposition can be undermined psychologically; that is to say, it can be made at all events probable that the herd instinct is not irreducible,

1. ['Political animal' (Aristotle, *Politics*, 1252b).]

that it is not primary in the same sense as the instinct of self-preservation and the sexual instinct.

It is naturally no easy matter to trace the ontogenesis of the herd instinct. The fear which is shown by small children when they are left alone, and which Trotter claims as being already a manifestation of the instinct, nevertheless suggests more readily another interpretation. The fear relates to the child's mother, and later to other familiar people, and it is the expression of an unfulfilled desire, which the child does not yet know how to deal with in any way except by turning it into anxiety.[1] Nor is the child's fear when it is alone pacified by the sight of any haphazard 'member of the herd', but on the contrary it is brought into existence by the approach of a 'stranger' of this sort. Then for a long time nothing in the nature of herd instinct or group feeling is to be observed in children. Something like it first grows up, in a nursery containing many children, out of the children's relation to their parents, and it does so as a reaction to the initial envy with which the elder child receives the younger one. The elder child would certainly like to put his successor jealously aside, to keep it away from the parents, and to rob it of all its privileges; but in the face of the fact that this younger child (like all that come later) is loved by the parents as much as he himself is, and in consequence of the impossibility of his maintaining his hostile attitude without damaging himself, he is forced into identifying himself with the other children. So there grows up in the troop of children a communal or group feeling, which is then further developed at school. The first demand made by this reaction-formation is for justice, for equal treatment for all. We all know how loudly and implacably this claim is put forward at school. If one cannot be the favourite oneself, at all events nobody else shall be the favourite. This transformation – the replacing of jealousy by a group feeling in the nursery and classroom – might be considered improbable, if the same process could not later on be observed again in

1. See the remarks upon anxiety in my *Introductory Lectures* (1916–17), Lecture 25. [*P.F.L.*, 1, 440 ff.]

other circumstances. We have only to think of the troop of women and girls, all of them in love in an enthusiastically sentimental way, who crowd round a singer or pianist after his performance. It would certainly be easy for each of them to be jealous of the rest; but, in the face of their numbers and the consequent impossibility of their reaching the aim of their love, they renounce it, and, instead of pulling out one another's hair, they act as a united group, do homage to the hero of the occasion with their common actions, and would probably be glad to have a share of *his* flowing locks. Originally rivals, they have succeeded in identifying themselves with one another by means of a similar love for the same object. When, as is usual, an instinctual situation is capable of various outcomes, we shall not be surprised that the actual outcome is one which brings with it the possibility of a certain amount of satisfaction, whereas some other outcome, in itself more obvious, is passed over because the circumstances of life prevent its leading to any such satisfaction.

What appears later on in society in the shape of *Gemeingeist, esprit de corps*, 'group spirit', etc., does not belie its derivation from what was originally envy. No one must want to put himself forward, every one must be the same and have the same. Social justice means that we deny ourselves many things so that others may have to do without them as well, or, what is the same thing, may not be able to ask for them. This demand for equality is the root of social conscience and the sense of duty. It reveals itself unexpectedly in the syphilitic's dread of infecting other people, which psychoanalysis has taught us to understand. The dread exhibited by these poor wretches corresponds to their violent struggles against the unconscious wish to spread their infection on to other people; for why should they alone be infected and cut off from so much? why not other people as well? And the same germ is to be found in the apt story of the judgement of Solomon. If one woman's child is dead, the other shall not have a live one either. The bereaved woman is recognized by this wish.

Thus social feeling is based upon the reversal of what was

first a hostile feeling into a positively-toned tie in the nature of an identification. So far as we have hitherto been able to follow the course of events, this reversal seems to occur under the influence of a common affectionate tie with a person outside the group. We do not ourselves regard our analysis of identification as exhaustive, but it is enough for our present purpose that we should revert to this one feature – its demand that equalization shall be consistently carried through. We have already heard in the discussion of the two artificial groups, Church and army, that their necessary precondition is that all their members should be loved in the same way by one person, the leader. Do not let us forget, however, that the demand for equality in a group applies only to its members and not to the leader. All the members must be equal to one another, but they all want to be ruled by one person. Many equals, who can identify themselves with one another, and a single person superior to them all – that is the situation that we find realized in groups which are capable of subsisting. Let us venture, then, to correct Trotter's pronouncement that man is a herd animal and assert that he is rather a horde animal, an individual creature in a horde led by a chief.

X

THE GROUP AND THE PRIMAL HORDE

In 1912 I took up a conjecture of Darwin's to the effect that the primitive form of human society was that of a horde ruled over despotically by a powerful male. I attempted to show that the fortunes of this horde have left indestructible traces upon the history of human descent; and, especially, that the development of totemism, which comprises in itself the beginnings of religion, morality, and social organization, is connected with the killing of the chief by violence and the transformation of the paternal horde into a community of brothers.[1] To be sure, this is only a hypothesis, like so many others with which archaeologists endeavour to lighten the darkness of prehistoric times – a 'Just-So Story', as it was amusingly called by a not unkind English critic;[2] but I think it is creditable to such a hypothesis if it proves able to bring coherence and understanding into more and more new regions.

Human groups exhibit once again the familiar picture of an individual of superior strength among a troop of equal companions, a picture which is also contained in our idea of the primal horde. The psychology of such a group, as we know it from the descriptions to which we have so often referred – the dwindling of the conscious individual personality, the focusing of thoughts and feelings into a common direction,

1. *Totem and Taboo* (1912–13) [Essay IV; *P.F.L.*, **13**. Freud uses the term 'horde' to signify a relatively small collection of people].

2. [In the first edition only, the name 'Kroeger' appeared here. This was evidently a misprint for 'Kroeber', the well-known American anthropologist, who had reviewed Freud's book (Kroeber, 1920). The comparison with a 'just-so story', however, was not made by him, as Kroeber himself pointed out in a second review (Kroeber, 1939), but by the English anthropologist R. R. Marett (Marett, 1920).]

the predominance of the affective side of the mind and of unconscious psychical life, the tendency to the immediate carrying out of intentions as they emerge – all this corresponds to a state of regression to a primitive mental activity, of just such a sort as we should be inclined to ascribe to the primal horde.[1]

Thus the group appears to us as a revival of the primal horde. Just as primitive man survives potentially in every individual, so the primal horde may arise once more out of any random collection; in so far as men are habitually under the sway of group formation we recognize in it the survival of the primal horde. We must conclude that the psychology of groups is the oldest human psychology; what we have isolated as individual psychology, by neglecting all traces of the group, has only since come into prominence out of the old group psychology, by a gradual process which may still, perhaps, be described as incomplete. We shall later venture upon an attempt at specifying the point of departure of this development. [See p. 168 ff.]

Further reflection will show us in what respect this statement requires correction. Individual psychology must, on the contrary, be just as old as group psychology, for from the first there were two kinds of psychologies, that of the individual members of the group and that of the father, chief, or leader. The members of the group were subject to ties just as we

1. What we have just described in our general characterization of mankind must apply especially to the primal horde. The will of the individual was too weak; he did not venture upon action. No impulses whatever came into existence except collective ones; there was only a common will, there were no single ones. An idea did not dare to turn itself into an act of will unless it felt itself reinforced by a perception of its general diffusion. This weakness of the idea is to be explained by the strength of the emotional tie which is shared by all the members of the horde; but the similarity in the circumstances of their life and the absence of any private property assist in determining the uniformity of their individual mental acts. As we may observe with children and soldiers, common activity is not excluded even in the excretory functions. The one great exception is provided by the sexual act, in which a third person is at best superfluous and in the extreme case is condemned to a state of painful expectancy. As to the reaction of the sexual need (for genital satisfaction) towards gregariousness, see below [p. 174].

see them to-day, but the father of the primal horde was free. His intellectual acts were strong and independent even in isolation, and his will needed no reinforcement from others. Consistency leads us to assume that his ego had few libidinal ties; he loved no one but himself, or other people only in so far as they served his needs. To objects his ego gave away no more than was barely necessary.

He, at the very beginning of the history of mankind, was the 'superman' whom Nietzsche only expected from the future. Even to-day the members of a group stand in need of the illusion that they are equally and justly loved by their leader; but the leader himself need love no one else, he may be of a masterful nature, absolutely narcissistic, self-confident and independent. We know that love puts a check upon narcissism, and it would be possible to show how, by operating in this way, it became a factor of civilization.

The primal father of the horde was not yet immortal, as he later became by deification. If he died, he had to be replaced; his place was probably taken by a youngest son, who had up to then been a member of the group like any other. There must therefore be a possibility of transforming group psychology into individual psychology; a condition must be discovered under which such a transformation is easily accomplished, just as it is possible for bees in case of necessity to turn a larva into a queen instead of into a worker. One can imagine only one possibility: the primal father had prevented his sons from satisfying their directly sexual impulsions; he forced them into abstinence and consequently into the emotional ties with him and with one another which could arise out of those of their impulsions that were inhibited in their sexual aim. He forced them, so to speak, into group psychology. His sexual jealousy and intolerance became in the last resort the causes of group psychology.[1]

1. It may perhaps also be assumed that the sons, when they were driven out and separated from their father, advanced from identification with one another to homosexual object-love, and in this way won freedom to kill their father. [See *Totem and Taboo*, *P.F.L.*, **13**, 205 ff.]

Whoever became his successor was also given the possibility of sexual satisfaction, and was by that means offered a way out of the conditions of group psychology. The fixation of the libido to woman and the possibility of satisfaction without any need for delay or accumulation made an end of the importance of those of his sexual impulsions that were inhibited in their aim, and allowed his narcissism always to rise to its full height. We shall return in a postscript [p. 170 ff.] to this connection between love and character formation.

We may further emphasize, as being specially instructive, the relation that holds between the contrivance by means of which an artificial group is held together and the constitution of the primal horde. We have seen that with an army and a Church this contrivance is the illusion that the leader loves all of the individuals equally and justly. But this is simply an idealistic remodelling of the state of affairs in the primal horde, where all of the sons knew that they were equally *persecuted* by the primal father, and *feared* him equally. This same recasting upon which all social duties are built up is already presupposed by the next form of human society, the totemic clan. The indestructible strength of the family as a natural group formation rests upon the fact that this necessary presupposition of the father's equal love can have a real application in the family.

But we expect even more of this derivation of the group from the primal horde. It ought also to help us to understand what is still incomprehensible and mysterious in group formations – all that lies hidden behind the enigmatic words 'hypnosis' and 'suggestion'. And I think it can succeed in this too. Let us recall that hypnosis has something positively uncanny about it; but the characteristic of uncanniness suggests something old and familiar that has undergone repression.[1] Let us consider how hypnosis is induced. The hypnotist asserts that he is in possession of a mysterious power that robs the subject of his own will; or, which is the same thing, the subject

---

1. Cf. 'The "Uncanny"' (1919*h*) [*P.F.L.*, **14**, 335].

believes it of him. This mysterious power (which is even now often described popularly as 'animal magnetism') must be the same power that is looked upon by primitive people as the source of taboo, the same that emanates from kings and chieftains and makes it dangerous to approach them (*mana*). The hypnotist, then, is supposed to be in possession of this power; and how does he manifest it? By telling the subject to look him in the eyes; his most typical method of hypnotizing is by his look. But it is precisely the *sight* of the chieftain that is dangerous and unbearable for primitive people, just as later that of the Godhead is for mortals. Even Moses had to act as an intermediary between his people and Jehovah, since the people could not support the sight of God; and when he returned from the presence of God his face shone – some of the *mana* had been transferred on to him, just as happens with the intermediary among primitive people.[1]

It is true that hypnosis can also be evoked in other ways, for instance by fixing the eyes upon a bright object or by listening to a monotonous sound. This is misleading and has given occasion to inadequate physiological theories. In point of fact these procedures merely serve to divert conscious attention and to hold it riveted. The situation is the same as if the hypnotist had said to the subject: 'Now concern yourself exclusively with my person; the rest of the world is quite uninteresting.' It would of course be technically inexpedient for a hypnotist to make such a speech; it would tear the subject away from his unconscious attitude and stimulate him to conscious opposition. The hypnotist avoids directing the subject's conscious thoughts towards his own intentions, and makes the person upon whom he is experimenting sink into an activity in which the world is bound to seem uninteresting to him; but at the same time the subject is in reality unconsciously concentrating his whole attention upon the hypnotist, and is getting into an attitude of *rapport*, of transference on to him. Thus the indirect methods of hypnotizing, like many

1. See *Totem and Taboo* [Essay II; *P.F.L.*, **13**] and the sources quoted there.

of the technical procedures used in making jokes,[1] have the effect of checking certain distributions of mental energy which would interfere with the course of events in the unconscious, and they lead eventually to the same result as the direct methods of influence by means of staring or stroking.[2]

Ferenczi [1909] has made the true discovery that when a hypnotist gives the command to sleep, which is often done at the beginning of hypnosis, he is putting himself in the place of the subject's parents. He thinks that two sorts of hypnotism are to be distinguished: one coaxing and soothing, which he considers is modelled on the mother, and another threatening, which is derived from the father. Now the command to sleep in hypnosis means nothing more nor less than an order to withdraw all interest from the world and to concentrate it on the person of the hypnotist. And it is so understood by the subject; for in this withdrawal of interest from the external world lies the psychological characteristic of sleep, and the kinship between sleep and the state of hypnosis is based on it.

By the measures that he takes, then, the hypnotist awakens

1. [The distracting of attention as part of the technique of joking is discussed at some length in the latter half of Chapter V of Freud's book on jokes (1905c), *P.F.L.*, **6**, 204–7. This idea is alluded to in connection with the 'pressure technique' in *Studies on Hysteria* (1895d), ibid., **3**, 355.]

2. This situation, in which the subject's attitude is unconsciously directed towards the hypnotist, while he is consciously occupied with monotonous and uninteresting perceptions, finds a parallel among the events of psycho-analytic treatment, which deserves to be mentioned here. At least once in the course of every analysis a moment comes when the patient obstinately maintains that just now positively nothing whatever occurs to his mind. His free associations come to a stop and the usual incentives for putting them in motion fail in their effect. If the analyst insists, the patient is at last induced to admit that he is thinking of the view from the consulting-room window, of the wall-paper that he sees before him, or of the gas-lamp hanging from the ceiling. Then one knows at once that he has gone off into the transference and that he is engaged upon what are still un-conscious thoughts relating to the physician; and one sees the stoppage in the patient's associations disappear, as soon as he has been given this explanation.

in the subject a portion of his archaic heritage which had also made him compliant towards his parents and which had experienced an individual re-animation in his relation to his father; what is thus awakened is the idea of a paramount and dangerous personality, towards whom only a passive-masochistic attitude is possible, to whom one's will has to be surrendered, – while to be alone with him, 'to look him in the face', appears a hazardous enterprise. It is only in some such way as this that we can picture the relation of the individual member of the primal horde to the primal father. As we know from other reactions, individuals have preserved a variable degree of personal aptitude for reviving old situations of this kind. Some knowledge that in spite of everything hypnosis is only a game, a deceptive renewal of these old impressions, may, however, remain behind and take care that there is a resistance against any too serious consequences of the suspension of the will in hypnosis.

The uncanny and coercive characteristics of group formations, which are shown in the phenomena of suggestion that accompany them, may therefore with justice be traced back to the fact of their origin from the primal horde. The leader of the group is still the dreaded primal father; the group still wishes to be governed by unrestricted force; it has an extreme passion for authority; in Le Bon's phrase, it has a thirst for obedience. The primal father is the group ideal, which governs the ego in the place of the ego ideal. Hypnosis has a good claim to being described as a group of two. There remains as a definition for suggestion: a conviction which is not based upon perception and reasoning but upon an erotic tie.[1]

---

1. It seems to me worth emphasizing the fact that the discussions in this section have induced us to give up Bernheim's conception of hypnosis and go back to the *naïf* earlier one. According to Bernheim all hypnotic phenomena are to be traced to the factor of suggestion, which is not itself capable of further explanation. We have come to the conclusion that suggestion is a partial manifestation of the state of hypnosis, and that hypnosis is solidly founded upon a predisposition which has survived in the unconscious from the early history of the human family.

A DIFFERENTIATING GRADE IN THE EGO

IF we survey the life of an individual man of to-day, bearing in mind the mutually complementary accounts of group psychology given by the authorities, we may lose the courage, in face of the complications that are revealed, to attempt a comprehensive exposition. Each individual is a component part of numerous groups, he is bound by ties of identification in many directions, and he has built up his ego ideal upon the most various models. Each individual therefore has a share in numerous group minds – those of his race, of his class, of his creed, of his nationality, etc. – and he can also raise himself above them to the extent of having a scrap of independence and originality. Such stable and lasting group formations, with their uniform and constant effects, are less striking to an observer than the rapidly formed and transient groups from which Le Bon has made his brilliant psychological character sketch of the group mind. And it is just in these noisy ephemeral groups, which are as it were superimposed upon the others, that we are met by the prodigy of the complete, even though only temporary, disappearance of exactly what we have recognized as individual acquirements.

We have interpreted this prodigy as meaning that the individual gives up his ego ideal and substitutes for it the group ideal as embodied in the leader. And we must add by way of correction that the prodigy is not equally great in every case. In many individuals the separation between the ego and the ego ideal is not very far advanced; the two still coincide readily; the ego has often preserved its earlier narcissistic self-complacency. The selection of the leader is very much facilitated by this circumstance. He need often only possess the typical qualities of the individuals concerned in a particularly clearly marked and pure form, and need only give an impression of greater force and of more freedom of libido; and in that case the need for a strong chief will often meet him half-way and invest him with a predominance to which he would otherwise perhaps have had no claim. The other members of the group, whose ego ideal would not, apart from this, have become embodied in his person without some correction, are then carried away with the rest by 'suggestion', that is to say, by means of identification.

We are aware that what we have been able to contribute towards the explanation of the libidinal structure of groups leads back to the distinction between the ego and the ego ideal and to the double kind of tie which this makes possible – identification, and putting the object in the place of the ego ideal. The assumption of this kind of differentiating grade in the ego as a first step in an analysis of the ego must gradually establish its justification in the most various regions of psychology. In my paper on narcissism [1914c] I have put together all the pathological material that could at the moment be used in support of this differentiation. But it may be expected that when we penetrate deeper into the psychology of the psychoses its significance will be discovered to be far greater. Let us reflect that the ego now enters into the relation of an object to the ego ideal which had been developed out of it, and that all the interplay between an external object and the ego as a whole, with which our study of the neuroses has made us acquainted, may possibly be repeated upon this new scene of action within the ego.

In this place I shall only follow up one of the consequences which seem possible from this point of view, thus resuming the discussion of a problem which I was obliged to leave unsolved elsewhere.[1] Each of the mental differentiations that we have become acquainted with represents a fresh aggravation of the difficulties of mental functioning, increases its instability,

1. 'Mourning and Melancholia' (1917e) [P.F.L., 11, 267–8].

and may become the starting-point for its breakdown, that is, for the onset of a disease. Thus, by being born we have made the step from an absolutely self-sufficient narcissism to the perception of a changing external world and the beginnings of the discovery of objects. And with this is associated the fact that we cannot endure the new state of things for long, that we periodically revert from it, in our sleep, to our former condition of absence of stimulation and avoidance of objects. It is true, however, that in this we are following a hint from the external world, which, by means of the periodical change of day and night, temporarily withdraws the greater part of the stimuli that affect us. The second example of such a step, pathologically more important, is subject to no such qualification. In the course of our development we have effected a separation of our mental existence into a coherent ego and into an unconscious and repressed portion which is left outside it; and we know that the stability of this new acquisition is exposed to constant shocks. In dreams and in neuroses what is thus excluded knocks for admission at the gates, guarded though they are by resistances; and in our waking health we make use of special artifices for allowing what is repressed to circumvent the resistances and for receiving it temporarily into our ego to the increase of our pleasure. Jokes and humour, and to some extent the comic in general, may be regarded in this light. Everyone acquainted with the psychology of the neuroses will think of similar examples of less importance; but I hasten on to the application I have in view.

It is quite conceivable that the separation of the ego ideal from the ego cannot be borne for long either, and has to be temporarily undone. In all renunciations and limitations imposed upon the ego a periodical infringement of the prohibition is the rule; this indeed is shown by the institution of festivals, which in origin are nothing less nor more than excesses provided by law and which owe their cheerful character to the release which they bring.[1] The Saturnalia

1. *Totem and Taboo* [Essay IV (5), *P.F.L.*, **13**].

of the Romans and our modern carnival agree in this essential feature with the festivals of primitive people, which usually end in debaucheries of every kind and the transgression of what are at other times the most sacred commandments. But the ego ideal comprises the sum of all the limitations in which the ego has to acquiesce, and for that reason the abrogation of the ideal would necessarily be a magnificent festival for the ego, which might then once again feel satisfied with itself.[1]

There is always a feeling of triumph when something in the ego coincides with the ego ideal. And the sense of guilt (as well as the sense of inferiority) can also be understood as an expression of tension between the ego and the ego ideal.

It is well known that there are people the general colour of whose mood oscillates periodically from an excessive depression through some kind of intermediate state to an exalted sense of well-being. These oscillations appear in very different degrees of amplitude, from what is just noticeable to those extreme instances which, in the shape of melancholia and mania, make the most tormenting or disturbing inroads upon the life of the person concerned. In typical cases of this cyclical depression external precipitating causes do not seem to play any decisive part; as regards internal motives, nothing more, or nothing else is to be found in these patients than in all others. It has consequently become the custom to consider these cases as not being psychogenic. We shall refer presently to those other exactly similar cases of cyclical depression which *can* easily be traced back to mental traumas.

Thus the foundation of these spontaneous oscillations of mood is unknown; we are without insight into the mechanism of the displacement of a melancholia by a mania. So we are free to suppose that these patients are people in whom our conjecture might find an actual application – their ego ideal

1. Trotter traces repression back to the herd instinct. It is a translation of this into another form of expression rather than a contradiction when I say in my paper on narcissism [1914*c*; *P.F.L.*, **11**, 88] that 'for the ego the formation of an ideal would be the conditioning factor of repression'.

might be temporarily resolved into their ego after having previously ruled it with especial strictness.

Let us keep to what is clear: On the basis of our analysis of the ego it cannot be doubted that in cases of mania the ego and the ego ideal have fused together, so that the person, in a mood of triumph and self-satisfaction, disturbed by no self-criticism, can enjoy the abolition of his inhibitions, his feelings of consideration for others, and his self-reproaches. It is not so obvious, but nevertheless very probable, that the misery of the melancholic is the expression of a sharp conflict between the two agencies of his ego, a conflict in which the ideal, in an excess of sensitiveness, relentlessly exhibits its condemnation of the ego in delusions of inferiority and in self-depreciation. The only question is whether we are to look for the causes of these altered relations between the ego and the ego ideal in the periodic rebellions, which we have postulated above, against the new institution, or whether we are to make other circumstances responsible for them.

A change into mania is not an indispensable feature of the symptomatology of melancholic depression. There are simple melancholias, some in single and some in recurrent attacks, which never show this development.

On the other hand there are melancholias in which the precipitating cause clearly plays an aetiological part. They are those which occur after the loss of a loved object, whether by death or as the result of circumstances which have necessitated the withdrawal of the libido from the object. A psychogenic melancholia of this sort can end in mania, and this cycle can be repeated several times, just as easily as in a case which appears to be spontaneous. Thus the state of things is somewhat obscure, especially as only a few forms and cases of melancholia have been submitted to psychoanalytic investigation.[1] So far we only understand those cases in which the object is given up because it has shown itself unworthy of

1. Cf. Abraham (1912).

love. It is then set up again inside the ego, by means of identification, and severely condemned by the ego ideal. The reproaches and attacks directed towards the object come to light in the shape of melancholic self-reproaches.[1]

A melancholia of this kind, too, may end in a change into mania; so that the possibility of this happening represents a feature which is independent of the other characteristics of the clinical picture.

Nevertheless I see no difficulty in assigning to the factor of the periodic rebellion of the ego against the ego ideal a share in both kinds of melancholia, the psychogenic as well as the spontaneous. In the spontaneous kind it may be supposed that the ego ideal is inclined to display a peculiar strictness, which then results automatically in its temporary suspension. In the psychogenic kind the ego would be incited to rebellion by ill-treatment on the part of its ideal – an ill-treatment which it encounters when there has been identification with a rejected object.[2]

---

1. To speak more accurately, they conceal themselves behind the reproaches directed towards the subject's own ego, and lend them the fixity, tenacity, and imperativeness which characterize the self-reproaches of a melancholic.

2. [Some further discussion of melancholia will be found in Chapter V of The Ego and the Id (1923b), P.F.L., 11, 394.]

XII

POSTSCRIPT

In the course of the inquiry which has just been brought to a provisional end we came across a number of side-paths which we avoided pursuing in the first instance but in which there was much that offered us promises of insight. We propose now to take up a few of the points that have been left on one side in this way.

A. The distinction between identification of the ego with an object and replacement of the ego ideal by an object finds an interesting illustration in the two great artificial groups which we began by studying, the army and the Christian Church.

It is obvious that a soldier takes his superior, that is, in fact, the leader of the army, as his ideal, while he identifies himself with his equals, and derives from this community of their egos the obligations for giving mutual help and for sharing possessions which comradeship implies. But he becomes ridiculous if he tries to identify himself with the general. The soldier in *Wallensteins Lager* laughs at the sergeant for this very reason:

> Wie er räuspert und wie er spuckt,
> Das habt ihr ihm glücklich abgeguckt![1]

It is otherwise in the Catholic Church. Every Christian loves Christ as his ideal and feels himself united with all other Christians by the tie of identification. But the Church requires

---

1. [I grant you, your counterfeit perfectly fits
   The way that he hawks and the way that he spits.
   (Scene 6 of Schiller's play.)]

more of him. He has also to identify himself with Christ and love all other Christians as Christ loved them. At both points, therefore, the Church requires that the position of the libido which is given by group formation should be supplemented. Identification has to be added where object-choice has taken place, and object-love where there is identification. This addition evidently goes beyond the constitution of the group. One can be a good Christian and yet be far from the idea of putting oneself in Christ's place and of having like him an all-embracing love for mankind. One need not think oneself capable, weak mortal that one is, of the Saviour's largeness of soul and strength of love. But this further development in the distribution of libido in the group is probably the factor upon which Christianity bases its claim to have reached a higher ethical level.

B. We have said that it would be possible to specify the point in the mental development of mankind at which the advance from group psychology to individual psychology was achieved also by the individual members of the group [p. 155].[1]

For this purpose we must return for a moment to the scientific myth of the father of the primal horde. He was later on exalted into the creator of the world, and with justice, for he had produced all the sons who composed the first group. He was the ideal of each one of them, at once feared and honoured, a fact which led later to the idea of taboo. These many individuals eventually banded themselves together, killed him and cut him in pieces. None of the group of victors could take his place, or, if one of them did, the battles began afresh, until they understood that they must all renounce their father's heritage. They then formed the totemic community of brothers, all with equal rights and united by the totem prohibitions which were to preserve and to expiate the memory

---

1. What follows at this point was written under the influence of an exchange of ideas with Otto Rank. [*Added* 1923:] See also Rank (1922). [This passage is to be read in conjunction with Sections 5, 6 and 7 of the fourth essay in *Totem and Taboo*, P.F.L., **13**.]

of the murder. But the dissatisfaction with what had been achieved still remained, and it became the source of new developments. The persons who were united in this group of brothers gradually came towards a revival of the old state of things at a new level. The male became once more the chief of a family, and broke down the prerogatives of the gynaecocracy which had become established during the father-less period. As a compensation for this he may at that time have acknowledged the mother deities, whose priests were castrated for the mother's protection, after the example that had been given by the father of the primal horde. And yet the new family was only a shadow of the old one; there were numbers of fathers and each one was limited by the rights of the others.

It was then, perhaps, that some individual, in the exigency of his longing, may have been moved to free himself from the group and take over the father's part. He who did this was the first epic poet; and the advance was achieved in his imagination. This poet disguised the truth with lies in accord-ance with his longing. He invented the heroic myth. The hero was a man who by himself had slain the father – the father who still appeared in the myth as a totemic monster. Just as the father had been the boy's first ideal, so in the hero who aspires to the father's place the poet now created the first ego ideal. The transition to the hero was probably afforded by the youngest son, the mother's favourite, whom she had protected from paternal jealousy, and who, in the era of the primal horde, had been the father's successor. In the lying poetic fancies of prehistoric times the woman, who had been the prize of battle and the temptation to murder, was probably turned into the active seducer and instigator to the crime.

The hero claims to have acted alone in accomplishing the deed, which certainly only the horde as a whole would have ventured upon. But, as Rank has observed, fairy tales have preserved clear traces of the facts which were disavowed. For we often find in them that the hero who has to carry out some difficult task (usually the youngest son, and not infrequently one who has represented himself to the father-substitute as being stupid, that is to say, harmless) – we often find, then, that this hero can carry out his task only by the help of a crowd of small animals, such as bees or ants. These would be the brothers in the primal horde, just as in the same way in dream symbolism insects or vermin signify brothers and sisters (contemptuously, considered as babies). Moreover every one of the tasks in myths and fairy tales is easily recognizable as a substitute for the heroic deed.

The myth, then, is the step by which the individual emerges from group psychology. The first myth was certainly the psychological, the hero myth; the explanatory nature myth must have followed much later. The poet who had taken this step, and had in this way set himself free from the group in his imagination, is nevertheless able (as Rank has further observed) to find his way back to it in reality. For he goes and relates to the group his hero's deeds which he has invented. At bottom this hero is no one but himself. Thus he lowers himself to the level of reality, and raises his hearers to the level of imagination. But his hearers understand the poet, and, in virtue of their having the same relation of longing towards the primal father, they can identify themselves with the hero.[1]

The lie of the heroic myth culminates in the deification of the hero. Perhaps the deified hero may have been earlier than the Father God and may have been a precursor to the return of the primal father as a deity. The series of gods, then, would run chronologically: Mother Goddess – Hero – Father God. But it is only with the elevation of the never-forgotten primal father that the deity acquires the features that we still recognize in him to-day.[2]

C. A great deal has been said in this paper about directly sexual instincts and those that are inhibited in their aims, and

1. Cf. Hanns Sachs (1920).
2. In this brief exposition I have made no attempt to bring forward any of the material existing in legends, myths, fairy tales, the history of manners, etc., in support of the construction.

it may be hoped that this distinction will not meet with too much resistance. But a detailed discussion of the question will not be out of place, even if it only repeats what has to a great extent already been said before.

The development of the libido in children has made us acquainted with the first but also the best example of sexual instincts which are inhibited in their aims. All the feelings which a child has towards its parents and those who look after it pass by an easy transition into the wishes which give expression to the child's sexual impulsions. The child claims from these objects of its love all the signs of affection which it knows of; it wants to kiss them, touch them, and look at them; it is curious to see their genitals, and to be with them when they perform their intimate excretory functions; it promises to marry its mother or nurse – whatever it may understand by marriage; it proposes to itself to bear its father a child, etc. Direct observation, as well as the subsequent analytic investigation of the residues of childhood, leave no doubt as to the complete fusion of tender and jealous feelings and of sexual intentions, and show us in what a fundamental way the child makes the person it loves into the object of all its still not properly centred sexual trends.[1]

This first configuration of the child's love, which in typical cases takes the shape of the Oedipus complex, succumbs, as we know, from the beginning of the period of latency onwards to a wave of repression. Such of it as is left over shows itself as a purely affectionate emotional tie, relating to the same people, but no longer to be described as 'sexual'. Psychoanalysis, which illuminates the depths of mental life, has no difficulty in showing that the sexual ties of the earliest years of childhood also persist, though repressed and unconscious. It gives us courage to assert that wherever we come across an affectionate feeling it is successor to a completely 'sensual' object-tie with the person in question or rather with that person's prototype (or *imago*). It cannot indeed disclose to us

1. Cf. my *Three Essays* (1905*d*) [*P.F.L.*, **7**, 118].

without a special investigation whether in a given case this former complete sexual current still exists under repression or whether it has already been exhausted. To speak still more precisely: it is quite certain that this current is still there as a form and possibility, and can always be cathected and put into activity again by means of regression; the only question is (and it cannot always be answered) what degree of cathexis and operative force it still has at the present moment. Equal care must be taken in this connection to avoid two sources of error – the Scylla of underestimating the importance of the repressed unconscious, and the Charybdis of judging the normal entirely by the standards of the pathological.

A psychology which will not or cannot penetrate the depths of what is repressed regards affectionate emotional ties as being invariably the expression of impulsions which have no sexual aim, even though they are derived from impulsions which have such an aim.[1]

We are justified in saying that they have been diverted from these sexual aims, even though there is some difficulty in giving a description of such a diversion of aim which will conform to the requirements of metapsychology. Moreover, those instincts which are inhibited in their aims always preserve some few of their original sexual aims; even an affectionate devotee, even a friend or an admirer, desires the physical proximity and the sight of the person who is now loved only in the 'Pauline' sense. If we choose, we may recognize in this diversion of aim a beginning of the *sublimation* of the sexual instincts, or on the other hand we may fix the limits of sublimation at some more distant point. Those sexual instincts which are inhibited in their aims have a great functional advantage over those which are uninhibited. Since they are not capable of really complete satisfaction, they are especially adapted to create permanent ties; while those instincts

1. Hostile feelings are doubtless a little more complicated in their construction. [In the 1st edition only, this footnote ran: 'Hostile feelings, which are a little more complicated in their construction, offer no exception to this rule.']

which are directly sexual incur a loss of energy each time they are satisfied, and must wait to be renewed by a fresh accumulation of sexual libido, so that meanwhile the object may have been changed. The inhibited instincts are capable of any degree of admixture with the uninhibited; they can be transformed back into them, just as they arose out of them. It is well known how easily erotic wishes develop out of emotional relations of a friendly character, based upon appreciation and admiration (compare Molière's 'Kiss me for the love of Greek'[1]), between a master and a pupil, between a performer and a delighted listener, and especially in the case of women. In fact the growth of emotional ties of this kind, with their purposeless beginnings, provides a much frequented pathway to sexual object-choice. Pfister, in his *Frömmigkeit des Grafen von Zinzendorf* (1910), has given an extremely clear and certainly not an isolated example of how easily even an intense religious tie can revert to ardent sexual excitement. On the other hand it is also very usual for directly sexual impulsions, short-lived in themselves, to be transformed into a lasting and purely affectionate tie; and the consolidation of a passionate love marriage rests to a large extent upon this process.

We shall naturally not be surprised to hear that the sexual impulsions that are inhibited in their aims arise out of the directly sexual ones when internal or external obstacles make the sexual aims unattainable. The repression during the period of latency is an internal obstacle of this kind – or rather one which has become internal. We have assumed that the father of the primal horde owing to his sexual intolerance compelled all his sons to be abstinent, and thus forced them into ties that were inhibited in their aims, while he reserved for himself freedom of sexual enjoyment and in this way remained without ties. All the ties upon which a group depends are of the character of instincts that are inhibited in their aims. But here we have

1. [Quoi! monsieur sait du grec! Ah! permettez, de grâce,
  Que, pour l'amour du grec, monsieur, on vous embrasse.
  Les femmes savantes, III, 5.]

approached the discussion of a new subject, which deals with the relation between directly sexual instincts and the formation of groups.

D. The last two remarks will have prepared us for finding that directly sexual impulsions are unfavourable to the formation of groups. In the history of the development of the family there have also, it is true, been group relations of sexual love (group marriages); but the more important sexual love became for the ego, and the more it developed the characteristics of being in love, the more urgently it required to be limited to two people – *una cum uno* – as is prescribed by the nature of the genital aim. Polygamous inclinations had to be content to find satisfaction in a succession of changing objects.

Two people coming together for the purpose of sexual satisfaction, in so far as they seek for solitude, are making a demonstration against the herd instinct, the group feeling. The more they are in love, the more completely they suffice for each other. Their rejection of the group's influence is expressed in the shape of a sense of shame. Feelings of jealousy of the most extreme violence are summoned up in order to protect the choice of a sexual object from being encroached upon by a group tie. It is only when the affectionate, that is, personal, factor of a love relation gives place entirely to the sensual one, that it is possible for two people to have sexual intercourse in the presence of others or for there to be simultaneous sexual acts in a group, as occurs at an orgy. But at that point a regression has taken place to an early stage in sexual relations, at which being in love as yet played no part, and all sexual objects were judged to be of equal value, somewhat in the sense of Bernard Shaw's malicious aphorism to the effect that being in love means greatly exaggerating the difference between one woman and another.

There are abundant indications that being in love only made its appearance late on in the sexual relations between men and women; so that the opposition between sexual love and group ties is also a late development. Now it may seem as though this assumption were incompatible with our myth of the primal family. For it was after all by their love for their mothers and sisters that the mob of brothers was, as we have supposed, driven to parricide; and it is difficult to imagine this love as being anything but undivided and primitive – that is, as an intimate union of the affectionate and sensual. But further consideration resolves this objection to our theory into a confirmation of it. One of the reactions to the parricide was after all the institution of totemic exogamy, the prohibition of any sexual relation with those women of the family who had been tenderly loved since childhood. In this way a wedge was driven in between a man's affectionate and sensual feelings, one still firmly fixed in his erotic life to-day.[1] As a result of this exogamy the sensual needs of men had to be satisfied with strange and unloved women.

In the great artificial groups, the Church and the army, there is no room for woman as a sexual object. The love relation between men and women remains outside these organizations. Even where groups are formed which are composed of both men and women the distinction between the sexes plays no part. There is scarcely any sense in asking whether the libido which keeps groups together is of a homosexual or of a heterosexual nature, for it is not differentiated according to the sexes, and particularly shows a complete disregard for the aims of the genital organization of the libido.

Even in a person who has in other respects become absorbed in a group, the directly sexual impulsions preserve a little of his individual activity. If they become too strong they disintegrate every group formation. The Catholic Church had the best of motives for recommending its followers to remain unmarried and for imposing celibacy upon its priests; but falling in love has often driven even priests to leave the Church. In the same way love for women breaks through the group ties of race, of national divisions, and of the social class system, and it thus produces important effects as a factor in civilization.

1. See Freud (1912*d*) [*P.F.L.*, **7**, 247–52].

It seems certain that homosexual love is far more compatible with group ties, even when it takes the shape of uninhibited sexual impulsions – a remarkable fact, the explanation of which might carry us far.

The psychoanalytic investigation of the psychoneuroses has taught us that their symptoms are to be traced back to directly sexual impulsions which are repressed but still remain active. We can complete this formula by adding – 'or, to aim-inhibited impulsions, whose inhibition has not been entirely successful or has made room for a return to the repressed sexual aim'. It is in accordance with this that a neurosis should make its victim asocial and should remove him from the usual group formations. It may be said that a neurosis has the same disintegrating effect upon a group as being in love. On the other hand it appears that where a powerful impetus has been given to group formation neuroses may diminish and, at all events temporarily, disappear. Justifiable attempts have also been made to turn this antagonism between neuroses and group formation to therapeutic account. Even those who do not regret the disappearance of religious illusions from the civilized world of to-day will admit that so long as they were in force they offered those who were bound by them the most powerful protection against the danger of neurosis.[1] Nor is it hard to discern that all the ties that bind people to mystico-religious or philosophico-religious sects and communities are expressions of crooked cures of all kinds of neuroses. All of this is correlated with the contrast between directly sexual impulsions and those which are inhibited in their aims.

If he is left to himself, a neurotic is obliged to replace by his own symptom formations the great group formations from which he is excluded. He creates his own world of imagination for himself, his own religion, his own system of delusions, and thus recapitulates the institutions of humanity in a distorted way which is clear evidence of the dominating part played by the directly sexual impulsions.[2]

1. [Cf. similar remarks on pp. 226–7 and 273 below.]
2. See *Totem and Taboo*, towards the end of Essay II [*P.F.L.*, **13**, 130–31].

E. In conclusion, we will add a comparative estimate, from the standpoint of the libido theory, of the states with which we have been concerned, of being in love, of hypnosis, of group formation, and of neurosis.

Being in love is based on the simultaneous presence of directly sexual impulsions and of sexual impulsions that are inhibited in their aims, while the object draws a part of the subject's narcissistic ego-libido to itself. It is a condition in which there is only room for the ego and the object.

Hypnosis resembles being in love in being limited to these two persons, but it is based entirely on sexual impulsions that are inhibited in their aims and puts the object in the place of the ego ideal.

The group multiplies this process; it agrees with hypnosis in the nature of the instincts which hold it together, and in the replacement of the ego ideal by the object; but to this it adds identification with other individuals, which was perhaps originally made possible by their having the same relation to the object.

Both states, hypnosis and group formation, are an inherited deposit from the phylogenesis of the human libido – hypnosis in the form of a predisposition, and the group, besides this, as a direct survival. The replacement of the directly sexual impulsions by those that are inhibited in their aims promotes in both states a separation between the ego and the ego ideal, a separation with which a beginning has already been made in the state of being in love.

Neurosis stands outside this series. It also is based upon a peculiarity in the development of the human libido – the twice repeated start made by the directly sexual function, with an intervening period of latency.[1] To this extent it resembles hypnosis and group formation in having the character of a regression, which is absent from being in love. It makes its appearance wherever the advance from directly sexual instincts to those that are inhibited in their aims has not been wholly successful;

---

1. See my *Three Essays* (1905*d*) [*P.F.L.*, **7**, 158–9].

and it represents a *conflict* between those portions of the instincts which have been received into the ego after having passed through this development and those portions of them which, springing from the repressed unconscious, strive – as do other, completely repressed, instinctual impulses – to attain direct satisfaction. Neuroses are extraordinarily rich in content, for they embrace all possible relations between the ego and the object – both those in which the object is retained and others in which it is abandoned or erected inside the ego itself – and also the conflicting relations between the ego and its ego ideal.

THE FUTURE OF AN ILLUSION
(1927)

EDITOR'S NOTE

DIE ZUKUNFT EINER ILLUSION

(A) GERMAN EDITIONS:

1927   Leipzig, Vienna and Zurich: Internationaler Psycho-analytischer Verlag. (2nd ed., 1928.)

1948   *Gesammelte Werke*, **14**, 325–80.

(B) ENGLISH TRANSLATIONS:
The Future of an Illusion

1928   London: Hogarth Press and Institute of Psycho-Analysis. (Tr. W. D. Robson-Scott.)

1961   *Standard Edition*, **21**, 1–56. (Based on the version of 1928.)

The present edition is a reprint of the *Standard Edition* version, with a few editorial changes.

This work was begun in the spring of 1927; it was finished by September and published in November of the same year.

In the 'Postscript' which Freud added in 1935 to his *Autobiographical Study* he remarked on 'a significant change' that had come about in his writings during the previous decade. 'My interest', he explained, 'after making a long *détour* through the natural sciences, medicine and psychotherapy, returned to the cultural problems which had fascinated me long before, when I was a youth scarcely old enough for thinking' (*P.F.L.*, **15**). He had, of course, touched several times on those problems in the intervening years – especially in *Totem and Taboo*

(1912–13);[1] but it was with *The Future of an Illusion* that he entered on the series of studies which were to be his major concern for the remainder of his life. Of these the most important were *Civilization and its Discontents* (1930a), which is the direct successor to the present work, the discussion of philosophies of life which forms the last of the *New Introductory Lectures* (1933a), *Why War?* (1933b), Freud's open letter to Einstein, and finally *Moses and Monotheism* (1939a), which he worked at from 1934 onwards.

The antagonism between man and civilization, which is an important theme in the earlier essays in the present volume, also plays a large part in the opening chapters of this work. Freud returned to the topic two years later, in *Civilization and its Discontents*, where it received more detailed treatment.

Freud remarks in the 'Postscript' (1935a) to his *Autobiographical Study*: 'In *The Future of an Illusion* I expressed an essentially negative valuation of religion. Later, I found a formula which did better justice to it: while granting that its power lies in the truth which it contains, I showed that that truth was not a material but a historical truth.' This formula is discussed further in *Moses and Monotheism* (Essay III, Part II (G). In brief, *The Future of an Illusion* is Freud's major work on religion as a contemporary social phenomenon. Its deeper roots in prehistory, history and psychology are more closely examined in *Totem and Taboo* and *Moses and Monotheism*.

In view of Freud's sweeping pronouncement on p. 184 ('I scorn to distinguish between culture and civilization') and of a similar remark towards the end of '*Why War?*', it seems unnecessary to embark on the tiresome problem of the proper translation of the German word '*Kultur*'. We have usually, but not invariably, chosen 'civilization' for the noun and 'cultural' for the adjective.

1. His earliest published approach to the problem of religion was in the paper on 'Obsessive Actions and Religious Practices' (1907b), *P.F.L.*, **13**.

THE FUTURE OF AN ILLUSION

I

W HEN one has lived for quite a long time in a particular civilization[1] and has often tried to discover what its origins were and along what path it has developed, one sometimes also feels tempted to take a glance in the other direction and to ask what further fate lies before it and what transformations it is destined to undergo. But one soon finds that the value of such an inquiry is diminished from the outset by several factors. Above all, because there are only a few people who can survey human activity in its full compass. Most people have been obliged to restrict themselves to a single, or a few, fields of it. But the less a man knows about the past and the present the more insecure must prove to be his judgement of the future. And there is the further difficulty that precisely in a judgement of this kind the subjective expectations of the individual play a part which it is difficult to assess; and these turn out to be dependent on purely personal factors in his own experience, on the greater or lesser optimism of his attitude to life, as it has been dictated for him by his temperament or by his success or failure. Finally, the curious fact makes itself felt that in general people experience their present naïvely, as it were, without being able to form an estimate of its contents; they have first to put themselves at a distance from it – the present, that is to say, must have become the past – before it can yield points of vantage from which to judge the future.

Thus anyone who gives way to the temptation to deliver

1. [See Editor's Note, p. 182.]

an opinion on the probable future of our civilization will do well to remind himself of the difficulties I have just pointed out, as well as of the uncertainty that attaches quite generally to any prophecy. It follows from this, so far as I am concerned, that I shall make a hasty retreat before a task that is too great, and shall promptly seek out the small tract of territory which has claimed my attention hitherto, as soon as I have determined its position in the general scheme of things.

Human civilization, by which I mean all those respects in which human life has raised itself above its animal status and differs from the life of beasts – and I scorn to distinguish between culture and civilization –, presents, as we know, two aspects to the observer. It includes on the one hand all the knowledge and capacity that men have acquired in order to control the forces of nature and extract its wealth for the satisfaction of human needs, and, on the other hand, all the regulations necessary in order to adjust the relations of men to one another and especially the distribution of the available wealth. The two trends of civilization are not independent of each other: firstly, because the mutual relations of men are profoundly influenced by the amount of instinctual satisfaction which the existing wealth makes possible; secondly, because an individual man can himself come to function as wealth in relation to another one, in so far as the other person makes use of his capacity for work, or chooses him as a sexual object; and thirdly, moreover, because every individual is virtually an enemy of civilization, though civilization is supposed to be an object of universal human interest. It is remarkable that, little as men are able to exist in isolation, they should nevertheless feel as a heavy burden the sacrifices which civilization expects of them in order to make a communal life possible. Thus civilization has to be defended against the individual, and its regulations, institutions and commands are directed to that task. They aim not only at effecting a certain distribution of wealth but at maintaining that distribution; indeed, they have to protect everything that contributes to the conquest of nature and the production of wealth against men's hostile impulses. Human creations are easily destroyed, and science and technology, which have built them up, can also be used for their annihilation.

One thus gets an impression that civilization is something which was imposed on a resisting majority by a minority which understood how to obtain possession of the means to power and coercion. It is, of course, natural to assume that these difficulties are not inherent in the nature of civilization itself but are determined by the imperfections of the cultural forms which have so far been developed. And in fact it is not difficult to indicate those defects. While mankind has made continual advances in its control over nature and may expect to make still greater ones, it is not possible to establish with certainty that a similar advance has been made in the management of human affairs; and probably at all periods, just as now once again, many people have asked themselves whether what little civilization has thus acquired is indeed worth defending at all. One would think that a re-ordering of human relations should be possible, which would remove the sources of dissatisfaction with civilization by renouncing coercion and the suppression of the instincts, so that, undisturbed by internal discord, men might devote themselves to the acquisition of wealth and its enjoyment. That would be the golden age, but it is questionable if such a state of affairs can be realized. It seems rather that every civilization must be built up on coercion and renunciation of instinct; it does not even seem certain that if coercion were to cease the majority of human beings would be prepared to undertake to perform the work necessary for acquiring new wealth. One has, I think, to reckon with the fact that there are present in all men destructive, and therefore anti-social and anti-cultural, trends and that in a great number of people these are strong enough to determine their behaviour in human society.

This psychological fact has a decisive importance for our judgement of human civilization. Whereas we might at first think that its essence lies in controlling nature for the purpose of acquiring wealth and that the dangers which threaten it could be eliminated through a suitable distribution of that wealth among men, it now seems that the emphasis has moved over from the material to the mental. The decisive question is whether and to what extent it is possible to lessen the burden of the instinctual sacrifices imposed on men, to reconcile men to those which must necessarily remain and to provide a compensation for them. It is just as impossible to do without control of the mass[1] by a minority as it is to dispense with coercion in the work of civilization. For masses are lazy and unintelligent; they have no love for instinctual renunciation, and they are not to be convinced by argument of its inevitability; and the individuals composing them support one another in giving free rein to their indiscipline. It is only through the influence of individuals who can set an example and whom masses recognize as their leaders that they can be induced to perform the work and undergo the renunciations on which the existence of civilization depends. All is well if these leaders are persons who possess superior insight into the necessities of life and who have risen to the height of mastering their own instinctual wishes. But there is a danger that in order not to lose their influence they may give way to the mass more than it gives way to them, and it therefore seems necessary that they shall be independent of the mass by having means to power at their disposal. To put it briefly, there are two widespread human characteristics which are responsible for the fact that the regulations of civilization can only be maintained by a certain degree of coercion – namely, that men are not spontaneously fond of work and that arguments are of no avail against their passions.

I know the objections which will be raised against these assertions. It will be said that the characteristic of human masses depicted here, which is supposed to prove that coercion cannot be dispensed with in the work of civilization, is itself only the result of defects in the cultural regulations, owing to which

---

1. ['*Masse*.' The German word has a very wide meaning. It is translated 'group' for special reasons in Freud's *Group Psychology* (1921c). See the Editor's footnote on p. 95 above. Here 'mass' seems more appropriate.

men have become embittered, revengeful and inaccessible. New generations, who have been brought up in kindness and taught to have a high opinion of reason, and who have experienced the benefits of civilization at an early age, will have a different attitude to it. They will feel it as a possession of their very own and will be ready for its sake to make the sacrifices as regards work and instinctual satisfaction that are necessary for its preservation. They will be able to do without coercion and will differ little from their leaders. If no culture has so far produced human masses of such a quality, it is because no culture has yet devised regulations which will influence men in this way, and in particular from childhood onwards.

It may be doubted whether it is possible at all, or at any rate as yet, at the present stage of our control over nature, to set up cultural regulations of this kind. It may be asked where the number of superior, unswerving and disinterested leaders are to come from who are to act as educators of the future generations, and it may be alarming to think of the enormous amount of coercion that will inevitably be required before these intentions can be carried out. The grandeur of the plan and its importance for the future of human civilization cannot be disputed. It is securely based on the psychological discovery that man is equipped with the most varied instinctual dispositions, whose ultimate course is determined by the experiences of early childhood. But for the same reason the limitations of man's capacity for education set bounds to the effectiveness of such a transformation in his culture. One may question whether, and in what degree, it would be possible for a different cultural environment to do away with the two characteristics of human masses which make the guidance of human affairs so difficult. The experiment has not yet been made. Probably a certain percentage of mankind (owing to a pathological disposition or an excess of instinctual strength) will always remain asocial; but if it were feasible merely to reduce the majority that is hostile towards civilization to-day into a minority, a great deal would have been accomplished – perhaps all that *can* be accomplished.

I should not like to give the impression that I have strayed a long way from the line laid down for my inquiry [p. 183]. Let me therefore give an express assurance that I have not the least intention of making judgements on the great experiment in civilization that is now in progress in the vast country that stretches between Europe and Asia.[1] I have neither the special knowledge nor the capacity to decide on its practicability, to test the expediency of the methods employed or to measure the width of the inevitable gap between intention and execution. What is in preparation there is unfinished and therefore eludes an investigation for which our own long-consolidated civilization affords us material.

1. [See, however, some remarks in Chapter V of *Civilization and its Discontents* (1930*a*), p. 303 ff. below, and at two points in *Why War?* (1933*b*), pp. 355 and 358 below. Cf. also the longer discussion in Lecture 35 of the *New Introductory Lectures* (1933*a*), *P.F.L.*, **2**, 213–19.]

WE have slipped unawares out of the economic field into the field of psychology. At first we were tempted to look for the assets of civilization in the available wealth and in the regulations for its distribution. But with the recognition that every civilization rests on a compulsion to work and a renunciation of instinct and therefore inevitably provokes opposition from those affected by these demands, it has become clear that civilization cannot consist principally or solely in wealth itself and the means of acquiring it and the arrangements for its distribution; for these things are threatened by the rebelliousness and destructive mania of the participants in civilization. Alongside of wealth we now come upon the means by which civilization can be defended – measures of coercion and other measures that are intended to reconcile men to it and to recompense them for their sacrifices. These latter may be described as the mental assets of civilization.

For the sake of a uniform terminology we will describe the fact that an instinct cannot be satisfied as a 'frustration', the regulation by which this frustration is established as a 'prohibition' and the condition which is produced by the prohibition as a 'privation'. The first step is to distinguish between privations which affect everyone and privations which do not affect everyone but only groups, classes or even single individuals. The former are the earliest; with the prohibitions that established them, civilization – who knows how many thousands of years ago? – began to detach man from his primordial animal condition. We have found to our surprise that these privations are still operative and still form the kernel of hostility to civilization. The instinctual wishes that suffer under them are born afresh with every child; there is a class of people, the neurotics, who already react to these frustrations with asocial behaviour. Among these instinctual wishes are those of incest, cannibalism and lust for killing. It sounds

189

strange to place alongside one another wishes which everyone seems united in repudiating and others about which there is so much lively dispute in our civilization as to whether they shall be permitted or frustrated; but psychologically it is justifiable to do so. Nor is the attitude of civilization to these oldest instinctual wishes by any means uniform. Cannibalism alone seems to be universally proscribed and − to the non-psychoanalytic view − to have been completely surmounted. The strength of the incestuous wishes can still be detected behind the prohibition against them; and under certain conditions killing is still practised, and indeed commanded, by our civilization. It is possible that cultural developments lie ahead of us in which the satisfaction of yet other wishes, which are entirely permissible to-day, will appear just as unacceptable as cannibalism does now.

These earliest instinctual renunciations already involve a psychological factor which remains important for all further instinctual renunciations as well. It is not true that the human mind has undergone no development since the earliest times and that, in contrast to the advances of science and technology, it is the same to-day as it was at the beginning of history. We can point out one of these mental advances at once. It is in keeping with the course of human development that external coercion gradually becomes internalized; for a special mental agency, man's super-ego, takes it over and includes it among its commandments.[1] Every child presents this process of transformation to us; only by that means does it become a moral and social being. Such a strengthening of the super-ego is a most precious cultural asset in the psychological field. Those in whom it has taken place are turned from being opponents of civilization into being its vehicles. The greater their number is in a cultural unit the more secure is its culture and the more it can dispense with external measures of coercion. Now the degree of this internalization differs greatly between the

1. [See Chapter III of *The Ego and the Id* (1923*b*), *P.F.L.*, **11**; cf. also Chapters VII and VIII of *Civilization and its Discontents* (1930*a*), in particular, pp. 317–19, 325 and 329–32 below.]

[handwritten marginal note: Degree of internalisation of prohibitive differ for different ethnics. Some need constant coercion]

various instinctual prohibitions. As regards the earliest cultural demands, which I have mentioned, the internalization seems to have been very extensively achieved, if we leave out of account the unwelcome exception of the neurotics. But the case is altered when we turn to the other instinctual claims. Here we observe with surprise and concern that a majority of people obey the cultural prohibitions on these points only under the pressure of external coercion — that is, only where that coercion can make itself effective and so long as it is to be feared. This is also true of what are known as the *moral* demands of civilization, which likewise apply to everyone. Most of one's experiences of man's moral untrustworthiness fall into this category. There are countless civilized people who would shrink from murder or incest but who do not deny themselves the satisfaction of their avarice, their aggressive urges or their sexual lusts, and who do not hesitate to injure other people by lies, fraud and calumny, so long as they can remain unpunished for it; and this, no doubt, has always been so through many ages of civilization.

If we turn to those restrictions that apply only to certain classes of society, we meet with a state of things which is flagrant and which has always been recognized. It is to be expected that these underprivileged classes will envy the favoured ones their privileges and will do all they can to free themselves from their own surplus of privation. Where this is not possible, a permanent measure of discontent will persist within the culture concerned and this can lead to dangerous revolts. If, however, a culture has not got beyond a point at which the satisfaction of one portion of its participants depends upon the suppression of another, and perhaps larger, portion — and this is the case in all present-day cultures — it is understandable that the suppressed people should develop an intense hostility towards a culture whose existence they make possible by their work, but in whose wealth they have too small a share. In such conditions an internalization of the cultural prohibitions among the suppressed people is not to be expected. On the contrary, they are not prepared to acknowledge the prohibitions, they are intent on destroying the culture itself, and possibly even on doing away with the postulates on which it is based. The hostility of these classes to civilization is so obvious that it has caused the more latent hostility of the social strata that are better provided for to be overlooked. It goes without saying that a civilization which leaves so large a number of its participants unsatisfied and drives them into revolt neither has nor deserves the prospect of a lasting existence.

The extent to which a civilization's precepts have been internalized – to express it popularly and unpsychologically: the moral level of its participants – is not the only form of mental wealth that comes into consideration in estimating a civilization's value. There are in addition its assets in the shape of ideals and artistic creations – that is, the satisfactions that can be derived from those sources.

People will be only too readily inclined to include among the psychical assets of a culture its ideals – its estimates of what achievements are the highest and the most to be striven after. It will seem at first as though these ideals would determine the achievements of the cultural unit; but the actual course of events would appear to be that the ideals are based on the first achievements which have been made possible by a combination of the culture's internal gifts and external circumstances, and that these first achievements are then held on to by the ideal as something to be carried further. The satisfaction which the ideal offers to the participants in the culture is thus of a narcissistic nature; it rests on their pride in what has already been successfully achieved. To make this satisfaction complete calls for a comparison with other cultures which have aimed at different achievements and have developed different ideals. On the strength of these differences every culture claims the right to look down on the rest. In this way cultural ideals become a source of discord and enmity between different cultural units, as can be seen most clearly in the case of nations.

The narcissistic satisfaction provided by the cultural ideal is also among the forces which are successful in combating the hostility to culture within the cultural unit. This satisfaction can be shared in not only by the favoured classes, which enjoy the benefits of the culture, but also by the suppressed ones, since the right to despise the people outside it compensates them for the wrongs they suffer within their own unit. No doubt one is a wretched plebeian, harassed by debts and military service; but, to make up for it, one is a Roman citizen, one has one's share in the task of ruling other nations and dictating their laws. This identification of the suppressed classes with the class who rules and exploits them is, however, only part of a larger whole. For, on the other hand, the suppressed classes can be emotionally attached to their masters; in spite of their hostility to them they may see in them their ideals; unless such relations of a fundamentally satisfying kind subsisted, it would be impossible to understand how a number of civilizations have survived so long in spite of the justifiable hostility of large human masses.

A different kind of satisfaction is afforded by art to the participants in a cultural unit, though as a rule it remains inaccessible to the masses, who are engaged in exhausting work and have not enjoyed any personal education. As we discovered long since,[1] art offers substitutive satisfactions for the oldest and still most deeply felt cultural renunciations, and for that reason it serves as nothing else does to reconcile a man to the sacrifices he has made on behalf of civilization. On the other hand, the creations of art heighten his feelings of identification, of which every cultural unit stands in so much need, by providing an occasion for sharing highly valued emotional experiences. And when those creations picture the achievements of his particular culture and bring to his mind its ideals in an impressive manner, they also minister to his narcissistic satisfaction.

No mention has yet been made of what is perhaps the most important item in the psychical inventory of a civilization. This consists in its religious ideas in the widest sense – in other words (which will be justified later) in its illusions.

1. [Cf., for instance, 'Creative Writers and Day-Dreaming' (1908e), P.F.L., 14, 129.]

III

IN what does the peculiar value of religious ideas lie?

We have spoken of the hostility to civilization which is produced by the pressure that civilization exercises, the renunciations of instinct which it demands. If one imagines its prohibitions lifted – if, then, one may take any woman one pleases as a sexual object, if one may without hesitation kill one's rival for her love or anyone else who stands in one's way, if, too, one can carry off any of the other man's belongings without asking leave – how splendid, what a string of satisfactions one's life would be! True, one soon comes across the first difficulty: everyone else has exactly the same wishes as I have and will treat me with no more consideration than I treat him. And so in reality only one person could be made unrestrictedly happy by such a removal of the restrictions of civilization, and he would be a tyrant, a dictator, who had seized all the means to power. And even he would have every reason to wish that the others would observe at least one cultural commandment: 'thou shalt not kill'.

But how ungrateful, how short-sighted after all, to strive for the abolition of civilization! What would then remain would be a state of nature, and that would be far harder to bear. It is true that nature would not demand any restrictions of instinct from us, she would let us do as we liked; but she has her own particularly effective method of restricting us. She destroys us – coldly, cruelly, relentlessly, as it seems to us, and possibly through the very things that occasioned our satisfaction. It was precisely because of these dangers with which nature threatens us that we came together and created civilization, which is also, among other things, intended to make our communal life possible. For the principal task of civilization, its actual *raison d'être*, is to defend us against nature.

We all know that in many ways civilization does this fairly well already, and clearly as time goes on it will do it much

194

better. But no one is under the illusion that nature has already been vanquished; and few dare hope that she will ever be entirely subjected to man. There are the elements, which seem to mock at all human control: the earth, which quakes and is torn apart and buries all human life and its works; water, which deluges and drowns everything in a turmoil; storms, which blow everything before them; there are diseases, which we have only recently recognized as attacks by other organisms; and finally there is the painful riddle of death, against which no medicine has yet been found, nor probably will be. With these forces nature rises up against us, majestic, cruel and inexorable; she brings to our mind once more our weakness and helplessness, which we thought to escape through the work of civilization. One of the few gratifying and exalting impressions which mankind can offer is when, in the face of an elemental catastrophe, it forgets the discordancies of its civilization and all its internal difficulties and animosities, and recalls the great common task of preserving itself against the superior power of nature.

For the individual, too, life is hard to bear, just as it is for mankind in general. The civilization in which he participates imposes some amount of privation on him, and other men bring him a measure of suffering, either in spite of the precepts of his civilization or because of its imperfections. To this are added the injuries which untamed nature – he calls it Fate – inflicts on him. One might suppose that this condition of things would result in a permanent state of anxious expectation in him and a severe injury to his natural narcissism. We know already how the individual reacts to the injuries which civilization and other men inflict on him: he develops a corresponding degree of resistance to the regulations of civilization and of hostility to it. But how does he defend himself against the superior powers of nature, of Fate, which threaten him as they threaten all the rest?

Civilization relieves him of this task; it performs it in the same way for all alike; and it is noteworthy that in this almost all civilizations act alike. Civilization does not call a halt in

THE FUTURE OF AN ILLUSION

the task of defending man against nature, it merely pursues it by other means. The task is a manifold one. Man's self-regard, seriously menaced, calls for consolation; life and the universe must be robbed of their terrors; moreover his curiosity, moved, it is true, by the strongest practical interest, demands an answer.

A great deal is already gained with the first step: the humanization of nature. Impersonal forces and destinies cannot be approached; they remain eternally remote. But if the elements have passions that rage as they do in our own souls, if death itself is not something spontaneous but the violent act of an evil Will, if everywhere in nature there are Beings around us of a kind that we know in our own society, then we can breathe freely, can feel at home in the uncanny and can deal by psychical means with our senseless anxiety. We are still defenceless, perhaps, but we are no longer helplessly paralysed; we can at least react. Perhaps, indeed, we are not even defenceless. We can apply the same methods against these violent supermen outside that we employ in our own society; we can try to adjure them, to appease them, to bribe them, and, by so influencing them, we may rob them of a part of their power. A replacement like this of natural science by psychology not only provides immediate relief, but also points the way to a further mastering of the situation.

For this situation is nothing new. It has an infantile prototype, of which it is in fact only the continuation. For once before one has found oneself in a similar state of helplessness: as a small child, in relation to one's parents. One had reason to fear them, and especially one's father; and yet one was sure of his protection against the dangers one knew. Thus it was natural to assimilate the two situations. Here, too, wishing played its part, as it does in dream-life. The sleeper may be seized with a presentiment of death, which threatens to place him in the grave. But the dream-work knows how to select a condition that will turn even that dreaded event into a wish-fulfilment: the dreamer sees himself in an ancient Etruscan grave which he has climbed down into, happy to find his archaeological interests satisfied.[1] In the same way, a man makes the forces of nature not simply into persons with whom he can associate as he would with his equals – that would not do justice to the overpowering impression which those forces make on him – but he gives them the character of a father. He turns them into gods, following in this, as I have tried to show,[2] not only an infantile prototype but a phylogenetic one.

In the course of time the first observations were made of regularity and conformity to law in natural phenomena, and with this the forces of nature lost their human traits. But man's helplessness remains and along with it his longing for his father, and the gods. The gods retain their threefold task: they must exorcize the terrors of nature, they must reconcile men to the cruelty of Fate, particularly as it is shown in death, and they must compensate them for the sufferings and privations which a civilized life in common has imposed on them.

But within these functions there is a gradual displacement of accent. It was observed that the phenomena of nature developed automatically according to internal necessities. Without doubt the gods were the lords of nature; they had arranged it to be as it was and now they could leave it to itself. Only occasionally, in what are known as miracles, did they intervene in its course, as though to make it plain that they had relinquished nothing of their original sphere of power. As regards the apportioning of destinies, an unpleasant suspicion persisted that the perplexity and helplessness of the human race could not be remedied. It was here that the gods were most apt to fail. If they themselves created Fate, then their counsels must be deemed inscrutable. The notion dawned on the most gifted people of antiquity that Moira [Fate] stood above the gods and that the gods themselves had their own destinies. And the more autonomous nature became and the more the gods withdrew from it, the more earnestly were

---

1. [This was an actual dream of Freud's, reported in Chapter VI (G) of *The Interpretation of Dreams* (1900a), *P.F.L.*, **4**, 587–8.]

2. [See Essay IV (6) in *Totem and Taboo* (1912–13), *P.F.L.*, **13**.]

all expectations directed to the third function of the gods – the more did morality become their true domain. It now became the task of the gods to even out the defects and evils of civilization, to attend to the sufferings which men inflict on one another in their life together and to watch over the fulfilment of the precepts of civilization, which men obey so imperfectly. Those precepts themselves were credited with a divine origin; they were elevated beyond human society and were extended to nature and the universe.

And thus a store of ideas is created, born from man's need to make his helplessness tolerable and built up from the material of memories of the helplessness of his own childhood and the childhood of the human race. It can clearly be seen that the possession of these ideas protects him in two directions – against the dangers of nature and Fate, and against the injuries that threaten him from human society itself. Here is the gist of the matter. Life in this world serves a higher purpose; no doubt it is not easy to guess what that purpose is, but it certainly signifies a perfecting of man's nature. It is probably the spiritual part of man, the soul, which in the course of time has so slowly and unwillingly detached itself from the body, that is the object of this elevation and exaltation. Everything that happens in this world is an expression of the intentions of an intelligence superior to us, which in the end, though its ways and byways are difficult to follow, orders everything for the best – that is, to make it enjoyable for us. Over each one of us there watches a benevolent Providence which is only seemingly stern and which will not suffer us to become a plaything of the over-mighty and pitiless forces of nature. Death itself is not extinction, is not a return to inorganic life-lessness, but the beginning of a new kind of existence which lies on the path of development to something higher. And, looking in the other direction, this view announces that the same moral laws which our civilizations have set up govern the whole universe as well, except that they are maintained by a supreme court of justice with incomparably more power and consistency. In the end all good is rewarded and all evil punished, if not actually in this form of life then in the later existences that begin after death. In this way all the terrors, the sufferings and the hardships of life are destined to be obliterated. Life after death, which continues life on earth just as the invisible part of the spectrum joins on to the visible part, brings us all the perfection that we may perhaps have missed here. And the superior wisdom which directs this course of things, the infinite goodness that expresses itself in it, the justice that achieves its aim in it – these are the attributes of the divine beings who also created us and the world as a whole, or rather, of the one divine being into which, in our civilization, all the gods of antiquity have been condensed. The people which first succeeded in thus concentrating the divine attributes was not a little proud of the advance. It had laid open to view the father who had all along been hidden behind every divine figure as its nucleus. Fundamentally this was a return to the historical beginnings of the idea of God. Now that God was a single person, man's relations to him could recover the intimacy and intensity of the child's relation to his father. But if one had done so much for one's father, one wanted to have a reward, or at least to be his only beloved child, his Chosen People. Very much later, pious America laid claim to being 'God's own Country'; and, as regards one of the shapes in which men worship the deity, the claim is undoubtedly valid.

The religious ideas that have been summarized above have of course passed through a long process of development and have been adhered to in various phases by various civilizations. I have singled out one such phase, which roughly corresponds to the final form taken by our present-day white Christian civilization. It is easy to see that not all the parts of this picture tally equally well with one another, that not all the questions that press for an answer receive one, and that it is difficult to dismiss the contradiction of daily experience. Nevertheless, such as they are, those ideas – ideas which are religious in the widest sense – are prized as the most precious possession of civilization, as the most precious thing it has to offer its participants. It is far more highly prized than all the devices for winning treasures from the earth or providing men with sustenance or preventing their illnesses, and so forth. People feel that life would not be tolerable if they did not attach to these ideas the value that is claimed for them. And now the question arises: what are these ideas in the light of psychology? Whence do they derive the esteem in which they are held? And, to take a further timid step, what is their real worth?

Motive for religion
Same as Now for love/fear
of father in infancy

IV

AN inquiry which proceeds like a monologue, without interruption, is not altogether free from danger. One is too easily
tempted into pushing aside thoughts which threaten to break
into it, and in exchange one is left with a feeling of uncertainty
which in the end one tries to keep down by over-decisiveness.
I shall therefore imagine that I have an opponent who follows
my arguments with mistrust, and here and there I shall allow
him to interject some remarks.

I hear him say: 'You have repeatedly used the expressions
"civilization creates these religious ideas", "civilization places
them at the disposal of its participants". There is something
about this that sounds strange to me. I cannot myself say why,
but it does not sound so natural as it does to say that civilization
has made rules about distributing the products of labour or
about rights concerning women and children.'

I think, all the same, that I am justified in expressing myself
in this way. I have tried to show that religious ideas have
arisen from the same need as have all the other achievements
of civilization: from the necessity of defending oneself against
the crushingly superior force of nature. To this a second motive
was added – the urge to rectify the shortcomings of civilization
which made themselves painfully felt. Moreover, it is especially
apposite to say that civilization gives the individual these ideas,
for he finds them there already; they are presented to him
ready-made, and he would not be able to discover them for
himself. What he is entering into is the heritage of many generations, and he takes it over as he does the multiplication table,
geometry, and similar things. There is indeed a difference in
this, but that difference lies elsewhere and I cannot examine
it yet. The feeling of strangeness that you mention may be
partly due to the fact that this body of religious ideas is usually
put forward as a divine revelation. But this presentation of
it is itself a part of the religious system, and it entirely ignores

the known historical development of these ideas and their differences in different epochs and civilizations.

'Here is another point, which seems to me to be more important. You argue that the humanization of nature is derived from the need to put an end to man's perplexity and helplessness in the face of its dreaded forces, to get into a relation with them and finally to influence them. But a motive of this kind seems superfluous. Primitive man has no choice, he has no other way of thinking. It is natural to him, something innate, as it were, to project his existence outwards into the world and to regard every event which he observes as the manifestation of beings who at bottom are like himself. It is his only method of comprehension. And it is by no means self-evident, on the contrary it is a remarkable coincidence, if by thus indulging his natural disposition he succeeds in satisfying one of his greatest needs.'

I do not find that so striking. Do you suppose that human thought has no practical motives, that it is simply the expression of a disinterested curiosity? That is surely very improbable. I believe rather that when man personifies the forces of nature he is again following an infantile model. He has learnt from the persons in his earliest environment that the way to influence them is to establish a relation with them; and so, later on, with the same end in view, he treats everything else that he comes across in the same way as he treated those persons. Thus I do not contradict your descriptive observation; it is in fact natural to man to personify everything that he wants to understand in order later to control it (psychical mastering as a preparation for physical mastering); but I provide in addition a motive and a genesis for this peculiarity of human thinking.

'And now here is yet a third point. You have dealt with the origin of religion once before, in your book *Totem and Taboo* [1912–13]. But there it appeared in a different light. Everything was the son–father relationship. God was the exalted father, and the longing for the father was the root of the need for religion. Since then, it seems, you have discovered the factor of human weakness and helplessness, to which indeed the chief role in the formation of religion is generally assigned, and now you transpose everything that was once the father complex into terms of helplessness. May I ask you to explain this transformation?'

With pleasure. I was only waiting for this invitation. But is it really a transformation? In *Totem and Taboo* it was not my purpose to explain the origin of religions but only of totemism. Can you, from any of the views known to you, explain the fact that the first shape in which the protecting deity revealed itself to men should have been that of an animal, that there was a prohibition against killing and eating this animal and that nevertheless the solemn custom was to kill and eat it communally once a year? This is precisely what happens in totemism. And it is hardly to the purpose to argue about whether totemism ought to be called a religion. It has intimate connections with the later god-religions. The totem animals become the sacred animals of the gods; and the earliest, but most fundamental moral restrictions – the prohibitions against murder and incest – originate in totemism. Whether or not you accept the conclusions of *Totem and Taboo*, I hope you will admit that a number of very remarkable, disconnected facts are brought together in it into a consistent whole.

The question of why in the long run the animal god did not suffice, and was replaced by a human one, was hardly touched on in *Totem and Taboo*, and other problems concerning the formation of religion were not mentioned in the book at all. Do you regard a limitation of that kind as the same thing as a denial? My work is a good example of the strict isolation of the particular contribution which psychoanalytic discussion can make to the solution of the problem of religion. If I am now trying to add the other, less deeply concealed part, you should not accuse me of contradicting myself, just as before you accused me of being one-sided. It is, of course, my duty to point out the connecting links between what I said earlier and what I put forward now, between the deeper

Inter-relation between
father-complex N
when more
manifest motives.

and the manifest motives, between the father-complex and man's helplessness and need for protection.

These connections are not hard to find. They consist in the relation of the child's helplessness to the helplessness of the adult which continues it. So that, as was to be expected, the motives for the formation of religion which psychoanalysis revealed now turn out to be the same as the infantile contribution to the *manifest* motives. Let us transport ourselves into the mental life of a child. You remember the choice of object according to the anaclitic [attachment] type, which psychoanalysis talks of?[1] The libido there follows the paths of narcissistic needs and attaches itself to the objects which ensure the satisfaction of those needs. In this way the mother, who satisfies the child's hunger, becomes its first love-object and certainly also its first protection against all the undefined dangers which threaten it in the external world – its first protection against anxiety, we may say.

In this function [of protection] the mother is soon replaced by the stronger father, who retains that position for the rest of childhood. But the child's attitude to its father is coloured by a peculiar ambivalence. The father himself constitutes a danger for the child, perhaps because of its earlier relation to its mother. Thus it fears him no less than it longs for him and admires him. The indications of this ambivalence in the attitude to the father are deeply imprinted in every religion, as was shown in *Totem and Taboo*. When the growing individual finds that he is destined to remain a child for ever, that he can never do without protection against strange superior powers, he lends those powers the features belonging to the figure of his father; he creates for himself the gods whom he dreads, whom he seeks to propitiate, and whom he nevertheless entrusts with his own protection. Thus his longing for a father is a motive identical with his need for protection against the consequences of his human weakness. The defence against childish helplessness is what lends its characteristic

1. [See Section II of Freud's paper on narcissism (1914*c*), *P.F.L.*, **11**, 81–4; see also p. 134 above.]

features to the adult's reaction to the helplessness which *he* has to acknowledge – a reaction which is precisely the formation of religion. But it is not my intention to inquire any further into the development of the idea of God; what we are concerned with here is the finished body of religious ideas as it is transmitted by civilization to the individual.

LET us now take up the thread of our inquiry.[1] What, then, is the psychological significance of religious ideas and under what heading are we to classify them? The question is not at all easy to answer immediately. After rejecting a number of formulations, we will take our stand on the following one. Religious ideas are teachings and assertions about facts and conditions of external (or internal) reality which tell one something one has not discovered for oneself and which lay claim to one's belief. Since they give us information about what is most important and interesting to us in life, they are particularly highly prized. Anyone who knows nothing of them is very ignorant; and anyone who has added them to his knowledge may consider himself much the richer.

There are, of course, many such teachings about the most various things in the world. Every school lesson is full of them. Let us take geography. We are told that the town of Constance lies on the Bodensee.[2] A student song adds: 'if you don't believe it, go and see.' I happen to have been there and can confirm the fact that that lovely town lies on the shore of a wide stretch of water which all those who live round it call the Bodensee; and I am now completely convinced of the correctness of this geographical assertion. In this connection I am reminded of another, very remarkable, experience. I was already a man of mature years when I stood for the first time on the hill of the Acropolis in Athens, between the temple ruins, looking out over the blue sea. A feeling of astonishment mingled with my joy. It seemed to say: 'So it really *is* true, just as we learnt at school!' How shallow and weak must have been the belief I then acquired in the real truth of what I heard, if I could be so astonished now! But I will not lay too much stress on the significance of this experience; for my

1. [From the end of Chapter III, p. 199 f.]
2. [The German name for what we call the Lake of Constance.]

astonishment could have had another explanation, which did not occur to me at the time and which is of a wholly subjective nature and has to do with the special character of the place.[1]

All teachings like these, then, demand belief in their contents, but not without producing grounds for their claim. They are put forward as the epitomized result of a longer process of thought based on observation and certainly also on inferences. If anyone wants to go through this process himself instead of accepting its result, they show him how to set about it. Moreover, we are always in addition given the source of the knowledge conveyed by them, where that source is not self-evident, as it is in the case of geographical assertions. For instance, the earth is shaped like a sphere; the proofs adduced for this are Foucault's pendulum experiment,[2] the behaviour of the horizon and the possibility of circumnavigating the earth. Since it is impracticable, as everyone concerned realizes, to send every schoolchild on a voyage round the world, we are satisfied with letting what is taught at school be taken on trust; but we know that the path to acquiring a personal conviction remains open.

Let us try to apply the same test to the teachings of religion. When we ask on what their claim to be believed is founded, we are met with three answers, which harmonize remarkably badly with one another. Firstly, these teachings deserve to be believed because they were already believed by our primal ancestors; secondly, we possess proofs which have been handed down to us from those same primaeval times; and thirdly, it is forbidden to raise the question of their authentication at all. In former days anything so presumptuous was visited with the severest penalties, and even to-day society looks askance at any attempt to raise the question again.

1. [This had happened in 1904, when Freud was almost fifty. He wrote a full account of the episode in an open letter to Romain Rolland some ten years after the present work (1936a), P.F.L., 11.]

2. [J. B. L. Foucault (1819–68) demonstrated the diurnal motion of the earth by means of a pendulum in 1851.]

This third point is bound to rouse our strongest suspicions. After all, a prohibition like this can only be for one reason – that society is very well aware of the insecurity of the claim it makes on behalf of its religious doctrines. Otherwise it would certainly be very ready to put the necessary data at the disposal of anyone who wanted to arrive at conviction. This being so, it is with a feeling of mistrust which it is hard to allay that we pass on to an examination of the other two grounds of proof. We ought to believe because our forefathers believed. But these ancestors of ours were far more ignorant than we are. They believed in things we could not possibly accept to-day; and the possibility occurs to us that the doctrines of religion may belong to that class too. The proofs they have left us are set down in writings which themselves bear every mark of untrustworthiness. They are full of contradictions, revisions and falsifications, and where they speak of factual confirmations they are themselves unconfirmed. It does not help much to have it asserted that their wording, or even their content only, originates from divine revelation; for this assertion is itself one of the doctrines whose authenticity is under examination, and no proposition can be a proof of itself.

Thus we arrive at the singular conclusion that of all the information provided by our cultural assets it is precisely the elements which might be of the greatest importance to us and which have the task of solving the riddles of the universe and of reconciling us to the sufferings of life – it is precisely those elements that are the least well authenticated of any. We should not be able to bring ourselves to accept anything of so little concern to us as the fact that whales bear young instead of laying eggs, if it were not capable of better proof than this.

This state of affairs is in itself a very remarkable psychological problem. And let no one suppose that what I have said about the impossibility of proving the truth of religious doctrines contains anything new. It has been felt at all times – undoubtedly, too, by the ancestors who bequeathed us this legacy. Many of them probably nourished the same doubts as ours, but the pressure imposed on them was too strong for them to have dared to utter them. And since then countless people have been tormented by similar doubts, and have striven to suppress them, because they thought it was their duty to believe; many brilliant intellects have broken down over this conflict, and many characters have been impaired by the compromises with which they have tried to find a way out of it.

If all the evidence put forward for the authenticity of religious teachings originates in the past, it is natural to look round and see whether the present, about which it is easier to form judgements, may not also be able to furnish evidence of the sort. If by this means we could succeed in clearing even a single portion of the religious system from doubt, the whole of it would gain enormously in credibility. The proceedings of the spiritualists meet us at this point; they are convinced of the survival of the individual soul and they seek to demonstrate to us beyond doubt the truth of this one religious doctrine. Unfortunately they cannot succeed in refuting the fact that the appearance and utterances of their spirits are merely the products of their own mental activity. They have called up the spirits of the greatest men and of the most eminent thinkers, but all the pronouncements and information which they have received from them have been so foolish and so wretchedly meaningless that one can find nothing credible in them but the capacity of the spirits to adapt themselves to the circle of people who have conjured them up.

I must now mention two attempts that have been made – both of which convey the impression of being desperate efforts – to evade the problem. One, of a violent nature, is ancient; the other is subtle and modern. The first is the 'Credo quia absurdum' of the early Father of the Church.[1] It maintains that religious doctrines are outside the jurisdiction of reason – are above reason. Their truth must be felt inwardly, and they need not be comprehended. But this Credo is only of interest as a self-confession. As an authoritative statement it

1. ['I believe because it is absurd.' This is attributed to Tertullian.]

has no binding force. Am I to be obliged to believe *every* absurdity? And if not, why this one in particular? There is no appeal to a court above that of reason. If the truth of religious doctrines is dependent on an inner experience which bears witness to that truth, what is one to do about the many people who do not have this rare experience? One may require every man to use the gift of reason which he possesses, but one cannot erect, on the basis of a motive that exists only for a very few, an obligation that shall apply to everyone. If one man has gained an unshakable conviction of the true reality of religious doctrines from a state of ecstasy which has deeply moved him, of what significance is that to others?

The second attempt is the one made by the philosophy of 'As if'. This asserts that our thought-activity includes a great number of hypotheses whose groundlessness and even absurdity we fully realize. They are called 'fictions', but for a variety of practical reasons we have to behave 'as if' we believed in these fictions. This is the case with religious doctrines because of their incomparable importance for the maintenance of human society.[1] This line of argument is not far removed from the '*Credo quia absurdum*'. But I think the demand made by the 'As if' argument is one that only a philosopher could put forward. A man whose thinking is not influenced by the artifices of philosophy will never be able to accept it; in such a man's view, the admission that something is absurd or contrary to reason leaves no more to be said. It cannot be expected of him that precisely in treating his most important interests he shall forgo the guarantees he requires for all his ordinary activities. I am reminded of one of my children who was distinguished at an early age by a peculiarly marked matter-

1. I hope I am not doing him an injustice if I take the philosopher of 'As if' as the representative of a view which is not foreign to other thinkers: 'We include as fictions not merely indifferent theoretical operations but ideational constructs emanating from the noblest minds, to which the noblest part of mankind cling and of which they will not allow themselves to be deprived. Nor is it our object so to deprive them – for as *practical fictions* we leave them all intact; they perish only as *theoretical truths*.' (Hans Vaihinger, 1922, 68 [C. K. Ogden's translation, 1924, 48–9].)

of-factness. When the children were being told a fairy story and were listening to it with rapt attention, he would come up and ask: 'Is that a true story?' When he was told it was not, he would turn away with a look of disdain. We may expect that people will soon behave in the same way towards the fairy tales of religion, in spite of the advocacy of 'As if'.

But at present they still behave quite differently; and in past times religious ideas, in spite of their incontrovertible lack of authentication, have exercised the strongest possible influence on mankind. This is a fresh psychological problem. We must ask where the inner force of those doctrines lies and to what it is that they owe their efficacy, independent as it is of recognition by reason.

VI

I THINK we have prepared the way sufficiently for an answer to both these questions. It will be found if we turn our attention to the psychical origin of religious ideas. These, which are given out as teachings, are not precipitates of experience or end-results of thinking: they are illusions, fulfilments of the oldest, strongest and most urgent wishes of mankind. The secret of their strength lies in the strength of those wishes. As we already know, the terrifying impression of helplessness in childhood aroused the need for protection – for protection through love – which was provided by the father; and the recognition that this helplessness lasts throughout life made it necessary to cling to the existence of a father, but this time a more powerful one. Thus the benevolent rule of a divine Providence allays our fear of the dangers of life; the establishment of a moral world-order ensures the fulfilment of the demands of justice, which have so often remained unfulfilled in human civilization; and the prolongation of earthly existence in a future life provides the local and temporal framework in which these wish-fulfilments shall take place. Answers to the riddles that tempt the curiosity of man, such as how the universe began or what the relation is between body and mind, are developed in conformity with the underlying assumptions of this system. It is an enormous relief to the individual psyche if the conflicts of its childhood arising from the father-complex – conflicts which it has never wholly overcome – are removed from it and brought to a solution which is universally accepted.

When I say that these things are all illusions, I must define the meaning of the word. An illusion is not the same thing as an error; nor is it necessarily an error. Aristotle's belief that vermin are developed out of dung (a belief to which ignorant people still cling) was an error; so was the belief of a former generation of doctors that *tabes dorsalis* is the result of sexual excess. It would be incorrect to call these errors illusions. On the other hand, it was an illusion of Columbus's that he had discovered a new sea-route to the Indies. The part played by his wish in this error is very clear. One may describe as an illusion the assertion made by certain nationalists that the Indo-Germanic race is the only one capable of civilization; or the belief, which was only destroyed by psychoanalysis, that children are creatures without sexuality. What is characteristic of illusions is that they are derived from human wishes. In this respect they come near to psychiatric delusions. But they differ from them, too, apart from the more complicated structure of delusions. In the case of delusions, we emphasize as essential their being in contradiction with reality. Illusions need not necessarily be false – that is to say, unrealizable or in contradiction to reality. For instance, a middle-class girl may have the illusion that a prince will come and marry her. This is possible; and a few such cases have occurred. That the Messiah will come and found a golden age is much less likely. Whether one classifies this belief as an illusion or as something analogous to a delusion will depend on one's personal attitude. Examples of illusions which have proved true are not easy to find, but the illusion of the alchemists that all metals can be turned into gold might be one of them. The wish to have a great deal of gold, as much gold as possible, has, it is true, been a good deal damped by our present-day knowledge of the determinants of wealth, but chemistry no longer regards the transmutation of metals into gold as impossible. Thus we call a belief an illusion when a wish-fulfilment is a prominent factor in its motivation, and in doing so we disregard its relations to reality, just as the illusion itself sets no store by verification.

Having thus taken our bearings, let us return once more to the question of religious doctrines. We can now repeat that all of them are illusions and insusceptible of proof. No one can be compelled to think them true, to believe in them. Some of them are so improbable, so incompatible with everything we have laboriously discovered about the reality of the world, that we may compare them – if we pay proper regard to the psychological differences – to delusions. Of the reality value of most of them we cannot judge; just as they cannot be proved, so they cannot be refuted. We still know too little to make a critical approach to them. The riddles of the universe reveal themselves only slowly to our investigation; there are many questions to which science to-day can give no answer. But scientific work is the only road which can lead us to a knowledge of reality outside ourselves. It is once again merely an illusion to expect anything from intuition and introspection; they can give us nothing but particulars about our own mental life, which are hard to interpret, never any information about the questions which religious doctrine finds it so easy to answer. It would be insolent to let one's own arbitrary will step into the breach and, according to one's personal estimate, declare this or that part of the religious system to be less or more acceptable. Such questions are too momentous for that; they might be called too sacred.

At this point one must expect to meet with an objection. 'Well then, if even obdurate sceptics admit that the assertions of religion cannot be refuted by reason, why should I not believe in them, since they have so much on their side – tradition, the agreement of mankind, and all the consolations they offer?' Why not, indeed? Just as no one can be forced to believe, so no one can be forced to disbelieve. But do not let us be satisfied with deceiving ourselves that arguments like these take us along the road of correct thinking. If ever there was a case of a lame excuse we have it here. Ignorance is ignorance; no right to believe anything can be derived from it. In other matters no sensible person will behave so irresponsibly or rest content with such feeble grounds for his opinions and for the line he takes. It is only in the highest and most sacred things that he allows himself to do so. In reality these are only attempts at pretending to oneself or to other people that one is still firmly attached to religion, when one has long since cut oneself loose from it. Where questions of religion are concerned, people are guilty of every possible sort of dishonesty and intellectual misdemeanour. Philosophers stretch the meaning of words until they retain scarcely anything of their original sense. They give

214

the name of 'God' to some vague abstraction which they have created for themselves; having done so they can pose before all the world as deists, as believers in God, and they can even boast that they have recognized a higher, purer concept of God, notwithstanding that their God is now nothing more than an insubstantial shadow and no longer the mighty personality of religious doctrines. Critics persist in describing as 'deeply religious' anyone who admits to a sense of man's insignificance or impotence in the face of the universe, although what constitutes the essence of the religious attitude is not this feeling but only the next step after it, the reaction to it which seeks a remedy for it. The man who goes no further, but humbly acquiesces in the small part which human beings play in the great world – such a man is, on the contrary, irreligious in the truest sense of the word.

To assess the truth-value of religious doctrines does not lie within the scope of the present inquiry. It is enough for us that we have recognized them as being, in their psychological nature, illusions. But we do not have to conceal the fact that this discovery also strongly influences our attitude to the question which must appear to many to be the most important of all. We know approximately at what periods and by what kind of men religious doctrines were created. If in addition we discover the motives which led to this, our attitude to the problem of religion will undergo a marked displacement. We shall tell ourselves that it would be very nice if there were a God who created the world and was a benevolent Providence, and if there were a moral order in the universe and an after-life; but it is a very striking fact that all this is exactly as we are bound to wish it to be. And it would be more remarkable still if our wretched, ignorant and down-trodden ancestors had succeeded in solving all these difficult riddles of the universe.

VII

HAVING recognized religious doctrines as illusions, we are at once faced by a further question: may not other cultural assets of which we hold a high opinion and by which we let our lives be ruled be of a similar nature? Must not the assumptions that determine our political regulations be called illusions as well? and is it not the case that in our civilization the relations between the sexes are disturbed by an erotic illusion or a number of such illusions? And once our suspicion has been aroused, we shall not shrink from asking too whether our conviction that we can learn something about external reality through the use of observation and reasoning in scientific work — whether this conviction has any better foundation. Nothing ought to keep us from directing our observation to our own selves or from applying our thought to criticism of itself. In this field a number of investigations open out before us, whose results could not but be decisive for the construction of a 'Weltanschauung'. We surmise, moreover, that such an effort would not be wasted and that it would at least in part justify our suspicion. But the author does not dispose of the means for undertaking so comprehensive a task; he needs must confine his work to following out one only of these illusions — that, namely, of religion.

But now the loud voice of our opponent brings us to a halt. We are called to account for our wrong-doing:

'Archaeological interests are no doubt most praiseworthy, but no one undertakes an excavation if by doing so he is going to undermine the habitations of the living so that they collapse and bury people under their ruins. The doctrines of religion are not a subject one can quibble about like any other. Our civilization is built up on them, and the maintenance of human society is based on the majority of men's believing in the truth of those doctrines. If men are taught that there is no almighty and all-just God, no divine world-order and no future life, they will feel exempt from all obligation to obey the precepts of civilization. Everyone will, without inhibition or fear, follow his asocial, egoistic instincts and seek to exercise his power; Chaos, which we have banished through many thousands of years of the work of civilization, will come again. Even if we knew, and could prove, that religion was not in possession of the truth, we ought to conceal the fact and behave in the way prescribed by the philosophy of "As if" – and this in the interest of the preservation of us all. And apart from the danger of the undertaking, it would be a purposeless cruelty. Countless people find their one consolation in religious doctrines, and can only bear life with their help. You would rob them of their support, without having anything better to give them in exchange. It is admitted that so far science has not achieved much, but even if it had advanced much further it would not suffice for man. Man has imperative needs of another sort, which can never be satisfied by cold science; and it is very strange – indeed, it is the height of inconsistency – that a psychologist who has always insisted on what a minor part is played in human affairs by the intelligence as compared with the life of the instincts – that such a psychologist should now try to rob mankind of a precious wish-fulfilment and should propose to compensate them for it with intellectual nourishment.'

What a lot of accusations all at once! Nevertheless I am ready with rebuttals for them all; and, what is more, I shall assert the view that civilization runs a greater risk if we maintain our present attitude to religion than if we give it up.

But I hardly know where to begin my reply. Perhaps with the assurance that I myself regard my undertaking as completely harmless and free of risk. It is not I who am overvaluing the intellect this time. If people are as my opponents describe them – and I should not like to contradict them – then there is no danger of a devout believer's being overcome by my arguments and deprived of his faith. Besides, I have said nothing which other and better men have not said before me in a much more complete, forcible and impressive manner. Their names are well known, and I shall not cite them, for I should not like to give an impression that I am seeking to rank myself as one of them. All I have done – and this is the only thing that is new in my exposition – is to add some psychological foundation to the criticisms of my great predecessors. It is hardly to be expected that precisely this addition will produce the effect which was denied to those earlier efforts. No doubt I might be asked here what is the point of writing these things if I am certain that they will be ineffective. But I shall come back to that later.

The one person this publication may injure is myself. I shall have to listen to the most disagreeable reproaches for my shallowness, narrow-mindedness and lack of idealism or of understanding for the highest interests of mankind. But on the one hand, such remonstrances are not new to me; and on the other, if a man has already learnt in his youth to rise superior to the disapproval of his contemporaries, what can it matter to him in his old age when he is certain soon to be beyond the reach of all favour or disfavour? In former times it was different. Then utterances such as mine brought with them a sure curtailment of one's earthly existence and an effective speeding-up of the opportunity for gaining a personal experience of the after-life. But, I repeat, those times are past and to-day writings such as this bring no more danger to their author than to their readers. The most that can happen is that the translation and distribution of his book will be forbidden in one country or another – and precisely, of course, in a country that is convinced of the high standard of its culture. But if one puts in any plea at all for the the renunciation of wishes and for acquiescence in Fate, one must be able to tolerate this kind of injury too.

The further question occurred to me whether the publication of this work might not after all do harm. Not to a person, however, but to a cause – the cause of psychoanalysis. For it cannot be denied that psychoanalysis is my creation, and it has met with plenty of mistrust and ill-will. If I now come forward with such displeasing pronouncements, people will be only too ready to make a displacement from my person to psychoanalysis. 'Now we see,' they will say, 'where psycho-analysis leads to. The mask has fallen; it leads to a denial of God and of a moral ideal, as we always suspected. To keep us from this discovery we have been deluded into thinking that psychoanalysis has no *Weltanschauung* and never can con-struct one.'[1]

An outcry of this kind will really be disagreeable to me on account of my many fellow-workers, some of whom do not by any means share my attitude to the problems of religion. But psychoanalysis has already weathered many storms and now it must brave this fresh one. In point of fact psycho-analysis is a method of research, an impartial instrument, like the infinitesimal calculus, as it were. If a physicist were to discover with the latter's help that after a certain time the earth would be destroyed, we would nevertheless hesitate to attribute destructive tendencies to the calculus itself and there-fore to proscribe it. Nothing that I have said here against the truth-value of religions needed the support of psycho-analysis; it had been said by others long before analysis came into existence. If the application of the psychoanalytic method makes it possible to find a new argument against the truths of religion, *tant pis* for religion; but defenders of religion will by the same right make use of psychoanalysis in order to give full value to the affective significance of religious doctrines.

And now to proceed with our defence. Religion has clearly performed great services for human civilization. It has contri-buted much towards the taming of the asocial instincts. But not enough. It has ruled human society for many thousands of years and has had time to show what it can achieve. If it had succeeded in making the majority of mankind happy, in comforting them, in reconciling them to life and in making them into vehicles of civilization, no one would dream of attempting to alter the existing conditions. But what do we see instead? We see that an appallingly large number of people

1. [See some remarks in Chapter II of *Inhibitions, Symptoms and Anxiety* (1926*d*), *P.F.L.*, 10, 247–8.]

are dissatisfied with civilization and unhappy in it, and feel it as a yoke which must be shaken off; and that these people either do everything in their power to change that civilization, or else go so far in their hostility to it that they will have nothing to do with civilization or with a restriction of instinct. At this point it will be objected against us that this state of affairs is due to the very fact that religion has lost a part of its influence over human masses precisely because of the deplorable effect of the advances of science. We will note this admission and the reason given for it, and we shall make use of it later for our own purposes; but the objection itself has no force.

It is doubtful whether men were in general happier at a time when religious doctrines held unrestricted sway; more moral they certainly were not. They have always known how to externalize the precepts of religion and thus to nullify their intentions. The priests, whose duty it was to ensure obedience to religion, met them half-way in this. God's kindness must lay a restraining hand on His justice. One sinned, and then one made a sacrifice or did penance and then one was free to sin once more. Russian introspectiveness has reached the pitch of concluding that sin is indispensable for the enjoyment of all the blessings of divine grace, so that, at bottom, sin is pleasing to God. It is no secret that the priests could only keep the masses submissive to religion by making such large concessions as these to the instinctual nature of man. Thus it was agreed: God alone is strong and good, man is weak and sinful. In every age immorality has found no less support in religion than morality has. If the achievements of religion in respect to man's happiness, susceptibility to culture[1] and moral control are no better than this, the question cannot but arise whether we are not over-rating its necessity for mankind, and whether we do wisely in basing our cultural demands upon it.

Let us consider the unmistakable situation as it is to-day.

1. [The nature of 'susceptibility to culture' is discussed by Freud in his paper on 'War and Death' (1915b), p. 70 above.]

We have heard the admission that religion no longer has the same influence on people that it used to. (We are here concerned with European Christian civilization.) And this is not because its promises have grown less but because people find them less credible. Let us admit that the reason – though perhaps not the only reason – for this change is the increase of the scientific spirit in the higher strata of human society. Criticism has whittled away the evidential value of religious documents, natural science has shown up the errors in them, and comparative research has been struck by the fatal resemblance between the religious ideas which we revere and the mental products of primitive peoples and times.

The scientific spirit brings about a particular attitude towards worldly matters; before religious matters it pauses for a little, hesitates, and finally there too crosses the threshold. In this process there is no stopping; the greater the number of men to whom the treasures of knowledge become accessible, the more widespread is the falling-away from religious belief – at first only from its obsolete and objectionable trappings, but later from its fundamental postulates as well. The Americans who instituted the 'monkey trial' at Dayton[1] have alone shown themselves consistent. Elsewhere the inevitable transition is accomplished by way of half-measures and insincerities.

Civilization has little to fear from educated people and brain-workers. In them the replacement of religious motives for civilized behaviour by other, secular motives would proceed unobtrusively; moreover, such people are to a large extent themselves vehicles of civilization. But it is another matter with the great mass of the uneducated and oppressed, who have every reason for being enemies of civilization. So long as they do not discover that people no longer believe in God, all is well. But they will discover it, infallibly, even if this piece of writing of mine is not published. And they are ready to accept the results of scientific thinking, but without the

1. [A small town in Tennessee where, in 1925, a science teacher was prosecuted for breach of a State law by teaching that 'man is descended from the lower animals'.]

change having taken place in them which scientific thinking brings about in people. Is there not a danger here that the hostility of these masses to civilization will throw itself against the weak spot that they have found in their task-mistress? If the sole reason why you must not kill your neighbour is because God has forbidden it and will severely punish you for it in this or the next life – then, when you learn that there is no God and that you need not fear His punishment, you will certainly kill your neighbour without hesitation, and you can only be prevented from doing so by mundane force. Thus either these dangerous masses must be held down most severely and kept most carefully away from any chance of intellectual awakening, or else the relationship between civilization and religion must undergo a fundamental revision.

VIII

ONE might think that there would be no special difficulties
in the way of carrying out this latter proposal. It is true that
it would involve a certain amount of renunciation, but more
would perhaps be gained than lost, and a great danger would
be avoided. Everyone is frightened of it, however, as though
it would expose civilization to a still greater danger. When
St Boniface[1] cut down the tree that was venerated as sacred
by the Saxons the bystanders expected some fearful event to
follow upon the sacrilege. But nothing happened, and the
Saxons accepted baptism.

When civilization laid down the commandment that a man
shall not kill the neighbour whom he hates or who is in his
way or whose property he covets, this was clearly done in
the interest of man's communal existence, which would not
otherwise be practicable. For the murderer would draw down
on himself the vengeance of the murdered man's kinsmen and
the secret envy of others, who within themselves feel as much
inclined as he does for such acts of violence. Thus he would
not enjoy his revenge or his robbery for long, but would
have every prospect of soon being killed himself. Even if he
protected himself against his single foes by extraordinary
strength and caution, he would be bound to succumb to a
combination of weaker men. If a combination of this sort
did not take place, the murdering would continue endlessly
and the final outcome would be that men would exterminate
one another. We should arrive at the same state of affairs
between individuals as still persists in Corsica between families,
though elsewhere only between nations. Insecurity of life,
which is an equal danger for everyone, now unites men into
a society which prohibits the individual from killing and
reserves to itself the right to communal killing of anyone who

1. [The eighth-century, Devonshire-born, 'Apostle of Germany'.]

violates the prohibition. Here, then, we have justice and punishment.

But we do not publish this rational explanation of the prohibition against murder. We assert that the prohibition has been issued by God. Thus we take it upon ourselves to guess His intentions, and we find that He, too, is unwilling for men to exterminate one another. In behaving in this way we are investing the cultural prohibition with a quite special solemnity, but at the same time we risk making its observance dependent on belief in God. If we retrace this step – if we no longer attribute to God what is our own will and if we content ourselves with giving the social reason – then, it is true, we have renounced the transfiguration of the cultural prohibition, but we have also avoided the risk to it. But we gain something else as well. Through some kind of diffusion or infection, the character of sanctity and inviolability – of belonging to another world, one might say – has spread from a few major prohibitions on to every other cultural regulation, law and ordinance. But on these the halo often looks far from becoming: not only do they invalidate one another by giving contrary decisions at different times and places, but apart from this they show every sign of human inadequacy. It is easy to recognize in them things that can only be the product of short-sighted apprehensiveness or an expression of selfishly narrow interests or a conclusion based on insufficient premisses. The criticism which we cannot fail to level at them also diminishes to an unwelcome extent our respect for other, more justifiable cultural demands. Since it is an awkward task to separate what God Himself has demanded from what can be traced to the authority of an all-powerful parliament or a high judiciary, it would be an undoubted advantage if we were to leave God out altogether and honestly admit the purely human origin of all the regulations and precepts of civilization. Along with their pretended sanctity, these commandments and laws would lose their rigidity and unchangeableness as well. People could understand that they are made, not so much to rule them as, on the contrary, to serve their interests; and they would adopt a more friendly attitude to them, and instead of aiming at their abolition, would aim only at their improvement. This would be an important advance along the road which leads to becoming reconciled to the burden of civilization.

But here our plea for ascribing purely rational reasons to the precepts of civilization – that is to say, for deriving them from social necessity – is interrupted by a sudden doubt. We have chosen as our example the origin of the prohibition against murder. But does our account of it tally with historical truth? We fear not; it appears to be nothing but a rationalistic construction. With the help of psychoanalysis, we have made a study of precisely this piece of the cultural history of mankind,[1] and, basing ourselves on it, we are bound to say that in reality things happened otherwise. Even in present-day man purely reasonable motives can effect little against passionate impulsions. How much weaker then must they have been in the human animal of primaeval times! Perhaps his descendants would even now kill one another without inhibition, if it were not that among those murderous acts there was one – the killing of the primitive father – which evoked an irresistible emotional reaction with momentous consequences. From it arose the commandment: Thou shalt not kill. Under totemism this commandment was restricted to the father-substitute; but it was later extended to other people, though even to-day it is not universally obeyed.

But, as was shown by arguments which I need not repeat here, the primal father was the original image of God, the model on which later generations have shaped the figure of God. Hence the religious explanation is right. God actually played a part in the genesis of that prohibition; it was His influence, not any insight into social necessity, which created it. And the displacement of man's will on to God is fully justified. For men knew that they had disposed of their father by violence, and in their reaction to that impious deed, they determined to respect his will thenceforward. Thus religious doctrine tells us the historical truth – though subject, it is

1. [Cf. the fourth essay in *Totem and Taboo* (1912–13), *P.F.L.*, **13**.]

Religion - the universal obsessional neurosis of mankind arising out of the Oedipus Complex

true, to some modification and disguise — whereas our rational account disavows it.

We now observe that the store of religious ideas includes not only wish-fulfilments but important historical recollections. This concurrent influence of past and present must give religion a truly incomparable wealth of power. But perhaps with the help of an analogy yet another discovery may begin to dawn on us. Though it is not a good plan to transplant ideas far from the soil in which they grew up, yet here is a conformity which we cannot avoid pointing out. We know that a human child cannot successfully complete its development to the civilized stage without passing through a phase of neurosis sometimes of greater and sometimes of less distinctness. This is because so many instinctual demands which will later be unserviceable cannot be suppressed by the rational operation of the child's intellect but have to be tamed by acts of repression, behind which, as a rule, lies the motive of anxiety. Most of these infantile neuroses are overcome spontaneously in the course of growing up, and this is especially true of the obsessional neuroses of childhood. The remainder can be cleared up later still by psychoanalytic treatment. In just the same way, one might assume, humanity as a whole, in its development through the ages, fell into states analogous to the neuroses,[1] and for the same reasons — namely because in the times of its ignorance and intellectual weakness the instinctual renunciations indispensable for man's communal existence had only been achieved by it by means of purely affective forces. The precipitates of these processes resembling repression which took place in prehistoric times still remained attached to civilization for long periods. Religion would thus be the universal obsessional neurosis of humanity; like the obsessional neurosis of children, it arose out of the Oedipus complex, out of the relation to the father. If this view is right, it is to be supposed

1. [Freud returned to this question in his *Civilization and its Discontents* (1930a), p. 338 below, in Lecture 35 of the *New Introductory Lectures* (1933a), *P.F.L.*, **2**, 202–4, and at greater length in Essay III, Part I (C) of *Moses and Monotheism* (1939a), ibid., **13**, 314 ff.]

→ leads to defence against need to construct more personal one

that a turning-away from religion is bound to occur with the fatal inevitability of a process of growth, and that we find ourselves at this very juncture in the middle of that phase of development. Our behaviour should therefore be modelled on that of a sensible teacher who does not oppose an impending new development but seeks to ease its path and mitigate the violence of its irruption. Our analogy does not, to be sure, exhaust the essential nature of religion. If, on the one hand, religion brings with it obsessional restrictions, exactly as an individual obsessional neurosis does, on the other hand it comprises a system of wishful illusions together with a disavowal[1] of reality, such as we find in an isolated form nowhere else but in amentia,[2] in a state of blissful hallucinatory confusion. But these are only analogies, by the help of which we endeavour to understand a social phenomenon; the pathology of the individual does not supply us with a fully valid counterpart.

It has been repeatedly pointed out (by myself and in particular by Theodor Reik[3]) in how great detail the analogy between religion and obsessional neurosis can be followed out, and how many of the peculiarities and vicissitudes in the formation of religion can be understood in that light. And it tallies well with this that devout believers are safeguarded in a high degree against the risk of certain neurotic illnesses; their acceptance of the universal neurosis spares them the task of constructing a personal one.[4]

Our knowledge of the historical worth of certain religious doctrines increases our respect for them, but does not invalidate our proposal that they should cease to be put forward as the reasons for the precepts of civilization. On the contrary! Those

1. [See the paper on 'Fetishism' (1927e), P.F.L., **7**, 353.]

2. ['Meynert's amentia': a state of acute hallucinatory confusion.]

3. [Cf. Freud, 'Obsessive Actions and Religious Practices' (1907b), P.F.L., **13**, and Reik (1927).]

4. [Freud had often made this point before: e.g. in a sentence added in 1919 to his study on Leonardo da Vinci (1910c), P.F.L., **14**, as well as in *Group Psychology* (1921c), p. 176 above. There is a further mention in *Civilization and its Discontents* (1930a), p. 273 below.]

religious teachings = neurotic relics.

historical residues have helped us to view religious teachings, as it were, as neurotic relics, and we may now argue that the time has probably come, as it does in an analytic treatment, for replacing the effects of repression by the results of the rational operation of the intellect. We may foresee, but hardly regret, that such a process of remoulding will not stop at renouncing the solemn transfiguration of cultural precepts, but that a general revision of them will result in many of them being done away with. In this way our appointed task of reconciling men to civilization will to a great extent be achieved. We need not deplore the renunciation of historical truth when we put forward rational grounds for the precepts of civilization. The truths contained in religious doctrines are after all so distorted and systematically disguised that the mass of humanity cannot recognize them as truth. The case is similar to what happens when we tell a child that new-born babies are brought by the stork. Here, too, we are telling the truth in symbolic clothing, for we know what the large bird signifies. But the child does not know it. He hears only the distorted part of what we say, and feels that he has been deceived; and we know how often his distrust of the grown-ups and his refractoriness actually take their start from this impression. We have become convinced that it is better to avoid such symbolic disguisings of the truth in what we tell children and not to withhold from them a knowledge of the true state of affairs commensurate with their intellectual level.[1]

---

1. [Freud later drew a distinction between what he termed 'material' and 'historical' truth in several passages. See, in particular, Essay III, Part II (G) in *Moses and Monotheism* (1939a), *P.F.L.*, **13**. The same idea also occurs, in connection with the formation of myths, in 'The Acquisition and Control of Fire' (1932a), ibid., **13**. Cf. also an Editor's footnote in *The Psychopathology of Everyday Life* (1901b), ibid., **5**, 318 *n.* 2.]

IX

'You permit yourself contradictions which are hard to reconcile with one another. You begin by saying that a piece of writing like yours is quite harmless: no one will let himself be robbed of his faith by considerations of the sort put forward in it. But since it is nevertheless your intention, as becomes evident later on, to upset that faith, we may ask why in fact you are publishing your work? In another passage, moreover, you admit that it may be dangerous, indeed very dangerous, for someone to discover that people no longer believe in God. Hitherto he has been docile, but now he throws off his obedience to the precepts of civilization. Yet your whole contention that basing the commandments of civilization on religious grounds constitutes a danger for civilization rests on the assumption that the believer can be turned into an unbeliever. Surely that is a complete contradiction.

'And here is another. On the one hand you admit that men cannot be guided through their intelligence, they are ruled by their passions and their instinctual demands. But on the other hand you propose to replace the affective basis of their obedience to civilization by a rational one. Let who can understand this. To me it seems that it must be either one thing or the other.

'Besides, have you learned nothing from history? Once before an attempt of this kind was made to substitute reason for religion, officially and in the grand manner. Surely you remember the French Revolution and Robespierre? And you must also remember how short-lived and miserably ineffectual the experiment was? The same experiment is being repeated in Russia at the present time, and we need not feel curious as to its outcome. Do you not think we may take it for granted that men cannot do without religion?

'You have said yourself that religion is more than an obsessional neurosis. But you have not dealt with this other side of it. You are content to work out the analogy with a neurosis. Men, you say, must be freed from a neurosis. What else may be lost in the process is of no concern to you.'

The appearance of contradiction has probably come about because I have dealt with complicated matters too hurriedly. But we can remedy this to some extent. I still maintain that what I have written is quite harmless in one respect. No believer will let himself be led astray from his faith by these or any similar arguments. A believer is bound to the teachings of religion by certain ties of affection. But there are undoubtedly countless other people who are not in the same sense believers. They obey the precepts of civilization because they let themselves be intimidated by the threats of religion, and they are afraid of religion so long as they have to consider it as a part of the reality which hems them in. They are the people who break away as soon as they are allowed to give up their belief in the reality-value of religion. But they too are unaffected by arguments. They cease to fear religion when they observe that others do not fear it; and it was of them that I asserted that they would get to know about the decline of religious influence even if I did not publish my work. [Cf. p. 221.]

But I think you yourself attach more weight to the other contradiction which you charge me with. Since men are so little accessible to reasonable arguments and are so entirely governed by their instinctual wishes, why should one set out to deprive them of an instinctual satisfaction and replace it by reasonable arguments? It is true that men are like this; but have you asked yourself whether they *must* be like this, whether their innermost nature necessitates it? Can an anthropologist give the cranial index of a people whose custom it is to deform their children's heads by bandaging them round from their earliest years? Think of the depressing contrast between the radiant intelligence of a healthy child and the feeble intellectual powers of the average adult. Can we be quite certain that it is not precisely religious education which bears a large share of the blame for this relative atrophy? I think it would be a very long time before a child who was not influenced began to trouble himself about God and things in another world. Perhaps his thoughts on these matters would then take the same paths as they did with his forefathers. But we do not wait for such a development; we introduce him to the doctrines of religion at an age when he is neither interested in them nor capable of grasping their import. Is it not true that the two main points in the programme for the education of children to-day are retardation of sexual development and premature religious influence? Thus by the time the child's intellect awakens, the doctrines of religion have already become unassailable. But are you of opinion that it is very conducive to the strengthening of the intellectual function that so important a field should be closed against it by the threat of Hell-fire? When a man has once brought himself to accept uncritically all the absurdities that religious doctrines put before him and even to overlook the contradictions between them, we need not be greatly surprised at the weakness of his intellect. But we have no other means of controlling our instinctual nature but our intelligence. How can we expect people who are under the dominance of prohibitions of thought to attain the psychological ideal, the primacy of the intelligence? You know, too, that women in general are said to suffer from 'physiological feeble-mindedness'[1] – that is, from a lesser intelligence than men. The fact itself is disputable and its interpretation doubtful, but one argument in favour of this intellectual atrophy being of a secondary nature is that women labour under the harshness of an early prohibition against turning their thoughts to what would most have interested them – namely, the problems of sexual life. So long as a person's early years are influenced not only by a sexual inhibition of thought but also by a religious inhibition and

---

1. [The phrase was used by Moebius (1903). Cf. Freud's early paper on 'civilized' sexual morality (1908d), p. 50 above, where the present argument is anticipated. The inhibition or prohibition of thought by religion is touched on in *Why War?* (1933b), p. 359 ff. below, and is discussed more fully in Lecture 35 of the *New Introductory Lectures* (1933a), *P.F.L.*, 2, 206–8.]

by a loyal inhibition[1] derived from this, we cannot really tell what in fact he is like.

But I will moderate my zeal and admit the possibility that I, too, am chasing an illusion. Perhaps the effect of the religious prohibition of thought may not be so bad as I suppose; perhaps it will turn out that human nature remains the same even if education is not abused in order to subject people to religion. I do not know and you cannot know either. It is not only the great problems of this life that seem insoluble at the present time; many lesser questions too are difficult to answer. But you must admit that here we are justified in having a hope for the future – that perhaps there is a treasure to be dug up capable of enriching civilization and that it is worth making the experiment of an irreligious education. Should the experiment prove unsatisfactory I am ready to give up the reform and to return to my earlier, purely descriptive judgement that man is a creature of weak intelligence who is ruled by his instinctual wishes.

On another point I agree with you unreservedly. It is certainly senseless to begin by trying to do away with religion by force and at a single blow. Above all, because it would be hopeless. The believer will not let his belief be torn from him, either by arguments or by prohibitions. And even if this did succeed with some it would be cruelty. A man who has been taking sleeping draughts for tens of years is naturally unable to sleep if his sleeping draught is taken away from him. That the effect of religious consolations may be likened to that of a narcotic is well illustrated by what is happening in America. There they are now trying – obviously under the influence of petticoat government – to deprive people of all stimulants, intoxicants, and other pleasure-producing substances, and instead, by way of compensation, are surfeiting them with piety. This is another experiment as to whose outcome we need not feel curious [p. 229].[2]

1. [I.e. in regard to the Monarchy.]
2. [This was written in the middle of the period of National Prohibition in the United States (1920–33).]

Thus I must contradict you when you go on to argue that men are completely unable to do without the consolation of the religious illusion, that without it they could not bear the troubles of life and the cruelties of reality. That is true, certainly, of the men into whom you have instilled the sweet – or bitter-sweet – poison from childhood onwards. But what of the other men, who have been sensibly brought up? Perhaps those who do not suffer from the neurosis will need no intoxicant to deaden it. They will, it is true, find themselves in a difficult situation. They will have to admit to themselves the full extent of their helplessness and their insignificance in the machinery of the universe; they can no longer be the centre of creation, no longer the object of tender care on the part of a beneficent Providence. They will be in the same position as a child who has left the parental house where he was so warm and comfortable. But surely infantilism is destined to be surmounted. Men cannot remain children for ever; they must in the end go out into 'hostile life'. We may call this *'education to reality'*. Need I confess to you that the sole purpose of my book is to point out the necessity for this forward step?

You are afraid, probably, that they will not stand up to the hard test? Well, let us at least hope they will. It is something, at any rate, to know that one is thrown upon one's own resources. One learns then to make a proper use of them. And men are not entirely without assistance. Their scientific knowledge has taught them much since the days of the Deluge, and it will increase their power still further. And, as for the great necessities of Fate, against which there is no help, they will learn to endure them with resignation. Of what use to them is the mirage of wide acres in the moon, whose harvest no one has ever yet seen? As honest smallholders on this earth they will know how to cultivate their plot in such a way that it supports them. By withdrawing their expectations from the other world and concentrating all their liberated energies into their life on earth, they will probably succeed in achieving a state of things in which life will become tolerable for everyone and civilization no longer oppressive to anyone. Then, with one of our fellow-unbelievers, they will be able to say without regret:

> Den Himmel überlassen wir
> Den Engeln und den Spatzen.[1]

1. ['We leave Heaven to the angels and the sparrows.' From Heine's poem *Deutschland* (Caput I). The word which is here translated 'fellow-unbelievers' – in German '*Unglaubensgenossen*' – was applied by Heine himself to Spinoza. It had been quoted by Freud as an example of a particular kind of joke-technique in his book on jokes (1905c), *P.F.L.*, **6**, 117.]

X

'THAT sounds splendid! A race of men who have renounced all illusions and have thus become capable of making their existence on earth tolerable! I, however, cannot share your expectations. And that is not because I am the obstinate reactionary you perhaps take me for. No, it is because I am sensible. We seem now to have exchanged roles: you emerge as an enthusiast who allows himself to be carried away by illusions, and I stand for the claims of reason, the rights of scepticism. What you have been expounding seems to me to be built upon errors which, following your example, I may call illusions, because they betray clearly enough the influence of your wishes. You pin your hope on the possibility that generations which have not experienced the influence of religious doctrines in early childhood will easily attain the desired primacy of the intelligence over the life of the instincts. This is surely an illusion: in this decisive respect human nature is hardly likely to change. If I am not mistaken – one knows so little about other civilizations – there are even to-day peoples which do not grow up under the pressure of a religious system, and yet they approach no nearer to your ideal than the rest. If you want to expel religion from our European civilization, you can only do it by means of another system of doctrines; and such a system would from the outset take over all the psychological characteristics of religion – the same sanctity, rigidity and intolerance, the same prohibition of thought – for its own defence. You have to have something of the kind in order to meet the requirements of education. And you cannot do without education. The path from the infant at the breast to the civilized man is a long one; too many human young would go astray on it and fail to reach their life-tasks at the proper time if they were left without guidance to their own development. The doctrines which had been applied in their upbringing would always set limits to the thinking of their riper years

– which is exactly what you reproach religion with doing to-day. Do you not observe that it is an ineradicable and innate defect of our and every other civilization, that it imposes on children, who are driven by instinct and weak in intellect, the making of decisions which only the mature intelligence of adults can vindicate? But civilization cannot do otherwise, because of the fact that mankind's age-long development is compressed into a few years of childhood; and it is only by emotional forces that the child can be induced to master the task set before it. Such, then, are the prospects for your "primacy of the intellect".

'And now you must not be surprised if I plead on behalf of retaining the religious doctrinal system as the basis of education and of man's communal life. This is a practical problem, not a question of reality-value. Since, for the sake of preserving our civilization, we cannot postpone influencing the individual until he has become ripe for civilization (and many would never become so in any case), since we are obliged to impose on the growing child some doctrinal system which shall operate in him as an axiom that admits of no criticism, it seems to me that the religious system is by far the most suitable for the purpose. And it is so, of course, precisely on account of its wish-fulfilling and consolatory power, by which you claim to recognize it as an "illusion". In view of the difficulty of discovering anything about reality – indeed, of the doubt whether it is possible for us to do so at all – we must not overlook the fact that human needs, too, are a piece of reality, and, in fact, an important piece and one that concerns us especially closely.

'Another advantage of religious doctrine resides, to my mind, in one of its characteristics to which you seem to take particular exception. For it allows of a refinement and sublimation of ideas, which make it possible for it to be divested of most of the traces which it bears of primitive and infantile thinking. What then remains is a body of ideas which science no longer contradicts and is unable to disprove. These modifications of religious doctrine, which you have condemned as half-measures and compromises, make it possible to avoid the cleft between the uneducated masses and the philosophic thinker, and to preserve the common bond between them which is so important for the safeguarding of civilization. With this, there would be no need to fear that the men of the people would discover that the upper strata of society "no longer believe in God". I think I have now shown that your endeavours come down to an attempt to replace a proved and emotionally valuable illusion by another one, which is unproved and without emotional value.'

You will not find me inaccessible to your criticism. I know how difficult it is to avoid illusions; perhaps the hopes I have confessed to are of an illusory nature, too. But I hold fast to one distinction. Apart from the fact that no penalty is imposed for not sharing them, my illusions are not, like religious ones, incapable of correction. They have not the character of a delusion. If experience should show – not to me, but to others after me, who think as I do – that we have been mistaken, we will give up our expectations. Take my attempt for what it is. A psychologist who does not deceive himself about the difficulty of finding one's bearings in this world, makes an endeavour to assess the development of man, in the light of the small portion of knowledge he has gained through a study of the mental processes of individuals during their development from child to adult. In so doing, the idea forces itself upon him that religion is comparable to a childhood neurosis, and he is optimistic enough to suppose that mankind will surmount this neurotic phase, just as so many children grow out of their similar neurosis. These discoveries derived from individual psychology may be insufficient, their application to the human race unjustified, and his optimism unfounded. I grant you all these uncertainties. But often one cannot refrain from saying what one thinks, and one excuses oneself on the ground that one is not giving it out for more than it is worth.

And there are two points that I must dwell on a little longer. Firstly, the weakness of my position does not imply any strengthening of yours. I think you are defending a lost cause.

We may insist as often as we like that man's intellect is powerless in comparison with his instinctual life, and we may be right in this. Nevertheless, there is something peculiar about this weakness. The voice of the intellect is a soft one, but it does not rest till it has gained a hearing. Finally, after a countless succession of rebuffs, it succeeds. This is one of the few points on which one may be optimistic about the future of mankind, but it is in itself a point of no small importance. And from it one can derive yet other hopes. The primacy of the intellect lies, it is true, in a distant, distant future, but probably not in an *infinitely* distant one. It will presumably set itself the same aims as those whose realization you expect from your God (of course within human limits – so far as external reality, 'Aνάγκη, allows it), namely the love of man and the decrease of suffering. This being so, we may tell ourselves that our antagonism is only a temporary one and not irreconcilable. We desire the same things, but you are more impatient, more exacting, and – why should I not say it? – more self-seeking than I and those on my side. You would have the state of bliss begin directly after death; you expect the impossible from it and you will not surrender the claims of the individual. Our God, Λόγος,[1] will fulfil whichever of these wishes nature outside us allows, but he will do it very gradually, only in the unforeseeable future, and for a new generation of men. He promises no compensation for us, who suffer grievously from life. On the way to this distant goal your religious doctrines will have to be discarded, no matter whether the first attempts fail, or whether the first substitutes prove to be untenable. You know why: in the long run nothing can withstand reason and experience, and the contradiction which religion offers to both is all too palpable. Even purified religious ideas cannot escape

1. The twin gods Λόγος [Logos: Reason] and 'Aνάγκη [Ananke: Necessity] of the Dutch writer Multatuli. ['Multatuli' (Latin for 'I have borne much') was the pseudonym of E. D. Dekker (1820–87), who had long been a favourite author of Freud's. He heads the list of 'ten good books' which Freud compiled in reply to a questionnaire (1906f). Cf. also an Editor's footnote to 'The Economic Problem of Masochism' (1924c), *P.F.L.*, II, 423 *n.* 4.]

this fate, so long as they try to preserve anything of the consolation of religion. No doubt if they confine themselves to a belief in a higher spiritual being, whose qualities are indefinable and whose purposes cannot be discerned, they will be proof against the challenge of science; but then they will also lose their hold on human interest.

And secondly: observe the difference between your attitude to illusions and mine. You have to defend the religious illusion with all your might. If it becomes discredited – and indeed the threat to it is great enough – then your world collapses. There is nothing left for you but to despair of everything, of civilization and the future of mankind. From that bondage I am, we are, free. Since we are prepared to renounce a good part of our infantile wishes, we can bear it if a few of our expectations turn out to be illusions.

Education freed from the burden of religious doctrines will not, it may be, effect much change in men's psychological nature. Our god Λόγος is perhaps not a very almighty one, and he may only be able to fulfil a small part of what his predecessors have promised. If we have to acknowledge this we shall accept it with resignation. We shall not on that account lose our interest in the world and in life, for we have one sure support which you lack. We believe that it is possible for scientific work to gain some knowledge about the reality of the world, by means of which we can increase our power and in accordance with which we can arrange our life. If this belief is an illusion, then we are in the same position as you. But science has given us evidence by its numerous and important successes that it is no illusion. Science has many open enemies, and many more secret ones, among those who cannot forgive her for having weakened religious faith and for threatening to overthrow it. She is reproached for the smallness of the amount she has taught us and for the incomparably greater field she has left in obscurity. But, in this, people forget how young she is, how difficult her beginnings were and how infinitesimally small is the period of time since the human intellect has been strong enough for the tasks she sets. Are we not all at fault, in basing our judgements on periods of time that are too short? We should make the geologists our pattern. People complain of the unreliability of science – how she announces as a law to-day what the next generation recognizes as an error and replaces by a new law whose accepted validity lasts no longer. But this is unjust and in part untrue. The transformations of scientific opinion are developments, advances, not revolutions. A law which was held at first to be universally valid proves to be a special case of a more comprehensive uniformity, or is limited by another law, not discovered till later; a rough approximation to the truth is replaced by a more carefully adapted one, which in turn awaits further perfectioning. There are various fields where we have not yet surmounted a phase of research in which we make trial with hypotheses that soon have to be rejected as inadequate; but in other fields we already possess an assured and almost unalterable core of knowledge. Finally, an attempt has been made to discredit scientific endeavour in a radical way, on the ground that, being bound to the conditions of our own organization, it can yield nothing else than subjective results, whilst the real nature of things outside ourselves remains inaccessible. But this is to disregard several factors which are of decisive importance for the understanding of scientific work. In the first place, our organization – that is, our mental apparatus – has been developed precisely in the attempt to explore the external world, and it must therefore have realized in its structure some degree of expediency; in the second place, it is itself a constituent part of the world which we set out to investigate, and it readily admits of such an investigation; thirdly, the task of science is fully covered if we limit it to showing how the world must appear to us in consequence of the particular character of our organization; fourthly, the ultimate findings of science, precisely because of the way in which they are acquired, are determined not only by our organization but by the things which have affected that organization; finally, the problem of the nature of the world without regard to our percipient mental apparatus is an empty abstraction, devoid of practical interest.

No, our science is no illusion. But an illusion it would be to suppose that what science cannot give us we can get elsewhere.

CIVILIZATION AND ITS DISCONTENTS
(1930 [1929])

EDITOR'S INTRODUCTION

DAS UNBEHAGEN IN DER KULTUR

(A) German Editions:

1930   Vienna: Internationaler Psychoanalytischer Verlag. (2nd ed., 1931, with some additions.)

1948   *Gesammelte Werke*, **14**, 421–506.

(B) English Translation:
Civilization and its Discontents

1930   London: Hogarth Press and Institute of Psycho-Analysis. New York: Cape and Smith. (Tr. Joan Riviere.)

1961   *Standard Edition*, **21**, 57–145. (Based on the translation of 1930.)

The present edition is a reprint of the *Standard Edition* version, with some editorial modifications.

The first chapter of the German original was published slightly in advance of the rest of the book in *Psychoanalytische Bewegung*, **1** (4), November–December 1929. The fifth chapter appeared separately in the next issue of the same periodical, **2** (1), January–February 1930. Two or three extra footnotes were included in the edition of 1931 and a new final sentence was added to the work. None of these additions appeared in the earlier version of the English translation.

Freud had finished *The Future of an Illusion* in the autumn of 1927. During the following two years, chiefly, no doubt, on account of his illness, he produced very little. But in the summer of 1929 he began writing another book, once more on a sociological subject. The first draft was finished by the end of July; the book was sent to the printers early in November and was actually published before the end of the year, though it carried the date '1930' on its title-page (Jones, 1957, 157–8).

The original title chosen for it by Freud was '*Das Unglück in der Kultur*' ('Unhappiness in Civilization'); but '*Unglück*' was later altered to '*Unbehagen*' – a word for which it was difficult to choose an English equivalent, though the French '*malaise*' might have served. Freud suggested '*Man's Discomfort in Civilization*' in a letter to his translator, Mrs Riviere; but it was she herself who found the ideal solution of the difficulty in the title that was finally adopted.

The main theme of the book – the irremediable antagonism between the demands of instinct and the restrictions of civilization – may be traced back to some of Freud's very earliest psychological writings. A number of references are given in the Editor's Note to the first paper in this volume, ' "Civilized" Sexual Morality and Modern Nervous Illness' (1908*d*), which is by far Freud's most detailed discussion of the topic. In his early writings Freud seems to have regarded the restrictions and repression of instinctual wishes as being in most cases due to external social influences. However, this is not consistently the case. Though in his *Three Essays* (1905*d*) he spoke of 'the inverse relation holding between civilization and the free development of sexuality' (*P.F.L.*, **7**, 168), elsewhere in the same work he had the following comment to make on the dams against the sexual instinct that emerge during the latency period: 'One gets an impression from civilized children that the construction of these dams is a product of education, and no doubt education has much to do with it. But in reality this development is organically determined and fixed by heredity, and it can occasionally occur without any help at all from education.' (Ibid., 93.)

The notion of there being an 'organic repression' paving the way to civilization – a notion that is expanded in the two long footnotes at the beginning and end of Chapter IV (pp. 208 f. and 295 ff. below) – goes back to the same early period. In a letter to Fliess of 14 November 1897, Freud wrote that he had often suspected 'that something organic played a part in repression' (Freud, 1950a, Letter 75). He went on, in precisely the sense of these footnotes, to suggest the importance as factors in repression of the adoption of an upright carriage and the replacement of smell by sight as the dominant sense. A still earlier hint at the same idea occurs in a letter of 11 January 1897 (ibid., Letter 55). In Freud's published writings the only mentions of these ideas before the present one seem to be a short passage in the 'Rat Man' analysis (1909d), P.F.L., **9**, 126–7, and another in the second paper on the psychology of love (1912d), ibid., **7**, 258. The idea of the 'process of civilization', which is linked with that of 'organic repression', occurs at several points in the present work, and is touched on again in the closing paragraphs of *Why War?* (1933b), p. 361 f. below. Compare also the related idea of an 'advance in intellectuality' in Essay III, Part II (c) of *Moses and Monotheism* (1939a), P.F.L., **13**, 358 ff.

But indeed no clear evaluation of the part played in these restrictions by internal and external influences and of their reciprocal effects was possible till Freud's investigations of ego-psychology had led him to his hypotheses of the super-ego and its origin from the individual's earliest object-relations. It is because of this that such a large part of the present work (especially in Chapters VII and VIII) is concerned with the further exploration and clarification of the nature of the sense of guilt, and that Freud (on p. 327) declares his 'intention to represent the sense of guilt as the most important problem in the development of civilization'. And this, in turn, is the ground for the second major side-issue of this work (though neither of them is in fact a side-issue) – the destructive instinct.

The history of Freud's views on the aggressive or destructive instinct is a complicated one and can only be summarily indicated here. Throughout his earlier writings the context in which he viewed it predominantly was that of sadism. His first lengthy discussions of this were in the *Three Essays on the Theory of Sexuality* (1905*d*), where it appeared as one of the 'component instincts' of the sexual instinct. 'Thus', he wrote in Section 2 (B) of the first essay, 'sadism would correspond to an aggressive component of the sexual instinct which has become independent and exaggerated and, by displacement, has usurped the leading position' (*P.F.L.*, **7**, 71). Nevertheless, later on, in Section 4 of the second essay, the original independence of the aggressive impulses was recognized: 'It may be assumed that the impulses of cruelty arise from sources which are in fact independent of sexuality, but may become united with it at an early stage' (ibid., 111 *n*. 1). The independent sources indicated were to be traced to the self-preservative instincts. This passage was altered in the edition of 1915, where it was stated that 'the impulse of cruelty arises from the instinct for mastery' and the phrase about its being 'independent of sexuality' was omitted. But already, in 1909, in the course of combating Adler's theories, Freud had made a much more sweeping pronouncement. In Section II of the third chapter of the 'Little Hans' case history (1909*b*), Freud wrote: 'I cannot bring myself to assume the existence of a special aggressive instinct alongside of the familiar instincts of self-preservation and of sex, and on an equal footing with them' (ibid., **8**, 297).[1] The reluctance to accept an aggressive instinct independent of the libido was assisted by the hypothesis of narcissism. Impulses of aggressiveness, and of hatred too, had from the first seemed to belong to the self-preservative instinct, and, since this was now subsumed under the libido, no independent aggressive instinct was called for. And this was so in spite of the bipolarity of object-relations, of the frequent admixtures of love and hate, and of

1. A footnote added in 1923 brought the inevitable qualification of this judgement. Since the time at which it was made 'I have myself', writes Freud, 'been obliged to assert the existence of an "aggressive instinct", but it is different from Adler's. I prefer to call it the "destructive" or "death instinct".' Adler's had in fact been more in the nature of an instinct of self-assertiveness.

the complex origin of hate itself. (See 'Instincts and their Vicissitudes' (1915c), ibid., **11**.) It was not until Freud's hypothesis of a 'death instinct' that a truly independent aggressive instinct came into view in *Beyond the Pleasure Principle* (1920g). (See, in particular, Chapter VI, ibid.) But it is to be remarked that even there, and in Freud's later writings (for instance, in Chapter IV of *The Ego and the Id*, ibid.), the aggressive instinct was still something secondary, derived from the primary self-destructive death instinct. This is still true of the present work, even though here the stress is much more upon the death instinct's manifestations *outwards*; and it is also true of the further discussions of the problem in the later part of Lecture 32 of the *New Introductory Lectures* (1933a), *P.F.L.*, **2**, 137 ff., and in *Why War?* (1933b), p. 358 f. below. It is nevertheless tempting to quote a couple of sentences from a letter written by Freud on 27 May 1937 to Princess Marie Bonaparte,[1] in which he appears to be hinting at a greater original independence of external destructiveness: 'The turning inwards of the aggressive instinct is of course the counterpart to the turning outwards of the libido when it passes over from the ego to objects. We should have a neat schematic picture if we supposed that originally, at the beginning of life, all libido was directed to the inside and all aggressiveness to the outside, and that in the course of life this gradually altered. But perhaps this may not be correct.' It is only fair to add that in his next letter Freud wrote: 'I beg you not to set too much value on my remarks about the destructive instinct. They were only made at random and would have to be carefully thought over before being published. Moreover there is little that is new in them.'

It will thus be obvious that *Civilization and its Discontents* is a work whose interest ranges far beyond sociology.

---

1. She has very kindly allowed us to reproduce it here. The whole passage will also be found (in a different translation) in Appendix A (No. 33) of Ernest Jones's biography (Jones, 1957, 494).

CIVILIZATION AND ITS DISCONTENTS

I

IT is impossible to escape the impression that people commonly use false standards of measurement – that they seek power, success and wealth for themselves and admire them in others, and that they underestimate what is of true value in life. And yet, in making any general judgement of this sort, we are in danger of forgetting how variegated the human world and its mental life are. There are a few men from whom their contemporaries do not withhold admiration, although their greatness rests on attributes and achievements which are completely foreign to the aims and ideals of the multitude. One might easily be inclined to suppose that it is after all only a minority which appreciates these great men, while the large majority cares nothing for them. But things are probably not as simple as that, thanks to the discrepancies between people's thoughts and their actions, and to the diversity of their wishful impulses.

One of these exceptional few calls himself my friend in his letters to me. I had sent him my small book that treats religion as an illusion,[1] and he answered that he entirely agreed with my judgement upon religion, but that he was sorry I had not properly appreciated the true source of religious sentiments. This, he says, consists in a peculiar feeling, which he himself is never without, which he finds confirmed by many others, and which he may suppose is present in millions of people. It is a feeling which he would like to call a sensation of 'eternity', a feeling as of something limitless, unbounded – as it were, 'oceanic'. This feeling, he adds, is a purely subjective fact, not

1. [*The Future of an Illusion* (1927c); see p. 183 above.]

an article of faith; it brings with it no assurance of personal immortality, but it is the source of the religious energy which is seized upon by the various Churches and religious systems, directed by them into particular channels, and doubtless also exhausted by them. One may, he thinks, rightly call oneself religious on the ground of this oceanic feeling alone, even if one rejects every belief and every illusion.

The views expressed by the friend whom I so much honour, and who himself once praised the magic of illusion in a poem,[1] caused me no small difficulty. I cannot discover this 'oceanic' feeling in myself. It is not easy to deal scientifically with feelings. One can attempt to describe their physiological signs. Where this is not possible – and I am afraid that the oceanic feeling too will defy this kind of characterization – nothing remains but to fall back on the ideational content which is most readily associated with the feeling. If I have understood my friend rightly, he means the same thing by it as the consolation offered by an original and somewhat eccentric dramatist to his hero who is facing a self-inflicted death. 'We cannot fall out of this world.'[2] That is to say, it is a feeling of an indissoluble bond, of being one with the external world as a whole. I may remark that to me this seems something rather in the nature of an intellectual perception, which is not, it is true, without an accompanying feeling-tone, but only such as would be present with any other act of thought of equal range. From my own experience I could not convince myself of the primary nature of such a feeling. But this gives me no right to deny that it does in fact occur in other people. The only question is whether it is being correctly interpreted and whether it ought to be regarded as the *fons et origo* of the whole need for religion.

1. [*Footnote added* 1931:] *Liluli* [1919]. – Since the publication of his two books *La vie de Ramakrishna* [1929] and *La vie de Vivekananda* (1930), I need no longer hide the fact that the friend spoken of in the text is Romain Rolland.

2. Christian Dietrich Grabbe [1801–36], *Hannibal*: 'Ja, aus der Welt werden wir nicht fallen. Wir sind einmal darin.' ['Indeed, we shall not fall out of this world. We are in it once and for all.']

I have nothing to suggest which could have a decisive influence on the solution of this problem. The idea of men's receiving an intimation of their connection with the world around them through an immediate feeling which is from the outset directed to that purpose sounds so strange and fits in so badly with the fabric of our psychology that one is justified in attempting to discover a psychoanalytic – that is, a genetic – explanation of such a feeling. The following line of thought suggests itself. Normally, there is nothing of which we are more certain than the feeling of our self, of our own ego. This ego appears to us as something autonomous and unitary, marked off distinctly from everything else. That such an appearance is deceptive, and that on the contrary the ego is continued inwards, without any sharp delimitation, into an unconscious mental entity which we designate as the id and for which it serves as a kind of façade – this was a discovery first made by psychoanalytic research, which should still have much more to tell us about the relation of the ego to the id. But towards the outside, at any rate, the ego seems to maintain clear and sharp lines of demarcation. There is only one state – admittedly an unusual state, but not one that can be stigmatized as pathological – in which it does not do this. At the height of being in love the boundary between ego and object threatens to melt away. Against all the evidence of his senses, a man who is in love declares that 'I' and 'you' are one, and is prepared to behave as if it were a fact. What can be temporarily done away with by a physiological [i.e. normal] function must also, of course, be liable to be disturbed by pathological processes. Pathology has made us acquainted with a great number of states in which the boundary lines between the ego and the external world become uncertain or in which they are actually drawn incorrectly. There are cases in which parts of a person's own body, even portions of his own mental life – his perceptions, thoughts and feelings –, appear alien to him and as not belonging to his ego; there are other cases in which he ascribes to the external world things that clearly originate in his own ego and that ought to be acknowledged by it. Thus even the feeling of our own ego is subject to disturbances and the boundaries of the ego are not constant.

Further reflection tells us that the adult's ego-feeling cannot have been the same from the beginning. It must have gone through a process of development, which cannot, of course, be demonstrated but which admits of being constructed with a fair degree of probability.[1] An infant at the breast does not as yet distinguish his ego from the external world as the source of the sensations flowing in upon him. He gradually learns to do so, in response to various promptings.[2] He must be very strongly impressed by the fact that some sources of excitation, which he will later recognize as his own bodily organs, can provide him with sensations at any moment, whereas other sources evade him from time to time – among them what he desires most of all, his mother's breast – and only reappear as a result of his screaming for help. In this way there is for the first time set over against the ego an 'object', in the form of something which exists 'outside' and which is only forced to appear by a special action. A further incentive to a disengagement of the ego from the general mass of sensations – that is, to the recognition of an 'outside', an external world – is provided by the frequent, manifold and unavoidable sensations of pain and unpleasure the removal and avoidance of which is enjoined by the pleasure principle, in the exercise of its unrestricted domination. A tendency arises to separate from the ego everything that can become a source of such unpleasure, to throw it outside and to create a pure pleasure-ego which is confronted by a strange and threatening 'outside'. The boundaries of this primitive pleasure-ego cannot escape rectification through experience. Some of the things that one is un-

1. Cf. the many writings on the topic of ego-development and ego-feeling, dating from Ferenczi's paper on 'Stages in the Development of the Sense of Reality' (1913) to Federn's contributions of 1926, 1927 and later.

2. [In this paragraph Freud was going over familiar ground. See, for instance, *The Interpretation of Dreams* (1900*a*), *P.F.L.*, **4**, 719; 'Instincts and their Vicissitudes' (1915*c*), ibid., **11**, 115, 131–4; and 'Negation' (1925*h*), ibid., **11**, 439–40.]

willing to give up, because they give pleasure, are nevertheless not ego but object; and some sufferings that one seeks to expel turn out to be inseparable from the ego in virtue of their internal origin. One comes to learn a procedure by which, through a deliberate direction of one's sensory activities and through suitable muscular action, one can differentiate between what is internal – what belongs to the ego – and what is external – what emanates from the outer world. In this way one makes the first step towards the introduction of the reality principle which is to dominate future development.[1] This differentiation, of course, serves the practical purpose of enabling one to defend oneself against sensations of unpleasure which one actually feels or with which one is threatened. In order to fend off certain unpleasurable excitations arising from within, the ego can use no other methods than those which it uses against unpleasure coming from without, and this is the starting-point of important pathological disturbances.

In this way, then, the ego detaches itself from the external world. Or, to put it more correctly, originally the ego includes everything, later it separates off an external world from itself. Our present ego-feeling is, therefore, only a shrunken residue of a much more inclusive – indeed, an all-embracing – feeling which corresponded to a more intimate bond between the ego and the world about it. If we may assume that there are many people in whose mental life this primary ego-feeling has persisted to a greater or less degree, it would exist in them side by side with the narrower and more sharply demarcated ego-feeling of maturity, like a kind of counterpart to it. In that case, the ideational contents appropriate to it would be precisely those of limitlessness and of a bond with the universe – the same ideas with which my friend elucidated the 'oceanic' feeling.

But have we a right to assume the survival of something that was originally there, alongside of what was later derived from it? Undoubtedly. There is nothing strange in such a

1. [Cf. 'Formulations on the Two Principles of Mental Functioning' (1911b), P.F.L., 11, 39–40.]

phenomenon, whether in the mental field or elsewhere. In the animal kingdom we hold to the view that the most highly developed species have proceeded from the lowest; and yet we find all the simple forms still in existence to-day. The race of the great saurians is extinct and has made way for the mammals; but a true representative of it, the crocodile, still lives among us. This analogy may be too remote, and it is also weakened by the circumstance that the lower species which survive are for the most part not the true ancestors of the present-day more highly developed species. As a rule the intermediate links have died out and are known to us only through reconstruction. In the realm of the mind, on the other hand, what is primitive is so commonly preserved alongside of the transformed version which has arisen from it that it is unnecessary to give instances as evidence. When this happens it is usually in consequence of a divergence in development: one portion (in the quantitative sense) of an attitude or instinctual impulse has remained unaltered, while another portion has undergone further development.

This brings us to the more general problem of preservation in the sphere of the mind. The subject has hardly been studied as yet; but it is so attractive and important that we may be allowed to turn our attention to it for a little, even though our excuse is insufficient. Since we overcame the error of supposing that the forgetting we are familiar with signified a destruction of the memory-trace – that is, its annihilation – we have been inclined to take the opposite view that in mental life nothing which has once been formed can perish – that everything is somehow preserved and that in suitable circumstances (when, for instance, regression goes back far enough) it can once more be brought to light. Let us try to grasp what this assumption involves by taking an analogy from another field. We will choose as an example the history of the Eternal City.[1] Historians tell us that the oldest Rome was the *Roma Quadrata*, a fenced settlement on the Palatine. Then followed the phase of

1. Based on *The Cambridge Ancient History*, 7 (1928): 'The Founding of Rome' by Hugh Last.

the *Septimontium*, a federation of the settlements on the different hills; after that came the city bounded by the Servian wall; and later still, after all the transformations during the periods of the republic and the early Caesars, the city which the Emperor Aurelian surrounded with his walls. We will not follow the changes which the city went through any further, but we will ask ourselves how much a visitor, whom we will suppose to be equipped with the most complete historical and topographical knowledge, may still find left of these early stages in the Rome of to-day. Except for a few gaps, he will see the wall of Aurelian almost unchanged. In some places he will be able to find sections of the Servian wall where they have been excavated and brought to light. If he knows enough – more than present-day archaeology does – he may perhaps be able to trace out in the plan of the city the whole course of that wall and the outline of the *Roma Quadrata*. Of the buildings which once occupied this ancient area he will find nothing, or only scanty remains, for they exist no longer. The best information about Rome in the republican era would only enable him at the most to point out the sites where the temples and public buildings of that period stood. Their place is now taken by ruins, but not by ruins of themselves but of later restorations made after fires or destruction. It is hardly necessary to remark that all these remains of ancient Rome are found dovetailed into the jumble of a great metropolis which has grown up in the last few centuries since the Renaissance. There is certainly not a little that is ancient still buried in the soil of the city or beneath its modern buildings. This is the manner in which the past is preserved in historical sites like Rome.

Now let us, by a flight of imagination, suppose that Rome is not a human habitation but a psychical entity with a similarly long and copious past – an entity, that is to say, in which nothing that has once come into existence will have passed away and all the earlier phases of development continue to exist alongside the latest one. This would mean that in Rome the palaces of the Caesars and the Septizonium of Septimius Severus would still be rising to their old height on the Palatine and the castle of S. Angelo would still be carrying on its battlements the beautiful statues which graced it until the siege by the Goths, and so on. But more than this. In the place occupied by the Palazzo Caffarelli would once more stand – without the Palazzo having to be removed – the Temple of Jupiter Capitolinus; and this not only in its latest shape, as the Romans of the Empire saw it, but also in its earliest one, when it still showed Etruscan forms and was ornamented with terracotta antefixes. Where the Coliseum now stands we could at the same time admire Nero's vanished Golden House. On the Piazza of the Pantheon we should find not only the Pantheon of to-day, as it was bequeathed to us by Hadrian, but, on the same site, the original edifice erected by Agrippa; indeed, the same piece of ground would be supporting the church of Santa Maria sopra Minerva and the ancient temple over which it was built. And the observer would perhaps only have to change the direction of his glance or his position in order to call up the one view or the other.

There is clearly no point in spinning our phantasy any further, for it leads to things that are unimaginable and even absurd. If we want to represent historical sequence in spatial terms we can only do it by juxtaposition in space: the same space cannot have two different contents. Our attempt seems to be an idle game. It has only one justification. It shows us how far we are from mastering the characteristics of mental life by representing them in pictorial terms.

There is one further objection which has to be considered. The question may be raised why we chose precisely the past of a *city* to compare with the past of the mind. The assumption that everything past is preserved holds good even in mental life only on condition that the organ of the mind has remained intact and that its tissues have not been damaged by trauma or inflammation. But destructive influences which can be compared to causes of illness like these are never lacking in the history of a city, even if it has had a less chequered past than Rome, and even if, like London, it has hardly ever suffered from the visitations of an enemy. Demolitions and replacement of buildings occur in the course of the most peaceful development of a city. A city is thus *a priori* unsuited for a comparison of this sort with a mental organism.

We bow to this objection; and, abandoning our attempt to draw a striking contrast, we will turn instead to what is after all a more closely related object of comparison – the body of an animal or a human being. But here, too, we find the same thing. The earlier phases of development are in no sense still preserved; they have been absorbed into the later phases for which they have supplied the material. The embryo cannot be discovered in the adult. The thymus gland of childhood is replaced after puberty by connective tissue, but is no longer present itself; in the marrow-bones of the grown man I can, it is true, trace the outline of the child's bone, but it itself has disappeared, having lengthened and thickened until it has attained it definitive form. The fact remains that only in the mind is such a preservation of all the earlier stages alongside of the final form possible, and that we are not in a position to represent this phenomenon in pictorial terms.

Perhaps we are going too far in this. Perhaps we ought to content ourselves with asserting that what is past in mental life *may* be preserved and is not *necessarily* destroyed. It is always possible that even in the mind some of what is old is effaced or absorbed – whether in the normal course of things or as an exception – to such an extent that it cannot be restored or revivified by any means; or that preservation in general is dependent on certain favourable conditions. It is possible, but we know nothing about it. We can only hold fast to the fact that it is rather the rule than the exception for the past to be preserved in mental life.

Thus we are perfectly willing to acknowledge that the 'oceanic' feeling exists in many people, and we are inclined to trace it back to an early phase of ego-feeling. The further question then arises, what claim this feeling has to be regarded as the source of religious needs.

To me the claim does not seem compelling. After all, a feeling can only be a source of energy if it is itself the expression of a strong need. The derivation of religious needs from the infant's helplessness and the longing for the father aroused by it seems to me incontrovertible, especially since the feeling is not simply prolonged from childhood days, but is permanently sustained by fear of the superior power of Fate. I cannot think of any need in childhood as strong as the need for a father's protection. Thus the part played by the oceanic feeling, which might seek something like the restoration of limitless narcissism, is ousted from a place in the foreground. The origin of the religious attitude can be traced back in clear outlines as far as the feeling of infantile helplessness. There may be something further behind that, but for the present it is wrapped in obscurity.

I can imagine that the oceanic feeling became connected with religion later on. The 'oneness with the universe' which constitutes its ideational content sounds like a first attempt at a religious consolation, as though it were another way of disclaiming the danger which the ego recognizes as threatening it from the external world. Let me admit once more that it is very difficult for me to work with these almost intangible quantities. Another friend of mine, whose insatiable craving for knowledge has led him to make the most unusual experiments and has ended by giving him encyclopaedic knowledge, has assured me that through the practices of Yoga, by withdrawing from the world, by fixing the attention on bodily functions and by peculiar methods of breathing, one can in fact evoke new sensations and coenaesthesias in oneself, which he regards as regressions to primordial states of mind which have long ago been overlaid. He sees in them a physiological basis, as it were, of much of the wisdom of mysticism. It would not be hard to find connections here with a number of obscure modifications of mental life, such as trances and ecstasies. But I am moved to exclaim in the words of Schiller's diver:

> '. . . Es freue sich,
> Wer da atmet im rosigten Licht.'[1]

1 ['Let him rejoice who breathes up here in the roseate light!' Schiller, 'Der Taucher'.]

IN my *Future of an Illusion* [1927c] I was concerned much less with the deepest sources of the religious feeling than with what the common man understands by his religion – with the system of doctrines and promises which on the one hand explains to him the riddles of this world with enviable completeness, and, on the other, assures him that a careful Providence will watch over his life and will compensate him in a future existence for any frustrations he suffers here. The common man cannot imagine this Providence otherwise than in the figure of an enormously exalted father. Only such a being can understand the needs of the children of men and be softened by their prayers and placated by the signs of their remorse. The whole thing is so patently infantile, so foreign to reality, that to anyone with a friendly attitude to humanity it is painful to think that the great majority of mortals will never be able to rise above this view of life. It is still more humiliating to discover how large a number of people living to-day, who cannot but see that this religion is not tenable, nevertheless try to defend it piece by piece in a series of pitiful rearguard actions. One would like to mix among the ranks of the believers in order to meet these philosophers, who think they can rescue the God of religion by replacing him by an impersonal, shadowy and abstract principle, and to address them with the warning words: 'Thou shalt not take the name of the Lord thy God in vain!' And if some of the great men of the past acted in the same way, no appeal can be made to their example: we know why they were obliged to.

Let us return to the common man and to his religion – the only religion which ought to bear that name. The first thing that we think of is the well-known saying of one of our great poets and thinkers concerning the relation of religion to art and science:

Wer Wissenschaft und Kunst besitzt, hat auch Religion;
Wer jene beide nicht besitzt, der habe Religion![1]

This saying on the one hand draws an antithesis between religion and the two highest achievements of man, and on the other, asserts that, as regards their value in life, those achievements and religion can represent or replace each other. If we also set out to deprive the common man, [who has neither science nor art] of his religion, we shall clearly not have the poet's authority on our side. We will choose a particular path to bring us nearer an appreciation of his words. Life, as we find it, is too hard for us; it brings us too many pains, disappointments and impossible tasks. In order to bear it we cannot dispense with palliative measures. 'We cannot do without auxiliary constructions', as Theodor Fontane tells us.[2] There are perhaps three such measures: powerful deflections, which cause us to make light of our misery; substitutive satisfactions, which diminish it; and intoxicating substances, which make us insensitive to it. Something of the kind is indispensable.[3] Voltaire has deflections in mind when he ends *Candide* with the advice to cultivate one's garden; and scientific activity is a deflection of this kind, too. The substitutive satisfactions, as offered by art, are illusions in contrast with reality, but they are none the less psychically effective, thanks to the role which phantasy has assumed in mental life. The intoxicating substances influence our body and alter its chemistry. It is no simple matter to see where religion has its place in this series. We must look further afield.

The question of the purpose of human life has been raised countless times; it has never yet received a satisfactory answer and perhaps does not admit of one. Some of those who have

1. ['He who possesses science and art also has religion; but he who possesses neither of those two, let him have religion!'] – Goethe, *Zahme Xenien* IX (Gedichte aus dem Nachlass).

2. [In his novel *Effi Briest* (1895).]

3. In *Die Fromme Helene* Wilhelm Busch has said the same thing on a lower plane: 'Wer Sorgen hat, hat auch Likör.' ['He who has cares has brandy too.']

asked it have added that if it should turn out that life has *no* purpose, it would lose all value for them. But this threat alters nothing. It looks, on the contrary, as though one had a right to dismiss the question, for it seems to derive from the human presumptuousness, many other manifestations of which are already familiar to us. Nobody talks about the purpose of the life of animals, unless, perhaps, it may be supposed to lie in being of service to man. But this view is not tenable either, for there are many animals of which man can make nothing, except to describe, classify and study them; and innumerable species of animals have escaped even this use, since they existed and became extinct before man set eyes on them. Once again, only religion can answer the question of the purpose of life. One can hardly be wrong in concluding that the idea of life having a purpose stands and falls with the religious system.

We will therefore turn to the less ambitious question of what men themselves show by their behaviour to be the purpose and intention of their lives. What do they demand of life and wish to achieve in it? The answer to this can hardly be in doubt. They strive after happiness; they want to become happy and to remain so. This endeavour has two sides, a positive and a negative aim. It aims, on the one hand, at an absence of pain and unpleasure, and, on the other, at the experiencing of strong feelings of pleasure. In its narrower sense the word 'happiness' only relates to the last. In conformity with this dichotomy in his aims, man's activity develops in two directions, according as it seeks to realize – in the main, or even exclusively – the one or the other of these aims.

As we see, what decides the purpose of life is simply the programme of the pleasure principle. This principle dominates the operation of the mental apparatus from the start. There can be no doubt about its efficacy, and yet its programme is at loggerheads with the whole world, with the macrocosm as much as with the microcosm. There is no possibility at all of its being carried through; all the regulations of the universe run counter to it. One feels inclined to say that the intention that man should be 'happy' is not included in the plan of

'Creation'. What we call happiness in the strictest sense comes from the (preferably sudden) satisfaction of needs which have been dammed up to a high degree, and it is from its nature only possible as an episodic phenomenon. When any situation that is desired by the pleasure principle is prolonged, it only produces a feeling of mild contentment. We are so made that we can derive intense enjoyment only from a contrast and very little from a state of things.[1] Thus our possibilities of happiness are already restricted by our constitution. Unhappiness is much less difficult to experience. We are threatened with suffering from three directions: from our own body, which is doomed to decay and dissolution and which cannot even do without pain and anxiety as warning signals; from the external world, which may rage against us with overwhelming and merciless forces of destruction; and finally from our relations to other men. The suffering which comes from this last source is perhaps more painful to us than any other. We tend to regard it as a kind of gratuitous addition, although it cannot be any less fatefully inevitable than the suffering which comes from elsewhere.

It is no wonder if, under the pressure of these possibilities of suffering, men are accustomed to moderate their claims to happiness – just as the pleasure principle itself, indeed, under the influence of the external world, changed into the more modest reality principle –, if a man thinks himself happy merely to have escaped unhappiness or to have survived his suffering, and if in general the task of avoiding suffering pushes that of obtaining pleasure into the background. Reflection shows that the accomplishment of this task can be attempted along very different paths; and all these paths have been recommended by the various schools of worldly wisdom and put into practice

1. Goethe, indeed, warns us that 'nothing is harder to bear than a succession of fair days.'

> [Alles in der Welt lässt sich ertragen,
> Nur nicht eine Reihe von schönen
> > Tagen.
> > (Weimar, 1810–12.)]

But this may be an exaggeration.

by men. An unrestricted satisfaction of every need presents itself as the most enticing method of conducting one's life, but it means putting enjoyment before caution, and soon brings its own punishment. The other methods, in which avoidance of unpleasure is the main purpose, are differentiated according to the source of unpleasure to which their attention is chiefly turned. Some of these methods are extreme and some moderate; some are one-sided and some attack the problem simultaneously at several points. Against the suffering which may come upon one from human relationships the readiest safeguard is voluntary isolation, keeping oneself aloof from other people. The happiness which can be achieved along this path is, as we see, the happiness of quietness. Against the dreaded external world one can only defend oneself by some kind of turning away from it, if one intends to solve the task by oneself. There is, indeed, another and better path: that of becoming a member of the human community, and, with the help of a technique guided by science, going over to the attack against nature and subjecting her to the human will. Then one is working with all for the good of all. But the most interesting methods of averting suffering are those which seek to influence our own organism. In the last analysis, all suffering is nothing else than sensation; it only exists in so far as we feel it, and we only feel it in consequence of certain ways in which our organism is regulated.

The crudest, but also the most effective among these methods of influence is the chemical one – intoxication. I do not think that anyone completely understands its mechanism, but it is a fact that there are foreign substances which, when present in the blood or tissues, directly cause us pleasurable sensations; and they also so alter the conditions governing our sensibility that we become incapable of receiving unpleasurable impulses. The two effects not only occur simultaneously, but seem to be intimately bound up with each other. But there must be substances in the chemistry of our own bodies which have similar effects, for we know at least one pathological state, mania, in which a condition similar to intoxication arises without the administration of any intoxicating drug. Besides this, our normal mental life exhibits oscillations between a comparatively easy liberation of pleasure and a comparatively difficult one, parallel with which there goes a diminished or an increased receptivity to unpleasure. It is greatly to be regretted that this toxic side of mental processes has so far escaped scientific examination. The service rendered by intoxicating media in the struggle for happiness and in keeping misery at a distance is so highly prized as a benefit that individuals and peoples alike have given them an established place in the economics of their libido. We owe to such media not merely the immediate yield of pleasure, but also a greatly desired degree of independence from the external world. For one knows that, with the help of this 'drowner of cares' one can at any time withdraw from the pressure of reality and find refuge in a world of one's own with better conditions of sensibility. As is well known, it is precisely this property of intoxicants which also determines their danger and their injuriousness. They are responsible, in certain circumstances, for the useless waste of a large quota of energy which might have been employed for the improvement of the human lot.

The complicated structure of our mental apparatus admits, however, of a whole number of other influences. Just as a satisfaction of instinct spells happiness for us, so severe suffering is caused us if the external world lets us starve, if it refuses to sate our needs. One may therefore hope to be freed from a part of one's sufferings by influencing the instinctual impulses. This type of defence against suffering is no longer brought to bear on the sensory apparatus; it seeks to master the internal sources of our needs. The extreme form of this is brought about by killing off the instincts, as is prescribed by the worldly wisdom of the East and practised by Yoga. If it succeeds, then the subject has, it is true, given up all other activities as well – he has sacrificed his life; and, by another path, he has once more only achieved the happiness of quietness. We follow the same path when our aims are less extreme and we merely attempt to *control* our instinctual life. In that case, the controlling

elements are the higher psychical agencies, which have subjected themselves to the reality principle. Here the aim of
satisfaction is not by any means relinquished; but a certain
amount of protection against suffering is secured, in that non-
satisfaction is not so painfully felt in the case of instincts kept
in dependence as in the case of uninhibited ones. As against
this, there is an undeniable diminution in the potentialities of
enjoyment. The feeling of happiness derived from the satisfaction of a wild instinctual impulse untamed by the ego is
incomparably more intense than that derived from sating an
instinct that has been tamed. The irresistibility of perverse
instincts, and perhaps the attraction in general of forbidden
things finds an economic explanation here.

Another technique for fending off suffering is the employment of the displacements of libido which our mental apparatus
permits of and through which its function gains so much in
flexibility. The task here is that of shifting the instinctual aims
in such a way that they cannot come up against frustration
from the external world. In this, sublimation of the instincts
lends its assistance. One gains the most if one can sufficiently
heighten the yield of pleasure from the sources of psychical
and intellectual work. When that is so, fate can do little against
one. A satisfaction of this kind, such as an artist's joy in creating,
in giving his phantasies body, or a scientist's in solving problems
or discovering truths, has a special quality which we shall
certainly one day be able to characterize in metapsychological
terms. At present we can only say figuratively that such
satisfactions seem 'finer and higher'. But their intensity is mild
as compared with that derived from the sating of crude and
primary instinctual impulses; it does not convulse our physical
being. And the weak point of this method is that it is not
applicable generally: it is accessible to only a few people. It
presupposes the possession of special dispositions and gifts
which are far from being common to any practical degree.
And even to the few who do possess them, this method cannot
give complete protection from suffering. It creates no
impenetrable armour against the arrows of fortune, and it

habitually fails when the source of suffering is a person's own body.[1]

While this procedure already clearly shows an intention of making oneself independent of the external world by seeking satisfaction in internal, psychical processes, the next procedure brings out those features yet more strongly. In it, the connection with reality is still further loosened; satisfaction is obtained from illusions, which are recognized as such without the discrepancy between them and reality being allowed to interfere with enjoyment. The region from which these illusions arise is the life of the imagination; at the time when the development of the sense of reality took place, this region was expressly exempted from the demands of reality-testing and was set apart for the purpose of fulfilling wishes which were difficult to carry out. At the head of these satisfactions through phantasy stands the enjoyment of works of art – an enjoyment which, by the agency of the artist, is made accessible even to those who are not themselves creative.[2] People who are receptive to the

---

1. When there is no special disposition in a person which imperatively prescribes what direction his interests in life shall take, the ordinary professional work that is open to everyone can play the part assigned to it by Voltaire's wise advice [p. 262 above]. It is not possible, within the limits of a short survey, to discuss adequately the significance of work for the economics of the libido. No other technique for the conduct of life attaches the individual so firmly to reality as laying emphasis on work; for his work at least gives him a secure place in a portion of reality, in the human community. The possibility it offers of displacing a large amount of libidinal components, whether narcissistic, aggressive or even erotic, on to professional work and on to the human relations connected with it lends it a value by no means second to what it enjoys as something indispensable to the preservation and justification of existence in society. Professional activity is a source of special satisfaction if it is a freely chosen one – if, that is to say, by means of sublimation, it makes possible the use of existing inclinations, of persisting or constitutionally reinforced instinctual impulses. And yet, as a path to happiness, work is not highly prized by men. They do not strive after it as they do after other possibilities of satisfaction. The great majority of people only work under the stress of necessity, and this natural human aversion to work raises most difficult social problems.

2. Cf. 'Formulations on the Two Principles of Mental Functioning' (1911b) [P.F.L., 11, 41–2] and Lecture 23 of my Introductory Lectures (1916–17) [ibid., 1, 405 ff.].

influence of art cannot set too high a value on it as a source of pleasure and consolation in life. Nevertheless the mild narcosis induced in us by art can do no more than bring about a transient withdrawal from the pressure of vital needs, and it is not strong enough to make us forget real misery.

Another procedure operates more energetically and more thoroughly. It regards reality as the sole enemy and as the source of all suffering, with which it is impossible to live, so that one must break off all relations with it if one is to be in any way happy. The hermit turns his back on the world and will have no truck with it. But one can do more than that; one can try to re-create the world, to build up in its stead another world in which its most unbearable features are eliminated and replaced by others that are in conformity with one's own wishes. But whoever, in desperate defiance, sets out upon this path to happiness will as a rule attain nothing. Reality is too strong for him. He becomes a madman, who for the most part finds no one to help him in carrying through his delusion. It is asserted, however, that each one of us behaves in some one respect like a paranoic, corrects some aspect of the world which is unbearable to him by the construction of a wish and introduces this delusion into reality. A special importance attaches to the case in which this attempt to procure a certainty of happiness and a protection against suffering through a delusional remoulding of reality is made by a considerable number of people in common. The religions of mankind must be classed among the mass-delusions of this kind. No one, need-less to say, who shares a delusion ever recognizes it as such.

I do not think that I have made a complete enumeration of the methods by which men strive to gain happiness and keep suffering away and I know, too, that the material might have been differently arranged. One procedure I have not yet mentioned – not because I have forgotten it but because it will concern us later in another connection. And how could one possibly forget, of all others, this technique in the art of living? It is conspicuous for a most remarkable combination of characteristic features. It, too, aims of course at making the subject independent of Fate (as it is best to call it), and to that end it locates satisfaction in internal mental processes, making use, in so doing, of the displaceability of the libido of which we have already spoken [p. 267]. But it does not turn away from the external world; on the contrary, it clings to the objects belonging to that world and obtains happiness from an emotional relationship to them. Nor is it content to aim at an avoidance of unpleasure – a goal, as we might call it, of weary resignation; it passes this by without heed and holds fast to the original, passionate striving for a positive fulfilment of happiness. And perhaps it does in fact come nearer to this goal than any other method. I am, of course, speaking of the way of life which makes love the centre of everything, which looks for all satisfaction in loving and being loved. A psychical attitude of this sort comes naturally enough to all of us; one of the forms in which love manifests itself – sexual love – has given us our most intense experience of an overwhelming sensation of pleasure and has thus furnished us with a pattern for our search for happiness. What is more natural than that we should persist in looking for happiness along the path on which we first encountered it? The weak side of this technique of living is easy to see; otherwise no human being would have thought of abandoning this path to happiness for any other. It is that we are never so defenceless against suffering as when we love, never so helplessly unhappy as when we have lost our loved object or its love. But this does not dispose of the technique of living based on the value of love as a means to happiness. There is much more to be said about it. [See below, p. 290.]

We may go on from here to consider the interesting case in which happiness in life is predominantly sought in the enjoyment of beauty, wherever beauty presents itself to our senses and our judgement – the beauty of human forms and gestures, of natural objects and landscapes and of artistic and even scientific creations. This aesthetic attitude to the goal of life offers little protection against the threat of suffering, but it can compensate for a great deal. The enjoyment of beauty has a peculiar, mildly intoxicating quality of feeling. Beauty has no obvious use; nor is there any clear cultural necessity for it. Yet civilization could not do without it. The science of aesthetics investigates the conditions under which things are felt as beautiful, but it has been unable to give any explanation of the nature and origin of beauty, and, as usually happens, lack of success is concealed beneath a flood of resounding and empty words. Psychoanalysis, unfortunately, has scarcely anything to say about beauty either. All that seems certain is its derivation from the field of sexual feeling. The love of beauty seems a perfect example of an impulse inhibited in its aim. 'Beauty' and 'attraction'[1] are originally attributes of the sexual object. It is worth remarking that the genitals themselves, the sight of which is always exciting, are nevertheless hardly ever judged to be beautiful; the quality of beauty seems, instead, to attach to certain secondary sexual characters.

In spite of the incompleteness [of my enumeration (p. 269)], I will venture on a few remarks as a conclusion to our inquiry. The programme of becoming happy, which the pleasure principle imposes on us [p. 263], cannot be fulfilled; yet we must not – indeed, we cannot – give up our efforts to bring it nearer to fulfilment by some means or other. Very different paths may be taken in that direction, and we may give priority either to the positive aspect of the aim, that of gaining pleasure, or to its negative one, that of avoiding unpleasure. By none of these paths can we attain all that we desire. Happiness, in the reduced sense in which we recognize it as possible, is a problem of the economics of the individual's libido. There is no golden rule which applies to everyone: every man must find out for himself in what particular fashion he can be saved.[2] All kinds of different factors will operate to direct his choice. It is a

1. [The German 'Reiz' means 'stimulus' as well as 'charm' or 'attraction'. Freud had argued on the same lines in the first edition of his Three Essays (1905d), P.F.L., 7, 130, as well as in a footnote added to that work in 1915, ibid., 69, n. 2.]

2. [The allusion is to a saying attributed to Frederick the Great: 'in my State every man can be saved after his own fashion.']

question of how much real satisfaction he can expect to get from the external world, how far he is led to make himself independent of it, and, finally, how much strength he feels he has for altering the world to suit his wishes. In this, his psychical constitution will play a decisive part, irrespectively of the external circumstances. The man who is predominantly erotic will give first preference to his emotional relationships to other people; the narcissistic man, who inclines to be self-sufficient, will seek his main satisfactions in his internal mental processes; the man of action will never give up the external world on which he can try out his strength.[1] As regards the second of these types, the nature of his talents and the amount of instinctual sublimation open to him will decide where he shall locate his interests. Any choice that is pushed to an extreme will be penalized by exposing the individual to the dangers which arise if a technique of living that has been chosen as an exclusive one should prove inadequate. Just as a cautious business-man avoids tying up all his capital in one concern, so, perhaps, worldly wisdom will advise us not to look for the whole of our satisfaction from a single aspiration. Its success is never certain, for that depends on the convergence of many factors, perhaps on none more than on the capacity of the psychical constitution to adapt its function to the environment and then to exploit that environment for a yield of pleasure. A person who is born with a specially unfavourable instinctual constitution, and who has not properly undergone the trans-formation and rearrangement of his libidinal components which is indispensable for later achievements, will find it hard to obtain happiness from his external situation, especially if he is faced with tasks of some difficulty. As a last technique of living, which will at least bring him substitutive satisfactions, he is offered that of a flight into neurotic illness – a flight which he usually accomplishes when he is still young. The man who sees his pursuit of happiness come to nothing in later years can

1. [Freud further develops his ideas on these different types in his paper on 'Libidinal Types' (1931a), P.F.L., 7, 359 ff.]

still find consolation in the yield of pleasure of chronic intoxication; or he can embark on the desperate attempt at rebellion seen in a psychosis.[1]

Religion restricts this play of choice and adaptation, since it imposes equally on everyone its own path to the acquisition of happiness and protection from suffering. Its technique consists in depressing the value of life and distorting the picture of the real world in a delusional manner – which presupposes an intimidation of the intelligence. At this price, by forcibly fixing them in a state of psychical infantilism and by drawing them into a mass-delusion, religion succeeds in sparing many people an individual neurosis.[2] But hardly anything more. There are, as we have said, many paths which *may* lead to such happiness as is attainable by men, but there is none which does so for certain. Even religion cannot keep its promise. If the believer finally sees himself obliged to speak of God's 'inscrutable decrees', he is admitting that all that is left to him as a last possible consolation and source of pleasure in his suffering is an unconditional submission. And if he is prepared for that, he could probably have spared himself the *détour* he has made.

1. [*Footnote added* 1931:] I feel impelled to point out one at least of the gaps that have been left in the account given above. No discussion of the possibilities of human happiness should omit to take into consideration the relation between narcissism and object libido. We require to know what being essentially self-dependent signifies for the economics of the libido.

2. Cf. *The Future of an Illusion*, pp. 226–7 f. and 227 *n.* 4 above.]

III

OUR inquiry concerning happiness has not so far taught us much that is not already common knowledge. And even if we proceed from it to the problem of why it is so hard for men to be happy, there seems no greater prospect of learning anything new. We have given the answer already [p. 264] by pointing to the three sources from which our suffering comes: the superior power of nature, the feebleness of our own bodies and the inadequacy of the regulations which adjust the mutual relationships of human beings in the family, the state and society. In regard to the first two sources, our judgement cannot hesitate long. It forces us to acknowledge those sources of suffering and to submit to the inevitable. We shall never completely master nature; and our bodily organism, itself a part of that nature, will always remain a transient structure with a limited capacity for adaptation and achievement. This recognition does not have a paralysing effect. On the contrary, it points the direction for our activity. If we cannot remove all suffering, we can remove some, and we can mitigate some: the experience of many thousands of years has convinced us of that. As regards the third source, the social source of suffering, our attitude is a different one. We do not admit it at all; we cannot see why the regulations made by ourselves should not, on the contrary, be a protection and a benefit for every one of us. And yet, when we consider how unsuccessful we have been in precisely this field of prevention of suffering, a suspicion dawns on us that here, too, a piece of unconquerable nature may lie behind – this time a piece of our own psychical constitution.

When we start considering this possibility, we come upon a contention which is so astonishing that we must dwell upon it. This contention holds that what we call our civilization is largely responsible for our misery, and that we should be much happier if we gave it up and returned to primitive conditions. I call this contention astonishing because, in whatever way we may define the concept of civilization, it is a certain fact that all the things with which we seek to protect ourselves against the threats that emanate from the sources of suffering are part of that very civilization.

How has it happened that so many people have come to take up this strange attitude of hostility to civilization?[1] I believe that the basis of it was a deep and long-standing dissatisfaction with the then existing state of civilization and that on that basis a condemnation of it was built up, occasioned by certain specific historical events. I think I know what the last and the last but one of those occasions were. I am not learned enough to trace the chain of them far back enough in the history of the human species; but a factor of this kind hostile to civilization must already have been at work in the victory of Christendom over the heathen religions. For it was very closely related to the low estimation put upon earthly life by the Christian doctrine. The last but one of these occasions was when the progress of voyages of discovery led to contact with primitive peoples and races. In consequence of insufficient observation and a mistaken view of their manners and customs, they appeared to Europeans to be leading a simple, happy life with few wants, a life such as was unattainable by their visitors with their superior civil-ization. Later experience has corrected some of those judge-ments. In many cases the observers had wrongly attributed to the absence of complicated cultural demands what was in fact due to the bounty of nature and the ease with which the major human needs were satisfied. The last occasion is especially familiar to us. It arose when people came to know about the mechanism of the neuroses, which threaten to undermine the modicum of happiness enjoyed by civilized men. It was dis-covered that a person becomes neurotic because he cannot tolerate the amount of frustration which society imposes on him in the service of its cultural ideals, and it was inferred from this that the abolition or reduction of those demands would result in a return to possibilities of happiness.

1. [Freud had discussed this question at considerable length two years earlier, in the opening chapters of *The Future of an Illusion*, p. 183 ff. above.]

There is also an added factor of disappointment. During the last few generations mankind has made an extraordinary advance in the natural sciences and in their technical application and has established his control over nature in a way never before imagined. The single steps of this advance are common knowledge and it is unnecessary to enumerate them. Men are proud of those achievements, and have a right to be. But they seem to have observed that this newly-won power over space and time, this subjugation of the forces of nature, which is the fulfilment of a longing that goes back thousands of years, has not increased the amount of pleasurable satisfaction which they may expect from life and has not made them feel happier. From the recognition of this fact we ought to be content to conclude that power over nature is not the *only* precondition of human happiness, just as it is not the *only* goal of cultural endeavour; we ought not to infer from it that technical progress is without value for the economics of our happiness. One would like to ask: is there, then, no positive gain in pleasure, no unequivocal increase in my feeling of happiness, if I can, as often as I please, hear the voice of a child of mine who is living hundreds of miles away or if I can learn in the shortest possible time after a friend has reached his destination that he has come through the long and difficult voyage unharmed? Does it mean nothing that medicine has succeeded in enormously reducing infant mortality and the danger of infection for women in childbirth, and, indeed, in considerably lengthening the average life of a civilized man? And there is a long list that might be added to benefits of this kind which we owe to the much-despised era of scientific and technical advances. But here the voice of pessimistic criticism makes itself heard and warns us that most of these satisfactions follow the model of the 'cheap enjoyment' extolled in the anecdote – the enjoyment obtained by putting a bare leg from under the bedclothes on a cold winter night and drawing it in again. If there had been no railway to conquer distances, my child would never have left his native town and I should need no telephone to hear his voice; if travelling across the ocean by ship had not been introduced, my friend would not have embarked on his sea-voyage and I should not need a cable to relieve my anxiety about him. What is the use of reducing infantile mortality when it is precisely that reduction which imposes the greatest restraint on us in the begetting of children, so that, taken all round, we nevertheless rear no more children than in the days before the reign of hygiene, while at the same time we have created difficult conditions for our sexual life in marriage, and have probably worked against the beneficial effects of natural selection? And, finally, what good to us is a long life if it is difficult and barren of joys, and if it is so full of misery that we can only welcome death as a deliverer?

It seems certain that we do not feel comfortable in our present-day civilization, but it is very difficult to form an opinion whether and in what degree men of an earlier age felt happier and what part their cultural conditions played in the matter. We shall always tend to consider people's distress objectively – that is, to place ourselves, with our own wants and sensibilities, in *their* conditions, and then to examine what occasions we should find in them for experiencing happiness or unhappiness. This method of looking at things, which seems objective because it ignores the variations in subjective sensibility, is, of course, the most subjective possible, since it puts one's own mental states in the place of any others, unknown though they may be. Happiness, however, is something essentially subjective. No matter how much we may shrink with horror from certain situations – of a galley-slave in antiquity, of a peasant during the Thirty Years' War, of a victim of the Holy Inquisition, of a Jew awaiting a pogrom – it is nevertheless impossible for us to feel our way into such people – to divine the changes which original obtuseness of mind, a gradual stupefying process, the cessation of expectations, and cruder or more refined methods of narcotization have produced upon their receptivity to sensations of pleasure and unpleasure. Moreover, in the case of the most extreme possibility of suffering, special mental protective devices are brought into operation. It seems to me unprofitable to pursue this aspect of the problem any further.

It is time for us to turn our attention to the nature of this civilization on whose value as a means to happiness doubts have been thrown. We shall not look for a formula in which to express that nature in a few words, until we have learned something by examining it. We shall therefore content ourselves with saying once more that the word 'civilization'[1] describes the whole sum of the achievements and the regulations which distinguish our lives from those of our animal ancestors and which serve two purposes – namely to protect men against nature and to adjust their mutual relations.[2] In order to learn more, we will bring together the various features of civilization individually, as they are exhibited in human communities. In doing so, we shall have no hesitation in letting ourselves be guided by linguistic usage or, as it is also called, linguistic feeling, in the conviction that we shall thus be doing justice to inner discernments which still defy expression in abstract terms.

The first stage is easy. We recognize as cultural all activities and resources which are useful to men for making the earth serviceable to them, for protecting them against the violence of the forces of nature, and so on. As regards this side of civilization, there can be scarcely any doubt. If we go back far enough, we find that the first acts of civilization were the use of tools, the gaining of control over fire and the construction of dwellings. Among these, the control over fire stands out as a quite extraordinary and unexampled achievement,[3] while

1. ['*Kultur.*' For the translation of this word see the Editor's Note to *The Future of an Illusion*, p. 182 above.]

2. See *The Future of an Illusion*, p. 184 above.

3. Psychoanalytic material, incomplete as it is and not susceptible to clear interpretation, nevertheless admits of a conjecture – a fantastic-sounding one – about the origin of this human feat. It is as though primal man had the habit, when he came in contact with fire, of satisfying an infantile desire connected with it, by putting it out with a stream of his urine. The legends that we possess leave no doubt about the originally phallic view taken of tongues of flame as they shoot upwards. Putting out fire by micturating – a theme to which modern giants, Gulliver in Lilliput and Rabelais' Gargantua, still hark back – was therefore a kind of sexual act with a male, an enjoyment of sexual potency in a homosexual competition. The first person to renounce this desire and spare the fire was able to carry it off with him and subdue

the others opened up paths which man has followed ever since, and the stimulus to which is easily guessed. With every tool man is perfecting his own organs, whether motor or sensory, or is removing the limits to their functioning. Motor power places gigantic forces at his disposal, which, like his muscles, he can employ in any direction; thanks to ships and aircraft neither water nor air can hinder his movements; by means of spectacles he corrects defects in the lens of his own eye; by means of the telescope he sees into the far distance; and by means of the microscope he overcomes the limits of visibility set by the structure of his retina. In the photographic camera he has created an instrument which retains the fleeting visual impressions, just as a gramophone disc retains the equally fleet-ing auditory ones; both are at bottom materializations of the power he possesses of recollection, his memory. With the help of the telephone he can hear at distances which would be respected as unattainable even in a fairy tale. Writing was in its origin the voice of an absent person; and the dwelling-house was a substitute for the mother's womb, the first lodging, for which in all likelihood man still longs, and in which he was safe and felt at ease.

These things that, by his science and technology, man has brought about on this earth, on which he first appeared as a feeble animal organism and on which each individual of his

---

it to his own use. By damping down the fire of his own sexual excitation, he had tamed the natural force of fire. This great cultural conquest was thus the reward for his renunciation of instinct. Further, it is as though woman had been appointed guardian of the fire which was held captive on the domestic hearth, because her anatomy made it impossible for her to yield to the temptation of this desire. It is remarkable, too, how regularly analytic experience testifies to the connection between ambition, fire and urethral erotism. [Freud pointed to the connection between urination and fire in the 'Dora' case history (1905e), P.F.L., **8**, 99 ff. The connection between urethral erotism and ambition was first explicitly stated in 'Character and Anal Erotism' (1908b), ibid., **7**, 215. See also 'The Acquisition and Control of Fire' (1932a), ibid., **13**, 229.]

species must once more make its entry ('oh inch of nature!'[1]) as a helpless suckling – these things do not only sound like a fairy tale, they are an actual fulfilment of every – or of almost every – fairy-tale wish. All these assets he may lay claim to as his cultural acquisition. Long ago he formed an ideal conception of omnipotence and omniscience which he embodied in his gods. To these gods he attributed everything that seemed unattainable to his wishes, or that was forbidden to him. One may say, therefore, that these gods were cultural ideals. To-day he has come very close to the attainment of this ideal, he has almost become a god himself. Only, it is true, in the fashion in which ideals are usually attained according to the general judgement of humanity. Not completely; in some respects not at all, in others only half way. Man has, as it were, become a kind of prosthetic God. When he puts on all his auxiliary organs he is truly magnificent; but those organs have not grown on to him and they still give him much trouble at times. Nevertheless, he is entitled to console himself with the thought that development will not come to an end precisely with the year 1930 A.D. Future ages will bring with them new and probably unimaginably great advances in this field of civilization and will increase man's likeness to God still more. But in the interests of our investigations, we will not forget that present-day man does not feel happy in his Godlike character.

We recognize, then, that countries have attained a high level of civilization if we find that in them everything which can assist in the exploitation of the earth by man and in his protection against the forces of nature – everything, in short, which

1. [In English in the original. This very Shakespearean phrase is not in fact to be found in the canon of Shakespeare. The words 'Poore inch of Nature' occur, however, in a novel by George Wilkins, *The Painfull Aduentures of Pericles Prince of Tyre*, where they are addressed by Pericles to his infant daughter. This work was first printed in 1608, just after the publication of Shakespeare's play, in which Wilkins has been thought to have had a hand. Freud's unexpected acquaintance with the phrase is explained by its appearance in a discussion of the origins of *Pericles* in Georg Brandes's well-known book on Shakespeare, a copy of the German translation of which had a place in Freud's library (Brandes, 1896).]

is of use to him – is attended to and effectively carried out. In such countries rivers which threaten to flood the land are regulated in their flow, and their water is directed through canals to places where there is a shortage of it. The soil is carefully cultivated and planted with the vegetation which it is suited to support; and the mineral wealth below ground is assiduously brought to the surface and fashioned into the required implements and utensils. The means of communication are ample, rapid and reliable. Wild and dangerous animals have been exterminated, and the breeding of domesticated animals flourishes. But we demand other things from civilization besides these, and it is a noticeable fact that we hope to find them realized in these same countries. As though we were seeking to repudiate the first demand we made, we welcome it as a sign of civilization as well if we see people directing their care too to what has no practical value whatever, to what is useless – if, for instance, the green spaces necessary in a town as playgrounds and as reservoirs of fresh air are also laid out with flower-beds, or if the windows of the houses are decorated with pots of flowers. We soon observe that this useless thing which we expect civilization to value is beauty. We require civilized man to reverence beauty wherever he sees it in nature and to create it in the objects of his handiwork so far as he is able. But this is far from exhausting our demands on civilization. We expect besides to see the signs of cleanliness and order. We do not think highly of the cultural level of an English country town in Shakespeare's time when we read that there was a big dung-heap in front of his father's house in Stratford; we are indignant and call it 'barbarous' (which is the opposite of civilized) when we find the paths in the Wiener Wald[1] littered with paper. Dirtiness of any kind seems to us incompatible with civilization. We extend our demand for cleanliness to the human body too. We are astonished to learn of the objectionable smell which emanated from the Roi Soleil;[2] and

1. [The wooded hills on the outskirts of Vienna.]
2. [Louis XIV of France.]

we shake our heads on the Isola Bella[1] when we are shown the tiny wash-basin in which Napoleon made his morning toilet. Indeed, we are not surprised by the idea of setting up the use of soap as an actual yardstick of civilization. The same is true of order. It, like cleanliness, applies solely to the works of man. But whereas cleanliness is not to be expected in nature, order, on the contrary, has been imitated from her. Man's observation of the great astronomical regularities not only furnished him with a model for introducing order into his life, but gave him the first points of departure for doing so. Order is a kind of compulsion to repeat which, when a regulation has been laid down once and for all, decides when, where and how a thing shall be done, so that in every similar circumstance one is spared hesitation and indecision. The benefits of order are incontestable. It enables men to use space and time to the best advantage, while conserving their psychical forces. We should have a right to expect that order would have taken its place in human activities from the start and without difficulty; and we may well wonder that this has not happened – that, on the contrary, human beings exhibit an inborn tendency to carelessness, irregularity and unreliability in their work, and that a laborious training is needed before they learn to follow the example of their celestial models.

Beauty, cleanliness and order obviously occupy a special position among the requirements of civilization. No one will maintain that they are as important for life as control over the forces of nature or as some other factors with which we shall become acquainted. And yet no one would care to put them in the background as trivialities. That civilization is not exclusively taken up with what is useful is already shown by the example of beauty, which we decline to omit from among the interests of civilization. The usefulness of order is quite evident. With regard to cleanliness, we must bear in mind that it is demanded of us by hygiene as well, and we may suspect that even before the days of scientific prophylaxis the con-

1. [The well-known island in Lake Maggiore, visited by Napoleon a few days before the battle of Marengo.]

nection between the two was not altogether strange to man. Yet utility does not entirely explain these efforts; something else must be at work besides.

No feature, however, seems better to characterize civilization than its esteem and encouragement of man's higher mental activities – his intellectual, scientific and artistic achievements – and the leading role that it assigns to ideas in human life. Foremost among those ideas are the religious systems, on whose complicated structure I have endeavoured to throw light elsewhere.[1] Next come the speculations of philosophy; and finally what might be called man's 'ideals' – his ideas of a possible perfection of individuals, or of peoples or of the whole of humanity, and the demands he sets up on the basis of such ideas. The fact that these creations of his are not independent of one another, but are on the contrary closely interwoven, increases the difficulty not only of describing them but of tracing their psychological derivation. If we assume quite generally that the motive force of all human activities is a striving towards the two confluent goals of utility and a yield of pleasure, we must suppose that this is also true of the manifestations of civilization which we have been discussing here, although this is easily visible only in scientific and aesthetic activities. But it cannot be doubted that the other activities, too, correspond to strong needs in men – perhaps to needs which are only developed in a minority. Nor must we allow ourselves to be misled by judgements of value concerning any particular religion, or philosophic system, or ideal. Whether we think to find in them the highest achievements of the human spirit, or whether we deplore them as aberrations, we cannot but recognize that where they are present, and, in especial, where they are dominant, a high level of civilization is implied.

The last, but certainly not the least important, of the characteristic features of civilization remains to be assessed: the manner in which the relationships of men to one another, their social relationships, are regulated – relationships which affect a person as a neighbour, as a source of help, as another person's sexual

1. [Cf. *The Future of an Illusion* (1927c), p. 183 ff. above.]

object, as a member of a family and of a State. Here it is especially difficult to keep clear of particular ideal demands and to see what is civilized in general. Perhaps we may begin by explaining that the element of civilization enters on the scene with the first attempt to regulate these social relationships. If the attempt were not made, the relationships would be subject to the arbitrary will of the individual: that is to say, the physically stronger man would decide them in the sense of his own interests and instinctual impulses. Nothing would be changed in this if this stronger man should in his turn meet someone even stronger than he. Human life in common is only made possible when a majority comes together which is stronger than any separate individual and which remains united against all separate individuals. The power of this community is then set up as 'right' in opposition to the power of the individual, which is condemned as 'brute force'. This replacement of the power of the individual by the power of a community constitutes the decisive step of civilization. The essence of it lies in the fact that the members of the community restrict themselves in their possibilities of satisfaction, whereas the individual knew no such restrictions. The first requisite of civilization, therefore, is that of justice – that is, the assurance that a law once made will not be broken in favour of an individual. This implies nothing as to the ethical value of such a law. The further course of cultural development seems to tend towards making the law no longer an expression of the will of a small community – a caste or a stratum of the population or a racial group – which, in its turn, behaves like a violent individual towards other, and perhaps more numerous, collections of people. The final outcome should be a rule of law to which all – except those who are not capable of entering a community – have contributed by a sacrifice of their instincts, and which leaves no one – again with the same exception – at the mercy of brute force.

The liberty of the individual is no gift of civilization. It was greatest before there was any civilization, though then, it is true, it had for the most part no value, since the individual was scarcely in a position to defend it. The development of civilization imposes restrictions on it, and justice demands that no one shall escape those restrictions. What makes itself felt in a human community as a desire for freedom may be their revolt against some existing injustice, and so may prove favourable to a further development of civilization; it may remain compatible with civilization. But it may also spring from the remains of their original personality, which is still untamed by civilization and may thus become the basis in them of hostility to civilization. The urge for freedom, therefore, is directed against particular forms and demands of civilization or against civilization altogether. It does not seem as though any influence could induce a man to change his nature into a termite's. No doubt he will always defend his claim to individual liberty against the will of the group. A good part of the struggles of mankind centre round the single task of finding an expedient accommodation – one, that is, that will bring happiness – between this claim of the individual and the cultural claims of the group; and one of the problems that touches the fate of humanity is whether such an accommodation can be reached by means of some particular form of civilization or whether this conflict is irreconcilable.

By allowing common feeling to be our guide in deciding what features of human life are to be regarded as civilized, we have obtained a clear impression of the general picture of civilization; but it is true that so far we have discovered nothing that is not universally known. At the same time we have been careful not to fall in with the prejudice that civilization is synonymous with perfecting, that it is the road to perfection pre-ordained for men. But now a point of view presents itself which may lead in a different direction. The development of civilization appears to us as a peculiar process which mankind undergoes, and in which several things strike us as familiar. We may characterize this process with reference to the changes which it brings about in the familiar instinctual dispositions of human beings, to satisfy which is, after all, the economic task of our lives. A few of these instincts are used up in such a manner that something appears in their place which, in an individual, we describe as a character-trait. The most remarkable example of such a process is found in the anal erotism of young human beings. Their original interest in the excretory function, its organs and products, is changed in the course of their growth into a group of traits which are familiar to us as parsimony, a sense of order and cleanliness – qualities which, though valuable and welcome in themselves, may be intensified till they become markedly dominant and produce what is called the anal character. How this happens we do not know, but there is no doubt about the correctness of the finding.[1] Now we have seen that order and cleanliness are important requirements of civilization, although their vital necessity is not very apparent, any more than their suitability as sources of enjoyment. At this point we cannot fail to be struck by the similarity between the process of civilization and the libidinal development of the individual. Other instincts [besides anal erotism] are induced to displace the conditions for their satisfaction, to lead them into other paths. In most cases this process coincides with that of the *sublimation* (of instinctual aims) with which we are familiar, but in some it can be differentiated from it. Sublimation of instinct is an especially conspicuous feature of cultural development; it is what makes it possible for higher psychical activities, scientific, artistic or ideological, to play such an important part in civilized life. If one were to yield to a first impression, one would say that sublimation is a vicissitude which has been forced upon the instincts entirely by civilization. But it would be wiser to reflect upon this a little longer. In the third place,[2] finally, and this seems the most important of all, it is impossible to overlook the extent to which civilization is built up upon a renunciation of instinct, how much it presupposes precisely the non-satisfaction (by suppression, repression or some other means?) of powerful instincts. This 'cultural frustration' dominates the large field of social relationships be-

1. Cf. my 'Character and Anal Erotism' (1908*b*) [*P.F.L.*, **7**, 205 ff.], and numerous further contributions, by Ernest Jones [1918] and others.

2. [Freud had already mentioned two other factors playing a part in the 'process' of civilization: character-formation and sublimation.]

tween human beings. As we already know, it is the cause of the hostility against which all civilizations have to struggle. It will also make severe demands on our scientific work, and we shall have much to explain here. It is not easy to understand how it can become possible to deprive an instinct of satisfaction. Nor is doing so without danger. If the loss is not compensated for economically, one can be certain that serious disorders will ensue.

But if we want to know what value can be attributed to our view that the development of civilization is a special process, comparable to the normal maturation of the individual, we must clearly attack another problem. We must ask ourselves to what influences the development of civilization owes its origin, how it arose, and by what its course has been determined.[1]

1. [Freud returns to the subject of civilization as a 'process' below, on p. 313 and again on p. 333 ff. He mentions it once more in his open letter to Einstein, *Why War?* (1933*b*), p. 361 below.]

THE task seems an immense one, and it is natural to feel diffidence in the face of it. But here are such conjectures as I have been able to make.

After primal man had discovered that it lay in his own hands, literally, to improve his lot on earth by working, it cannot have been a matter of indifference to him whether another man worked with or against him. The other man acquired the value for him of a fellow-worker, with whom it was useful to live together. Even earlier, in his ape-like prehistory, man had adopted the habit of forming families, and the members of his family were probably his first helpers. One may suppose that the founding of families was connected with the fact that a moment came when the need for genital satisfaction no longer made its appearance like a guest who drops in suddenly, and, after his departure, is heard of no more for a long time, but instead took up its quarters as a permanent lodger. When this happened, the male acquired a motive for keeping the female, or, speaking more generally, his sexual objects, near him; while the female, who did not want to be separated from her helpless young, was obliged, in their interests, to remain with the stronger male.[1] In this primitive family one essential feature of

---

1. The organic periodicity of the sexual process has persisted, it is true, but its effect on psychical sexual excitation has rather been reversed. This change seems most likely to be connected with the diminution of the olfactory stimuli by means of which the menstrual process produced an effect on the male psyche. Their role was taken over by visual excitations, which, in contrast to the intermittent olfactory stimuli, were able to maintain a permanent effect. The taboo on menstruation is derived from this 'organic repression', as a defence against a phase of development that has been surmounted. All other motives are probably of a secondary nature. (Cf. C. D. Daly, 1927.) This process is repeated on another level when the gods of a superseded period of civilization turn into demons. The diminution of the olfactory stimuli seems itself to be a consequence of man's raising himself from the ground, of his assumption of an upright gait; this made his genitals, which

civilization is still lacking. The arbitrary will of its head, the father, was unrestricted. In *Totem and Taboo*[1] I have tried to

---

were previously concealed, visible and in need of protection, and so provoked feelings of shame in him.

The fateful process of civilization would thus have set in with man's adoption of an erect posture. From that point the chain of events would have proceeded through the devaluation of olfactory stimuli and the isolation of the menstrual period to the time when visual stimuli were paramount and the genitals became visible, and thence to the continuity of sexual excitation, the founding of the family and so to the threshold of human civilization. This is only a theoretical speculation, but it is important enough to deserve careful checking with reference to the conditions of life which obtain among animals closely related to man.

A social factor is also unmistakably present in the cultural trend towards cleanliness, which has received *ex post facto* justification in hygienic considerations but which manifested itself before their discovery. The incitement to cleanliness originates in an urge to get rid of the excreta, which have become disagreeable to the sense perceptions. We know that in the nursery things are different. The excreta arouse no disgust in children. They seem valuable to them as being a part of their own body which has come away from it. Here upbringing insists with special energy on hastening the course of development which lies ahead, and which should make the excreta worthless, disgusting, abhorrent and abominable. Such a reversal of values would scarcely be possible if the substances that are expelled from the body were not doomed by their strong smells to share the fate which overtook olfactory stimuli after man adopted the erect posture. Anal erotism, therefore, succumbs in the first instance to the 'organic repression' which paved the way to civilization. The existence of the social factor which is responsible for the further transformation of anal erotism is attested by the circumstance that, in spite of all man's developmental advances, he scarcely finds the smell of *his own* excreta repulsive, but only that of other people's. Thus a person who is not clean – who does not hide his excreta – is offending other people; he is showing no consideration for them. And this is confirmed by our strongest and commonest terms of abuse. It would be incomprehensible, too, that man should use the name of his most faithful friend in the animal world – the dog – as a term of abuse if that creature had not incurred his contempt through two characteristics: that it is an animal whose dominant sense is that of smell and one which has no horror of excrement, and that it is not ashamed of its sexual functions. [Cf. some remarks on the history of Freud's views on this subject in the Editor's Note, p. 246 f. above.]

1. [What Freud here calls the 'primitive family' he speaks of more often as the 'primal horde'; it corresponds to what Atkinson (1903), to whom the notion is largely due, named the 'Cyclopean family'. See, for all this, *Totem and Taboo* (1912–13), Essay IV (5), *P.F.L.*, **13**.]

show how the way led from this family to the succeeding stage of communal life in the form of bands of brothers. In over-powering their father, the sons had made the discovery that a combination can be stronger than a single individual. The totemic culture is based on the restrictions which the sons had to impose on one another in order to keep this new state of affairs in being. The taboo-observances were the first 'right' or 'law'.[1] The communal life of human beings had, therefore, a two-fold foundation: the compulsion to work, which was created by external necessity, and the power of love, which made the man unwilling to be deprived of his sexual object – the woman –, and made the woman unwilling to be deprived of the part of herself which had been separated off from her – her child. Eros and Ananke [Love and Necessity] have become the parents of human civilization too. The first result of civil-ization was that even a fairly large number of people were now able to live together in a community. And since these two great powers were co-operating in this, one might expect that the further development of civilization would proceed smoothly towards an even better control over the external world and towards a further extension of the number of people included in the community. Nor is it easy to understand how this civilization could act upon its participants otherwise than to make them happy.

Before we go on to inquire from what quarter an interference might arise, this recognition of love as one of the foundations of civilization may serve as an excuse for a digression which will enable us to fill in a gap which we left in an earlier dis-cussion [p. 270]. We said there that man's discovery that sexual (genital) love afforded him the strongest experiences of satis-faction, and in fact provided him with the prototype of all happiness, must have suggested to him that he should continue to seek the satisfaction of happiness in his life along the path of sexual relations and that he should make genital erotism the central point of his life. We went on to say that in doing so he made himself dependent in a most dangerous way on a

1. [The German 'Recht' means both 'right' and 'law'.]

portion of the external world, namely, his chosen love-object, and exposed himself to extreme suffering if he should be rejected by that object or should lose it through unfaithfulness or death. For that reason the wise men of every age have warned us most emphatically against this way of life; but in spite of this it has not lost its attraction for a great number of people.

A small minority are enabled by their constitution to find happiness, in spite of everything, along the path of love. But far-reaching mental changes in the function of love are necessary before this can happen. These people make themselves independent of their object's acquiescence by displacing what they mainly value from being loved on to loving; they protect themselves against the loss of the object by directing their love, not to single objects but to all men alike; and they avoid the uncertainties and disappointments of genital love by turning away from its sexual aims and transforming the instinct into an impulse with an *inhibited aim*. What they bring about in themselves in this way is a state of evenly suspended, steadfast, affectionate feeling, which has little external resemblance any more to the stormy agitations of genital love, from which it is nevertheless derived. Perhaps St Francis of Assisi went furthest in thus exploiting love for the benefit of an inner feeling of happiness. Moreover, what we have recognized as one of the techniques for fulfilling the pleasure principle has often been brought into connection with religion; this connection may lie in the remote regions where the distinction between the ego and objects or between objects themselves is neglected. According to one ethical view, whose deeper motivation will become clear to us presently [p. 302], this readiness for a universal love of mankind and the world represents the highest standpoint which man can reach. Even at this early stage of the discussion I should like to bring forward my two main objections to this view. A love that does not discriminate seems to me to forfeit a part of its own value, by doing an injustice to its object; and secondly, not all men are worthy of love.

The love which founded the family continues to operate in civilization both in its original form, in which it does not renounce direct sexual satisfaction, and in its modified form as aim-inhibited affection. In each, it continues to carry on its function of binding together considerable numbers of people, and it does so in a more intensive fashion than can be effected through the interest of work in common. The careless way in which language uses the word 'love' has its genetic justification. People give the name 'love' to the relation between a man and a woman whose genital needs have led them to found a family; but they also give the name 'love' to the positive feelings between parents and children, and between the brothers and sisters of a family, although *we* are obliged to describe this as 'aim-inhibited love' or 'affection'. Love with an inhibited aim was in fact originally fully sensual love, and it is so still in man's unconscious. Both – fully sensual love and aim-inhibited love – extend outside the family and create new bonds with people who before were strangers. Genital love leads to the formation of new families, and aim-inhibited love to 'friendships' which become valuable from a cultural standpoint because they escape some of the limitations of genital love, as, for instance, its exclusiveness. But in the course of development the relation of love to civilization loses its unambiguity. On the one hand love comes into opposition to the interests of civilization; on the other, civilization threatens love with substantial restrictions.

This rift between them seems unavoidable. The reason for it is not immediately recognizable. It expresses itself at first as a conflict between the family and the larger community to which the individual belongs. We have already perceived that one of the main endeavours of civilization is to bring people together into large unities. But the family will not give the individual up. The more closely the members of a family are attached to one another, the more often do they tend to cut themselves off from others, and the more difficult is it for them to enter into the wider circle of life. The mode of life in common which is phylogenetically the older, and which is the only one that exists in childhood, will not let itself be superseded by the cultural mode of life which has been acquired later.

Detaching himself from his family becomes a task that faces every young person, and society often helps him in the solution of it by means of puberty and initiation rites. We get the impression that these are difficulties which are inherent in all psychical – and, indeed, at bottom, in all organic – development.

Furthermore, women soon come into opposition to civilization and display their retarding and restraining influence – those very women who, in the beginning, laid the foundations of civilization by the claims of their love. Women represent the interests of the family and of sexual life. The work of civilization has become increasingly the business of men, it confronts them with ever more difficult tasks and compels them to carry out instinctual sublimations of which women are little capable. Since a man does not have unlimited quantities of psychical energy at his disposal, he has to accomplish his tasks by making an expedient distribution of his libido. What he employs for cultural aims he to a great extent withdraws from women and sexual life. His constant association with men, and his dependence on his relations with them, even estrange him from his duties as a husband and father. Thus the woman finds herself forced into the background by the claims of civilization and she adopts a hostile attitude towards it.

The tendency on the part of civilization to restrict sexual life is no less clear than its other tendency to expand the cultural unit. Its first, totemic, phase already brings with it the prohibition against an incestuous choice of object, and this is perhaps the most drastic mutilation which man's erotic life has in all time experienced. Taboos, laws and customs impose further restrictions, which affect both men and women. Not all civilizations go equally far in this; and the economic structure of the society also influences the amount of sexual freedom that remains. Here, as we already know, civilization is obeying the laws of economic necessity, since a large amount of the psychical energy which it uses for its own purposes has to be withdrawn from sexuality. In this respect civilization behaves towards sexuality as a people or a stratum of its population does which has subjected another one to its exploitation. Fear of a revolt by the suppressed elements drives it to stricter precautionary measures. A high-water mark in such a development has been reached in our Western European civilization. A cultural community is perfectly justified, psychologically, in starting by proscribing manifestations of the sexual life of children, for there would be no prospect of curbing the sexual lusts of adults if the ground had not been prepared for it in childhood. But such a community cannot in any way be justified in going to the length of actually *disavowing* such easily demonstrable, and, indeed, striking phenomena. As regards the sexually mature individual, the choice of an object is restricted to the opposite sex, and most extra-genital satisfactions are forbidden as perversions. The requirement, demonstrated in these prohibitions, that there shall be a single kind of sexual life for everyone, disregards the dissimilarities, whether innate or acquired, in the sexual constitution of human beings; it cuts off a fair number of them from sexual enjoyment, and so becomes the source of serious injustice. The result of such restrictive measures might be that in people who are normal – who are not prevented by their constitution – the whole of their sexual interests would flow without loss into the channels that are left open. But heterosexual genital love, which has remained exempt from outlawry, is itself restricted by further limitations, in the shape of insistence upon legitimacy and monogamy. Present-day civilization makes it plain that it will only permit sexual relationships on the basis of a solitary, indissoluble bond between one man and one woman, and that it does not like sexuality as a source of pleasure in its own right and is only prepared to tolerate it because there is so far no substitute for it as a means of propagating the human race.

This, of course, is an extreme picture. Everybody knows that it has proved impossible to put it into execution, even for quite short periods. Only the weaklings have submitted to such an extensive encroachment upon their sexual freedom, and stronger natures have only done so subject to a compensatory condition, which will be mentioned later.[1] Civilized society has found itself obliged to pass over in silence many transgressions which, according to its own rescripts, it ought to have punished. But we must not err on the other side and assume that, because it does not achieve all its aims, such an attitude on the part of society is entirely innocuous. The sexual life of civilized man is notwithstanding severely impaired; it sometimes gives the impression of being in process of involution as a function, just as our teeth and hair seem to be as organs. One is probably justified in assuming that its importance as a source of feelings of happiness, and therefore in the fulfilment of our aim in life, has sensibly diminished.[2] Sometimes one seems to perceive that it is not only the pressure of civilization but something in the nature of the function itself which denies us full satisfaction and urges us along other paths. This may be wrong; it is hard to decide.[3]

1. [The compensation is the obtaining of some measure of security. See below, p. 306.]

2. Among the works of that sensitive English writer, John Galsworthy, who enjoys general recognition to-day, there is a short story of which I early formed a high opinion. It is called 'The Apple-Tree', and it brings home to us how the life of present-day civilized people leaves no room for the simple natural love of two human beings.

3. The view expressed above is supported by the following considerations. Man is an animal organism with (like others) an unmistakably bisexual disposition. The individual corresponds to a fusion of two symmetrical halves, of which, according to some investigators, one is purely male and the other female. It is equally possible that each half was originally hermaphrodite. Sex is a biological fact which, although it is of extraordinary importance in mental life, is hard to grasp psychologically. We are accustomed to say that every human being displays both male and female instinctual impulses, needs and attributes; but though anatomy, it is true, can point out the characteristic of maleness and femaleness, psychology cannot. For psychology the contrast between the sexes fades away into one between activity and passivity, in which we far too readily identify activity with maleness and passivity with femaleness, a view which is by no means universally confirmed in the animal kingdom. The theory of bisexuality is still surrounded by many obscurities and we cannot but feel it as a serious impediment in psycho-

analysis that it has not yet found any link with the theory of the instincts. However this may be, if we assume it as a fact that each individual seeks to satisfy both male and female wishes in his sexual life, we are prepared for the possibility that those [two sets of] demands are not fulfilled by the same object, and that they interfere with each other unless they can be kept apart and each impulse guided into a particular channel that is suited to it. Another difficulty arises from the circumstance that there is so often associated with the erotic relationship, over and above its own sadistic components, a quota of plain inclination to aggression. The love-object will not always view these complications with the degree of understanding and tolerance shown by the peasant woman who complained that her husband did not love her any more, since he had not beaten her for a week.

The conjecture which goes deepest, however, is the one which takes its start from what I have said above in my footnote on p. 288 f. It is to the effect that, with the assumption of an erect posture by man and with the depreciation of his sense of smell, it was not only his anal erotism which threatened to fall a victim to organic repression, but the whole of his sexuality; so that since this, the sexual function has been accompanied by a repugnance which cannot further be accounted for, and which prevents its complete satisfaction and forces it away from the sexual aim into sublimations and libidinal displacements. I know that Bleuler (1913) once pointed to the existence of a primary repelling attitude like this towards sexual life. All neurotics, and many others besides, take exception to the fact that *'inter urinas et faeces nascimur* [we are born between urine and faeces]'. The genitals, too, give rise to strong sensations of smell which many people cannot tolerate and which spoil sexual intercourse for them. Thus we should find that the deepest root of the sexual repression which advances along with civilization is the organic defence of the new form of life achieved with man's erect gait against his earlier animal existence. This result of scientific research coincides in a remarkable way with commonplace prejudices that have often made themselves heard. Nevertheless, these things are at present no more than unconfirmed possibilities which have not been substantiated by science. Nor should we forget that, in spite of the undeniable depreciation of olfactory stimuli, there exist even in Europe peoples among whom the strong genital odours which are so repellent to us are highly prized as sexual stimulants and who refuse to give them up. (Cf. the collections of folklore obtained from Iwan Bloch's questionnaire on the sense of smell in sexual life ['*Über den Geruchssinn in der vita sexualis*'] published in different volumes of Friedrich S. Krauss's *Anthropophyteia*.)

[On the difficulty of finding a psychological meaning for 'maleness' and 'femaleness', see a long footnote added in 1915 to the third of Freud's *Three Essays* (1905d), *P.F.L.*, **7**, 141–2, and a discussion at the beginning of Lecture 33 of the *New Introductory Lectures* (1933a), ibid., **2**, 146–50. – The important consequences of the proximity between the sexual and excretory organs were first indicated by Freud in the unpublished Draft K sent to Fliess on 1 January 1896 (Freud, 1950a). He returned to the point frequently. Cf., for instance, the 'Dora' case history (1905e), *P.F.L.*, **8**, 62–3, and the second paper on 'The Psychology of Love' (1912d), ibid., **7**, 258–9. Cf. also the Editor's Note, p. 246 f. above.]

V

PSYCHOANALYTIC work has shown us that it is precisely these frustrations of sexual life which people known as neurotics cannot tolerate. The neurotic creates substitutive satisfactions for himself in his symptoms, and these either cause him suffering in themselves or become sources of suffering for him by raising difficulties in his relations with his environment and the society he belongs to. The latter fact is easy to understand; the former presents us with a new problem. But civilization demands other sacrifices besides that of sexual satisfaction.

We have treated the difficulty of cultural development as a general difficulty of development by tracing it to the inertia of the libido, to its disinclination to give up an old position for a new one.[1] We are saying much the same thing when we derive the antithesis between civilization and sexuality from the circumstance that sexual love is a relationship between two individuals in which a third can only be superfluous or disturbing, whereas civilization depends on relationships between a considerable number of individuals. When a love-relationship is at its height there is no room left for any interest in the environment; a pair of lovers are sufficient to themselves, and do not even need the child they have in common to make them happy. In no other case does Eros so clearly betray the core of his being, his purpose of making one out of more than one; but when he has achieved this in the proverbial way through the love of two human beings, he refuses to go further.

So far, we can quite well imagine a cultural community consisting of double individuals like this, who, libidinally satisfied in themselves, are connected with one another through the bonds of common work and common interests. If this were so, civilization would not have to withdraw any energy from

1. [See, for instance, p. 292 above. On the concept of 'psychical inertia' in general, see the paper 'A Case of Paranoia' (1915*f*), *P.F.L.*, **10**, 157–8 and *n.*]

sexuality. But this desirable state of things does not, and never did, exist. Reality shows us that civilization is not content with the ties we have so far allowed it. It aims at binding the members of the community together in a libidinal way as well and employs every means to that end. It favours every path by which strong identifications can be established between the members of the community, and it summons up aim-inhibited libido on the largest scale so as to strengthen the communal bond by relations of friendship. In order for these aims to be fulfilled, a restriction upon sexual life is unavoidable. But we are unable to understand what the necessity is which forces civilization along this path and which causes its antagonism to sexuality. There must be some disturbing factor which we have not yet discovered.

The clue may be supplied by one of the ideal demands, as we have called them,[1] of civilized society. It runs: 'Thou shalt love thy neighbour as thyself.' It is known throughout the world and is undoubtedly older than Christianity, which puts it forward as its proudest claim. Yet it is certainly not very old; even in historical times it was still strange to mankind. Let us adopt a naïve attitude towards it, as though we were hearing it for the first time; we shall be unable then to suppress a feeling of surprise and bewilderment. Why should we do it? What good will it do us? But, above all, how shall we achieve it? How can it be possible? My love is something valuable to me which I ought not to throw away without reflection. It imposes duties on me for whose fulfilment I must be ready to make sacrifices. If I love someone, he must deserve it in some way. (I leave out of account the use he may be to me, and also his possible significance for me as a sexual object, for neither of these two kinds of relationship comes into question where the precept to love my neighbour is concerned.) He deserves it if he is so like me in important ways that I can love myself in him; and he deserves it if he is so much more perfect than myself that I can love my ideal of my own self

---

1. [See p. 283 above. Cf. also ' "Civilized" Sexual Morality' (1908*d*), p. 51 above.]

in him. Again, I have to love him if he is my friend's son, since the pain my friend would feel if any harm came to him would be my pain too – I should have to share it. But if he is a stranger to me and if he cannot attract me by any worth of his own or any significance that he may already have acquired for my emotional life, it will be hard for me to love him. Indeed, I should be wrong to do so, for my love is valued by all my own people as a sign of my preferring them, and it is an injustice to them if I put a stranger on a par with them. But if I am to love him (with this universal love) merely because he, too, is an inhabitant of this earth, like an insect, an earth-worm or a grass-snake, then I fear that only a small modicum of my love will fall to his share – not by any possibility as much as, by the judgement of my reason, I am entitled to retain for myself. What is the point of a precept enunciated with so much solemnity if its fulfilment cannot be recommended as reasonable?

On closer inspection, I find still further difficulties. Not merely is this stranger in general unworthy of my love; I must honestly confess that he has more claim to my hostility and even my hatred. He seems not to have the least trace of love for me and shows me not the slightest consideration. If it will do him any good he has no hesitation in injuring me, nor does he ask himself whether the amount of advantage he gains bears any proportion to the extent of the harm he does to me. Indeed, he need not even obtain an advantage; if he can satisfy any sort of desire by it, he thinks nothing of jeering at me, insulting me, slandering me and showing his superior power; and the more secure he feels and the more helpless I am, the more certainly I can expect him to behave like this to me. If he behaves differently, if he shows me consideration and forbearance as a stranger, I am ready to treat him in the same way, in any case and quite apart from any precept. Indeed, if this grandiose commandment had run 'Love thy neighbour as thy neighbour loves thee', I should not take exception to it. And there is a second commandment, which seems to me even more incom-prehensible and arouses still stronger opposition in me. It is

'Love thine enemies'. If I think it over, however, I see that I am wrong in treating it as a greater imposition. At bottom it is the same thing.[1]

I think I can now hear a dignified voice admonishing me: 'It is precisely because your neighbour is not worthy of love, and is on the contrary your enemy, that you should love him as yourself.' I then understand that the case is one like that of *Credo quia absurdum*.[2]

Now it is very probable that my neighbour, when he is enjoined to love me as himself, will answer exactly as I have done and will repel me for the same reasons. I hope he will not have the same objective grounds for doing so, but he will have the same idea as I have. Even so, the behaviour of human beings shows differences, which ethics, disregarding the fact that such differences are determined, classifies as 'good' or 'bad'. So long as these undeniable differences have not been removed, obedience to high ethical demands entails damage to the aims of civilization, for it puts a positive premium on being bad. One is irresistibly reminded of an incident in the French Chamber when capital punishment was being debated. A member had been passionately supporting its abolition and his speech was being received with tumultuous applause, when a voice from the hall called out: 'Que messieurs les assassins commencent!'[3]

---

1. A great imaginative writer may permit himself to give expression – jokingly, at all events – to psychological truths that are severely proscribed. Thus Heine confesses: 'Mine is a most peaceable disposition. My wishes are: a humble cottage with a thatched roof, but a good bed, good food, the freshest milk and butter, flowers before my window, and a few fine trees before my door; and if God wants to make my happiness complete, he will grant me the joy of seeing some six or seven of my enemies hanging from those trees. Before their death I shall, moved in my heart, forgive them all the wrong they did me in their lifetime. One must, it is true, forgive one's enemies – but not before they have been hanged.' (*Gedanken und Einfälle* [Section I].)

2. [See Chapter V of *The Future of an Illusion* (1927c), p. 209 above. Freud returns to the question of the commandment to love one's neighbour as oneself below, on p. 336 f.].

3. ['It's the murderers who should make the first move.']

The element of truth behind all this, which people are so ready to disavow, is that men are not gentle creatures who want to be loved, and who at the most can defend themselves if they are attacked; they are, on the contrary, creatures among whose instinctual endowments is to be reckoned a powerful share of aggressiveness. As a result, their neighbour is for them not only a potential helper or sexual object, but also someone who tempts them to satisfy their aggressiveness on him, to exploit his capacity for work without compensation, to use him sexually without his consent, to seize his possessions, to humiliate him, to cause him pain, to torture and to kill him. *Homo homini lupus.*[1] Who, in the face of all his experience of life and of history, will have the courage to dispute this assertion? As a rule this cruel aggressiveness waits for some provocation or puts itself at the service of some other purpose, whose goal might also have been reached by milder measures. In circumstances that are favourable to it, when the mental counter-forces which ordinarily inhibit it are out of action, it also manifests itself spontaneously and reveals man as a savage beast to whom consideration towards his own kind is something alien. Anyone who calls to mind the atrocities committed during the racial migrations or the invasions of the Huns, or by the people known as Mongols under Jenghiz Khan and Tamerlane, or at the capture of Jerusalem by the pious Crusaders, or even, indeed, the horrors of the recent World War – anyone who calls these things to mind will have to bow humbly before the truth of this view.

The existence of this inclination to aggression, which we can detect in ourselves and justly assume to be present in others, is the factor which disturbs our relations with our neighbour and which forces civilization into such a high expenditure [of energy]. In consequence of this primary mutual hostility of human beings, civilized society is perpetually threatened with disintegration. The interest of work in common would not hold it together; instinctual passions are stronger than reasonable interests. Civilization has to use its utmost efforts in order to

1. ['Man is a wolf to man.' Derived from Plautus, *Asinaria* II, iv, 88.]

set limits to man's aggressive instincts and to hold the manifestations of them in check by psychical reaction-formations.
Hence, therefore, the use of methods intended to incite people
into identifications and aim-inhibited relationships of love,
hence the restriction upon sexual life, and hence too the ideal's
commandment to love one's neighbour as oneself — a commandment which is really justified by the fact that nothing
else runs so strongly counter to the original nature of man.
In spite of every effort, these endeavours of civilization have
not so far achieved very much. It hopes to prevent the crudest
excesses of brutal violence by itself assuming the right to use
violence against criminals, but the law is not able to lay hold
of the more cautious and refined manifestations of human
aggressiveness. The time comes when each one of us has to
give up as illusions the expectations which, in his youth, he
pinned upon his fellow-men, and when he may learn how much
difficulty and pain has been added to his life by their ill-will.
At the same time, it would be unfair to reproach civilization
with trying to eliminate strife and competition from human
activity. These things are undoubtedly indispensable. But
opposition is not necessarily enmity; it is merely misused and
made an *occasion* for enmity.

The communists believe that they have found the path to
deliverance from our evils. According to them, man is wholly
good and is well-disposed to his neighbour; but the institution
of private property has corrupted his nature. The ownership
of private wealth gives the individual power, and with it the
temptation to ill-treat his neighbour; while the man who is
excluded from possession is bound to rebel in hostility against
his oppressor. If private property were abolished, all wealth
held in common, and everyone allowed to share in the enjoyment of it, ill-will and hostility would disappear among men.
Since everyone's needs would be satisfied, no one would have
any reason to regard another as his enemy; all would willingly
undertake the work that was necessary. I have no concern with
any economic criticisms of the communist system; I cannot
inquire into whether the abolition of private property is ex-

pedient or advantageous.[1] But I am able to recognize that the psychological premises on which the system is based are an untenable illusion. In abolishing private property we deprive the human love of aggression of one of its instruments, certainly a strong one, though certainly not the strongest; but we have in no way altered the differences in power and influence which are misused by aggressiveness, nor have we altered anything in its nature. Aggressiveness was not created by property. It reigned almost without limit in primitive times, when property was still very scanty, and it already shows itself in the nursery almost before property has given up its primal, anal form; it forms the basis of every relation of affection and love among people (with the single exception, perhaps, of the mother's relation to her male child[2]). If we do away with personal rights over material wealth, there still remains prerogative in the field of sexual relationships, which is bound to become the source of the strongest dislike and the most violent hostility among men who in other respects are on an equal footing. If we were to remove this factor, too, by allowing complete freedom of sexual life and thus abolishing the family, the germ-cell of civilization, we cannot, it is true, easily foresee what new paths the development of civilization could take; but one thing we can expect, and that is that this indestructible feature of human nature will follow it there.

It is clearly not easy for men to give up the satisfaction of this inclination to aggression. They do not feel comfortable

1. Anyone who has tasted the miseries of poverty in his own youth and has experienced the indifference and arrogance of the well-to-do, should be safe from the suspicion of having no understanding or good will towards endeavours to fight against the inequality of wealth among men and all that it leads to. To be sure, if an attempt is made to base this fight upon an abstract demand, in the name of justice, for equality for all men, there is a very obvious objection to be made – that nature, by endowing individuals with extremely unequal physical attributes and mental capacities, has introduced injustices against which there is no remedy.

2. [Cf. a footnote to *Group Psychology* (1921*c*), p. 130 *n*. 2 above. A rather longer discussion of the point occurs in Lecture 33 of the *New Introductory Lectures* (1933*a*), *P.F.L.*, **2**, 167–8.]

without it. The advantage which a comparatively small cultural group offers of allowing this instinct an outlet in the form of hostility against intruders is not to be despised. It is always possible to bind together a considerable number of people in love, so long as there are other people left over to receive the manifestations of their aggressiveness. I once discussed the phenomenon that it is precisely communities with adjoining territories, and related to each other in other ways as well, who are engaged in constant feuds and in ridiculing each other – like the Spaniards and Portuguese, for instance, the North Germans and South Germans, the English and Scotch, and so on.[1] I gave this phenomenon the name of 'the narcissism of minor differences', a name which does not do much to explain it. We can now see that it is a convenient and relatively harmless satisfaction of the inclination to aggression, by means of which cohesion between the members of the community is made easier. In this respect the Jewish people, scattered everywhere, have rendered most useful services to the civilizations of the countries that have been their hosts; but unfortunately all the massacres of the Jews in the Middle Ages did not suffice to make that period more peaceful and secure for their Christian fellows. When once the Apostle Paul had posited universal love between men as the foundation of his Christian community, extreme intolerance on the part of Christendom towards those who remained outside it became the inevitable consequence. To the Romans, who had not founded their communal life as a State upon love, religious intolerance was something foreign, although with them religion was a concern of the State and the State was permeated by religion. Neither was it an unaccountable chance that the dream of a Germanic world-dominion called for anti-semitism as its complement; and it is intelligible that the attempt to establish a new, communist

---

1. [See *Group Psychology* (1921*c*), p. 131 above, and 'The Taboo of Virginity' (1918*a*), *P.F.L.*, **7**, 272. The idea is mentioned again in connection with anti-semitism in Essay III, Part I (D), of *Moses and Monotheism* (1939*a*), *P.F.L.*, **13**, 335.]

civilization in Russia should find its psychological support in the persecution of the bourgeois. One only wonders, with concern, what the Soviets will do after they have wiped out their bourgeois.

If civilization imposes such great sacrifices not only on man's sexuality but on his aggressivity, we can understand better why it is hard for him to be happy in that civilization. In fact, primitive man was better off in knowing no restrictions of instinct. To counterbalance this, his prospects of enjoying this happiness for any length of time were very slender. Civilized man has exchanged a portion of his possibilities of happiness for a portion of security. We must not forget, however, that in the primal family only the head of it enjoyed this instinctual freedom; the rest lived in slavish suppression. In that primal period of civilization, the contrast between a minority who enjoyed the advantages of civilization and a majority who were robbed of those advantages was, therefore, carried to extremes. As regards the primitive peoples who exist to-day, careful researches have shown that their instinctual life is by no means to be envied for its freedom. It is subject to restrictions of a different kind but perhaps of greater severity than those attaching to modern civilized man.

When we justly find fault with the present state of our civilization for so inadequately fulfilling our demands for a plan of life that shall make us happy, and for allowing the existence of so much suffering which could probably be avoided – when, with unsparing criticism, we try to uncover the roots of its imperfection, we are undoubtedly exercising a proper right and are not showing ourselves enemies of civilization. We may expect gradually to carry through such alterations in our civilization as will better satisfy our needs and will escape our criticisms. But perhaps we may also familiarize ourselves with the idea that there are difficulties attaching to the nature of civilization which will not yield to any attempt at reform. Over and above the tasks of restricting the instincts, which we are prepared for, there forces itself on our notice the danger of a state of things which might be termed 'the psychological poverty of groups'.[1] This danger is most threatening where the bonds of a society are chiefly constituted by the identification of its members with one another, while individuals of the leader type do not acquire the importance that should fall to them in the formation of a group.[2] The present cultural state of America would give us a good opportunity for studying the damage to civilization which is thus to be feared. But I shall avoid the temptation of entering upon a critique of American civilization; I do not wish to give an impression of wanting myself to employ American methods.

1. [The German *'psychologisches Elend'* seems to be a version of Janet's expression *'misère psychologique'* applied by him to describe the incapacity for mental synthesis which he attributes to neurotics.]

2. Cf. *Group Psychology and the Analysis of the Ego* (1921*c*) [p. 134 ff. above].

IN none of my previous writings have I had so strong a feeling as now that what I am describing is common knowledge and that I am using up paper and ink and, in due course, the compositor's and printer's work and material in order to expound things which are, in fact, self-evident. For that reason I should be glad to seize the point if it were to appear that the recognition of a special, independent aggressive instinct means an alteration of the psychoanalytic theory of the instincts.

We shall see, however, that this is not so and that it is merely a matter of bringing into sharper focus a turn of thought arrived at long ago and of following out its consequences. Of all the slowly developed parts of analytic theory, the theory of the instincts is the one that has felt its way the most painfully forward. And yet that theory was so indispensable to the whole structure that something had to be put in its place. In what was at first my utter perplexity, I took as my starting-point a saying of the poet-philosopher, Schiller, that 'hunger and love are what moves the world'.[1] Hunger could be taken to represent the instincts which aim at preserving the individual; while love strives after objects, and its chief function, favoured in every way by nature, is the preservation of the species. Thus, to begin with, ego-instincts and object-instincts confronted each other. It was to denote the energy of the latter and only the latter instincts that I introduced the term 'libido'.[2] Thus the antithesis was between the ego-instincts and the 'libidinal' instincts of love (in its widest sense[3]) which were directed to an object. One of these object-instincts, the sadistic instinct, stood out from the rest, it is true, in that its aim was so very far from being loving. Moreover it was obviously in some

1. ['Die Weltweisen.']
2. [In the first paper on anxiety neurosis (1895b), P.F.L., 10, 48.]
3. [I.e. as used by Plato. See Group Psychology (1921c), p. 119 above.]

respects attached to the ego-instincts: it could not hide its close affinity with instincts of mastery which have no libidinal purpose. But these discrepancies were got over; after all, sadism was clearly a part of sexual life, in the activities of which affection could be replaced by cruelty. Neurosis was regarded as the outcome of a struggle between the interest of self-preservation and the demands of the libido, a struggle in which the ego had been victorious but at the price of severe sufferings and renunciations.

Every analyst will admit that even to-day this view has not the sound of a long-discarded error. Nevertheless, alterations in it became essential, as our inquiries advanced from the re-pressed to the repressing forces, from the object-instincts to the ego. The decisive step forward was the introduction of the concept of narcissism – that is to say, the discovery that the ego itself is cathected with libido, that the ego, indeed, is the libido's original home, and remains to some extent its head-quarters. This narcissistic libido turns towards objects, and thus becomes object-libido; and it can change back into narcissistic libido once more. The concept of narcissism made it possible to obtain an analytic understanding of the traumatic neuroses and of many of the affections bordering on the psychoses, as well as of the latter themselves. It was not necessary to give up our interpretation of the transference neuroses as attempts made by the ego to defend itself against sexuality; but the concept of libido was endangered. Since the ego-instincts, too, were libidinal, it seemed for a time inevitable that we should make libido coincide with instinctual energy in general, as C. G. Jung had already advocated earlier. Nevertheless, there still remained in me a kind of conviction, for which I was not as yet able to find reasons, that the instincts could not all be of the same kind. My next step was taken in *Beyond the Pleasure Principle* (1920g), when the compulsion to repeat and the con-servative character of instinctual life first attracted my attention. Starting from speculations on the beginning of life and from biological parallels, I drew the conclusion that, besides the instinct to preserve living substance and to join it into ever larger units,[1] there must exist another, contrary instinct seeking to dissolve those units and to bring them back to their primaeval, inorganic state. That is to say, as well as Eros there was an instinct of death. The phenomena of life could be explained from the concurrent or mutually opposing action of these two instincts. It was not easy, however, to demonstrate the activities of this supposed death instinct. The manifestations of Eros were conspicuous and noisy enough. It might be assumed that the death instinct operated silently within the organism towards its dissolution, but that, of course, was no proof. A more fruitful idea was that a portion of the instinct is diverted towards the external world and comes to light as an instinct of aggressiveness and destructiveness. In this way the instinct itself could be pressed into the service of Eros, in that the organism was destroying some other thing, whether animate or inanimate, instead of destroying its own self. Conversely, any restriction of this aggressiveness directed outwards would be bound to increase the self-destruction, which is in any case proceeding. At the same time one can suspect from this example that the two kinds of instinct seldom – perhaps never – appear in isolation from each other, but are alloyed with each other in varying and very different proportions and so become unrecognizable to our judgement. In sadism, long since known to us as a component instinct of sexuality, we should have before us a particularly strong alloy of this kind between trends of love and the destructive instinct; while its counterpart, masochism, would be a union between destructiveness directed inwards and sexuality – a union which makes what is otherwise an imperceptible trend into a conspicuous and tangible one.

The assumption of the existence of an instinct of death or destruction has met with resistance even in analytic circles; I am aware that there is a frequent inclination rather to ascribe

1. The opposition which thus emerges between the ceaseless trend by Eros towards extension and the general conservative nature of the instincts is striking, and it may become the starting-point for the study of further problems.

whatever is dangerous and hostile in love to an original bi-polarity in its own nature. To begin with it was only tentatively that I put forward the views I have developed here,[1] but in the course of time they have gained such a hold upon me that I can no longer think in any other way. To my mind, they are far more serviceable from a theoretical standpoint than any other possible ones; they provide that simplification, without either ignoring or doing violence to the facts, for which we strive in scientific work. I know that in sadism and masochism we have always seen before us manifestations of the destructive instinct (directed outwards and inwards), strongly alloyed with erotism; but I can no longer understand how we can have overlooked the ubiquity of non-erotic aggressivity and destructiveness and can have failed to give it its due place in our interpretation of life. (The desire for destruction when it is directed *inwards* mostly eludes our perception, of course, unless it is tinged with erotism.) I remember my own defensive attitude when the idea of an instinct of destruction first emerged in psychoanalytic literature, and how long it took before I became receptive to it.[2] That others should have shown, and still show, the same attitude of rejection surprises me less. For 'little children do not like it'[3] when there is talk of the inborn human inclination to 'badness', to aggressiveness and destructiveness, and so to cruelty as well. God has made them in the image of His own perfection; nobody wants to be reminded how hard it is to reconcile the undeniable existence of evil – despite the protestations of Christian Science – with His all-powerfulness or His all-goodness. The Devil would be the best way out as an excuse for God; in that way he would be playing the same part as an agent of economic discharge as the Jew does in the world of the Aryan ideal.[4] But even so, one can hold God responsible for the existence of the Devil just as well

1. [Cf. *Beyond the Pleasure Principle* (1920g), *P.F.L*, **11**, 332–3.]

2. [Cf. the Editor's Introduction, p. 247 ff above.]

3. ['Denn die Kindlein, Sie hören es nicht gerne.' A quotation from Goethe's poem 'Die Ballade vom vertriebenen und heimgekehrten Grafen'.]

4. [Cf. p. 305 above.]

as for the existence of the wickedness which the Devil embodies. In view of these difficulties, each of us will be well advised, on some suitable occasion, to make a low bow to the deeply moral nature of mankind; it will help us to be generally popular and much will be forgiven us for it.[1]

The name 'libido' can once more be used to denote the manifestations of the power of Eros in order to distinguish them from the energy of the death instinct.[2] It must be confessed that we have much greater difficulty in grasping that instinct; we can only suspect it, as it were, as something in the background

1. In Goethe's Mephistopheles we have a quite exceptionally convincing identification of the principle of evil with the destructive instinct:

> Denn alles, was entsteht,
> Ist wert, dass es zu Grunde geht ...
> So ist dann alles, was Ihr Sünde,
> Zerstörung, kurz das Böse nennt,
> Mein eigentliches Element.

> [For all things, from the Void
> Called forth, deserve to be destroyed ...
> Thus, all which you as Sin have rated –
> Destruction, – aught with Evil blent, –
> That is my proper element.]

The Devil himself names as his adversary, not what is holy and good, but Nature's power to create, to multiply life – that is, Eros:

> Der Luft, dem Wasser, wie der Erden
> Entwinden tausend Keime sich,
> Im Trocknen, Feuchten, Warmen, Kalten!
> Hätt' ich mir nicht die Flamme vorbehalten,
> Ich hätte nichts Aparts für mich.

> [From Water, Earth, and Air unfolding,
> A thousand germs break forth and grow,
> In dry, and wet, and warm, and chilly:
> And had I not the Flame reserved, why, really,
> There's nothing special of my own to show.

Both passages are from Goethe's *Faust*, Part I, Scene 3. Translated by Bayard Taylor.]

2. Our present point of view can be roughly expressed in the statement that libido has a share in every instinctual manifestation, but that not everything in that manifestation is libido.

behind Eros, and it escapes detection unless its presence is betrayed by its being alloyed with Eros. It is in sadism, where the death instinct twists the erotic aim in its own sense and yet at the same time fully satisfies the erotic urge, that we succeed in obtaining the clearest insight into its nature and its relation to Eros. But even where it emerges without any sexual purpose, in the blindest fury of destructiveness, we cannot fail to recognize that the satisfaction of the instinct is accompanied by an extraordinarily high degree of narcissistic enjoyment, owing to its presenting the ego with a fulfilment of the latter's old wishes for omnipotence. The instinct of destruction, moderated and tamed, and, as it were, inhibited in its aim, must, when it is directed towards objects, provide the ego with the satisfaction of its vital needs and with control over nature. Since the assumption of the existence of the instinct is mainly based on theoretical grounds, we must also admit that it is not entirely proof against theoretical objections. But this is how things appear to us now, in the present state of our knowledge; future research and reflection will no doubt bring further light which will decide the matter.

In all that follows I adopt the standpoint, therefore, that the inclination to aggression is an original, self-subsisting instinctual disposition in man, and I return to my view [p. 302] that it constitutes the greatest impediment to civilization. At one point in the course of this inquiry [p. 285] I was led to the idea that civilization was a special process which mankind undergoes, and I am still under the influence of that idea. I may now add that civilization is a process in the service of Eros, whose purpose is to combine single human individuals, and after that families, then races, peoples and nations, into one great unity, the unity of mankind. Why this has to happen, we do not know; the work of Eros is precisely this.[1] These collections of men are to be libidinally bound to one another. Necessity alone, the advantages of work in common, will not hold them together. But man's natural aggressive instinct, the hostility of each against all and of all against each, opposes this programme of

1. [See *Beyond the Pleasure Principle* (1920*g*) passim, *P.F.L.*, **11**.]

civilization. This aggressive instinct is the derivative and the main representative of the death instinct which we have found alongside of Eros and which shares world-dominion with it. And now, I think, the meaning of the evolution of civilization is no longer obscure to us. It must present the struggle between Eros and Death, between the instinct of life and the instinct of destruction, as it works itself out in the human species. This struggle is what all life essentially consists of, and the evolution of civilization may therefore be simply described as the struggle for life of the human species.[1] And it is this battle of the giants that our nurse-maids try to appease with their lullaby about Heaven.[2]

1. And we may probably add more precisely, a struggle for life in the shape it was bound to assume after a certain event which still remains to be discovered.

2. ['*Eiapopeia vom Himmel.*' A quotation from Heine's poem *Deutschland*, Caput I.]

WHY do our relatives, the animals, not exhibit any such cultural struggle? We do not know. Very probably some of them – the bees, the ants, the termites – strove for thousands of years before they arrived at the State institutions, the distribution of functions and the restrictions on the individual, for which we admire them to-day. It is a mark of our present condition that we know from our own feelings that we should not think ourselves happy in any of these animal States or in any of the roles assigned in them to the individual. In the case of other animal species it may be that a temporary balance has been reached between the influences of their environment and the mutually contending instincts within them, and that thus a cessation of development has come about. It may be that in primitive man a fresh access of libido kindled a renewed burst of activity on the part of the destructive instinct. There are a great many questions here to which as yet there is no answer.

Another question concerns us more nearly. What means does civilization employ in order to inhibit the aggressiveness which opposes it, to make it harmless, to get rid of it, perhaps? We have already become acquainted with a few of these methods, but not yet with the one that appears to be the most important. This we can study in the history of the development of the individual. What happens in him to render his desire for aggression innocuous? Something very remarkable, which we should never have guessed and which is nevertheless quite obvious. His aggressiveness is introjected, internalized; it is, in point of fact, sent back to where it came from – that is, it is directed towards his own ego. There it is taken over by a portion of the ego, which sets itself over against the rest of the ego as super-ego, and which now, in the form of 'conscience', is ready to put into action against the ego the same harsh aggressiveness that the ego would have liked to satisfy upon other, extraneous individuals. The tension between the harsh super-ego and the ego that is subjected to it, is called by us the sense of guilt; it expresses itself as a need for punishment. Civilization, therefore, obtains mastery over the individual's dangerous desire for aggression by weakening and disarming it and by setting up an agency within him to watch over it, like a garrison in a conquered city.

As to the origin of the sense of guilt, the analyst has different views from other psychologists; but even he does not find it easy to give an account of it. To begin with, if we ask how a person comes to have a sense of guilt, we arrive at an answer which cannot be disputed: a person feels guilty (devout people would say 'sinful') when he has done something which he knows to be 'bad'. But then we notice how little this answer tells us. Perhaps, after some hesitation, we shall add that even when a person has not actually *done* the bad thing but has only recognized in himself an *intention* to do it, he may regard himself as guilty; and the question then arises of why the intention is regarded as equal to the deed. Both cases, however, presuppose that one had already recognized that what is bad is reprehensible, is something that must not be carried out. How is this judgement arrived at? We may reject the existence of an original, as it were natural, capacity to distinguish good from bad. What is bad is often not at all what is injurious or dangerous to the ego; on the contrary, it may be something which is desirable and enjoyable to the ego. Here, therefore, there is an extraneous influence at work, and it is this that decides what is to be called good or bad. Since a person's own feelings would not have led him along this path, he must have had a motive for submitting to this extraneous influence. Such a motive is easily discovered in his helplessness and his dependence on other people, and it can best be designated as fear of loss of love. If he loses the love of another person upon whom he is dependent, he also ceases to be protected from a variety of dangers. Above all, he is exposed to the danger that this stronger person will show his superiority in the form of punishment. At the beginning, therefore, what is bad is whatever causes one to be threatened with loss of love. For fear of that loss, one must avoid it. This, too, is the reason why it makes little difference whether one has already done the bad thing or only intends to do it. In either case the danger only sets in if and when the authority discovers it, and in either case the authority would behave in the same way.

This state of mind is called a 'bad conscience'; but actually it does not deserve this name, for at this stage the sense of guilt is clearly only a fear of loss of love, 'social' anxiety. In small children it can never be anything else, but in many adults, too, it has only changed to the extent that the place of the father or the two parents is taken by the larger human community. Consequently, such people habitually allow themselves to do any bad thing which promises them enjoyment, so long as they are sure that the authority will not know anything about it or cannot blame them for it; they are afraid only of being found out.[1] Present-day society has to reckon in general with this state of mind.

A great change takes place only when the authority is internalized through the establishment of a super-ego. The phenomena of conscience then reach a higher stage. Actually, it is not until now that we should speak of conscience or a sense of guilt.[2] At this point, too, the fear of being found out comes to an end; the distinction, moreover, between doing something bad and wishing to do it disappears entirely, since nothing can be hidden from the super-ego, not even thoughts. It is true that the seriousness of the situation from a real point of view has passed away, for the new authority, the super-ego, has no motive that we know of for ill-treating the ego, with which it is intimately bound up; but genetic influence, which leads to the survival of what is past and has been surmounted, makes

1. This reminds one of Rousseau's famous mandarin. [The problem raised by Rousseau had been quoted in full in Freud's paper on 'Our Attitude towards Death' (1915b), p. 87 above.]

2. Everyone of discernment will understand and take into account the fact that in this summary description we have sharply delimited events which in reality occur by gradual transitions, and that it is not merely a question of the *existence* of a super-ego but of its relative strength and sphere of influence. All that has been said above about conscience and guilt is, moreover, common knowledge and almost undisputed.

itself felt in the fact that fundamentally things remain as they were at the beginning. The super-ego torments the sinful ego with the same feeling of anxiety and is on the watch for opportunities of getting it punished by the external world.

At this second stage of development, the conscience exhibits a peculiarity which was absent from the first stage and which is no longer easy to account for. For the more virtuous a man is, the more severe and distrustful is its behaviour, so that ultimately it is precisely those people who have carried saintliness[1] furthest who reproach themselves with the worst sinfulness. This means that virtue forfeits some part of its promised reward; the docile and continent ego does not enjoy the trust of its mentor, and strives in vain, it would seem, to acquire it. The objection will at once be made that these difficulties are artificial ones, and it will be said that a stricter and more vigilant conscience is precisely the hallmark of a moral man. Moreover, when saints call themselves sinners, they are not so wrong, considering the temptations to instinctual satisfaction to which they are exposed in a specially high degree – since, as is well known, temptations are merely increased by constant frustration, whereas an occasional satisfaction of them causes them to diminish, at least for the time being. The field of ethics, which is so full of problems, presents us with another fact: namely that ill-luck – that is, external frustration – so greatly enhances the power of the conscience in the super-ego. As long as things go well with a man, his conscience is lenient and lets the ego do all sorts of things; but when misfortune befalls him, he searches his soul, acknowledges his sinfulness, heightens the demands of his conscience, imposes abstinences on himself and punishes himself with penances.[2] Whole peoples have behaved

1. ['*Heiligkeit*.' The same term, used in the different sense of 'sacredness', is discussed by Freud in some other passages. Cf. the paper on 'civilized' sexual morality (1908*d*), p. 39 above. Cf. also *P.F.L.*, **13**, 367.]

2. This enhancing of morality as a consequence of ill-luck has been illustrated by Mark Twain in a delightful little story, *The First Melon I ever Stole*. This first melon happened to be unripe. I heard Mark Twain tell the story himself in one of his public readings. After he had given out the title, he stopped and asked himself as though he was in doubt: '*Was* it the first?'

in this way, and still do. This, however, is easily explained by the original infantile stage of conscience, which, as we see, is not given up after the introjection into the super-ego, but persists alongside of it and behind it. Fate is regarded as a substitute for the parental agency. If a man is unfortunate it means that he is no longer loved by this highest power; and, threatened by such a loss of love, he once more bows to the parental representative in his super-ego – a representative whom, in his days of good fortune, he was ready to neglect. This becomes especially clear where Fate is looked upon in the strictly religious sense of being nothing else than an expression of the Divine Will. The people of Israel had believed themselves to be the favourite child of God, and when the great Father caused misfortune after misfortune to rain down upon this people of his, they were never shaken in their belief in his relationship to them or questioned his power or righteousness. Instead, they produced the prophets, who held up their sinfulness before them; and out of their sense of guilt they created the over-strict commandments of their priestly religion.[1] It is remarkable how differently a primitive man behaves. If he has met with a misfortune, he does not throw the blame on himself but on his fetish, which has obviously not done its duty, and he gives it a thrashing instead of punishing himself.

Thus we know of two origins of the sense of guilt: one arising from fear of an authority, and the other, later on, arising from fear of the super-ego. The first insists upon a renunciation of instinctual satisfactions; the second, as well as doing this, presses for punishment, since the continuance of the forbidden wishes cannot be concealed from the super-ego. We have also learned how the severity of the super-ego – the demands of conscience –

With this, everything had been said. The first melon was evidently not the only one. [This last sentence was added in 1931. – In a letter to Fliess of 9 February 1898, Freud reported that he had attended a reading by Mark Twain a few days earlier. (Freud, 1950a, Letter 83.)]

1. [A very much more extended account of the relations of the people of Israel to their God is to be found in Freud's *Moses and Monotheism* (1939a), P.F.L., **13**.]

is to be understood. It is simply a continuation of the severity of the external authority, to which it has succeeded and which it has in part replaced. We now see in what relationship the renunciation of instinct stands to the sense of guilt. Originally, renunciation of instinct was the result of fear of an external authority: one renounced one's satisfactions in order not to lose its love. If one has carried out this renunciation, one is, as it were, quits with the authority and no sense of guilt should remain. But with fear of the super-ego the case is different. Here, instinctual renunciation is not enough, for the wish persists and cannot be concealed from the super-ego. Thus, in spite of the renunciation that has been made, a sense of guilt comes about. This constitutes a great economic disadvantage in the erection of a super-ego, or, as we may put it, in the formation of a conscience. Instinctual renunciation now no longer has a completely liberating effect; virtuous continence is no longer rewarded with the assurance of love. A threatened external unhappiness – loss of love and punishment on the part of the external authority – has been exchanged for a permanent internal unhappiness, for the tension of the sense of guilt.

These interrelations are so complicated and at the same time so important that, at the risk of repeating myself, I shall approach them from yet another angle. The chronological sequence, then, would be as follows. First comes renunciation of instinct owing to fear of aggression by the *external* authority. (This is, of course, what fear of the loss of love amounts to, for love is a protection against this punitive aggression.) After that comes the erection of an *internal* authority, and renunciation of instinct owing to fear of it – owing to fear of conscience.[1] In this second situation bad intentions are equated with bad actions, and hence come a sense of guilt and a need for punishment. The aggressiveness of conscience keeps up the aggressiveness of the authority. So far things have no doubt been made clear; but where does this leave room for the reinforcing in-

1. ['*Gewissensangst.*' Some remarks on this term will be found in an Editor's footnote to Chapter VII of *Inhibitions, Symptoms and Anxiety* (1926d), *P.F.L.*, 10, 284 *n.*]

fluence of misfortune (of renunciation imposed from without) [p. 318], and for the extraordinary severity of conscience in the best and most tractable people [p. 317 f.]? We have already explained both these peculiarities of conscience, but we probably still have an impression that those explanations do not go to the bottom of the matter, and leave a residue still unexplained. And here at last an idea comes in which belongs entirely to psychoanalysis and which is foreign to people's ordinary way of thinking. This idea is of a sort which enables us to understand why the subject-matter was bound to seem so confused and obscure to us. For it tells us that conscience (or more correctly, the anxiety which later becomes conscience) is indeed the cause of instinctual renunciation to begin with, but that later the relationship is reversed. Every renunciation of instinct now becomes a dynamic source of conscience and every fresh renunciation increases the latter's severity and intolerance. If we could only bring it better into harmony with what we already know about the history of the origin of conscience, we should be tempted to defend the paradoxical statement that conscience is the result of instinctual renunciation, or that instinctual renunciation (imposed on us from without) creates conscience, which then demands further instinctual renunciation.

The contradiction between this statement and what we have previously said about the genesis of conscience is in point of fact not so very great, and we see a way of further reducing it. In order to make our exposition easier, let us take as our example the aggressive instinct, and let us assume that the renunciation in question is always a renunciation of aggression. (This, of course, is only to be taken as a temporary assumption.) The effect of instinctual renunciation on the conscience then is that every piece of aggression whose satisfaction the subject gives up is taken over by the super-ego and increases the latter's aggressiveness (against the ego). This does not harmonize well with the view that the original aggressiveness of conscience is a continuance of the severity of the external authority and therefore has nothing to do with renunciation. But the discrepancy is removed if we postulate a different derivation for this first instalment of the super-ego's aggressivity. A considerable amount of aggressiveness must be developed in the child against the authority which prevents him from having his first, but none the less his most important, satisfactions, whatever the kind of instinctual deprivation that is demanded of him may be; but he is obliged to renounce the satisfaction of this revengeful aggressiveness. He finds his way out of this economically difficult situation with the help of familiar mechanisms. By means of identification he takes the unattackable authority into himself. The authority now turns into his super-ego and enters into possession of all the aggressiveness which a child would have liked to exercise against it. The child's ego has to content itself with the unhappy role of the authority – the father – who has been thus degraded. Here, as so often, the [real] situation is reversed: 'If I were the father and you were the child, I should treat you badly.' The relationship between the super-ego and the ego is a return, distorted by a wish, of the real relationships between the ego, as yet undivided, and external object. That is typical, too. But the essential difference is that the original severity of the super-ego does not – or does not so much – represent the severity which one has experienced from it [the object], or which one attributes to it; it represents rather one's own aggressiveness towards it. If this is correct, we may assert truly that in the beginning conscience arises through the suppression of an aggressive impulse, and that it is subsequently reinforced by fresh suppressions of the same kind.

Which of these two views is correct? The earlier one, which genetically seemed so unassailable, or the newer one, which rounds off the theory in such a welcome fashion? Clearly, and by the evidence, too, of direct observations, both are justified. They do not contradict each other, and they even coincide at one point, for the child's revengeful aggressiveness will be in part determined by the amount of punitive aggression which he expects from his father. Experience shows, however, that the severity of the super-ego which a child develops in no way corresponds to the severity of treatment which he has himself met with.[1] The severity of the former seems to be independent of that of the latter. A child who has been very leniently brought up can acquire a very strict conscience. But it would also be wrong to exaggerate this independence; it is not difficult to convince oneself that severity of upbringing does also exert a strong influence on the formation of the child's super-ego. What it amounts to is that in the formation of the super-ego and the emergence of a conscience innate constitutional factors and influences from the real environment act in combination. This is not at all surprising; on the contrary, it is a universal aetiological condition for all such processes.[2]

It can also be asserted that when a child reacts to his first great instinctual frustrations with excessively strong aggressiveness and with a correspondingly severe super-ego, he is following a phylogenetic model and is going beyond the response that would be currently justified; for the father of prehistoric times was undoubtedly terrible, and an extreme amount of aggressiveness may be attributed to him. Thus, if one shifts over from individual to phylogenetic development, the differences between the two theories of the genesis of conscience are still further diminished. On the other hand, a new and important difference makes its appearance between these two

1. As has rightly been emphasized by Melanie Klein and by other, English, writers.

2. The two main types of pathogenic methods of upbringing – over-strictness and spoiling – have been accurately assessed by Franz Alexander in his book *The Psychoanalysis of the Total Personality* (1927) in connection with Aichhorn's study of delinquency [*Wayward Youth*, 1925]. The 'unduly lenient and indulgent father' is the cause of children's forming an over-severe super-ego, because, under the impression of the love that they receive, they have no other outlet for their aggressiveness but turning it inwards. In delinquent children, who have been brought up without love, the tension between ego and super-ego is lacking, and the whole of their aggressiveness can be directed outwards. Apart from a constitutional factor which may be supposed to be present, it can be said, therefore, that severe conscience arises from the joint operation of two factors: the frustration of instinct, which unleashes aggressiveness, and the experience of being loved, which turns the aggressiveness inwards and hands it over to the super-ego.

developmental processes. We cannot get away from the assumption that man's sense of guilt springs from the Oedipus complex and was acquired at the killing of the father by the brothers banded together.[1] On that occasion an act of aggression was not suppressed but carried out; but it was the same act of aggression whose suppression in the child is supposed to be the source of his sense of guilt. At this point I should not be surprised if the reader were to exclaim angrily: 'So it makes no difference whether one kills one's father or not – one gets a feeling of guilt in either case! We may take leave to raise a few doubts here. Either it is not true that the sense of guilt comes from suppressed aggressiveness, or else the whole story of the killing of the father is a fiction and the children of primaeval man did not kill their fathers any more often than children do nowadays. Besides, if it is not fiction but a plausible piece of history, it would be a case of something happening which everyone expects to happen – namely, of a person feeling guilty because he really has done something which cannot be justified. And of this event, which is after all an everyday occurrence, psychoanalysis has not yet given any explanation.'

That is true, and we must make good the omission. Nor is there any great secret about the matter. When one has a sense of guilt after having committed a misdeed, and because of it, the feeling should more properly be called *remorse*. It relates only to a deed that has been done, and, of course, it presupposes that a *conscience* – the readiness to feel guilty – was already in existence before the deed took place. Remorse of this sort can, therefore, never help us to discover the origin of conscience and of the sense of guilt in general. What happens in these everyday cases is usually this: an instinctual need acquires the strength to achieve satisfaction in spite of the conscience, which is, after all, limited in its strength; and with the natural weakening of the need owing to its having been satisfied, the former balance of power is restored, Psychoanalysis is thus justified in excluding from the present discussion the case of

1. [*Totem and Taboo* (1912–13), Essay IV (5), *P.F.L.*, **13**, 204.]

a sense of guilt due to remorse, however frequently such cases occur and however great their practical importance.

But if the human sense of guilt goes back to the killing of the primal father, that was after all a case of 'remorse'. Are we to assume that [at that time] a conscience and a sense of guilt were not, as we have presupposed, in existence before the deed? If not, where, in this case, did the remorse come from? There is no doubt that this case should explain the secret of the sense of guilt to us and put an end to our difficulties. And I believe it does. This remorse was the result of the primordial ambivalence of feeling towards the father. His sons hated him, but they loved him, too. After their hatred had been satisfied by their act of aggression, their love came to the fore in their remorse for the deed. It set up the super-ego by identification with the father; it gave that agency the father's power, as though as a punishment for the deed of aggression they had carried out against him, and it created the restrictions which were intended to prevent a repetition of the deed. And since the inclination to aggressiveness against the father was repeated in the following generations, the sense of guilt, too, persisted, and it was reinforced once more by every piece of aggressiveness that was suppressed and carried over to the super-ego. Now, I think, we can at last grasp two things perfectly clearly: the part played by love in the origin of conscience and the fatal inevitability of the sense of guilt. Whether one has killed one's father or has abstained from doing so is not really the decisive thing. One is bound to feel guilty in either case, for the sense of guilt is an expression of the conflict due to ambivalence, of the eternal struggle between Eros and the instinct of destruction or death. This conflict is set going as soon as men are faced with the task of living together. So long as the community assumes no other form than that of the family, the conflict is bound to express itself in the Oedipus complex, to establish the conscience and to create the first sense of guilt. When an attempt is made to widen the community, the same conflict is continued in forms which are dependent on the past; and it is strengthened and results in a further intensification of the sense of guilt. Since civilization obeys an internal erotic impulsion which causes human beings to unite in a closely-knit group, it can only achieve this aim through an ever-increasing reinforcement of the sense of guilt. What began in relation to the father is completed in relation to the group. If civilization is a necessary course of development from the family to humanity as a whole, then – as a result of the inborn conflict arising from ambivalence, of the eternal struggle between the trends of love and death – there is inextricably bound up with it an increase of the sense of guilt, which will perhaps reach heights that the individual finds hard to tolerate. One is reminded of the great poet's moving arraignment of the 'Heavenly Powers':

> Ihr führt in's Leben uns hinein.
> Ihr lasst den Armen schuldig werden,
> Dann überlasst Ihr ihn der Pein,
> Denn jede Schuld rächt sich auf Erden.[1]

And we may well heave a sigh of relief at the thought that it is nevertheless vouchsafed to a few to salvage without effort from the whirlpool of their own feelings the deepest truths, towards which the rest of us have to find our way through tormenting uncertainty and with restless groping.

1. One of the Harp-player's songs in Goethe's *Wilhelm Meister*.
   [To earth, this weary earth, ye bring us
   To guilt ye let us heedless go,
   Then leave repentance fierce to wring us:
   A moment's guilt, an age of woe!
                                        Carlyle's translation.]

VIII

HAVING reached the end of his journey, the author must ask his readers' forgiveness for not having been a more skilful guide and for not having spared them empty stretches of road and troublesome *détours*. There is no doubt that it could have been done better. I will attempt, late in the day, to make some amends.

In the first place, I suspect that the reader has the impression that our discussions on the sense of guilt disrupt the framework of this essay: that they take up too much space, so that the rest of its subject-matter, with which they are not always closely connected, is pushed to one side. This may have spoilt the structure of my paper; but it corresponds faithfully to my intention to represent the sense of guilt as the most important problem in the development of civilization and to show that the price we pay for our advance in civilization is a loss of happiness through the heightening of the sense of guilt.[1] Anything that still sounds strange about this statement, which is the final conclusion of our investigation, can probably be traced to the quite peculiar relationship – as yet completely un-

---

1. 'Thus conscience does make cowards of us all ...' [*Hamlet*, Act III, Scene 1.]

That the education of young people at the present day conceals from them the part which sexuality will play in their lives is not the only reproach which we are obliged to make against it. Its other sin is that it does not prepare them for the aggressiveness of which they are destined to become the objects. In sending the young out into life with such a false psychological orientation, education is behaving as though one were to equip people starting on a Polar expedition with summer clothing and maps of the Italian Lakes. In this it becomes evident that a certain misuse is being made of ethical demands. The strictness of those demands would not do so much harm if education were to say: 'This is how men ought to be, in order to be happy and to make others happy; but you have to reckon on their not being like that.' Instead of this the young are made to believe that everyone else fulfils those ethical demands – that is, that everyone else is virtuous. It is on this that the demand is based that the young, too, shall become virtuous.

explained – which the sense of guilt has to our consciousness. In the common case of remorse, which we regard as normal, this feeling makes itself clearly enough perceptible to consciousness. Indeed, we are accustomed to speak of a 'consciousness of guilt' instead of a 'sense of guilt'.[1] Our study of the neuroses, to which, after all, we owe the most valuable pointers to an understanding of normal conditions, brings us up against some contradictions. In one of those affections, obsessional neurosis, the sense of guilt makes itself noisily heard in consciousness; it dominates the clinical picture and the patient's life as well, and it hardly allows anything else to appear alongside of it. But in most other cases and forms of neurosis it remains completely unconscious, without on that account producing any less important effects. Our patients do not believe us when we attribute an 'unconscious sense of guilt' to them. In order to make ourselves at all intelligible to them, we tell them of an unconscious need for punishment, in which the sense of guilt finds expression. But its connection with a particular form of neurosis must not be over-estimated. Even in obsessional neurosis there are types of patients who are not aware of their sense of guilt, or who only feel it as a tormenting uneasiness, a kind of anxiety, if they are prevented from carrying out certain actions. It ought to be possible eventually to understand these things; but as yet we cannot. Here perhaps we may be glad to have it pointed out that the sense of guilt is at bottom nothing else but a topographical variety of anxiety; in its later phases it coincides completely with *fear of the super-ego*. And the relations of anxiety to consciousness exhibit the same extraordinary variations. Anxiety is always present somewhere or other behind every symptom; but at one time it takes noisy possession of the whole of consciousness, while at another it conceals itself so completely that we are obliged to speak of unconscious anxiety or, if we want to have a clearer psycho-

1. ['*Schuldbewusstsein*' instead of '*Schuldgefühl*'. The second of these terms is the one which Freud has been using for the most part. They are synonyms apart from their literal meaning, and both are translated by the usual English 'sense of guilt' except on such special occasions as this.]

logical conscience, since anxiety is in the first instance simply a feeling,[1] of possibilities of anxiety. Consequently it is very conceivable that the sense of guilt produced by civilization is not perceived as such either, and remains to a large extent unconscious, or appears as a sort of *malaise*,[2] a dissatisfaction, for which people seek other motivations. Religions, at any rate, have never overlooked the part played in civilization by a sense of guilt. Furthermore – a point which I failed to appreciate elsewhere[3] – they claim to redeem mankind from this sense of guilt, which they call sin. From the manner in which, in Christianity, this redemption is achieved – by the sacrificial death of a single person, who in this manner takes upon himself a guilt that is common to everyone – we have been able to infer what the first occasion may have been on which this primal guilt, which was also the beginning of civilization, was acquired.[4]

Though it cannot be of great importance, it may not be superfluous to elucidate the meaning of a few words such as 'super-ego', 'conscience', 'sense of guilt', 'need for punishment' and 'remorse', which we have often, perhaps, used too loosely and interchangeably. They all relate to the same state of affairs, but denote different aspects of it. The super-ego is an agency which has been inferred by us, and conscience is a function which we ascribe, among other functions, to that agency. This function consists in keeping a watch over the actions and intentions of the ego and judging them, in exercising a censorship. The sense of guilt, the harshness of the super-ego, is thus the same thing as the severity of the conscience. It is the perception which the ego has of being watched over in this way, the assessment of the tension between its own strivings and the demands of the super-ego. The fear of this critical agency (a fear which is at the bottom of the whole relationship), the need for

---

1. [See Chapter VIII of *Inhibitions, Symptoms and Anxiety* (1926d), P.F.L., **10**, 288. – Feelings cannot properly be described as 'unconscious' (cf. *The Ego and the Id*, ibid., **11**, 361).]

2. ['*Unbehagen*': the word which appears in the title of this work.]

3. In *The Future of an Illusion* (1927c). [P. 183 ff. above.]

4. *Totem and Taboo* (1912–13). [Essay IV (6), P.F.L., **13**, 216–17.]

punishment, is an instinctual manifestation on the part of the ego, which has become masochistic under the influence of a sadistic super-ego; it is a portion, that is to say, of the instinct towards internal destruction present in the ego, employed for forming an erotic attachment to the super-ego. We ought not to speak of a conscience until a super-ego is demonstrably present. As to a sense of guilt, we must admit that it is in existence before the super-ego, and therefore before conscience, too. At that time it is the immediate expression of fear of the external authority, a recognition of the tension between the ego and that authority. It is the direct derivative of the conflict between the need for the authority's love and the urge towards instinctual satisfaction, whose inhibition produces the inclination to aggression. The superimposition of these two strata of the sense of guilt – one coming from fear of the *external* authority, the other from fear of the *internal* authority – has hampered our insight into the position of conscience in a number of ways. Remorse is a general term for the ego's reaction in a case of sense of guilt. It contains, in little altered form, the sensory material of the anxiety which is operating behind the sense of guilt; it is itself a punishment and can include the need for punishment. Thus remorse, too, can be older than conscience.

Nor will it do any harm if we once more review the contradictions which have for a while perplexed us during our inquiry. Thus, at one point the sense of guilt was the consequence of acts of aggression that had been abstained from; but at another point – and precisely at its historical beginning, the killing of the father – it was the consequence of an act of aggression that had been carried out [p. 324]. But a way out of this difficulty was found. For the institution of the internal authority, the super-ego, altered the situation radically. Before this, the sense of guilt coincided with remorse. (We may remark, incidentally, that the term 'remorse' should be reserved for the reaction after an act of aggression has actually been carried out.) After this, owing to the omniscience of the super-ego, the difference between an aggression intended and an aggression carried out lost its force. Henceforward a sense of guilt could be produced not only by an act of violence that is actually carried out (as all the world knows), but also by one that is merely intended (as psychoanalysis has discovered). Irrespectively of this alteration in the psychological situation, the conflict arising from ambivalence – the conflict between the two primal instincts – leaves the same result behind [p. 325]. We are tempted to look here for the solution of the problem of the varying relation in which the sense of guilt stands to consciousness. It might be thought that a sense of guilt arising from remorse for an evil *deed* must always be conscious, whereas a sense of guilt arising from the perception of an evil *impulse* may remain unconscious. But the answer is not so simple as that. Obsessional neurosis speaks energetically against it.

The second contradiction concerned the aggressive energy with which we suppose the super-ego to be endowed. According to one view, that energy merely carries on the punitive energy of the external authority and keeps it alive in the mind [p. 315]; while, according to another view, it consists, on the contrary, of one's own aggressive energy which has not been used and which one now directs against that inhibiting authority [p. 321]. The first view seemed to fit in better with the *history*, and the second with the *theory*, of the sense of guilt. Closer reflection has resolved this apparently irreconcilable contradiction almost too completely; what remained as the essential and common factor was that in each case we were dealing with an aggressiveness which had been displaced inwards. Clinical observation, moreover, allows us in fact to distinguish two sources for the aggressiveness which we attribute to the super-ego; one or the other of them exercises the stronger effect in any given case, but as a general rule they operate in unison.

This is, I think, the place at which to put forward for serious consideration a view which I have earlier recommended for provisional acceptance.[1] In the most recent analytic literature a predilection is shown for the idea that any kind of frustration, any thwarted instinctual satisfaction, results, or may result, in

1. [Cf. the 'temporary assumption' on p. 321 above.]

a heightening of the sense of guilt.[1] A great theoretical simplification will, I think, be achieved if we regard this as applying only to the *aggressive* instincts, and little will be found to contradict this assumption. For how are we to account, on dynamic and economic grounds, for an increase in the sense of guilt appearing in place of an unfulfilled *erotic* demand? This only seems possible in a round-about way – if we suppose, that is, that the prevention of an erotic satisfaction calls up a piece of aggressiveness against the person who has interfered with the satisfaction, and that this aggressiveness has itself to be suppressed in turn. But if this is so, it is after all only the aggressiveness which is transformed into a sense of guilt, by being suppressed and made over to the super-ego. I am convinced that many processes will admit of a simpler and clearer exposition if the findings of psychoanalysis with regard to the derivation of the sense of guilt are restricted to the aggressive instincts. Examination of the clinical material gives us no unequivocal answer here, because, as our hypothesis tells us, the two classes of instinct hardly ever appear in a pure form, isolated from each other; but an investigation of extreme cases would probably point in the direction I anticipate.

I am tempted to extract a first advantage from this more restricted view of the case by applying it to the process of repression. As we have learned, neurotic symptoms are, in their essence, substitutive satisfactions for unfulfilled sexual wishes. In the course of our analytic work we have discovered to our surprise that perhaps every neurosis conceals a quota of unconscious sense of guilt, which in its turn fortifies the symptoms by making use of them as a punishment. It now seems plausible to formulate the following proposition. When an instinctual trend undergoes repression, its libidinal elements are turned into symptoms, and its aggressive components into a sense of guilt. Even if this proposition is only an average approximation to the truth, it is worthy of our interest.

1. This view is taken in particular by Ernest Jones, Susan Isaacs and Melanie Klein; and also, I understand, by Reik and Alexander.

Some readers of this work may further have an impression that they have heard the formula of the struggle between Eros and the death instinct too often. It was alleged to characterize the process of civilization which mankind undergoes [p. 313] but it was also brought into connection with the development of the individual [p. 310], and, in addition, it was said to have revealed the secret of organic life in general [p. 309 f.]. We cannot, I think, avoid going into the relations of these three processes to one another. The repetition of the same formula is justified by the consideration that both the process of human civilization and of the development of the individual are also vital processes – which is to say that they must share in the most general characteristic of life. On the other hand, evidence of the presence of this general characteristic fails, for the very reason of its general nature, to help us to arrive at any differentiation [between the processes], so long as it is not narrowed down by special qualifications. We can only be satisfied, therefore, if we assert that the process of civilization is a modification which the vital process experiences under the influence of a task that is set it by Eros and instigated by Ananke – by the exigencies of reality; and that this task is one of uniting separate individuals into a community bound together by libidinal ties. When, however, we look at the relation between the process of human civilization and the developmental or educative process of individual human beings, we shall conclude without much hesitation that the two are very similar in nature, if not the very same process applied to different kinds of object. The process of the civilization of the human species is, of course, an abstraction of a higher order than is the development of the individual and it is therefore harder to apprehend in concrete terms, nor should we pursue analogies to an obsessional extreme; but in view of the similarity between the aims of the two processes – in the one case the integration of a separate individual into a human group, and in the other case the creation of a unified group out of many individuals – we cannot be surprised at the similarity between the means employed and the resultant phenomena.

In view of its exceptional importance, we must not long postpone the mention of one feature which distinguishes between the two processes. In the developmental process of the individual, the programme of the pleasure principle, which consists in finding the satisfaction of happiness, is retained as the main aim. Integration in, or adaptation to, a human community appears as a scarcely avoidable condition which must be fulfilled before this aim of happiness can be achieved. If it could be done without that condition, it would perhaps be preferable. To put it in other words, the development of the individual seems to us to be a product of the interaction between two urges, the urge towards happiness, which we usually call 'egoistic', and the urge towards union with others in the community, which we call 'altruistic'. Neither of these descriptions goes much below the surface. In the process of individual development, as we have said, the main accent falls mostly on the egoistic urge (or the urge towards happiness); while the other urge, which may be described as a 'cultural' one, is usually content with the role of imposing restrictions. But in the process of civilization things are different. Here by far the most important thing is the aim of creating a unity out of the individual human beings. It is true that the aim of happiness is still there, but it is pushed into the background. It almost seems as if the creation of a great human community would be most successful if no attention had to be paid to the happiness of the individual. The developmental process of the individual can thus be expected to have special features of its own which are not reproduced in the process of human civilization. It is only in so far as the first of these processes has union with the community as its aim that it need coincide with the second process.

Just as a planet revolves around a central body as well as rotating on its own axis, so the human individual takes part in the course of development of mankind at the same time as he pursues his own path in life. But to our dull eyes the play of forces in the heavens seems fixed in a never-changing order; in the field of organic life we can still see how the forces

334

contend with one another, and how the effects of the conflict are continually changing. So, also, the two urges, the one towards personal happiness and the other towards union with other human beings must struggle with each other in every individual; and so, also, the two processes of individual and of cultural development must stand in hostile opposition to each other and mutually dispute the ground. But this struggle between the individual and society is not a derivative of the contradiction – probably an irreconcilable one – between the primal instincts of Eros and death. It is a dispute within the economics of the libido, comparable to the contest concerning the distribution of libido between ego and objects; and it does admit of an eventual accommodation in the individual, as, it may be hoped, it will also do in the future of civilization, however much that civilization may oppress the life of the individual to-day.

The analogy between the process of civilization and the path of individual development may be extended in an important respect. It can be asserted that the community, too, evolves a super-ego under whose influence cultural development proceeds. It would be a tempting task for anyone who has a knowledge of human civilizations to follow out this analogy in detail. I will confine myself to bringing forward a few striking points. The super-ego of an epoch of civilization has an origin similar to that of an individual. It is based on the impression left behind by the personalities of great leaders – men of overwhelming force of mind or men in whom one of the human impulsions has found its strongest and purest, and therefore often its most one-sided, expression. In many instances the analogy goes still further, in that during their lifetime these figures were – often enough, even if not always – mocked and maltreated by others and even despatched in a cruel fashion. In the same way, indeed, the primal father did not attain divinity until long after he had met his death by violence. The most arresting example of this fateful conjunction is to be seen in the figure of Jesus Christ – if, indeed, that figure is not a part of mythology, which called it into being from an obscure memory of that primal event. Another point of agreement between the cultural and the individual super-ego is that the former, just like the latter, sets up strict ideal demands, disobedience to which is visited with 'fear of conscience' [p. 320]. Here, indeed, we come across the remarkable circumstance that the mental processes concerned are actually more familiar to us and more accessible to consciousness as they are seen in the group than they can be in the individual man. In him, when tension arises, it is only the aggressiveness of the super-ego which, in the form of reproaches, makes itself noisily heard; its actual demands often remain unconscious in the background. If we bring them to conscious knowledge, we find that they coincide with the precepts of the prevailing cultural super-ego. At this point the two processes, that of the cultural development of the group and that of the cultural development of the individual, are, as it were, always interlocked. For that reason some of the manifestations and properties of the super-ego can be more easily detected in its behaviour in the cultural community than in the separate individual.

The cultural super-ego has developed its ideals and set up its demands. Among the latter, those which deal with the relations of human beings to one another are comprised under the heading of ethics. People have at all times set the greatest value on ethics, as though they expected that it in particular would produce especially important results. And it does in fact deal with a subject which can easily be recognized as the sorest spot in every civilization. Ethics is thus to be regarded as a therapeutic attempt − as an endeavour to achieve, by means of a command of the super-ego, something which has so far not been achieved by means of any other cultural activities. As we already know, the problem before us is how to get rid of the greatest hindrance to civilization − namely, the constitutional inclination of human beings to be aggressive towards one another; and for that very reason we are especially interested in what is probably the most recent of the cultural commands of the super-ego, the commandment to love one's neighbour as oneself. [Cf. p. 299 ff. above.] In our research into, and therapy of, a neurosis, we are led to make two reproaches against the super-ego of the individual. In the severity of its commands and prohibitions it troubles itself too little about the happiness of the ego, in that it takes insufficient account of the resistances against obeying them – of the instinctual strength of the id [in the first place], and of the difficulties presented by the real external environment [in the second]. Consequently we are very often obliged, for therapeutic purposes, to oppose the super-ego, and we endeavour to lower its demands. Exactly the same objections can be made against the ethical demands of the cultural super-ego. It, too, does not trouble itself enough about the facts of the mental constitution of human beings. It issues a command and does not ask whether it is possible for people to obey it. On the contrary, it assumes that a man's ego is psychologically capable of anything that is required of it, that his ego has unlimited mastery over his id. This is a mistake; and even in what are known as normal people the id cannot be controlled beyond certain limits. If more is demanded of a man, a revolt will be produced in him or a neurosis, or he will be made unhappy. The commandment, 'Love thy neighbour as thyself', is the strongest defence against human aggressiveness and an excellent example of the unpsychological proceedings of the cultural super-ego. The commandment is impossible to fulfil; such an enormous inflation of love can only lower its value, not get rid of the difficulty. Civilization pays no attention to all this; it merely admonishes us that the harder it is to obey the precept the more meritorious it is to do so. But anyone who follows such a precept in present-day civilization only puts himself at a disadvantage *vis-à-vis* the person who disregards it. What a potent obstacle to civilization aggressiveness must be, if the defence against it can cause as much unhappiness as aggressiveness itself! 'Natural' ethics, as it is called, has nothing to offer here except the narcissistic satisfaction of being able to think oneself better than others. At this point the ethics based on religion introduces its promises of a better after-life. But so long as virtue is not rewarded here on earth, ethics will, I fancy, preach in vain. I too think it quite certain that a real change in the relations of human beings to possessions would be of more help in this direction than any ethical commands; but the recognition of this fact among socialists has been obscured and made useless for practical purposes by a fresh idealistic misconception of human nature. [Cf. p. 304 above.]

I believe the line of thought which seeks to trace in the phenomena of cultural development the part played by a super-ego promises still further discoveries. I hasten to come to a close. But there is one question which I can hardly evade. If the development of civilization has such a far-reaching similarity to the development of the individual and if it employs the same methods, may we not be justified in reaching the diagnosis that, under the influence of cultural urges, some civilizations, or some epochs of civilization – possibly the whole of mankind – have become 'neurotic'?[1] An analytic dissection of such neuroses might lead to therapeutic recommendations which could lay claim to great practical interest. I would not say that an attempt of this kind to carry psychoanalysis over to the cultural community was absurd or doomed to be fruitless. But we should have to be very cautious and not forget that, after all, we are only dealing with analogies and that it is dangerous, not only with men but also with concepts, to tear them from the sphere in which they have originated and been evolved. Moreover, the diagnosis of communal neuroses is faced with a special difficulty. In an individual neurosis we take as our starting-point the contrast that distinguishes the patient from his environment, which is assumed to be 'normal'. For a group all of whose members are affected by one and the same disorder no such background could exist; it would have to be found elsewhere. And as regards the therapeutic application of our knowledge, what would be the use of the most correct analysis of social neuroses, since no one possesses authority to impose such a therapy upon the group? But in spite of all these difficulties, we may expect that one day some-

---

1. [Cf. some remarks in *The Future of an Illusion* (1927c), p. 226 f. above.]

one will venture to embark upon a pathology of cultural communities.

For a wide variety of reasons, it is very far from my intention to express an opinion upon the value of human civilization. I have endeavoured to guard myself against the enthusiastic prejudice which holds that our civilization is the most precious thing that we possess or could acquire and that its path will necessarily lead to heights of unimagined perfection. I can at least listen without indignation to the critic who is of the opinion that when one surveys the aims of cultural endeavour and the means it employs, one is bound to come to the conclusion that the whole effort is not worth the trouble, and that the outcome of it can only be a state of affairs which the individual will be unable to tolerate. My impartiality is made all the easier to me by my knowing very little about all these things. One thing only do I know for certain and that is that man's judgements of value follow directly his wishes for happiness – that, accordingly, they are an attempt to support his illusions with arguments. I should find it very understandable if someone were to point out the obligatory nature of the course of human civilization and were to say, for instance, that the tendencies to a restriction of sexual life or to the institution of a humanitarian ideal at the expense of natural selection were developmental trends which cannot be averted or turned aside and to which it is best for us to yield as though they were necessities of nature. I know, too, the objection that can be made against this, to the effect that in the history of mankind, trends such as these, which were considered unsurmountable, have often been thrown aside and replaced by other trends. Thus I have not the courage to rise up before my fellow-men as a prophet, and I bow to their reproach that I can offer them no consolation: for at bottom that is what they are all demanding – the wildest revolutionaries no less passionately than the most virtuous believers.

The fateful question for the human species seems to me to be whether and to what extent their cultural development will succeed in mastering the disturbance of their communal life by the human instinct of aggression and self-destruction. It may be that in this respect precisely the present time deserves a special interest. Men have gained control over the forces of nature to such an extent that with their help they would have no difficulty in exterminating one another to the last man. They know this, and hence comes a large part of their current unrest, their unhappiness and their mood of anxiety. And now it is to be expected that the other of the two 'Heavenly Powers' [p. 326], eternal Eros, will make an effort to assert himself in the struggle with his equally immortal adversary. But who can foresee with what success and with what result?[1]

1. [The final sentence was added in 1931 – when the menace of Hitler was already beginning to be apparent.]

WHY WAR?
(1933 [1932])

(EINSTEIN AND FREUD)

EDITOR'S NOTE

WARUM KRIEG?

(A) GERMAN EDITIONS:

1933   Paris: Internationales Institut für Geistige Zusammen-
arbeit (Völkerbund).

1934   *Gesammelte Schriften*, **12**, 349–63. (With only a very brief
summary of Einstein's letter.)

1950   *Gesammelte Werke*, **16**, 13–27. (Reprint of above.)

(B) ENGLISH TRANSLATIONS:
Why War?

1933   Paris: International Institute of Intellectual Co-operation
(League of Nations). (Tr. Stuart Gilbert.)

1939   London: Peace Pledge Union. (Reprint of above.)

1950   *Collected Papers*, **5**, 273–87. (Omitting Einstein's letter.)
(Tr. James Strachey.)

1964   *Standard Edition*, **22**, 195–215. (Corrected version of 1950
translation, including Einstein's letter.)

The present edition is a reprint of the *Standard Edition* version.

Einstein's letter is included here by permission of his executors
and at their request is given in the original English version by
Stuart Gilbert. Part of the German text of Freud's letter was
published in *Psychoanalytische Bewegung*, **5** (1933), 207–16.

It was in 1931 that the International Institute of Intellectual
Co-operation was instructed by the Permanent Committee for
Literature and the Arts of the League of Nations to arrange
for exchanges of letters between representative intellectuals 'on

subjects calculated to serve the common interests of the League of Nations and of intellectual life', and to publish these letters periodically. Among the first to be approached by the Institute was Einstein and it was he who suggested Freud's name. Accordingly, in June 1932, the Secretary of the Institute wrote to Freud inviting his participation, to which he at once agreed. Einstein's letter reached him at the beginning of August and his reply was finished a month later. The correspondence was published in Paris by the Institute in March 1933, in German, French and English simultaneously. Its circulation was, however, forbidden in Germany.

Freud himself was not enthusiastic about the work, and wrote of it as a tedious and sterile discussion (Jones, 1957, 187). The two men were never at all intimate with each other and only met once, at the beginning of 1927, in the house of Freud's youngest son in Berlin. In a letter to Ferenczi describing the occasion, Freud wrote: 'He understands as much about psychology as I do about physics, so we had a very pleasant talk.' (Ibid., 139.) Some very friendly letters were exchanged between them in 1936 and 1939. (Ibid., 217–18 and 259.)

Freud had written on the subject of war before: in the first section ('The Disillusionment of War') of his paper 'Thoughts for the Times on War and Death' (1915b), produced soon after the beginning of the First World War (p. 61 ff. above). But though some of the considerations discussed in the present paper appear in the earlier one, they are more closely related to the thoughts expressed in his recent writings on sociological subjects – The Future of an Illusion (1927c) and Civilization and its Discontents (1930a). Particular interest attaches to some further development here of Freud's view of civilization as a 'process', which had been brought up by him at several points in the latter work (e.g. pp. 313 and 333 ff.). He also takes up once more the topic of the destructive instinct, of which he had given a first considerable account in Chapters V and VI of the same book, and to which he was to return in later writings. (Cf. the Editor's Introduction to Civilization and its Discontents, pp. 247–9 above.)

WHY WAR?

Caputh near Potsdam, 30 July 1932

Dear Professor Freud,

The proposal of the League of Nations and its International Institute of Intellectual Co-operation at Paris that I should invite a person, to be chosen by myself, to a frank exchange of views on any problem that I might select affords me a very welcome opportunity of conferring with you upon a question which, as things now are, seems the most insistent of all the problems civilization has to face. This is the problem: Is there any way of delivering mankind from the menace of war? It is common knowledge that, with the advance of modern science, this issue has come to mean a matter of life and death for civilization as we know it; nevertheless, for all the zeal displayed, every attempt at its solution has ended in a lamentable breakdown.

I believe, moreover, that those whose duty it is to tackle the problem professionally and practically are growing only too aware of their impotence to deal with it, and have now a very lively desire to learn the views of men who, absorbed in the pursuit of science, can see world-problems in the perspective distance lends. As for me, the normal objective of my thought affords no insight into the dark places of human will and feeling. Thus, in the inquiry now proposed, I can do little more than seek to clarify the question at issue and, clearing the ground of the more obvious solutions, enable you to bring the light of your far-reaching knowledge of man's instinctive life to bear upon the problem. There are certain psychological obstacles whose existence a layman in the mental sciences may dimly surmise, but whose interrelations and vagaries he is incompetent to fathom; you, I am convinced, will be able to

345

suggest educative methods, lying more or less outside the scope of politics, which will eliminate these obstacles.

As one immune from nationalist bias, I personally see a simple way of dealing with the superficial (i.e. administrative) aspect of the problem: the setting up, by international consent, of a legislative and judicial body to settle every conflict arising between nations. Each nation would undertake to abide by the orders issued by this legislative body, to invoke its decision in every dispute, to accept its judgements unreservedly and to carry out every measure the tribunal deems necessary for the execution of its decrees. But here, at the outset, I come up against a difficulty; a tribunal is a human institution which, in proportion as the power at its disposal is inadequate to enforce its verdicts, is all the more prone to suffer these to be deflected by extrajudicial pressure. This is a fact with which we have to reckon; law and might inevitably go hand in hand, and juridical decisions approach more nearly the ideal justice demanded by the community (in whose name and interests these verdicts are pronounced) in so far as the community has effective power to compel respect of its juridical ideal. But at present we are far from possessing any supranational organization competent to render verdicts of incontestable authority and enforce absolute submission to the execution of its verdicts. Thus I am led to my first axiom: the quest of international security involves the unconditional surrender by every nation, in a certain measure, of its liberty of action, its sovereignty that is to say, and it is clear beyond all doubt that no other road can lead to such security.

The ill-success, despite their obvious sincerity, of all the efforts made during the last decade to reach this goal leaves us no room to doubt that strong psychological factors are at work, which paralyse these efforts. Some of these factors are not far to seek. The craving for power which characterizes the governing class in every nation is hostile to any limitation of the national sovereignty. This political power-hunger is wont to batten on the activities of another group, whose aspirations are on purely mercenary, economic lines. I have specially in mind that small but determined group, active in every nation, composed of individuals who, indifferent to social considerations and restraints, regard warfare, the manufacture and sale of arms, simply as an occasion to advance their personal interests and enlarge their personal authority.

But recognition of this obvious fact is merely the first step towards an appreciation of the actual state of affairs. Another question follows hard upon it: How is it possible for this small clique to bend the will of the majority, who stand to lose and suffer by a state of war, to the service of their ambitions? (In speaking of the majority, I do not exclude soldiers of every rank who have chosen war as their profession, in the belief that they are serving to defend the highest interests of their race, and that attack is often the best method of defence.) An obvious answer to this question would seem to be that the minority, the ruling class at present, has the schools and press, usually the Church as well, under its thumb. This enables it to organize and sway the emotions of the masses, and make its tool of them.

Yet even this answer does not provide a complete solution. Another question arises from it: How is it these devices succeed so well in rousing men to such wild enthusiasm, even to sacrifice their lives? Only one answer is possible. Because man has within him a lust for hatred and destruction. In normal times this passion exists in a latent state, it emerges only in unusual circumstances; but it is a comparatively easy task to call it into play and raise it to the power of a collective psychosis. Here lies, perhaps, the crux of all the complex of factors we are considering, an enigma that only the expert in the lore of human instincts can resolve.

And so we come to our last question. Is it possible to control man's mental evolution so as to make him proof against the psychoses of hate and destructiveness? Here I am thinking by no means only of the so-called uncultured masses. Experience proves that it is rather the so-called 'Intelligentzia' that is most apt to yield to these disastrous collective suggestions, since the intellectual has no direct contact with life in the raw, but encounters it in its easiest synthetic form – upon the printed page.

To conclude: I have so far been speaking only of wars between nations; what are known as international conflicts. But I am well aware that the aggressive instinct operates under other forms and in other circumstances. (I am thinking of civil wars, for instance, due in earlier days to religious zeal, but nowadays to social factors; or, again, the persecution of racial minorities.) But my insistence on what is the most typical, most cruel and extravagant form of conflict between man and man was deliberate, for here we have the best occasion of discovering ways and means to render all armed conflicts impossible.

I know that in your writings we may find answers, explicit or implied, to all the issues of this urgent and absorbing problem. But it would be of the greatest service to us all were you to present the problem of world peace in the light of your most recent discoveries, for such a presentation well might blaze the trail for new and fruitful modes of action.

Yours very sincerely,
A. EINSTEIN

Dear Professor Einstein,

When I heard that you intended to invite me to an exchange of views on some subject that interested you and that seemed to deserve the interest of others besides yourself, I readily agreed. I expected you to choose a problem on the frontiers of what is knowable to-day, a problem to which each of us, a physicist and a psychologist, might have our own particular angle of approach and where we might come together from different directions upon the same ground. You have taken me by surprise, however, by posing the question of what can be done to protect mankind from the curse of war.[1] I was scared at first by the thought of my – I had almost written 'our' – incapacity for dealing with what seemed to be a practical problem, a concern for statesmen. But I then realized that you had raised the question not as a natural scientist and physicist but as a philanthropist: you were following the promptings of the League of Nations just as Fridtjof Nansen, the polar explorer, took on the work of bringing help to the starving and homeless victims of the World War. I reflected, moreover, that I was not being asked to make practical proposals but only to set out the problem of avoiding war as it appears to a psychological observer. Here again you yourself have said almost all there is to say on the subject. But though you have taken the wind out of my sails I shall be glad to follow in your wake and content myself with confirming all you have said by amplifying it to the best of my knowledge – or conjecture.

You begin with the relation between Right and Might.[2] There can be no doubt that that is the correct starting-point

1. ['Das Verhängnis des Krieges.' Freud quotes Einstein's actual words, which are, however, translated differently on p. 345 above.]

2. [In the original the words 'Recht' and 'Macht' are used throughout Freud's letter and in Einstein's. It has unfortunately been necessary to sacrifice this stylistic unity in the translation. 'Recht' has been rendered indifferently by 'right', 'law' and 'justice'; and 'Macht' by 'might', 'force' and 'power'.]

for our investigation. But may I replace the word 'might' by the balder and harsher word 'violence'? To-day right and violence appear to us as antitheses. It can easily be shown, however, that the one has developed out of the other; and, if we go back to the earliest beginnings and see how that first came about, the problem is easily solved. You must forgive me if in what follows I go over familiar and commonly accepted ground as though it were new, but the thread of my argument requires it.

It is a general principle, then, that conflicts of interest between men are settled by the use of violence. This is true of the whole animal kingdom, from which men have no business to exclude themselves. In the case of men, no doubt, conflicts of *opinion* occur as well which may reach the highest pitch of abstraction and which seem to demand some other technique for their settlement. That, however, is a later complication. To begin with, in a small human horde,[1] it was superior muscular strength which decided who owned things or whose will should prevail. Muscular strength was soon supplemented and replaced by the use of tools: the winner was the one who had the better weapons or who used them the more skilfully. From the moment at which weapons were introduced, intellectual superiority already began to replace brute muscular strength; but the final purpose of the fight remained the same – one side or the other was to be compelled to abandon his claim or his objection by the damage inflicted on him and by the crippling of his strength. That purpose was most completely achieved if the victor's violence eliminated his opponent permanently – that is to say, killed him. This had two advantages: he could not renew his opposition and his fate deterred others from following his example. In addition to this, killing an enemy satisfied an instinctual inclination which I shall have to mention later. The intention to kill might be countered by a reflection that the enemy could be employed in performing useful services if he were left alive in an intimidated condition. In that case the victor's violence was content with subjugating

1. [Freud uses the term 'horde' to mean comparatively small groups.]

him instead of killing him. This was a first beginning of the idea of sparing an enemy's life, but thereafter the victor had to reckon with his defeated opponent's lurking thirst for revenge and sacrificed some of his own security.

Such, then, was the original state of things: domination by whoever had the greater might – domination by brute violence or by violence supported by intellect. As we know, this régime was altered in the course of evolution. There was a path that led from violence to right or law. What was that path? It is my belief that there was only one: the path which led by way of the fact that the superior strength of a single individual could be rivalled by the union of several weak ones. *'L'union fait la force.'* Violence could be broken by union, and the power of those who were united now represented law in contrast to the violence of the single individual. Thus we see that right is the might of a community. It is still violence, ready to be directed against any individual who resists it; it works by the same methods and follows the same purposes. The only real difference lies in the fact that what prevails is no longer the violence of an individual but that of a community. But in order that the transition from violence to this new right or justice may be effected, one psychological condition must be fulfilled. The union of the majority must be a stable and lasting one. If it were only brought about for the purpose of combating a single dominant individual and were dissolved after his defeat, nothing would have been accomplished. The next person who thought himself superior in strength would once more seek to set up a dominion by violence and the game would be repeated *ad infinitum*. The community must be maintained permanently, must be organized, must draw up regulations to anticipate the risk of rebellion and must institute authorities to see that those regulations – the laws – are respected and to superintend the execution of legal acts of violence. The recognition of a community of interests such as these leads to the growth of emotional ties between the members of a united group of people – communal feelings which are the true source of its strength.

★

Here, I believe, we already have all the essentials: violence overcome by the transference of power to a larger unity, which is held together by emotional ties between its members. What remains to be said is no more than an expansion and a repetition of this.

The situation is simple so long as the community consists only of a number of equally strong individuals. The laws of such an association will determine the extent to which, if the security of communal life is to be guaranteed, each individual must surrender his personal liberty to turn his strength to violent uses. But a state of rest of that kind is only theoretically conceivable. In actuality the position is complicated by the fact that from its very beginning the community comprises elements of unequal strength – men and women, parents and children – and soon, as a result of war and conquest, it also comes to include victors and vanquished, who turn into masters and slaves. The justice of the community then becomes an expression of the unequal degrees of power obtaining within it; the laws are made by and for the ruling members and find little room for the rights of those in subjection. From that time forward there are two factors at work in the community which are sources of unrest over matters of law but tend at the same time to a further growth of law. First, attempts are made by certain of the rulers to set themselves above the prohibitions which apply to everyone – they seek, that is, to go back from a dominion of law to a dominion of violence. Secondly, the oppressed members of the group make constant efforts to obtain more power and to have any changes that are brought about in that direction recognized in the laws – they press forward, that is, from unequal justice to equal justice for all. This second tendency becomes especially important if a real shift of power occurs within a community, as may happen as a result of a number of historical factors. In that case right may gradually adapt itself to the new distribution of power; or, as is more frequent, the ruling class is unwilling to recognize the change, and rebellion and civil war follow, with a temporary suspension of law and new attempts at a solution by violence, ending in the establishment of a fresh rule of law. There is yet another source from which modifications of law may arise, and one of which the expression is invariably peaceful: it lies in the cultural transformation of the members of the community. This, however, belongs properly in another connection and must be considered later. [P. 360.]

Thus we see that the violent solution of conflicts of interest is not avoided even inside a community. But the everyday necessities and common concerns that are inevitable where people live together in one place tend to bring such struggles to a swift conclusion and under such conditions there is an increasing probability that a peaceful solution will be found. Yet a glance at the history of the human race reveals an endless series of conflicts between one community and another or several others, between larger and smaller units – between cities, provinces, races, nations, empires – which have almost always been settled by force of arms. Wars of this kind end either in the spoliation or in the complete overthrow and conquest of one of the parties. It is impossible to make any sweeping judgement upon war of conquest. Some, such as those waged by the Mongols and Turks, have brought nothing but evil. Others, on the contrary, have contributed to the transformation of violence into law by establishing larger units within which the use of violence was made impossible and in which a fresh system of law led to the solution of conflicts. In this way the conquests of the Romans gave the countries round the Mediterranean the priceless *pax Romana*, and the greed of the French kings to extend their dominions created a peacefully united and flourishing France. Paradoxical as it may sound, it must be admitted that war might be a far from inappropriate means of establishing the eagerly desired reign of 'everlasting' peace, since it is in a position to create the large units within which a powerful central government makes further wars impossible. Nevertheless it fails in this purpose, for the results of conquest are as a rule short-lived: the newly created units fall apart once again, usually owing to a lack of cohesion between the portions that have been united by violence.

Hitherto, moreover, the unifications created by conquest, though of considerable extent, have only been *partial*, and the conflicts between these have called out more than ever for violent solution. Thus the result of all these warlike efforts has only been that the human race has exchanged numerous, and indeed unending, minor wars for wars on a grand scale that are rare but all the more destructive.

If we turn to our own times, we arrive at the same conclusion which you have reached by a shorter path. Wars will only be prevented with certainty if mankind unites in setting up a central authority to which the right of giving judgement upon all conflicts of interest shall be handed over. There are clearly two separate requirements involved in this: the creation of a supreme agency and its endowment with the necessary power. One without the other would be useless. The League of Nations is designed as an agency of this kind, but the second condition has not been fulfilled: the League of Nations has no power of its own and can only acquire it if the members of the new union, the separate States, are ready to resign it. And at the moment there seems very little prospect of this. The institution of the League of Nations would, however, be wholly unintelligible if one ignored the fact that here was a bold attempt such as has seldom (perhaps, indeed, never on such a scale) been made before. It is an attempt to base upon an appeal to certain idealistic attitudes of mind the authority (that is, the coercive influence) which otherwise rests on the possession of power. We have seen [p. 351] that a community is held together by two things: the compelling force of violence and the emotional ties (identifications is the technical name) between its members. If one of the factors is absent, the community may possibly be held together by the other. The ideas that are appealed to can, of course, only have any significance if they give expression to important affinities between the members and the question arises of how much strength such ideas can exert. History teaches us that they have been to some extent effective. For instance, the Panhellenic idea, the sense of being superior to the surrounding barbarians – an idea which was so powerfully expressed in the Amphictyonic Council, the Oracles and the Games – was sufficiently strong to mitigate the customs of war among Greeks, though evidently not sufficiently strong to prevent warlike disputes between the different sections of the Greek nation or even to restrain a city or confederation of cities from allying itself with the Persian foe in order to gain an advantage over a rival. The community of feeling among Christians, powerful though it was, was equally unable at the time of the Renaissance to deter Christian States, whether large or small, from seeking the Sultan's aid in their wars with one another. Nor does any idea exist to-day which could be expected to exert a unifying authority of the sort. Indeed it is all too clear that the national ideals by which nations are at present swayed operate in a contrary direction. Some people are inclined to prophesy that it will not be possible to make an end of war until Communist ways of thinking have found universal acceptance. But that aim is in any case a very remote one to-day, and perhaps it could only be reached after the most fearful civil wars. Thus the attempt to replace actual force by the force of ideas seems at present to be doomed to failure. We shall be making a false calculation if we disregard the fact that law was originally brute violence and that even to-day it cannot do without the support of violence.

I can now proceed to add a gloss to another of your remarks. You express astonishment at the fact that it is so easy to make men enthusiastic about a war and add your suspicions [p. 347] that there is something at work in them – an instinct for hatred and destruction – which goes halfway to meet the efforts of the warmongers. Once again, I can only express my entire agreement. We believe in the existence of an instinct of that kind and have in fact been occupied during the last few years in studying its manifestations. Will you allow me to take this opportunity of putting before you a portion of the theory of the instincts which, after much tentative groping and many fluctuations of opinion, has been reached by workers in the field of psychoanalysis?

According to our hypothesis human instincts are of only two kinds: those which seek to preserve and unite – which we call 'erotic', exactly in the sense in which Plato uses the word 'Eros' in his *Symposium*, or 'sexual', with a deliberate extension of the popular conception of 'sexuality' – and those which seek to destroy and kill and which we group together as the aggressive or destructive instinct. As you see, this is in fact no more than a theoretical clarification of the universally familiar opposition between Love and Hate which may perhaps have some fundamental relation to the polarity of attraction and repulsion that plays a part in your own field of knowledge. But we must not be too hasty in introducing ethical judgements of good and evil. Neither of these instincts is any less essential than the other; the phenomena of life arise from the concurrent or mutually opposing action of both. Now it seems as though an instinct of the one sort can scarcely ever operate in isolation; it is always accompanied – or, as we say, alloyed – with a certain quota from the other side, which modifies its aim or is, in some cases, what enables it to achieve that aim. Thus, for instance, the instinct of self-preservation is certainly of an erotic kind, but it must nevertheless have aggressiveness at its disposal if it is to fulfil its purpose. So, too, the instinct of love, when it is directed towards an object, stands in need of some contribution from the instinct for mastery if it is in any way to obtain possession of that object. The difficulty of isolating the two classes of instinct in their actual manifestations is indeed what has so long prevented us from recognizing them.

If you will follow me a little further, you will see that human actions are subject to another complication of a different kind. It is very rarely that an action is the work of a *single* instinctual impulse (which must in itself be compounded of Eros and destructiveness). In order to make an action possible there must be as a rule a combination of such compounded motives. This was perceived long ago by a specialist in your own subject, a Professor G. C. Lichtenberg who taught physics at Göttingen during our classical age – though perhaps he was even more remarkable as a psychologist than as a physicist.[1] He invented a Compass of Motives, for he wrote: 'The motives that lead us to do anything might be arranged like the thirty-two winds and might be given names in a familiar way: for instance, "bread-bread-fame" or "fame-fame-bread".' So that when human beings are incited to war they may have a whole number of motives for assenting – some noble and some base, some which are openly declared and others which are never mentioned. There is no need to enumerate them all. A lust for aggression and destruction is certainly among them: the countless cruelties in history and in our everyday lives vouch for its existence and its strength. The satisfaction of these destructive impulses is of course facilitated by their admixture with others of an erotic and idealistic kind. When we read of the atrocities of the past, it sometimes seems as though the idealistic motives served only as an excuse for the destructive appetites; and sometimes – in the case, for instance, of the cruelties of the Inquisition – it seems as though the idealistic motives had pushed themselves forward in consciousness, while the destructive ones lent them an unconscious reinforcement. Both may be true.

I fear I may be abusing your interest, which is after all concerned with the prevention of war and not with our theories. Nevertheless I should like to linger for a moment over our destructive instinct, whose popularity is by no means equal to its importance. As a result of a little speculation, we have come to suppose that this instinct is at work in every living creature and is striving to bring it to ruin and to reduce life to its original condition of inanimate matter. Thus it quite seriously deserves to be called a death instinct, while the erotic instincts represent the effort to live. The death instinct turns into the destructive instinct when, with the help of special organs, it is directed outwards, on to objects. The organism preserves its own life, so to say, by destroying an extraneous one. Some portion of

1. [Georg Christoph Lichtenberg (1742–99) was a favourite author of Freud's. The present analogy had already been quoted in his book on jokes (1905c), *P.F.L.*, **6**, 127–8, in which a great number of Lichtenberg's epigrams will be found.]

the death instinct, however, remains operative *within* the organism, and we have sought to trace quite a number of normal and pathological phenomena to this internalization of the destructive instinct. We have even been guilty of the heresy of attributing the origin of conscience to this diversion inwards of aggressiveness. You will notice that it is by no means a trivial matter if this process is carried too far: it is positively unhealthy. On the other hand if these forces are turned to destruction in the external world, the organism will be relieved and the effect must be beneficial. This would serve as a biological justification for all the ugly and dangerous impulses against which we are struggling. It must be admitted that they stand nearer to Nature than does our resistance to them for which an explanation also needs to be found. It may perhaps seem to you as though our theories are a kind of mythology and, in the present case, not even an agreeable one. But does not every science come in the end to a kind of mythology like this? Cannot the same be said to-day of your own physics?

For our immediate purpose then, this much follows from what has been said: there is no use in trying to get rid of men's aggressive inclinations. We are told that in certain happy regions of the earth, where nature provides in abundance everything that man requires, there are races whose life is passed in tranquillity and who know neither coercion nor aggression. I can scarcely believe it and I should be glad to hear more of these fortunate beings. The Russian Communists, too, hope to be able to cause human aggressiveness to disappear by guaranteeing the satisfaction of all material needs and by establishing equality in other respects among all the members of the community. That, in my opinion, is an illusion. They themselves are armed to-day with the most scrupulous care and not the least important of the methods by which they keep their supporters together is hatred of everyone beyond their frontiers. In any case, as you yourself have remarked, there is no question of getting rid entirely of human aggressive impulses; it is enough to try to divert them to such an extent that they need not find expression in war.

Our mythological theory of instincts makes it easy for us to find a formula for *indirect* methods of combating war. If willingness to engage in war is an effect of the destructive instinct, the most obvious plan will be to bring Eros, its antagonist, into play against it. Anything that encourages the growth of emotional ties between men must operate against war. These ties may be of two kinds. In the first place they may be relations resembling those towards a loved object, though without having a sexual aim. There is no need for psychoanalysis to be ashamed to speak of love in this connection, for religion itself uses the same words: 'Thou shalt love thy neighbour as thyself.' This, however, is more easily said than done.[1] The second kind of emotional tie is by means of identification. Whatever leads men to share important interests produces this community of feeling, these identifications. And the structure of human society is to a large extent based on them.

A complaint which you make about the abuse of authority [p. 346] brings me to another suggestion for the indirect combating of the propensity to war. One instance of the innate and ineradicable inequality of men is their tendency to fall into the two classes of leaders and followers. The latter constitute the vast majority; they stand in need of an authority which will make decisions for them and to which they for the most part offer an unqualified submission. This suggests that more care should be taken than hitherto to educate an upper stratum of men with independent minds, not open to intimidation and eager in the pursuit of truth, whose business it would be to give direction to the dependent masses. It goes without saying that the encroachments made by the executive power of the State and the prohibition laid by the Church upon freedom of thought are far from propitious for the production of a class of this kind. The ideal condition of things would of course be a community of men who had subordinated their instinctual life to the dictatorship of reason. Nothing else could unite men

1. [Cf. the discussion of this in Chapter V of *Civilization and its Discontents* (1930*a*), p. 299 ff. above.]

so completely and so tenaciously, even if there were no emotional ties between them.[1] But in all probability that is a Utopian expectation. No doubt the other indirect methods of preventing war are more practicable, though they promise no rapid success. An unpleasant picture comes to one's mind of mills that grind so slowly that people may starve before they get their flour.

The result, as you see, is not very fruitful when an unworldly theoretician is called in to advise on an urgent practical problem. It is a better plan to devote oneself in every particular case to meeting the danger with whatever means lie to hand. I should like, however, to discuss one more question, which you do not mention in your letter but which specially interests me. Why do you and I and so many other people rebel so violently against war? Why do we not accept it as another of the many painful calamities of life? After all, it seems to be quite a natural thing, to have a good biological basis and in practice to be scarcely avoidable. There is no need to be shocked at my raising this question. For the purpose of an investigation such as this, one may perhaps be allowed to wear a mask of assumed detachment. The answer to my question will be that we react to war in this way because everyone has a right to his own life, because war puts an end to human lives that are full of hope, because it brings individual men into humiliating situations, because it compels them against their will to murder other men, and because it destroys precious material objects which have been produced by the labours of humanity. Other reasons besides might be given, such as that in its present-day form war is no longer an opportunity for achieving the old ideals of heroism and that owing to the perfection of instruments of destruction a future war might involve the extermination of one or perhaps both of the antagonists. All this is true, and so incontestably true that one can only feel astonished that the waging of war has not yet been unanimously repudiated. No doubt debate

1. [Cf. some remarks in Lecture 35 of the *New Introductory Lectures* (1933*a*), P.F.L., **2**, 207.]

is possible upon one or two of these points. It may be questioned whether a community ought not to have a right to dispose of individual lives; every war is not open to condemnation to an equal degree; so long as there exist countries and nations that are prepared for the ruthless destruction of others, those others must be armed for war. But I will not linger over any of these issues; they are not what you want to discuss with me, and I have something different in mind. It is my opinion that the main reason why we rebel against war is that we cannot help doing so. We are pacifists because we are obliged to be for organic reasons. And we then find no difficulty in producing arguments to justify our attitude.

No doubt this requires some explanation. My belief is this. For incalculable ages mankind has been passing through a process of evolution of culture. (Some people, I know, prefer to use the term 'civilization'.)[1] We owe to that process the best of what we have become, as well as a good part of what we suffer from. Though its causes and beginnings are obscure and its outcome uncertain, some of its characteristics are easy to perceive. It may perhaps be leading to the extinction of the human race, for in more than one way it impairs the sexual function; uncultivated races and backward strata of the population are already multiplying more rapidly than highly cultivated ones. The process is perhaps comparable to the domestication of certain species of animals and it is undoubtedly accompanied by physical alterations; but we are still unfamiliar with the notion that the evolution of civilization is an organic process of this kind.[2] The *psychical* modifications that go along with the process of civilization are striking and unambiguous. They consist in a progressive displacement of instinctual aims and a restriction of instinctual impulses. Sensations which were pleasurable to our ancestors have become indifferent or even intolerable to ourselves; there are organic grounds for the changes in our ethical and aesthetic ideals. Of the psychological characteristics of civilization two appear to be the most

1. [See p. 184 above.]
2. [Cf. the Editor's Note, p. 344 above.]

important: a strengthening of the intellect, which is beginning to govern instinctual life, and an internalization of the aggressive impulses, with all its consequent advantages and perils. Now war is in the crassest opposition to the psychical attitude imposed on us by the process of civilization, and for that reason we are bound to rebel against it; we simply cannot any longer put up with it. This is not merely an intellectual and emotional repudiation; we pacifists have a *constitutional* intolerance of war, an idiosyncrasy magnified, as it were, to the highest degree. It seems, indeed, as though the lowering of aesthetic standards in war plays a scarcely smaller part in our rebellion than do its cruelties.

And how long shall we have to wait before the rest of mankind become pacifists too? There is no telling. But it may not be Utopian to hope that these two factors, the cultural attitude and the justified dread of the consequences of a future war, may result within a measurable time in putting an end to the waging of war. By what paths or by what side-tracks this will come about we cannot guess. But one thing we *can* say: whatever fosters the growth of civilization works at the same time against war.[1]

I trust you will forgive me if what I have said has disappointed you, and I remain, with kindest regards,

Sincerely yours,

SIGM. FREUD

1. [The idea of a 'process of civilization' may be traced back to Freud's very early period. But he developed it still further. In rather different terms it figures prominently in Essay III, Part II (C), of *Moses and Monotheism* (1939*a*). Its two main characteristics (as illustrated in the religion of Moses derived from Akhenaten) are the same as those mentioned here – strengthening of intellectual life and renunciation of instinct.]

BIBLIOGRAPHY
AND AUTHOR INDEX

Titles of books and periodicals are in italics, titles of papers are in inverted commas. Abbreviations are in accordance with the *World List of Scientific Periodicals* (London, 1963–5). Further abbreviations used in this volume will be found in the List at the end of this bibliography. Numerals in bold type refer to volumes, ordinary numerals refer to pages. The figures in round brackets at the end of each entry indicate the page or pages of this volume on which the work in question is mentioned.

In the case of the Freud entries, only English translations are given. The initial dates are those of the German, or other, original publications. (The date of writing is added in square brackets where it differs from the latter.) The letters attached to the dates of publication are in accordance with the corresponding entries in the complete bibliography of Freud's writings included in Volume 24 of the *Standard Edition*. Details of the original publications, including the original German (or other) title, are given in the editorial introduction to each work included in the *Pelican Freud Library*.

For non-technical authors, and for technical authors where no specific work is mentioned, see the General Index.

ABRAHAM, K. (1912) 'Ansätze zur psychoanalytischen Erforschung und Behandlung des manisch-depressiven Irreseins und verwandter Zustände', *Zentbl. Psychoanal.*, **2**, 302. (165)
    [*Trans.:* 'Notes on the Psycho-Analytical Investigation and Treatment of Manic-Depressive Insanity and Allied Conditions', *Selected Papers*, London, 1927; New York, 1953, Chap. VI.]
  (1916) 'Untersuchungen über die früheste prägenitale Entwicklungsstufe der Libido', *Int. Z. ärztl. Psychoanal.*, **4**, 71. (135)
    [*Trans.:* 'The First Pregenital Stage of the Libido', *Selected Papers*, London, 1927; New York, 1953, Chap. XII.]
  (1965) With FREUD, S. *See* FREUD, S. (1965*a*)
AICHHORN, A. (1925) *Verwahrloste Jugend*, Vienna. (323)
    [*Trans.:* *Wayward Youth*, New York, 1935; London, 1936; revised reprint, London, 1951.]

ALEXANDER, F. (1927) *Die Psychoanalyse der Gesamtpersönlichkeit*, Vienna. (323)
[*Trans.*: *The Psychoanalysis of the Total Personality*, New York, 1930.]

ANDREAS-SALOMÉ, L., and FREUD, S. (1966) *See* FREUD, S. (1966*a*)

ATKINSON, J. J. (1903) *Primal Law*, London. Included in A. Lang's *Social Origins*, London. (289)

BEARD, G. M. (1881) *American Nervousness, Its Causes and Consequences*, New York. (36)
(1884) *Sexual Neurasthenia (Nervous Exhaustion), Its Hygiene, Causes, Symptoms and Treatment*, New York. (36)

BINSWANGER, O. L. (1896) *Die Pathologie und Therapie der Neurasthenie*, Jena. (36)

BLEULER, E. (1912) *Das autistische Denken*, Leipzig and Vienna. (96)
(1913) 'Der Sexualwiderstand', *Jb. psychoanalyt. psychopath. Forsch.*, **5**, 442. (296)

BRANDES, G. (1896) *William Shakespeare*, Paris, Leipzig and Munich. (280)

BREUER, J., and FREUD, S. (1893) *See* FREUD, S. (1893*a*)
(1895) *See* FREUD, S. (1895*d*)

BRUGEILLES, R. (1913) 'L'essence du phénomène social: la suggestion', *Rev. phil.*, **75**, 593. (116)

DALY, C. D. (1927) 'Hindumythologie und Kastrationskomplex', *Imago*, **13**, 145. (288)

EHRENFELS, C. VON (1907) *Sexualethik. Grenzfr. Nerv.- u. Seelenleb.*, No. 56, Wiesbaden. (33, 34)

EINSTEIN, A., and FREUD, S. (1933) *See* FREUD, S. (1933*b*)

ERB, W. (1893) *Über die wachsende Nervosität unserer Zeit*, Heidelberg. (35)

FEDERN, P. (1919) *Die vaterlose Gesellschaft*, Vienna. (128)
(1926) 'Einige Variationen des Ichgefühls', *Int. Z. Psychoanal.*, **12**, 263. (254)
[*Trans.*: 'Some Variations in Ego Feeling', *Ego Psychology and the Psychoses*, New York, 1952, 25.]
(1927) 'Narzissmus im Ichgefüge', *Int. Z. Psychoanal.*, **13**, 420. (254)
[*Trans.*: 'Narcissism in the Structure of the Ego', *Ego Psychology and the Psychoses*, New York, 1952, 38.]

FELSZEGHY, B. VON (1920) 'Panik und Pankomplex', *Imago*, **6**, 1. (127)

FERENCZI, S. (1909) 'Introjektion und Übertragung', *Jb. psychoanalyt. psychopath. Forsch.*, **1**, 422. (144, 159)
[*Trans.*: 'Introjection and Transference', *First Contributions to Psycho-Analysis*, London, 1952, Chap. II.]

(1913) 'Entwicklungsstufen des Wirklichkeitssinnes', *Int. Z. ärztl. Psychoanal.*, **1**, 124. (254)
[*Trans.*: 'Stages in the Development of the Sense of Reality', *First Contributions to Psycho-Analysis*, London, 1952, Chap. VIII.]

FREUD, M. (1957) *Glory Reflected*, London. (22)

FREUD, S. (1891b) *On Aphasia*, London and New York, 1953. (14, 24)

(1893a) With BREUER, J., 'On the Psychical Mechanism of Hysterical Phenomena: Preliminary Communication', in *Studies on Hysteria*, Standard Ed., **2**, 3; P.F.L., **3**, 53. (25, 37)

(1895b [1894]) 'On the Grounds for Detaching a Particular Syndrome from Neurasthenia under the Description "Anxiety Neurosis"', Standard Ed., **3**, 87; P.F.L., **10**, 31. (36, 37, 308)

(1895d) With BREUER, J., *Studies on Hysteria*, London, 1956; Standard Ed., **2**; P.F.L., **3**. (25, 159)

(1898a) 'Sexuality in the Aetiology of the Neuroses', Standard Ed., **3**, 261. (30, 46)

(1900a) *The Interpretation of Dreams*, London and New York, 1955; Standard Ed., **4–5**; P.F.L., **4**. (21, 25, 64, 74, 105, 197, 254)

(1901b) *The Psychopathology of Everyday Life*, Standard Ed., **6**; P.F.L., **5**. (21, 25, 228)

(1905c) *Jokes and their Relation to the Unconscious*, Standard Ed., **8**; P.F.L., **6**. (33, 51, 159, 234, 357)

(1905d) *Three Essays on the Theory of Sexuality*, London, 1962; Standard Ed., **7**, 125; P.F.L., **7**, 31 (25, 30, 40, 43, 68, 107, 121, 132, 135, 142, 171, 177, 246, 248, 271, 296)

(1905e [1901]) 'Fragment of an Analysis of a Case of Hysteria', Standard Ed., **7**, 3; P.F.L., **8**, 29. (136, 279, 297)

(1906a [1905]) 'My Views on the Part played by Sexuality in the Aetiology of the Neuroses', Standard Ed., **7**, 271; P.F.L., **10**, 71. (37)

(1906f) 'Contribution to a Questionnaire on Reading', Standard Ed., **9**, 245. (238)

FREUD, S. (*cont.*)

(1907*b*) 'Obsessive Actions and Religious Practices', *Standard Ed.*, 9, 116; *P.F.L.*, **13**, 27. (182, 227)

(1907*c*) 'The Sexual Enlightenment of Children', *Standard Ed.*, 9, 131; *P.F.L.*, **7**, 171. (48)

(1908*b*) 'Character and Anal Erotism', *Standard Ed.*, 9, 169; *P.F.L.*, **7**, 205. (279, 286)

(1908*d*) '"Civilized" Sexual Morality and Modern Nervous Illness', *Standard Ed.*, 9, 179; *P.F.L.*, **12**, 27. (59, 231, 246, 299)

(1908*e* [1907]) 'Creative Writers and Day-Dreaming', *Standard Ed.*, 9, 143; *P.F.L.*, **14**, 129. (193)

(1909*a* [1908]) 'Some General Remarks on Hysterical Attacks', *Standard Ed.*, 9, 229; *P.F.L.*, **10**, 95. (44)

(1909*b*) 'Analysis of a Phobia in a Five-Year-Old Boy', *Standard Ed.*, **10**, 3; *P.F.L.*, **8**, 165. (25, 248)

(1909*d*) 'Notes upon a Case of Obsessional Neurosis', *Standard Ed.*, **10**, 155; *P.F.L.*, **9**, 31. (51, 247)

(1910*a* [1909]) *Five Lectures on Psycho-Analysis*, *Standard Ed.*, **11**, 3; in *Two Short Accounts of Psycho-Analysis*, Penguin Books, Harmondsworth, 1962. (16, 25)

(1910*c*) *Leonardo da Vinci and a Memory of his Childhood*, *Standard Ed.*, **11**, 59; *P.F.L.*, **14**, 143. (138, 227)

(1911*b*) 'Formulations on the Two Principles of Mental Functioning', *Standard Ed.*, **12**, 215; *P.F.L.*, **11**, 29. (255, 268)

(1911*c* [1910]) 'Psycho-Analytic Notes on an Autobiographical Account of a Case of Paranoia (Dementia Paranoides)', *Standard Ed.*, **12**, 3; *P.F.L.*, **9**, 129. (25)

(1912*c*) 'Types of Onset of Neurosis', *Standard Ed.*, **12**, 229; *P.F.L.*, **10**, 115. (40)

(1912*d*) 'On the Universal Tendency to Debasement in the Sphere of Love', *Standard Ed.*, **11**, 179; *P.F.L.*, **7**, 243. (30, 142, 175, 247, 297)

(1912–13) *Totem and Taboo*, London, 1950; New York, 1952; *Standard Ed.*, **13**, 1; *P.F.L.*, **13**, 43. (25, 59, 81, 82, 84 ff., 94, 104, 107, 140, 154, 156, 158, 163, 168, 176, 181, 197, 202 ff., 225, 289, 324, 329)

(1914*c*) 'On Narcissism: An Introduction', *Standard Ed.*, **14**, 69; *P.F.L.*, **11**, 59. (94, 132, 134, 139, 140, 143, 162, 164, 204)

(1914*d*) 'On the History of the Psycho-Analytic Movement', *Standard Ed.*, **14**, 3; *P.F.L.*, **15**, 57. (25)

FREUD, S. (*cont.*)

(1915*b*) 'Thoughts for the Times on War and Death', *Standard Ed.*, **14**, 275; *P.F.L.*, **12**, 57. (30, 220, 317, 344)

(1915*c*) 'Instincts and their Vicissitudes', *Standard Ed.*, **14**, 111; *P.F.L.*, **11**, 105. (249, 254)

(1915*f*) 'A Case of Paranoia Running Counter to the Psycho-Analytic Theory of the Disease', *Standard Ed.*, **14**, 263; *P.F.L.*, **10**, 145. (298)

(1916*a*) 'On Transcience', *Standard Ed.*, **14**, 305; *P.F.L.*, **14**, 283. (59)

(1916–17 [1915–17]) *Introductory Lectures on Psycho-Analysis*, New York, 1966; London, 1971; *Standard Ed.*, **15–16**; *P.F.L.*, **1**. (26, 126, 151, 268)

(1917*d* [1915]) 'A Metapsychological Supplement to the Theory of Dreams', *Standard Ed.*, **14**, 219; *P.F.L.*, **11**, 223. (145)

(1917*e* [1915]) 'Mourning and Melancholia', *Standard Ed.*, **14**, 239; *P.F.L.*, **11**, 245. (94, 139, 162)

(1918*a* [1917]) 'The Taboo of Virginity', *Standard Ed.*, **11**, 193; *P.F.L.*, **7**, 261. (144, 305)

(1918*b* [1914]) 'From the History of an Infantile Neurosis', *Standard Ed.*, **17**, 3; *P.F.L.*, **9**, 225. (26)

(1919*h*) 'The Uncanny', *Standard Ed.*, **17**, 219; *P.F.L.*, **14**, 335. (157)

(1920*a*) 'The Psychogenesis of a Case of Female Homosexuality', *Standard Ed.*, **18**, 147; *P.F.L.*, **9**, 367. (138)

(1920*g*) *Beyond the Pleasure Principle*, London, 1961; *Standard Ed.*, **18**, 7; *P.F.L.*, **11**, 269. (26, 94, 131, 149, 249, 309, 311, 313)

(1921*c*) *Group Psychology and the Analysis of the Ego*, London and New York, 1959; *Standard Ed.*, **18**, 69; *P.F.L.*, **12**, 91. (26, 186, 227, 304, 305, 307, 308)

(1922*b* [1921]) 'Some Neurotic Mechanisms in Jealousy, Paranoia and Homosexuality', *Standard Ed.*, **18**, 223; *P.F.L.*, **10**, 195. (138)

(1923*b*) *The Ego and the Id*, London and New York, 1962; *Standard Ed.*, **19**, 3; *P.F.L.*, **11**, 339. (26, 86, 94, 135, 145, 166, 190, 249, 329)

(1924*c*) 'The Economic Problem of Masochism', *Standard Ed.*, **19**, 157; *P.F.L.*, **11**, 409. (238)

(1925*d* [1924]) *An Autobiographical Study*, *Standard Ed.*, **20**, 3; *P.F.L.*, **15**. (12)

(1925*h*) 'Negation', *Standard Ed.*, **19**, 235; *P.F.L.*, **11**, 435. (254)

(1926*d* [1925]) *Inhibitions, Symptoms and Anxiety*, London, 1960; *Standard Ed.*, **20**, 77; *P.F.L.*, **10**, 227. (26, 86, 126, 219, 320, 329)

FREUD, S. (cont.)

(1927a) 'Postscript to *The Question of Lay Analysis*', Standard Ed., **20**, 251; P.F.L., **15**, 355. (12)

(1927c) *The Future of an Illusion*, London, 1962; Standard Ed., **21**, 3; P.F.L., **12**, 179. (26, 30, 31, 245, 251, 261, 273, 275, 278, 283, 301, 329, 338, 344)

(1927e) 'Fetishism', Standard Ed., **21**, 149; P.F.L., **7**, 345. (227)

(1930a) *Civilization and its Discontents*, New York, 1961; London, 1963; Standard Ed., **21**, 59; P.F.L., **12**, 243. (26, 30, 67, 182, 188, 190, 226, 227, 344, 359)

(1931a) 'Libidinal Types', Standard Ed., **21**, 215; P.F.L., **7**, 359. (272)

(1932a) 'The Acquisition and Control of Fire', Standard Ed., **22**, 185; P.F.L., **13**, 225. (228, 279)

(1933a [1932]) *New Introductory Lectures on Psycho-Analysis*, New York, 1966; London, 1971; Standard Ed., **22**; P.F.L., **2**. (182, 188, 226, 231, 249, 296, 304, 360)

(1933b [1932]) *Why War?*, Paris, 1933; Standard Ed., **22**, 197; P.F.L., **12**, 341. (30, 59, 182, 188, 231, 247, 249, 287)

(1935a) Postscript (1935) to *An Autobiographical Study*, new edition, London and New York; Standard Ed., **20**, 71; P.F.L., **15**, 256. (12, 181, 182)

(1936a) 'A Disturbance of Memory on the Acropolis', Standard Ed., **22**, 239; P.F.L., **11**, 443. (207)

(1939a [1934–8]) *Moses and Monotheism*, Standard Ed., **23**, 3; P.F.L., **13**, 237. (26, 39, 182, 226, 228, 247, 305, 318, 319, 362)

(1940a [1938]) *An Outline of Psycho-Analysis*, New York, 1968; London, 1969; Standard Ed., **23**, 141; P.F.L., **15**, 369. (26)

(1950a [1887–1902]) *The Origins of Psycho-Analysis*, London and New York, 1954. (Partly, including 'A Project for a Scientific Psychology', in Standard Ed., **1**, 175.) (15, 23 ff., 30, 39, 247, 297, 319)

(1960a) *Letters 1873–1939* (ed. E. L. Freud) (trans. T. and J. Stern), New York, 1960; London, 1961. (23)

(1963a [1909–39]) *Psycho-Analysis and Faith. The Letters of Sigmund Freud and Oskar Pfister* (ed. H. Meng and E. L. Freud) (trans. E. Mosbacher), London and New York, 1963. (23)

(1965a [1907–26]) *A Psycho-Analytic Dialogue. The Letters of Sigmund Freud and Karl Abraham* (ed. H. C. Abraham and E. L. Freud) (trans. B. Marsh and H. C. Abraham), London and New York, 1965. (23)

FREUD, S. (*cont.*)

    (1966*a* [1912–36]) *Sigmund Freud and Lou Andreas-Salomé: Letters* (ed. E. Pfeiffer) (trans. W. and E. Robson-Scott), London and New York, 1972. (23)

    (1968*a* [1927–39]) *The Letters of Sigmund Freud and Arnold Zweig* (ed. E. L. Freud) (trans. W. and E. Robson-Scott), London and New York, 1970. (23)

    (1970*a* [1919–35]) *Sigmund Freud as a Consultant. Recollections of a Pioneer in Psychoanalysis* (Letters from Freud to Edoardo Weiss, including a Memoir and Commentaries by Weiss, with Foreword and Introduction by M. Grotjahn), New York, 1970. (23)

    (1974*a* [1906–23]) *The Freud/Jung Letters* (ed. W. McGuire) (trans. R. Manheim and R. F. C. Hull), London and Princeton, N.J., 1974. (23)

JONES, E. (1918) 'Anal-Erotic Character Traits', *J. abnorm. Psychol.*, **13**, 261; *Papers on Psycho-Analysis*, London and New York, 2nd ed., Chap. XL. (3rd ed., 1923, London and New York; 4th ed., 1938, and 5th ed., 1948, London and Baltimore.) (286)

    (1953) *Sigmund Freud: Life and Work*, Vol. 1, London and New York. (23)

    (1955) *Sigmund Freud: Life and Work*, Vol. 2, London and New York. (Page references are to the English edition.) (23, 58)

    (1957) *Sigmund Freud: Life and Work*, Vol. 3, London and New York. (Page references are to the English edition.) (23, 246, 249, 344)

JUNG, C. G., and FREUD, S. (1974) *See* FREUD, S. (1974*a*)

KELSEN, H. (1922) 'Der Begriff des Staates und die Sozialpsychologie', *Imago*, **8**, 97. (115)

KRAFFT-EBING, R. VON (1895) *Nervosität und neurasthenische Zustände*, Vienna. (36)

KRASKOVIC, C. B. (1915) *Die Psychologie der Kollektivitäten*, Vukovar. (110)

KROEBER, A. L. (1920) 'Totem and Taboo: An Ethnologic Psychoanalysis', *Amer. Anthropol.*, N.S., **22**, 48. (154)

    (1939) '*Totem and Taboo* in Retrospect', *Amer. J. Sociol.*, **45**, 446. (154)

LAST, H. (1928) 'The Founding of Rome', *Cambridge Ancient History*, Vol. VII: *The Hellenistic Monarchies and the Rise of Rome* (ed. S. A. Cook, F. E. Adcock and M. P. Charlesworth), Cambridge, Chap. XI. (256)

LE BON, G. (1895) *Psychologie des foules*, Paris. (98–109, 111)
[*Trans.*: *The Crowd: a Study of the Popular Mind*, London, 1920.]

McDOUGALL, W. (1920a) *The Group Mind*, Cambridge. (112–14, 125, 127)

(1920b) 'A Note on Suggestion', *J. Neurol. Psychopath.*, **1**, 1. (118)

MARCUSZEWICZ, R. (1920) 'Beitrag zum autistischen Denken bei Kindern', *Int. Z. Psychoanal.*, **6**, 248. (138)

MARETT, R. R. (1920) 'Psycho-Analysis and the Savage', *Athenaeum*, No. 4685 (13 Feb.), 205–6. (154)

MOEBIUS, P. J. (1903) *Über den physiologischen Schwachsinn des Weibes* (5th ed.), Halle. (50, 231)

MOEDE, W. (1915) 'Die Massen- und Sozialpsychologie im kritischen Überblick', *Z. pädag. Psychol.*, **16**, 385. (110)

NACHMANSOHN, M. (1915) 'Freuds Libidotheorie verglichen mit der Eroslehre Platos', *Int. Z. ärztl. Psychoanal.*, **3**, 65. (119)

PFISTER, O. (1910) *Die Frömmigkeit des Grafen Ludwig von Zinzendorf*, Vienna. (173)

(1921) 'Plato als Vorläufer der Psychoanalyse', *Int. Z. Psychoanal.*, **7**, 264. (119)

(1963) With FREUD, S. *See* FREUD, S. (1963a)

RANK, O. (1922) 'Die Don-Juan-Gestalt', *Imago*, **8**, 142. (168)

REIK, T. (1927) 'Dogma und Zwangsidee: eine psychoanalytische Studie zur Entwicklung der Religion', *Imago*, **13**, 247; in book form, Vienna, 1927. (227)
[*Trans.*: In *Dogma and Compulsion: Psychoanalytic Studies of Religion and Myths*, New York, 1951.]

SACHS, H. (1912) 'Traumdeutung und Menschenkenntnis', *Jb. psychoanalyt. psychopath. Forsch.*, **3**, 568. (105)

(1920) 'Gemeinsame Tagträume', *Int. Z. Psychoanal.*, **6**, 395. (170)

SCHOPENHAUER, A. (1851) 'Gleichnisse, Parabeln und Fabeln', *Parerga und Paralipomena*, Vol. 2, Leipzig. (2nd ed., Berlin, 1862.) In *Sämtliche Werke* (ed. Hübscher), Leipzig, 1938, Vol. 5. (130)

SIMMEL, E. (1918) *Kriegsneurosen und 'Psychisches Trauma'*, Munich. (124)

SMITH, W. ROBERTSON (1885) *Kinship and Marriage*, London. (140)

TARDE, G. (1890) *Les lois de l'imitation*, Paris. (116)

TROTTER, W. (1916) *Instincts of the Herd in Peace and War*, London. (115)

VAIHINGER, H. (1922) *Die Philosophie des Als Ob*, Berlin. (7th and
    8th eds.; 1st ed., 1911.) (210)
    [*Trans.: The Philosophy of 'As If'*, London, 1924.]
WEISS, E., and FREUD, S. (1970) *See* FREUD, S. (1970*a*)
ZWEIG, A., and FREUD, S. (1968) *See* FREUD, S. (1968*a*)

LIST OF ABBREVIATIONS

Gesammelte Schriften	=	Freud, *Gesammelte Schriften* (12 vols.), Vienna, 1924–34.
Gesammelte Werke	=	Freud, *Gesammelte Werke* (18 vols.), Vols. 1–17 London, 1940–52, Vol. 18 Frankfurt am Main, 1968. From 1960 the whole edition published by S. Fischer Verlag, Frankfurt am Main.
S.K.S.N.	=	Freud, *Sammlung kleiner Schriften zur Neurosenlehre* (5 vols.), Vienna, 1906–22.
Sexualtheorie und Traumlehre	=	Freud, *Kleine Schriften zur Sexualtheorie und zur Traumlehre*, Vienna, 1931.
Theoretische Schriften	=	Freud, *Theoretische Schriften (1911–1925)*, Vienna, 1931.
Collected Papers	=	Freud, *Collected Papers* (5 vols.), London, 1924–50.
Standard Edition	=	*The Standard Edition of the Complete Psychological Works of Sigmund Freud* (24 vols.), Hogarth Press and The Institute of Psycho-Analysis, London, 1953–74.
P.F.L.	=	*Pelican Freud Library* (15 vols.), Penguin Books, Harmondsworth, from 1973.

GENERAL INDEX

This index includes the names of non-technical authors. It also includes the names of technical authors where no reference is made in the text to specific works. For references to specific technical works, the Bibliography should be consulted.